THE
VEST
POCKET
CPA

D0427766

Third Edition

THE
VEST
POCKET
CPA

Third Edition

Joel G. Siegel, Ph.D., CPA
Financial Consultant
Professor of Accounting and Finance
Queens College of the City University of
New York

Nick Dauber, MS, CPA
Accounting Practitioner
Instructor of Auditing and Taxation
Queens College of the City University of
New York

Jae K. Shim, Ph.D.
Chief Financial Officer
NBRF Incorporated
Professor of Accounting and Finance
California State University, Long Beach

WILEY
John Wiley & Sons, Inc.

Copyright @ 2005 by John Wiley & Sons, Inc. All rights reserved

Published by John Wiley & Sons, Inc., Hoboken, New Jersey

Published simultaneously in Canada

For general information on our other products and services, or technical support, please contact our Customer Care Department within the United States at 800-762-2974, outside the United States at 317-572-3993 or fax 317-572-4002.

Wiley also publishes its books in a variety of electronic formats. Some content that appears in print may not be available in electronic books.

Library of Congress Cataloging-in-Publication Data:

Siegel, Joel G.
   The vest pocket CPA / Joel G. Siegel, Nick Dauber, Jae K. Shim.--
3rd ed.
      p. cm.
   Dauber's name appears first in earlier ed.
   Includes index.
   ISBN 0-471-70875-5 (pbk.)
   1. Accounting--Handbook, manuals, etc. I. Dauber, Nicky A. II.
Shim, Jae K. III. Title.
   HF5635.D226 2005
   657'.076--dc22
                                                    2004059604

Printed in the United States of America
10 9 8 7 6 5 4 3 2 1

ABOUT THE AUTHORS

JOEL G. SIEGEL, Ph.D., CPA, is professor of Accounting at Queens College of the City University of New York. He is also an accounting practitioner to various clients.

Dr. Siegel was previously a member of the audit staff of Coopers and Lybrand, CPAs, and a faculty resident with Arthur Andersen, CPAs. Dr. Siegel has acted as a consultant in accounting issues to many organizations, including International Telephone & Telegraph, United Technologies, Person-Wolinsky CPA Review Courses, and Citicorp.

Dr. Siegel is the author of 67 books and approximately 300 articles on accounting topics. His books have been published by Prentice Hall, McGraw-Hill, John Wiley & Sons, Inc. Barron's, Richard Irwin, Probus, Macmillan, HarperCollins, International Publishing, Southwestern, Commerce Clearing House, American Management Association, and the AICPA.

He has been published in numerous accounting and financial journals including *Massachusetts CPA, Ohio CPA, Michigan CPA, Virginia Accountant Quarterly, Delaware CPA, The CPA Journal, National Public Accountant, Financial Executive,* and *The Financial Analysts Journal.*

In 1972, he was the recipient of the Outstanding Educator of America Award. He is listed in *Who's Who Among Writers* and *Who's Who in the World.* He is the former chairperson of the National Oversight Board.

NICK DAUBER, MS, CPA, is an accounting practitioner, specializing in auditing and taxation. Prior to starting his practice 20 years ago, he was an audit and tax manager at a CPA firm.

Mr. Dauber is also an instructor of Auditing and Taxation at Queens College of the City University of New Year. He was the president of Person/Wolinsky CPA Review Courses and has instructed over 50,000 CPA Exam candidates during the past 25 years. Mr. Dauber was the writer of the review course's auditing and taxation material and served as the editor of the law and financial accounting material.

In 1992, Mr. Dauber was named Professor of the Year at Queens College of the City University of New York, and recipient of the Golden Apple Award bestowed by the Golden Key National Honor Society. He has also served as an award-winning lecturer in auditing and taxation for the

Foundation for Accounting Education at the New York State Society of CPAs as well as for the American Institute of Certified Public Accountants.

Mr. Dauber has served as a book reviewer for major book publishers and has published articles in many professional accounting journals including *The CPA Journal* (New York), *Massachusetts CPA*, *Virginia Accountant Quarterly*, and *National Public Accountant*.

Books that Mr. Dauber has authored include *The GAAS Book*, *Corporate Controller's Handbook of Financial Management*, and *Barron's How to Prepare for the CPA Exam*. He has also been a contributor to professional books in accounting and auditing.

DR. JAE K. SHIM is one of the most prolific accounting and finance experts in the world. He is a professor of accounting and finance at California State University, Long Beach, and CEO of Delta Consulting Company, a financial consulting and training firm. Dr. Shim received his M.B.A. and Ph.D. degrees from the University of California at Berkeley (Haas School of Business). He has been a consultant to commercial and nonprofit organizations for over 30 years.

Dr. Shim has over 50 college and professional books to his credit, including *2004 US Master Finance Guide*, *Barron's Accounting Handbook*, *Barron's Dictionary of Accounting Terms*, *GAAP 2005*, *Dictionary of Personal Finance*, *Investment Sourcebook*, *Dictionary of Real Estate*, *Dictionary of Economics*, *Dictionary of International Investment Terms*, *Encyclopedic Dictionary of Accounting and Finance*, *2004–2005 Corporate Controller's Handbook of Financial Management*, *The Vest Pocket CPA*, *The Vest Pocket CFO*, and the best-selling *Vest Pocket MBA*. Seventeen of his publications have been translated into foreign languages including Spanish, Chinese, Russian, Italian, Japanese, and Korean. Professor Shim's books have been published by Prentice Hall, McGraw-Hill, Barron's, Commerce Clearing House (CCH), Southwestern, John Wiley & Sons, Inc., American Management Association (Amacom), and the American Institute of CPAs (AICPA).

Dr. Shim has been frequently quoted by such media as the *Los Angeles Times*, *Orange County Register*, *Business Start-ups*, *Personal Finance*, and *Money Radio*. He has also published numerous articles in professional and academic journals. Dr. Shim was the recipient of the *Credit Research Foundation Award* for his article on cash flow forecasting and financial modeling.

ACKNOWLEDGMENTS

Permission to quote from the *Audit and Accounting Manual, Professional Standards, Statements on Auditing Standards, Statements on Standards for Accounting and Review Services, Statements on Standards for Attestation Engagements* and May 1983 Auditing CPA Exam (Question 5) was received from the American Institute of Certified Public Accountants (AICPA). Copyright by the American Institute of Certified Public Accountants, 1211 Avenue of the Americas, New York, New York 10036.

Permission to reprint Example 1 of Appendix C (pages 44–51) of *FASB Statement 95—Statement of Cash Flows* and the example on page 32 of *FASB Statement 96—Accounting for Income Taxes* were received from the Financial Accounting Standards Board. Copyright by the Financial Accounting Standards Board, High Ridge Park, Stamford, Connecticut 06905, U.S.A. Reprinted with permission. Copies of the complete document are available from the Financial Accounting Standards Board.

CONTENTS

INTRODUCTION

Now completely revised and updated, *The Vest Pocket CPA, Third Edition* is a handy pocket reference and problem-solver for today's busy accountant. Organized in a handy question-and-answer format, it will help you quickly pinpoint:

- What to look for
- What to watch out for
- What to do
- How to do it

This valuable book will guide you through the complex, ever-changing world of accounting. You'll find financial measures, ratios, procedures, techniques, and rules of thumb to help you analyze, evaluate, and solve most accounting-related problems as they come up. Throughout, you'll find this book practical, quick, comprehensive, and useful. Carry it with you for constant reference wherever you go—on a business trip, visiting a client's office, meeting corporate executives, and at your office. The content of the book applies to public and private accountants whether employed by large, medium, or small firms. The uses for this book are as varied as the topics presented.

This practical reference contains the latest information on proven approaches and techniques for understanding and solving problems of:

- Financial accounting
- Financial statement analysis
- Financial planning
- Managerial accounting
- Quantitative analysis and modeling
- Auditing
- Taxation

Part 1 takes you through accounting principles, financial reporting requirements, disclosures, and specialized accounting topics, to keep you up to date with generally accepted accounting principles.

Part 2 examines the financial health and operating performance of an entity. You'll learn about:

- Analytical tools used in appraising a company as a basis for determining the extent of audit testing, financial reliance thereon, and going-concern problems

○ The viability of a targeted company for a merger
○ Means of corporate and personal financial planning
○ Achievement of optimal investment return while controlling risk
○ Investment analysis techniques
○ Adequacy of insurance for the viability of the entity
○ Retirement and estate planning issues

Part 3 presents internal accounting applications to help you:

○ Evaluate your own company's performance, profitability, effectiveness, efficiency, marketing, and budgeting processes
○ Highlight problem areas with variance analysis
○ Move your company toward greater profits through breakeven analysis

Guidelines are presented for evaluating proposals, whether they be short or long term, for profit potential and risk-return comparison. Operations research, quantitative, and modeling techniques are clearly presented so that the accountant can use up-to-date approaches in solving business problems.

Part 4 relates to audit planning, procedures, and reporting. Means of gathering audit evidence, evaluating internal control, appraising financial statement items, and preparating audit workpapers are addressed. Review and compilation services are also discussed. The practitioner is provided with a handy guide for designing audit programs. Checklists are provided to assist the auditor in developing work programs for any client environment. The practitioner is guided through the many Statements on Auditing Standards and Auditing Standards of the Public Company Accounting Oversight Board. The practitioner is exposed to the many types of reports pertinent to various engagements. Given a standard report, the practitioner can prepare modifications with a minimum of effort. The pronouncements relevant to the various reporting situations have been streamlined for easier application. The major provisions of the Sarbanes-Oxley Act are discussed from the practitioner's point of view.

Part 5 applies to conducting income tax research.

The Vest-Pocket CPA, Third Edition, provides instant answers to any accounting or finance question you may have.

The content of the book is clear, concise, and current. It is a valuable reference tool with guidelines, checklists, illustrations, step-by-step instructions, practical applications, and "how-to's" for you, the up-to-date, knowledgable accountant. Keep this book handy for easy reference and daily use.

PART 1

COMMONLY USED GENERALLY ACCEPTED ACCOUNTING PRINCIPLES

CHAPTER 1

FINANCIAL STATEMENT REPORTING: THE INCOME STATEMENT

*T*he reporting requirements of the income statement, balance sheet, statement of changes in cash flows, and interim reporting guidelines must be carefully examined. Individuals preparing personal financial statements have to follow certain unique reporting requirements, also true in accounting for a partnership. Points to note are:

- ○ Income statement preparation involves proper revenue and expense recognition. The income statement format is highlighted along with the earnings per share computation.

- ○ Balance sheet reporting covers accounting requirements for the various types of assets, liabilities, and stockholders' equity.

- ○ The Statement of Cash Flows presents cash receipts and cash payments classified according to investing, financing, and operating activities. Disclosure is also provided for certain noncash investment and financial transactions. A reconciliation is provided between reported earnings and cash flow from operations.

- ○ Interim financial reporting allows for some departures from annual reporting such as the gross profit method to estimate inventory. The tax provision is based on the effective tax rate expected for the year.

- ○ Personal financial statements show the worth of the individual. Assets and liabilities are reflected at current value in the order of maturity.

- ○ This chapter will deal with the reporting requirements on the income statement. Chapter 2 will deal with the balance sheet, and Chapter 3 will cover the remaining statements.

INCOME STATEMENT FORMAT

With respect to the income statement, the CPA's attention is addressed to:

- o Income statement format
- o Comprehensive income
- o Extraordinary items
- o Nonrecurring items
- o Discontinued operations
- o Revenue recognition methods
- o Accounting for research and development costs
- o Presentation of earnings per share

How are items on the income statement arranged?

In the preparation of the income statement, continuing operations are presented before discontinued operations.

Starting with income from continuing operations, the format of the income statement is as follows:

Income from continuing operations before tax
Less: Taxes
Income from continuing operations after tax
Discontinued operations:
   Income from discontinued operations (net of tax)
   Loss or gain on disposal of a division (net of tax)
Income before extraordinary items
Extraordinary items (net of tax)
Cumulative effect of a change in accounting principle (net of tax)
Net income

NOTE
Earnings per share is shown on the above items as well.

COMPREHENSIVE INCOME

What is comprehensive income?

Comprehensive income is the change in equity occurring from transactions and other events with nonowners. It excludes investment (disinvestment) by owners.

What are the two components of comprehensive income?

Comprehensive income consists of two components: net income and "other comprehensive income." Net income plus "other comprehensive income" equals comprehensive income.

What does "other comprehensive income" include?

As per FASB Statement No. 130 (Reporting Comprehensive Income), "other comprehensive income" includes the following:

- Foreign currency translation gain or loss
- Unrealized gain or loss on available-for-sale securities
- Minimum pension liability adjustment (excess of additional pension liability over unamortized prior service cost)
- Change in market value of a futures contract that is a hedge of an asset reported at present value

How is comprehensive income reported?

FASB Statement No. 130 has three acceptable options of reporting comprehensive income and its components. We present the best and most often used option which is an income statement-type format as follows:

STATEMENT OF INCOME AND COMPREHENSIVE INCOME		
Net Income		$400,000
Other Comprehensive Income		
Foreign currency translation gain	$20,000	
Unrealized loss on available-for-sale securities	(2,000)	
Minimum pension liability adjustment	(1,000)	
		17,000
Comprehensive Income		$417,000

The "other comprehensive income" items reported in the income statement are for the *current year* amounts only. The total "other comprehensive income" for all the years is presented in the stockholders' equity section of the balance sheet as "accumulated other comprehensive income."

EXTRAORDINARY ITEMS

What are extraordinary items?

Extraordinary items are those that are *both* unusual in nature and infrequent in occurrence.

- "Unusual in nature" means the event is abnormal and not related to the typical operations of the entity.
- "Infrequent in occurrence" means the transaction is not anticipated to take place in the foreseeable future, taking into account the corporate environment.
- The environment of a company includes consideration of industry characteristics, geographic location of operations, and extent of government regulation.

○ Materiality is considered by judging the items individually and not in the aggregate. However, if they arise from a single specific event or plan, they should be aggregated.

Extraordinary items are shown net of tax between income from discontinued operations and cumulative effect of a change in accounting principle.

What are some typical extraordinary items?

Extraordinary items include:

○ Casualty losses
○ Losses on expropriation of property by a foreign government
○ Gain on life insurance proceeds.
○ Gain on troubled debt restructuring
○ Loss from prohibition under a newly enacted law or regulation

---

EXCEPTION

Losses on receivables and inventory occur in the normal course of business and therefore are not extraordinary. Losses on receivables and inventory are extraordinary, however, if they relate to a casualty loss (e.g., earthquake) or governmental expropriation (e.g., banning of product because of a health hazard).

NONRECURRING ITEMS

What are nonrecurring items?

Nonrecurring items are items that are *either* unusual in nature or infrequent in occurrence. They are shown as a separate line item before tax in arriving at income from continuing operations. EXAMPLE: The gain or loss on the sale of a fixed asset.

DISCONTINUED OPERATIONS

How is a discontinued operation defined?

A discontinued operation is an operation that has been discontinued during the year or will be discontinued shortly after year-end. A discontinued operation may be a business segment that has been sold, abandoned, or spun off.

The two components of discontinued operations are:

1. Income or loss from operations
2. Loss or gain on disposal of division

What disclosure requirements apply to a discontinued activity?

Footnote disclosure regarding the discontinued operation should include:

- An identification of the segment
- Disposal date
- The manner of disposal
- Description of remaining net assets of the segment at year-end

(A business segment is a major line of business or customer class.) Even though it may be operating, a formal plan to dispose exists.

How do we present discontinued operations?

In an annual report, the income of a component classified as held-for-sale is presented in discontinued operations in the year(s) in which they *occur*. Phase-out losses are *not* accrued.

EXAMPLE 1.1

ABC Company produces and sells consumer products. It has a number of product groups, each with different product lines and brands. For this company, a product group is the lowest level at which the operations and cash flows can be distinguished, operationally and for financial reporting purposes, from the rest of the company. ABC Company has suffered losses related to specific brands in its beauty product group. It has opted to get out of this group.

ABC commits to a plan to sell the product group, and as such classifies it as held-for-sale at that date. The operations and cash flows of the group will be eliminated from the ongoing operations of ABC because of the sale transaction, and the company will not have any continuing involvement in the activities of the component. Therefore, ABC should report in discontinued operations the activities of the product group while it is classified as held-for-sale.

Assume ABC decided to continue in the beauty care business but discontinued the brands with which the losses are associated. Because the brands are part of a larger cash-flow-generating product group and, in the aggregate, do not constitute a group that on its own is a component of ABC, the conditions for reporting in discontinued operations the losses associated with the brands that are discontinued would not be satisfied.

The income of a component of a business that either has been disposed of or is held-for-sale is reported in discontinued operations only when *both* the following criteria have been satisfied:

○ The profit and cash flows of the component have been (or will be) eliminated from the ongoing operations of the company due to the disposal decision.

○ The company will not have any major ongoing involvement in the activities of the component subsequent to the disposal decision.

In general, gain or loss from operations of the discontinued component should include operating gain or loss incurred and the gain or loss on disposal of a component taking place in the current period. Gains should not be recognized until the year actually realized.

REVENUE RECOGNITION

What are the various ways of recording revenue?

Revenue, which is associated with a gross increase in assets or a decrease in liabilities, may be recognized under different methods depending on the circumstances. (Special revenue recognition guidelines exist for franchisors and in sales involving a right of return. A product financing arrangement may also exist.) The basic methods of recognition include:

○ Realization
○ Completion of production
○ During production
○ Cash basis

Realization

When is revenue normally realized?

Revenue is recognized when goods are sold or services are performed. It results in an increase in net assets. This method is used almost all of the time. At realization, the earnings process is complete. Further, realization is consistent with the accrual basis, meaning that revenue is recognized when earned rather than when received. Realization should be used when:

○ The selling price is determinable
○ Future costs can be estimated
○ An exchange has taken place that can be objectively measured

NOTE
There must be a reasonable basis for determining anticipated bad debts.

Three other methods of revenue recognition are used in exceptional situations, as discussed below.

At the completion of production

When can revenue be recognized upon completion of production?

Revenue is recognized prior to sale or exchange.

REQUIREMENTS

There must be

- o A stable selling price
- o Absence of material marketing costs to complete the final transfer.
- o Interchangeability in units

This approach is used:

- o With agricultural products, byproducts, and precious metals when the aforementioned criteria are met.
- o In accounting for construction contracts under the completed contract method.

During Production

When can I recognize revenue during production?

In the case of long-term production situations, revenue recognition is made when:

- o An assured price for the completed item exists by contractual agreement, and
- o A reliable measure of the degree of completion at various stages of the production process is possible.

EXAMPLE: The percentage of completion method used in accounting for long-term construction contracts.

Which is preferable—completed contract or percentage of completion method?

Under the completed contract method, revenue should not be recognized until completion of a contract. In general, the completed contract method should be used only when the use of the percentage of completion method is inappropriate.

How is revenue matched with costs in the percentage of completion method?

Under the percentage of completion method, revenue is recognized as production activity is occurring. The gradual recognition of revenue levels out earnings over the years and is more realistic since revenue is recognized as performance takes place.

RECOMMENDATION
Percentage completed method is preferred over the completed contract method and should be used when reliable estimates of the extent of completion each period are possible. If not, the completed contract method should be used. Percentage of completion results in a matching of revenue against related expenses in the benefit period.

Using the cost-to-cost method, revenue recognized for the period equals:

$$\frac{\text{Actual Costs to Date}}{\text{Total Estimated Costs}} \times \text{Contract Price}$$
$$= \text{Cumulative Revenue}$$

Revenue recognized in prior years is deducted from the cumulative revenue to determine the revenue in the current period.

EXAMPLE 1.2

Cumulative Revenue (1–4 years)
Revenue Recognized (1–3 years)
Revenue (Year 4-current year)
Revenue less expenses equals profit.

In year 4 of a contract, the actual costs to date are $50,000. Total estimated costs are $200,000. The contract price is $1,000,000. Revenue recognized in the prior years (years 1–3) are $185,000.

$$\frac{\$50,000}{\$200,000} \times \$1,000,000$$
$$= \$250,000 \text{ Cumulative Revenue}$$

Cumulative Revenue	$250,000
Prior Year Revenue	185,000
Current Year Revenue	$ 65,000

Journal entries under the construction methods using assumed figures follow:

	Percentage of Completion		Completed Contract	
Construction-in-				
Progress	100,000		100,000	
Cash		100,000		100,000
Construction Costs				
Progress Billings				
Receivable	80,000		80,000	

EXAMPLE 1.2 (continued)		
Progress Billings on Construction-in-Progress	80,000	80,000
Periodic billings		
Construction-in-Progress	25,000	No Entry
Profit		25,000
Yearly profit recognition based on percentage of completion during the year		

In the last year when the construction project is completed, the following additional entry is made to record the profit in the final year:

	Percentage of Completion		Completed Contract	
Progress Billings on Construction-in-Progress	Total Billings		Total Billings	
Construction-in-Progress		Cost +		Cost
Profit		Profit Incremental Profit for Last Year		Profit for All the Years

Construction-in-Progress less Progress Billings is shown net. Usually, a debit figure results. This is shown as a current asset. Construction-in-Progress is an inventory account for a construction company. If a credit balance occurs, the net amount is shown as a current liability.

Cash Basis

When is cash basis, rather than accrual, preferable or required?

In the case of a company selling inventory, the accrual basis is used. However, the cash basis of revenue recognition is used under certain circumstances, namely, when revenue is recognized upon collection of the account. The cash basis instead of the accrual basis must be used when one or more of the following exist:

- Inability to objectively determine selling price at the time of sale
- Inability to estimate expenses at the time of sale
- Risks as to collections from customers
- Uncertain collection period

How do I compute revenue under the installment method?

Revenue recognition under the installment method equals the cash collected times the gross profit percent. Any gross profit not collected is deferred on the balance sheet until collection occurs. When collections are received, realized gross profit is recognized by debiting the deferred gross profit account. The balance sheet presentation is:

Accounts Receivable (Cost + Profit)
Less: Deferred Gross Profit
Net Accounts Receivable (Cost)

NOTE
A service business that does not deal in inventory (e.g., accountant, doctor, lawyer) has the option of either using the accrual basis or cash basis.

How is revenue recognized if the buyer can return the goods?

When a buyer has a right to return the merchandise bought, the seller can only recognize revenue at the time of sale in accordance with FASB 48 provided that *all* of the following conditions are satisfied:

- Selling price is known.
- Buyer has to pay for the goods even if the buyer is unable to resell them. EXAMPLE: A sale of goods from a manufacturer to wholesaler. No provision must exist that the wholesaler has to be able to sell the items to the retailer.
- If the buyer loses the item or it is damaged in some way, the buyer still has to pay for it.
- Purchase by the buyer of the item has economic feasibility.

- Seller does not have to render future performance in order that the buyer will be able to resell the goods.
- Returns may be reasonably estimated.

If any of the above criteria are not met, revenue must be deferred along with deferral of related expenses until the criteria have been satisfied or the right of return provision has expired. As an alternative to deferring the revenue, record a memo entry as to the sale.

What factors affect the ability of a company to predict future returns?

The following considerations may be used in predicting returns:

- Predictability is hampered when there is technological obsolescence risk of the product, uncertain product demand changes, or other material external factors.
- Predictability is lessened when there is a long time period involved for returns.
- Predictability is enhanced when there exists a large volume of similar transactions.
- The seller's previous experience should be weighed in estimating returns for similar products.
- The nature of customer relationship and types of product involved need to be evaluated.

CAUTION
FASB 48 does not apply to dealer leases, real estate transactions, or service industries.

What is the definition of a financing arrangement?

Per FASB 49, the arrangement involving the sale and repurchase of inventory is, in substance, a financing arrangement. It mandates that the product financing arrangement be accounted for as a borrowing instead of a sale. In many cases, the product is stored on the company's (sponsor's) premises. Further, often the sponsor will guarantee the debt of the other entity.

Typically, the sponsor eventually uses or sells most of the product in the financing arrangement. However, in some cases, the financing entity may sell small amounts of the product to other parties.

The entity that gives financing to the sponsor is usually an existing creditor, nonbusiness entity, or trust. It is also possible that the finansor may have been established for the *only* purpose of providing financing for the sponsor.

NOTE
Footnote disclosure should be made of the particulars of the product-financing arrangement.

What are some types of financing arrangements?

Types of product financing arrangements include:

o Sponsor sells a product to another business and agrees to reacquire the product or one basically identical to it. The established price to be paid by the sponsor typically includes financing and holding costs.
o Sponsor has another company buy the product for it and agrees to repurchase the product from the other entity.
o Sponsor controls the distribution of the product that has been bought by another company in accord with the aforementioned terms.

NOTE
In all situations, the company (sponsor) either agrees to repurchase the product at given prices over specified time periods, or guarantees resale prices to third parties.

How are financing arrangements reported?

o When the sponsor sells the product to the other firm and in a related transaction agrees to repurchase it, the sponsor should record a liability when the proceeds are received to the degree the product applies to the financing arrangement.

CAUTION
A sale should *not* be recorded, and the product should be retained as inventory on the sponsor's books.

o In the case where another firm buys the product for the sponsor, inventory is debited and liability is credited at the time of purchase.
o Costs of the product, except for processing costs, in excess of the sponsor's original production cost or acquisition cost or the other company's purchase cost constitute finance and holding costs. The sponsor accounts for these costs according to its typical accounting policies. Interest costs will also be incurred in connection with the financing arrangement. These should be shown separately and may be deferred.

EXAMPLE 1.3		

On 1/1/20X4, a sponsor borrows $100,000 from another company and gives the inventory as collateral for the loan. The entry is:

| Cash | 100,000 | |
| Liability | | 100,000 |

NOTE

A sale is not recorded here, and the inventory remains on the books of the sponsor. In effect, inventory serves as collateral for a loan.

On 12/31/20X4, the sponsor pays back the other company. The collateralized inventory item is returned. The interest rate on the loan was 8%. Storage costs were $2,000. The entry is:

Liability	100,000	
Interest Expense	8,000	
Storage Expense	2,000	
Cash		110,000

Recognition of Franchise Fee Revenue by the Franchisor

When can franchise fees be recognized?

According to FASB 45, the franchisor can record revenue from the initial sale of the franchise only when all significant services and obligations applicable to the sale have been substantially performed. Substantial performance is indicated when:

- There is absence of intent to give cash refunds or relieve the accounts receivable due from the franchisee.
- Nothing material remains to be done by the franchisor.
- Initial services have been rendered.

The earliest date on which substantial performance can occur is the franchisee's commencement of operations unless special circumstances can be shown to exist. In the case where it is probable that the franchisor will ultimately repurchase the franchise, the initial fee must be deferred and treated as a reduction of the repurchase price.

How are deferred franchise fee revenues reported?

If revenue is deferred, the related expenses must be deferred for later matching in the year in which the revenue is recognized. This is illustrated below:

Year of initial fee:
Cash
    Deferred Revenue
Deferred Expenses
    Cash
Year when substantial performance takes place:
Deferred Revenue
    Revenue
Expenses
    Deferred Expenses

What are the requirements for initial franchise fees?

In the case where the initial fee includes both initial services and property (real or personal), there should be an appropriate allocation based on fair market values.

When part of the initial franchise fee applies to *tangible property* (e.g., equipment, signs, inventory), revenue recognition is based on the fair value of the assets. Revenue recognition may take place prior to or after recognizing the portion of the fee related to initial services. **EXAMPLE: Part of the fee for equipment may be recognized at the time title passes with the balance of the fee being recorded as revenue when future services are performed.**

How do I handle recurring franchise fees?

Recurring franchise fees are recognized as earned and receivable. Related costs are expensed.

EXCEPTION
If the price charged for the continuing services or goods to the franchisee is below the price charged to third parties, it indicates that the initial franchise fee was in essence a partial *pre-payment* for the recurring franchise fee. In this situation, part of the initial fee has to be deferred and recognized as an adjustment of the revenue from the sale of goods and services at bargain prices.

SUGGESTION
The deferred amount should be adequate to meet future costs and generate an adequate profit on the recurring services. This situation may occur if the continuing fees are minimal relative to services provided or if the franchisee has the privilege of making bargain purchases for a particular time period.

When *continuing franchise fees will probably not cover the cost of the continuing services and provide for a reasonable profit* to the franchisor, the part of the initial franchise fee should be deferred to satisfy the deficiency and amortized over the life of the franchise.

What accounting requirements exist?

o *Unearned franchise fees* are recorded at present value. Where a part of the initial fee constitutes a nonrefundable amount for services already performed, revenue should be accordingly recognized.

o The *initial franchise fee is not typically allocated to specific franchisor services* before all services are performed. This practice can only be done if actual transaction prices are available for individual services.

o If the franchisor *sells equipment and inventory* to the franchisee *at no profit*, a receivable and payable is recorded. No revenue or expense recognition is given.

o In the case of *a repossessed franchise,* refunded amounts to the franchisee reduce current revenue. If there is no refund, the franchisor books additional revenue for the consideration retained which was not previously recorded. In either situation, *prospective* accounting treatment is given for the repossession.

CAUTION
Do not adjust previously recorded revenue for the repossession.

o Indirect costs of an operating and recurring nature are expensed immediately. Future costs to be incurred are accrued no later than the period in which related revenue is recognized. Bad debts applicable to expected uncollectability of franchise fees should be recorded in the year of revenue recognition.

o Installment or cost recovery accounting may be employed to account for franchisee fee revenue *only* if a long collection period is involved and future uncollectability of receivables cannot be accurately predicted.

REQUIREMENTS
Footnote disclosure is required of: o Outstanding obligations under agreement. o Segregation of franchise fee revenue between initial and continuing.

OTHER REVENUE CONSIDERATIONS

What happens if the vendor gives consideration to a customer?

In general, if the vendor provides the customer something to purchase the vendor's product, such consideration should reduce the vendor's revenue applicable to that sale.

What if the vendor is reimbursed for its "out-of-pocket" expenses?

The vendor records the recovery of reimbursable expenses (e.g., shipping costs billed to customers, travel costs on service contracts) as revenue.

NOTE
These costs are *not* to be netted as a reduction of cost.

How are contributions received recorded?

As per FASB Statement No. 116 (Accounting for Contributions Received and Contributions Made), contributions received by a donee are recorded at fair market value by debiting the Asset and crediting Revenue.

The donor debits contribution expense at fair market value. A gain or loss is recognized if fair market value differs from the book value of the donated Asset.

RESEARCH AND DEVELOPMENT COSTS

How are research and development costs defined?

○ *Research* is the testing done in search of a new product, service, process, or technique. Research can be aimed at deriving a material improvement to an existing product or process. Development is the translation of the research into a design for the new product or process.

○ *Development* may also result in material improvement in an existing product or process.

How are R&D costs accounted for?

Per FASB 2, research and development costs are expensed as incurred.

What are R&D costs?

R&D costs include:

○ Salaries of personnel involved in R&D activities

○ Rational allocation of indirect (general and administrative) costs

> **NOTE**
>
> R&D costs incurred under contract for others that are reimbursable are charged to a receivable account rather than expensed. Further, materials, equipment, and intangibles purchased from others that have alternative future benefit in R&D activities are capitalized. The depreciation or amortization on such assets is classified as an R&D expense. If no alternative future use exists, the costs should be expensed.

If a group of assets is acquired, allocation should be made to those that relate to R&D efforts. When a business combination is accounted for as a purchase, R&D costs are assigned their fair market value.

Expenditures paid to others to conduct R&D activities are expensed.

> **NOTE**
>
> FASB 2 does not apply to regulated industries and to the extractive industries (e.g., mining).

What are typical activities that may or may not be included as R&D?

R&D activities include:

- o Formulation and design of product alternatives and testing thereof
- o Laboratory research
- o Engineering functions until the point the product satisfies operation requirements for manufacture
- o Design of tools, molds, and dies involving new technology
- o Pre-production prototypes and models
- o Pilot plant costs

Examples of activities that are not for R&D include:

- o Quality control
- o Seasonal design changes
- o Legal costs of obtaining a patent
- o Market research
- o Identification of breakdowns during commercial production
- o Engineering of followup in the initial stages of commercial production
- o Rearrangement and start-up activities including design and construction engineering
- o Recurring and continuous efforts to improve the product
- o Commercial use of the product

NOTE

According to FASB 86, costs incurred for computer software to be sold, leased, or otherwise marketed are expensed as R&D costs until technological feasibility exists as indicated by the development of a detailed program or working model. After technological feasibility exists, software production costs should be deferred and recorded at the lower of unamortized cost or net realizable value. **EXAMPLES: Debugging the software; improvements to subroutines; and adaptations for other uses.**

Amortization begins when the product is available for customer release. The amortization expense should be based on the higher of:

- ○ The percent of current revenue to total revenue from the product or
- ○ The straight line amortization amount

What are the requirements if another party funds R&D?

Per FASB 68, if a business enters into an arrangement with other parties to fund the R&D efforts, the nature of the obligation must be determined. In the case where the entity has an obligation to repay the funds regardless of the R&D results, a liability has to be recognized with the related R&D expense. The journal entries are:

Cash
  Liability
Research and Development Expense
  Cash

A liability does not exist when the transfer of financial risk involved to the other party is substantive and genuine. If the financial risk applicable to R&D is transferred because repayment depends only on the R&D possessing future economic benefit, the company accounts for its obligation as a contract to conduct R&D for others. In this case R&D costs are capitalized, and revenue is recognized as earned and becomes billable under the contract.

REQUIREMENT

Footnote disclosure is made of the terms of the R&D agreement, the amount of compensation earned, and the costs incurred under the contract.

What if loans or advances are to be repaid depending on R&D results?

When repayment of loans or advances to the company depends *only* on R&D results, such amounts are deemed R&D costs incurred by the company and charged to expense.

How are warrants or other financial vehicles handled?

If warrants or other financial instruments are issued in an R&D arrangement, the company records part of the proceeds to be provided by the other parties as paid-in-capital based on their fair market value on the arrangement date.

ADVERTISING COSTS

How are advertising costs accounted for?

Advertising must be expensed as incurred or when the advertising program first occurs. The cost of a billboard should be deferred and amortized.

RESTRUCTURING CHARGES

How are restructuring charges treated?

Restructuring charges are expensed as incurred. In general, an expense and liability should be accrued for employee termination costs. Disclosure should be made of the group and number of employees laid off.

OTHER EXPENSE CONSIDERATIONS

Startup costs including organization costs and moving costs are expensed as incurred.

EARNINGS PER SHARE (EPS)

Who must compute earnings per share?

FASB Statement No. 128 (Earnings Per Share) requires that publicly held companies must compute earnings per share. This is not required of nonpublic companies. In a simple capital structure, no potentially dilutive securities exist. Potentially dilutive means the security will be converted into common stock at a later date, reducing EPS. Thus, only one EPS figure is necessary. In a complex capital structure, dilutive securities exist, requiring dual presentation.

What does Basic Earnings Per Share and Diluted Earnings Per Share take into account?

Basic EPS takes into account only the actual number of outstanding common shares during the period (and those contingently issuable in certain cases). Diluted EPS includes the effect of common shares actually outstanding and the impact of convertible securities, stock options, stock warrants, and their equivalents if dilutive.

How are Basic EPS and Diluted EPS calculated?

Basic EPS = Net income available to common stockholders divided by the weighted-average number of common shares outstanding.

Diluted EPS = Net income available to common stockholders + net of tax interest and/or dividend savings on convertible securities divided by the weighted-average number of common shares outstanding + effect of convertible securities + net effect of stock options

How do I calculate the weighted average common stock outstanding?

Weighted-average common stock shares outstanding takes into account the number of months in which those shares were outstanding.

EXAMPLE 1.4

On 1/1/20X1, 10,000 shares were issued. On 4/1/20X1, 2,000 of those shares were bought back by the company. The weighted-average common stock outstanding is:

$$\left(10,000 \times \frac{3}{12}\right) + \left(8,000 \times \frac{9}{12}\right) = 8,500 \text{ shares}$$

NOTE

When shares are issued because of a stock dividend or stock split, the computation of weighted-average common stock shares outstanding mandates retroactive adjustment as if the shares were outstanding at the beginning of the year.

EXAMPLE 1.5

The following occurred during the year regarding common stock:

Shares outstanding—1/1	30,000
2-for-1 stock split—4/1	30,000
Shares issued—8/1	5,000

The common shares to be used in the denominator of Basic EPS is 62,083 shares, computed:

1/1-3/31	30,000 × 3/12 × 2	15,000
4/1-8/1	60,000 × 4/12	20,000
8/1-12/31	65,000 × 5/12	27,083
Total		62,083

What are the mechanics of the calculation of EPS?

In the numerator of the EPS fraction, net income less preferred dividends represents earnings available to common stockholders. On cumulative preferred stock, preferred dividends for the current year are subtracted out whether or not paid. Further, preferred dividends are only subtracted out for the current year. EXAMPLE: If preferred dividends in arrears were for five years, all of which were paid plus the sixth year dividend, only the sixth year dividend (current year) is deducted. Preferred dividends for each of the prior years would have been deducted in those years.

In computing EPS, preferred dividends are subtracted out only on preferred stock that was not included as a common stock equivalent. If the preferred stock is a common stock equivalent, the preferred divided would *not* be subtracted out since the equivalency of preferred shares into common shares is included in the denominator.

As for the denominator of EPS, if convertible bonds are included, they are considered as equivalent to common shares. Thus, interest expense (net of tax) has to be added back in the numerator.

EXAMPLE 1.6

The following information is presented for a company:

Preferred stock, $10 par, 6% cumulative, 30,000 shares issued and outstanding	$300,000
Common stock, $5 par, 100,000 shares issued and outstanding	500,000
Net income	400,000

The company paid a cash dividend on preferred stock. The preferred dividend would therefore equal $18,000

EXAMPLE 1.6 *(continued)*

(6% × $300,000). Basic EPS equals $3.82, computed as follows:

Earnings Available to Common Stockholders

Net income	400,000
Less: Preferred dividends	(18,000)
Earnings available to common stockholders	$382,000

Basic EPS = $382,000/100,000 shares = $3.82.

EXAMPLE 1.7

On January 1, 20X2, Dauber Company had the following shares outstanding:

6% Cumulative preferred stock, $100 par value	150,000 shares
Common stock, $5 par value	500,000 shares

During the year, the following occurred:

- On April 1, 20X2, the company issued 100,000 shares of common stock.
- On September 1, 20X2, the company declared and issued a 10% stock dividend.
- For the year ended December 31, 20X2, the net income was $2,200,000.

Basic EPS for 20X2 equals $2.06 ($1,300,000/632,500 shares), calculated as follows:

Earnings Available to Common Stockholders

Net income	$2,200,000
Less: Preferred dividend (150,000 shares × $6)	900,000
Earnings available to common stockholders	$1,300,000
Weighted-Average Number of Outstanding Common Shares	
1/1/20X2-3/31/20X2 (500,000 × 3/12 × 110%)	137,500
4/1/20X2-8/31/20X2 (600,000 × 5/12 × 110%)	275,000
9/1/20X2-12/31/20X2 (660,000 × 4/12)	220,000
Weighted-average outstanding common shares	632,500

Diluted Earnings Per Share

If potentially dilutive securities exist that are outstanding, such as convertible bonds, convertible preferred stock, stock options, or stock warrants, both basic and diluted earnings per share must be presented.

How does the "if-converted" method work?

In the case of convertible securities, the *if-converted method* must be used. Under this approach, it is assumed that the dilutive convertible security is converted into common stock at the beginning of the period or date of issue, if later. If conversion is assumed, the interest expense (net of tax) that would have been incurred on the convertible bonds must be added back to net income in the numerator. Any dividend on convertible preferred stock would also be added back (dividend savings) to net income in the numerator. The add-back of interest expense (net of tax) on convertible bonds and preferred dividends on convertible preferred stock results in an adjusted net income figure used to determine earnings per share. Correspondingly, the number of common shares the convertible securities are convertible into (or their weighted-average effect if conversion to common stock actually took place during the year) must also be added to the weighted-average outstanding common shares in the denominator.

How does the treasury stock method work?

In the case of dilutive stock options, stock warrants, or their equivalent, the *treasury stock method* is used. Under this method, there is an assumption that the option or warrant was exercised at the beginning of the period, or date of grant if later. The assumed proceeds received from the exercise of the option or warrant are assumed to be used to buy treasury stock at the average market price for the period. However, exercise is presumed to occur only if the average market price of the underlying shares during the period is greater than the exercise price of the option or warrant. This presumption ensures that the assumed exercise of a stock option or warrant will have a dilutive effect on the earnings per share computation. Correspondingly, the denominator of diluted earnings per share increases by the number of shares assumed issued owing to the exercise of options or warrants reduced by the assumed treasury shares bought.

EXAMPLE 1.8

One hundred shares are under a stock option plan at an exercise price of $10. The average market price of stock during the period is $25. The assumed issuance of common shares because of the assumed exercise of the stock options is $60, computed as follows:

Issued shares from option	100 shares × $10 = $1,000
Less: Treasury shares	40 shares* × $25 = $1,000
Additional shares that must be issued to satisfy option holders	60 shares

*It is assumed that $1,000/$25 = 40 shares were acquired

If options are granted as part of a stock-based compensation arrangement, the assumed proceeds from the exercise of the options under the treasury stock method include deferred compensation and the resulting tax benefit that would be credited to paid-in-capital arising from the exercise of the options.

What about the denominator of diluted EPS?

As a result of the if-converted method for convertible dilutive securities and the treasury stock method for stock option plans and warrants, the denominator of diluted earnings per share computation equals the weighted-average outstanding common shares for the period plus the assumed issue of common shares arising from convertible securities plus the assumed shares issued because of the exercise of stock options or stock warrants, or their equivalent.

EXAMPLE 1.9

This example assumes the same information about the Dauber Company given in Example 1.7. It is further assumed that potentially dilutive securities outstanding include 5% convertible bonds (each $1,000 bond is convertible into 25 shares of common stock) having a face value of $5,000,000. There are options to buy 50,000 shares of common stock at $10 per share. The average market price for common shares is $25 per share for 20X1. The tax rate is 30 percent.

> Basic Earnings Per Share = Net income available to common stockholders divided by weighted-average number of common shares outstanding = $1,300,000/632,500 shares = $2.06

Diluted Earnings Per Share equals:		
Income for diluted earnings per share:		
Earnings available to common stockholders		$1,300,000
Interest expense on convertible bonds ($5,000,000 × 0.05)	$250,000	
Less: Tax savings ($250,000 × 0.30)	(75,000)	
Interest expense (net of tax)		175,000
Income for diluted earnings per share		$1,475,000
Shares outstanding for diluted EPS:		
Weighted-average outstanding common shares		632,500
Assumed issued common shares for convertible bonds (5,000 bonds × 25 shares)		125,000

EXAMPLE 1.9 *(continued)*		
Assumed issued common shares from exercise of option	50,000	
Less: Assumed repurchase of treasury shares (50,000 × $10) = ($500,000/$25)	(20,000)	30,000
Shares outstanding for diluted EPS		787,500

Diluted EPS for 20X1 is $1.87 ($1,475,000/787,500 shares). Diluted EPS must be disclosed because the two securities (the 5% convertible bond and the stock options) had an aggregately dilutive effect on EPS. That is, EPS decreased from $2.06 to $1.87. The required disclosures are indicated below:

EARNINGS PER SHARE DISCLOSURE

Basic Earnings Per Share	$2.06
Diluted Earnings Per Share	$1.87

Antidilutive Securities

Are antidilutive securities included in EPS?

In computing EPS, all antidilutive securities should be ignored. A security is considered to be antidilutive if its inclusion does not cause EPS to go down. In computing EPS, the aggregate of all dilutive securities must be taken into account. However, in order to exclude the ones that should not be used in the computation, it is necessary to determine which securities are individually dilutive and which ones are antidilutive. As was previously noted, a stock option will be antidilutive if the underlying market price of the stock that can be bought is less than the exercise price of the option. A convertible security is antidilutive if the exercise of the convertible bond or preferred stock results in an increase in the EPS computation compared to that derived before the assumed conversion. In this case, the additive effect to the numerator and denominator as a result of the conversion causes EPS to increase. In both cases, the antidilutive securities should be ignored in the calculation.

EXAMPLE 1.10
A company's net income for the year is $100,000. A 10% $2,000,000 convertible bond was outstanding all year that was convertible into 2,000 shares of common stock. The weighted-average number of shares of common stock outstanding all year was 200,000. The income tax rate was 30%.

EXAMPLE 1.10 *(continued)*

Basic EPS = $100,000/200,000 shares = $0.50

Diluted EPS = $100,000 + $200,000 (1 − 0.30)
             divided by $200,000 + 2,000

= $240,000/202,000 shares = $1.19

Because EPS increased as a result of the inclusion of the convertible bond, the bond is antidilutive and should be excluded from the calculation. Only Basic EPS should be disclosed here.

EXAMPLE 1.11

Davis Company has Basic EPS of $14 for 20X2. There were no conversions or exercises of convertible securities during the year. However, possible conversion of convertible bonds would have reduced EPS by $2. The impact of possible exercise of stock options would have increased EPS by $0.38. Diluted EPS for 20X2 equals $12 ($14 − $2).

NOTE

The dilutive convertible bonds are taken into account in deriving Diluted EPS, but the stock options are ignored because they have an antidilutive effect.

What are the reporting requirements for EPS?

Disclosure of EPS should include:

- Information on the capital structure
- Explanation of the computation of EPS
- Identification of common stock equivalents
- Assumptions made
- Number of shares converted

Rights and privileges of the securities should also be disclosed, including:

- Dividend and participation rights
- Call prices
- Conversion ratios
- Sinking fund requirements

Other points to remember are:

- A stock conversion occurring during the year or between year-end and the audit report date may have

materially affected EPS if it had taken place at the
beginning of the year.

RECOMMENDATION
Supplementary footnote disclosure should be made reflecting on an "as if" basis what the effects of these conversions would have had on EPS if they were made at the start of the accounting period.

o If a subsidiary has been acquired under the *purchase
  accounting method* during the year, the weighted-
  average shares outstanding for the year are used
  from the purchase date.
o If common stock or a common stock equivalent is
  sold during the year and the proceeds are used to buy
  back debt or retire preferred stock, there should be a
  presentation of supplemental EPS figures.
o When comparative financial statements are presented,
  there is a retroactive adjustment for stock splits and
  stock dividends.

EXAMPLE 1.12
Assume in 20X5 a 10 percent stock dividend occurs. The weighted-average shares used for previous years' computations has to be increased by 10 percent to make EPS data comparable.
o When a prior period adjustment occurs that causes a restatement of previous years' earnings, EPS should also be restated.

Chapter 2

Financial Statement Reporting: The Balance Sheet

On the balance sheet, the CPA is concerned with the accounting for and reporting of assets, liabilities, and stockholders' equity.

ASSETS

What valuation is used for assets?

Assets are recorded at the price paid plus related incidental costs (e.g., insurance, freight). If an asset is acquired for the incurrence of a liability, the asset is recorded at the present value (discounted value) of the payments.

EXAMPLE 2.1

If a machine was acquired in exchange for making ten $10,000 payments at an interest rate of 10 percent, the asset would be recorded at:

10,000 × 6.145* = $61,450

*Factor using the present value of ordinary annuity table
for n = 10, i = 10%

NOTE

The asset is recorded at the principal amount excluding the interest payments. If an asset is acquired for stock, the asset is recorded at the fair value of the stock issued. If it is impossible to determine the fair market value of the stock (e.g., closely held corporation), the asset will be recorded at its appraised value.

Unearned discounts (except for cost or quantity), finance charges, and interest included in the face of receivables should be deducted therefrom to derive the net receivable.

Some of the major current and noncurrent assets include:

o Accounts receivable
o Inventory
o Fixed assets
o Intangibles

Accounts Receivable

What is the difference between an assignment and factoring?

The *assignment* of accounts receivable typically requires the incurrence of a financing charge as well as interest expense on the note.

EXAMPLE 2.2

In an assignment of accounts receivable, the entries are:

Accounts Receivable Assigned	50,000	
Accounts Receivable		50,000

To designate specific accounts for assignment and collateralization for the loan.

Cash	45,000	
Notes Payable		45,000

To recognize a liability for the advance received from the lending institution.

Allowance for Bad Debts	XX	
Accounts Receivable Assigned		XX

To write off an uncollectible assigned accounts receivable.

At a particular date, the transferor's equity in the assigned receivables equals the difference between the accounts receivable assigned and the balance of the line ($5,000). When payments on the receivables are received, they are remitted by the company to the lending institution to reduce the liability. Assignment is on a nonnotification basis to customers. It is made with recourse, where the company has to make good for uncollectible customer accounts.

In a *factoring* of accounts receivable, the receivables are in effect sold. Customers are typically notified. Factoring is usually done without recourse, where the risk of uncollectibility of the customer's account rests with the financing institution. Billing and collection is typically done by the factor. The difference between the factored receivable and the amount received represents a gain or loss as follows:

Cash
Loss (or Gain)
  Accounts Receivable
Receivables from officers and affiliates require disclosure.

When are transfers of receivables treated as sales?

According to FASB 77, a sale is recorded for the transfer of receivables with recourse if *all* of the following criteria are satisfied:

o The transferor gives up control of the future economic benefits applicable to the receivables (e.g., repurchase right).

o The liability of the transferor under the recourse provisions is estimable.

o The transferee cannot require the transferor to repurchase the receivables unless there is a recourse provision in the contract.

How are transfer sales disclosed?

When the transfer is treated as a sale, gain or loss is recognized for the difference between the selling price and the net receivables.

o The selling price includes normal servicing fees of the transferor and appropriate probable adjustments (e.g., debtor's failure to pay on time, effects of prepayment, and defects in the transferred receivable).

o Net receivables equals gross receivables plus finance and service charges minus unearned finance and service charges.

In the case where selling price varies during the term of the receivables owing to a variable interest rate provision, the selling price is estimated with the use of an appropriate "going market interest rate" at the transfer date.

NOTE

Later changes in the rate cause a change in estimated selling price, *not* in interest income or interest expense.

If any one of the aforementioned criteria is not satisfied, a liability is recognized for the proceeds received.

The footnote disclosure includes:

o Amount received by transferor

o Balance of the receivables at the balance sheet date

Inventory

How may inventory be valued?

Inventory may be valued at the lower of cost or market value. Specialized inventory methods may be used such as:

- o Retail
- o Retail lower of cost or market
- o Retail LIFO
- o Dollar value LIFO

Losses on purchase commitments should be recognized in the accounts.

If ending inventory is overstated, cost of sales is understated, and net income is overstated. If beginning inventory is overstated, cost of sales is overstated, and net income is understated.

How does the lower of cost or market value method work?

Inventories are recorded at the lower of cost or market value for conservatism purposes applied on a total, category, or individual basis.

NOTE
The method used must be consistently applied.

If cost is below market value (replacement cost), cost is taken. If market value is below cost, we start with market value.

- o Market value cannot exceed the ceiling which is net realizable value (selling price less costs to complete and dispose). If it does, the ceiling is chosen.
- o Market value cannot be less than the floor which is net realizable value less a normal profit margin. If market value is less than the floor, the floor value is used.
- o Market value is used when it lies between the ceiling and floor. The following diagram may be helpful:

EXAMPLE 2.3

The lower of cost or market value method is being applied on an item-by-item basis. The circled figure is the appropriate valuation.

Product	Cost	Market	Ceiling	Floor
A	($5)	$7	$9	$6
B	14	12	(11)	7
C	18	(15)	16	12
D	20	12	18	(16)
E	(6)	5	12	7

In case E, a market value of $5 was originally selected. Because the market value of $5 exceeded the floor of $7, so the floor value would be used. However, if after applying the lower of cost or market value rule, the valuation derived ($7) exceeds the cost ($6), the cost figure is more conservative and thus is used.

NOTE

If market (replacement cost) is below the original cost but the selling price has not likewise declined, no loss should be recognized. To do so would create an abnormal profit margin in the future period.

The lower of cost or market value method is not used with LIFO since under LIFO current revenue is matched against current costs.

When and how should the retail method be applied?

The retail method is used by department stores and other large retail businesses that carry inventory items at retail selling price. The retail method is used to estimate the ending inventory at cost by employing a cost to retail (selling price) ratio. The ending inventory is first determined at selling price and then converted to cost. Markups and markdowns are both considered in arriving at the cost to retail ratio, resulting in a higher ending inventory than the retail lower of cost or market value method.

How do I apply the retail lower of cost or market value method?

The "conventional retail" method is a modification of the retail method and is preferable to it. In computing the cost to retail ratio, markups but not markdowns are considered. This results in a lower inventory figure.

The following example illustrates the accounting difference between the retail method and the retail lower of cost or market value method.

EXAMPLE 2.4			
		Cost	Retail
Inventory—1/1		16,000	30,000
Purchases		30,000	60,000
Purchase returns		(5,000)	(10,000)
Purchase discount		(2,000)	
Freight In		1,000	
Markups	25,000		
Markup cancellations	(5,000)		
Net markups			20,000
Total		40,000	100,000 (40%)
Markdowns	22,000		
Markdown cancellations	(2,000)		
Net markdowns			20,000
Cost of goods available		40,000	80,000 (50%)
Deduct:			
Sales	55,000		
–Sales returns	(5,000)		50,000
Inventory—Retail			30,000
Retail method: At cost 50% × 30,000			15,000
Retail lower of cost or mark method: 40% × 30,000			12,000

How does retail LIFO work?

In computing ending inventory, the mechanics of the retail method are basically followed. Beginning inventory is *excluded*, and both markups and markdowns are *included* in computing the cost to retail ratio. A decrease in inventory during the period is deducted from the most recently added layer and then subtracted from layers in the inverse order of addition. A retail price index is used in restating inventory.

EXAMPLE 2.5	
Retail price indices follow:	
20X7	100
20X8	104
20X9	110

EXAMPLE 2.5 (continued)

	Cost	Retail		
20X8				
Inventory—Jan. 1 (Base Inv.)	80,000	130,000		
Purchases	240,000	410,000		
Markups		10,000		
Markdowns		(20,000)		
Total (exclude Beg. Inv.)	240,000	400,000	60%	
Total (include Beg. Inv.)	320,000	530,000		
Sales		389,600		
20X8 Inv-End-Retail		140,400		
Cost Basis				
20X8 Inventory in terms of 20X7 Prices				
140,400 ÷ 1.04				
20X7 Base	80,000	135,000	$130,000 \times 1.04$	135,200
20X8 Layer in 20X7 prices		130,000 5,000		
20X8 Layer in 20X8 prices		5,000 5,200	5000×1.04	5,200
		140,400		140,400
20X8 LIFO cost 60% × 5,200	3,120			
	83,120			

EXAMPLE 2.5 *(continued)*

	Cost		Retail	
20X9				
Inventory—Jan. 1	83,120		140,400	
Purchases	260,400		430,000	
Markups			20,000	
Markdowns			(30,000)	
Total (exclude Beg. Inv.)	260,400	62%	420,000	
Total (include Beg. Inv.)	343,520		560,400	
Sales			408,600	
20X9 Inventory—End at Retail			151,800	
Cost Basis				
20X9 Inventory in 20X7 prices 151,800 ÷ 1.10			138,000	
20X7 Base	80,000		130,000	130,000 × 1.10 143,000
Excess over base year			8,000	
20X8 Layer in 20X8 prices	3,120		5,000	5,000 × 1.10 5,500
20X9 Layer in 20X7 prices			3,000	
20X9 Layer in 20X9 prices			3,300	3,000 × 1.10 3,300
20X9 Increase in 20X9 prices				
LIFO cost 62% × 3,300	2,046		151,800	151,800
	85,166			

37

What are the steps in dollar value LIFO?

Dollar value LIFO is an extension of the historical cost principle. This method aggregates dollars instead of units into homogeneous groupings. The method assumes that an inventory decrease came from the last year.

The steps under dollar value LIFO are:

○ Restate ending inventory in the current year into base dollars by applying a price index.

○ Subtract the year zero inventory in base dollars from the current year's inventory in base dollars.

○ Multiply the incremental inventory in the current year in base dollars by the price index to obtain the incremental inventory in current dollars.

○ Obtain the reportable inventory for the current year by adding to the year zero inventory in base dollars the incremental inventory for the current year in current dollars.

EXAMPLE 2.6

At 12/31/20X1, the ending inventory is $130,000, and the price index is 1.30. The base inventory on 1/1/20X1 was $80,000. The 12/31/20X1 inventory is computed below:

12/31/20X1 inventory in base dollars	
$130,000/1.30	$100,000
1/1/20X1 beginning base inventory	80,000
20X1 Increment in base dollars	$ 20,000
20X1 Increment in current year	× 1.3
dollars	$ 26,000
Inventory in base dollars	$ 80,000
Increment in current year dollars	26,000
Reportable inventory	$106,000

What are some problems in determining inventory?

Although the basics of inventory cost measurement are easily stated, difficulties arise because of cost allocation problems.

EXAMPLES:

○ Idle capacity costs and abnormal spoilage costs may have to be written off immediately in the current year instead of being allocated as an element of inventory valuation.

○ General and administrative expenses are inventoriable when they specifically relate to production activity.

What if there is a loss on a prospective purchase?

Significant net losses on purchase commitments should be recognized at the end of the reporting period.

EXAMPLE 2.7

In 20X8, ABC Company committed itself to buy raw materials at $1.20 per pound. At the end of the year, before fulfilling the purchase commitment, the price of the materials dropped to $1.00 per pound. Conservatism dictates that a loss on purchase commitment of $.20 per pound be recognized in 20X8. Loss on Purchase Commitment is debited and Allowance for Purchase Commitment Loss is credited.

When can inventory be stated at market value in excess of cost?

Inventories may be stated in excess of cost under unusual circumstances when:

- ○ There is no basis for cost apportionment (e.g., meat packing industry).
- ○ Immediate marketability exists at quoted prices (e.g., certain precious metals or agricultural products).

Disclosure is necessary when inventory is stated above cost.

What footnote disclosure is required for inventory?

Footnote disclosure for inventory includes the valuation basis method, inventory categorization by major type, unusual losses, and inventory pledged or collateralized.

Fixed Assets

How are fixed assets recorded?

A fixed asset is recorded at its fair market value or the fair market value of the consideration given, whichever is more clearly evident.

- ○ The cost of *buying an asset* includes all costs necessary to put that asset into existing use and location, including freight, insurance, taxes, installation, and breaking-in costs (e.g., instruction).
- ○ *Additions to an existing asset* (e.g., garage attached to a house) are capitalized and depreciated over the shorter of the life of the addition or the life of the

house. Rearrangement and reinstallation costs should be capitalized if they have future benefit. If not, they should be expensed.

RECOMMENDATION
Obsolete fixed assets should be reclassified from property, plant, and equipment to other assets and shown at salvage value reflecting a loss.

- When *two or more assets are bought for one price,* cost is allocated to the assets based on their relative fair market values. If an old building is demolished to make way for the construction of a new building, the costs of demolishing the old building are charged to the land account.
- Assets that are *self-constructed* are recorded at the incremental costs to build assuming idle capacity. However, they should not be reflected at more than the outside price.

EXAMPLE 2.8
Incremental costs to self-construct a machine is $15,000. The machine could have been purchased from outside at $10,000. The journal entry is:

Machine	10,000	
Loss	5,000	
Cash		15,000

- A fixed asset *donated to the company* should be recorded at fair market value. The entry is to debit fixed assets and credit revenue.

NOTE
Fixed assets cannot be written up except in the case of a discovery of a natural resource or in a purchase combination. In a discovery of a natural resource (e.g., oil), the land account is charged at appraised value and then depleted by the units of production method.

- *Land improvements* (e.g., sidewalks, driveways, fencing) are capitalized and depreciated over useful life. Land held for investment purposes or for a future plant site should be classified under investments and not fixed assets.
- *Ordinary repairs* to an asset (e.g., tune-up for a car) are expensed since they have a life of less than one year.
- *Extraordinary repairs* are capitalized since they benefit a period of one year or more (e.g., new motor for a car).

Extraordinary repairs add to an asset's life or make the asset more useful. Capital expenditures improve the quality or quantity of services to be derived from the asset.

Depreciation

How do I calculate depreciation?

Fractional year depreciation is computing depreciation when the asset is acquired during the year. A proration is required.

EXAMPLE 2.9

On 10/1/20X7, a fixed asset costing $10,000 with a salvage value of $1,000 and a life of 5 years is acquired.

Depreciation expense for 20X8 using the sum-of-the-years' digits method is:

1/1/20X8–9/30/20X8	
5/15 × $9,000 × 9/12	$2,250
10/1/20X8–12/21/20X8	
4/15 × $9,000 × 3/12	600
	$2,850

Depreciation expense for 20X8 using double declining balance is:

Year	Computation	Depreciation	Book Value
0			$10,000
10/1/20X7–12/31/20X7	3/12 × $10,000 × 40%	$1,000	9,000
1/1/20X8–12/31/20X8	$9,000 × 40%	3,600	5,400

How is depreciation calculated by group and composite methods?

Group and composite depreciation methods involve similar accounting. The group method is used for similar assets, while the composite method is used for dissimilar assets. Both methods are generally accepted. There is one accumulated depreciation account for the entire group.

$$\text{Depreciation rate} = \frac{\text{Depreciation}}{\text{Gross Cost}}$$

For a period:
Depreciation expense

$$= \text{Depreciation Rate} \times \text{Gross Cost}$$

$$\text{Depreciable life} = \frac{\text{Depreciable Cost}}{\text{Depreciation}}$$

When an asset is sold in the group, the entry is:

Cash (proceeds received)
Accumulated Depreciation (plug figure)
    Fixed Asset (cost)

NOTE
Upon sale of a fixed asset in the group the difference between the proceeds received and the cost of the fixed asset is plugged to accumulated depreciation. No gain or loss is recognized upon the sale. The only time a gain or loss would be recognized is if the entire assets were sold.

EXAMPLE 2.10

Calculations for composite depreciation follow:

Asset	Cost	Salvage	Depreciable Cost	Life	Depreciation
A	$ 25,000	$ 5,000	$ 20,000	10	$ 2,000
B	40,000	2,000	38,000	5	7,600
C	52,000	4,000	48,000	6	8,000
	$117,000	$11,000	$106,000		$17,600

Composite Rate:

$$\frac{\$17,600}{\$117,000} = \underline{15.04\%}$$

Composite Life:

$$\frac{\$106,000}{\$17,600} = \underline{6.02} \text{ years}$$

The entry to record depreciation is:

Depreciation	17,600	
Accumulated Depreciation		17,600

The entry to sell asset B for $36,000 is:

Cash	36,000	
Accumulated Depreciation	4,000	
Fixed Asset		40,000

Disclosure should be made of the interest capitalized and expensed.

Capitalized Interest

When is interest expensed or capitalized?

Disclosure should be made of the interest capitalized and expensed. Interest incurred on borrowed funds is expensed. However, interest on borrowed money is capitalized to the asset account and then amortized in the following instances:

- o Self-constructed assets for the entity's own use. To justify interest capitalization, a time period must exist for assets to be prepared for use.

○ Assets purchased for the company's own use by arrangements mandating a down payment and/or progress payments.

○ Assets for sale or lease constructed as discrete, individual projects (e.g., real estate development).

Interest is *not* capitalized for:

○ Assets produced in large volume or on a repetitive basis

○ Assets in use or ready for use

○ Assets not in use and not being prepared for use

What interest rate is used?

Interest capitalized is based on the average accumulated expenditures for that asset. The interest rate used is either:

○ Weighted-average interest rate of corporate debt

○ Interest rate on the specific borrowing

When does the capitalization period begin and end?

The interest capitalization period commences when the following exist:

○ Expenditures have been incurred.

○ Work is proceeding to make the asset ready for intended use. These activities are not limited to actual construction but may also include administrative and technical functions prior to the time of construction. Included are costs of unforeseen events taking place during construction. EXAMPLES: Labor problems and litigation.

○ Interest is being incurred.

The capitalization period ceases when the asset is materially complete and usable. When an asset has individual parts (e.g., condominium units), the capitalization period of interest costs applicable to one of the separate units ends when the specific unit is materially finished and usable. Capitalization of interest is not continued when construction ends, except for brief or unexpected delays.

When the total asset must be finished to be useful, interest capitalization continues until the total asset is materially complete. EXAMPLE: A manufacturing plant where sequential production activities must take place.

Nonmonetary Transactions

How is an exchange of assets recorded?

Nonmonetary transactions covered under APB 29 deal primarily with exchanges or distributions of fixed assets.

In an exchange of *similar assets* (e.g., truck for truck), the new asset received is recorded at the book value of the old asset plus the cash paid. Since book value of the old asset is the basis to charge the new asset, no gain is possible. However, a loss is possible, because in no case can the new asset exceed the fair market value of the new asset.

In an exchange of *dissimilar assets* (e.g., truck for machine), the new asset is recorded at the fair market value of the old asset plus the cash paid. Thus, a gain or loss may arise because the fair market value of the old asset will be different from the book value of the old asset. However, the new asset cannot be shown at more than its fair market value.

Fair market value in a nonmonetary exchange may be based upon:

○ Quoted market price
○ Appraisal
○ Cash transaction for similar items

EXAMPLE 2.11

An old fixed asset costing $10,000 with accumulated depreciation of $2,000 is traded in for a similar, new fixed asset having a fair market value of $22,000. Cash paid on the exchange is $4,000. The fair market value of the old asset is $5,000.

If a similar exchange is involved the entry is:

Fixed Asset (8,000 + 4,000)	12,000	
Accumulated Depreciation	2,000	
Fixed Asset		10,000
Cash		4,000

Assume instead that the fair market value of the new asset was $11,000, resulting in the exception where the new fixed asset must be recorded at $11,000.

NOTE

The new fixed asset cannot be shown at more than its fair market value.

In this case, the entry is:

Fixed Asset	11,000	
Accumulated Depreciation	2,000	
Loss	1,000	
Fixed Asset		10,000
Cash		4,000

Assume the original facts except that a *dissimilar* exchange is involved. The entry is:

Fixed Asset (5,000 + 4,000)	9,000	
Accumulated Depreciation	2,000	
Fixed Asset		10,000
Gain		1,000

How is "boot" recorded?

In a nonmonetary exchange, the entity receiving the monetary payment ("boot") recognizes a gain to the degree the monetary receipt is greater than the proportionate share of the book value of the asset given up.

$$\text{Gain} = \text{Monetary Receipt}$$
$$- \left(\frac{\text{Monetary Receipt}}{\begin{array}{c}\text{Fair Market Value of Total}\\ \text{Consideration Recieved}\end{array}} \right)$$
$$\times (\text{Book value of Asset Given up})$$

○ The company receiving the boot records the asset acquired at the carrying value of the asset surrendered minus the portion considered sold.

○ The company paying the boot records the asset purchased at the carrying value of the asset surrendered plus the "boot" paid.

Impairment or Disposal of Long-Lived Assets

How do we account for the impairment or disposal of long-lived assets?

FASB Statement No. 144 (Accounting for the Impairment or Disposal of Long-Lived Assets) applies to a company's long-term assets to be retained or to be disposed of.

With respect to long-term assets to be retained and used, an impairment takes place when the fair value of the long-term asset group is below its book (carrying) value. The impairment loss is recorded only when the carrying value of the asset group is not recoverable and exceeds its fair value. A lack of recoverability exists when the book value of the asset group is more than the total undiscounted cash flows expected to arise from the use and eventual disposition of the asset group. The impairment loss equals the carrying value of the asset group less its fair value.

EXAMPLE 2.12

The following data are given for an asset group:

Carrying value	$50,000
Fair value	40,000
Sum of the undiscounted cash flows	47,500

Because the sum of the undiscounted cash flows is less than the carrying value, a nonrecoverability situation exists. The impairment loss to be recognized equals $10,000 ($50,000 – $40,000).

EXAMPLE 2.13

The following information is provided for another asset group:

Carrying value	$50,000
Fair value	53,000
Sum of the undiscounted cash flows	47,000

    Because the sum of the undiscounted cash flows is less than the carrying value, a nonrecoverability situation exists. However, an impairment loss is *not* recognized because the fair value exceeds the carrying value.

EXAMPLE 2.14

Carrying value	$50,000
Fair value	46,000
Sum of the undiscounted cash flows	52,000

    Because the sum of the undiscounted cash flows exceeds the carrying value, a recoverability situation exists. Therefore, no impairment loss has occurred.

What should be footnoted for an impairment loss?

Footnote disclosure required for an impairment loss follows:

- Description of the impaired asset along with impairment circumstances
- Method used to derive fair value
- Amount of impairment loss and where such loss is included in the income statement
- The business segment associated with the impaired asset.

Involuntary Conversion

What is an involuntary conversion?

There may exist an involuntary conversion of nonmonetary assets into monetary assets, followed by replacement of the involuntarily converted assets. EXAMPLE: A warehouse is destroyed by a fire, and the insurance proceeds received are used to purchase a similar warehouse.

How is an involuntary conversion recorded?

Per Interpretation 30, gain or loss is recognized for the difference between the insurance recovery and the book value of the destroyed asset. EXAMPLE: The new warehouse (replacing the destroyed one) is recorded at its purchase price.

> **CAUTION**
>
> A contingency results if the old fixed asset is damaged in one period, but the insurance recovery is not received until a later period. A contingent gain or loss is reported in the period the old fixed asset was damaged. The gain or loss may be recognized for book and tax purposes in different years causing a temporary difference requiring interperiod income tax allocation.

Asset Retirement Obligations

How are asset retirement obligations accounted for?

FASB Statement No. 143 (Accounting for Asset Retirement Obligations) requires companies to record at fair value a liability when a retirement obligation is incurred, provided fair value can be reasonably estimated even though it is years before the asset's planned retirement. The asset retirement obligation must be measured and recorded along with its associated asset retirement cost. Asset retirements may be from sale, recycling, abandonment, or disposal.

When the initial obligation arises, the company books a liability and defers the cost to the long-term asset for the same amount. After the initial recognition, the liability will change over time so the obligation must be accreted to its present value each year. The long-term asset's capitalized cost is depreciated over its useful life. When the liability is settled, the company either settles the liability for the amount recorded or will have a settlement gain or loss.

Any incremental liability incurred in a later year is an additional layer of the original obligation. Each layer is initially measured at fair value.

Disclosure

What footnote disclosure is given for fixed assets?

Footnote disclosure for fixed assets include:

- Fixed assets by major category
- Contracts to buy new fixed assets
- Description of depreciation method and estimates used
- Fixed assets subject to pledges, liens, or other commitments
- Fixed assets held to be disposed of and any expected losses
- Idle fixed assets
- Fully depreciated assets still in use

Intangibles

What are intangible assets?

Intangible assets are assets that have a life of one year or more and which lack physical substance (e.g., goodwill) or represent a right granted by the government (e.g., patent) or by another company (e.g., franchise fee).

NOTE
"Goodwill" does not include identifiable assets.

How are intangible assets accounted for?

FASB Statement No. 142 (Goodwill and Other Intangible Assets) covers accounting for intangible assets whether purchased or internally developed. The costs of intangibles *acquired* from others should be reported as assets. The cost equals the cash or fair market value of the consideration given.

Individual intangibles that can be separately identified must be costed separately. If not separately identified, the intangibles are assigned a cost equal to the difference between the total purchase price and the cost of identifiable tangible and intangible assets.

According to FASB Statement No. 142, intangibles have either a *limited useful life* or an *indefinite useful life*. An intangible asset with a *limited life* is amortized into expense over its useful life. Examples are patents, trademarks, tradenames, franchises, licenses, and copyrights. A loss on impairment is recognized on a *limited life* intangible asset when carrying value exceeds its fair market value. After the impairment is recognized, the reduced carrying amount is the asset's new cost basis. An intangible asset with an *indefinite life* is *not* amortized but rather subject to a yearly impairment test. An example is goodwill.

The cost of developing and maintaining intangibles should be charged against earnings if the assets are not specifically identifiable, have indeterminate lives, or are inherent in the continuing business (e.g., goodwill).

EXAMPLE
With respect to internally developed goodwill, the costs incurred in developing a name (e.g., "Burger King") are expensed.

How is useful life determined?

The factors in estimating useful lives for limited life intangibles include:

○ Legal, contractual, and regulatory provisions
○ Renewal or extension provisions (if a renewal occurs, the life of the intangible may be increased)

- o Obsolescence and competitive factors
- o Product demand
- o Service lives of essential employees within the organization

NOTE
Footnote disclosure is made of the amortization period for limited life intangibles.

How is goodwill valued?

Goodwill is theoretically equal to the present value of future excess earnings of a company over other companies in the industry.

In buying a new business, a determination must often be made as to the estimated value of the goodwill. Two methods that can be used are:

- o Capitalization of earnings
- o Capitalization of excess earnings

EXAMPLE 2.15

The following information is available for a business that we are contemplating acquiring:

Expected average annual earnings	$10,000
Expected fair value of net assets exclusive of goodwill	$45,000
Normal rate of return	20%

Using the capitalization of earnings approach, goodwill is estimated at:

Total asset value implied ($10,000/20%)	$50,000
Estimated fair value of assets	45,000
Estimated goodwill	$5,000

Assuming the same facts as above except a capitalization rate of excess earnings of 22 percent, and using the capitalization of excess earnings method, goodwill is estimated at:

Expected average annual earnings	+ $10,000
Return on expected average assets ($45,000 × 20%)	9,000
Excess earnings	$1,000
Goodwill ($1,000/0.22) = $4,545	

EXAMPLE 2.16

The net worth of ABC Company excluding goodwill is $800,000, and profits for the last four years were $750,000. Included in the latter figure are extraordinary gains of $50,000 and nonrecurring losses of $30,000. It is desired to determine a selling price of the business. A 12 percent return on net worth is deemed typical for the industry. The capitalization of excess earnings is 45 percent in determining goodwill.

Net Income for 4 years	$750,000
Less: Extraordinary gains	50,000
Add: Nonrecurring losses	30,000
Adjusted 4-year earnings	$730,000
Average earnings ($730,000/4)	$182,500
Normal earnings ($800,000 × 0.12)	96,000
Excess annual earnings	$86,500
Excess earnings capitalized at 45%:	

$$\frac{\$86,500}{0.45} = \$192,222$$

How is goodwill accounted for?

If a firm buys, on a step-by-step basis, an investment using the equity method, the fair value of the acquired assets and the goodwill for each step purchased must be separately identified.

When the purchase of assets results in goodwill, later sale of a separable portion of the equity acquired mandates a proportionate reduction of the goodwill account.

Goodwill is only recorded in a business combination accounted for under the purchase method when the cost to the acquirer exceeds the fair market value of the net assets acquired. Goodwill is then subject to an annual impairment test. If the cost to the acquirer is less than the fair market value of the net assets acquired, a credit arises. This credit represents negative goodwill that is proportionately allocated as a reduction of the acquired assets except for certain deferred assets (e.g., deferred pension and tax assets). If these assets are reduced to zero, the credit balance remaining is recorded as an extraordinary gain.

How should I handle new product costs, organization costs, leaseholds?

Internally generated costs to derive a patented product are expensed (e.g., R&D incurred in developing a new product). The patent is recorded at the registration fees to secure and register it, legal fees in successfully defending it in court, and the cost of acquiring competing patents from outsiders. The patent account is amortized over its useful life not exceeding 20 years.

How are trademarks, tradenames, franchises, licenses, and copyrights accounted for?

Trademarks and tradenames have legal protection for 10 years and may be renewed for an indefinite number of times. Franchises and licenses with a limited life should be amortized over its useful life. Copyrights are granted for the life of the creator plus 70 years. Registration fees and successful legal fees are deferred to the intangible asset.

NOTE
If an intangible asset is deemed worthless, it should be written off, recognizing an extraordinary or nonrecurring item depending on the circumstances.

Organization costs are the costs incurred to incorporate a business (e.g., legal fees). They are expensed as incurred.

Leaseholds are rents paid in advance and are amortized over the life of the lease.

What footnote disclosures should be made for goodwill and other intangible assets?

The footnote disclosures for goodwill and other intangible assets include:

- Amortization period for limited life intangibles and expected amortization expense for the next five years
- Amount of any significant residual value
- Amount of goodwill included in the gain or loss on disposal of all or a part of a reporting unit
- Description of impaired intangible assets and the reasons for such impairment
- Amount of impairment loss
- Method to compute fair value

Insurance

How is cash surrender value defined?

Cash surrender value of life insurance is the sum payable upon cancellation of the policy by the insured; the insured will of course receive less than the premiums paid in.

NOTE
Cash surrender value is classified under long-term investments.

How is possible reimbursement calculated?

Casualty insurance covers such items as fire loss and water damage. Casualty insurance reimburses the holder for the fair market value of property lost. Insurance companies typically have a coinsurance clause so that the insured bears part of the loss. The following insurance reimbursement formula assumes an 80 percent coinsurance clause:

$$\frac{\text{Face of Policy}}{0.80 \times \text{Fair Market Value of insured Property}} \times \text{Fair Market Value of Loss}$$

$$= \text{Possible Reimbursement}$$

Insurance reimbursement is based on the lower of the face of the policy, fair market value of loss, or possible reimbursement.

EXAMPLE 2.17

Case	Face of Policy	Fair Market Value of Property	Fair Market Value of Loss
A	$4,000	$10,000	$6,000
B	6,000	10,000	10,000
C	10,000	10,000	4,000

Insurance reimbursement follows:

Case A:

$$\frac{\$4,000}{0.8 \times \$10,000} \times \$6,000 = \$3,000$$

Case B:

$$\frac{\$6,000}{0.8 \times \$10,000} \times \$10,000 = \$7,500$$

Case C:

$$\frac{\$10,000}{0.8 \times \$10,000} \times \$4,000 = \$5,000$$

What does a blanket policy cover?

A blanket policy covers several items of property. The face of the policy is allocated based upon the fair market values of the insured assets.

EXAMPLE 2.18

A blanket policy of $15,000 applies to equipment I and equipment II. The fair values of equipment I and II are $30,000 and $15,000, respectively. Equipment II is partially destroyed, resulting in a fire loss of $3,000.

EXAMPLE 2.18 *(continued)*

The policy allocation to equipment II is computed below:

	Fair Market Value	Policy
Equipment I	$30,000	$10,000
Equipment II	15,000	5,000
	$45,000	$15,000

The insurance reimbursement is:

$$\frac{\$5,000}{0.8 \times \$15,000} \times \$3,000 = \$1,500$$

How is a fire loss recorded?

When a fire loss occurs, the asset destroyed has to be removed from the accounts, with the resulting fire loss recorded based on book value. The insurance reimbursement reduces the fire loss. The fire loss is an extraordinary item (net of tax).

EXAMPLE 2.19

The following fire loss information applies to ABC Company. Merchandise costing $5,000 is fully destroyed. There is no insurance for it. Furniture costing $10,000 with accumulated depreciation of $1,000 and having a fair market value of $7,000 is entirely destroyed. The policy is for $10,000. A building costing $30,000 with accumulated depreciation of $3,000 and having a fair market value of $20,000 is 50 percent destroyed: The face of the policy is $15,000. The journal entries to record the book loss are:

Fire Loss	5,000	
Inventory		5,000
Fire Loss	9,000	
Accumulated Depreciation	1,000	
Furniture		10,000
Fire Loss	13,500	
Accumulated Depreciation	1,500	
Building		15,000

Insurance reimbursement totals $16,375 computed as follows:

Furniture:

$$\frac{\$10,000}{0.8 \times \$7,000} \times \$7,000 = \$12,500$$

Building:

$$\frac{\$15,000}{0.8 \times \$20,000} \times \$10,000 = \$9,375$$

EXAMPLE 2.19 *(continued)*	
The journal entry for the insurance reimbursement is:	
Cash 16,375	
Fire Loss	16,375
The net fire loss is $11,125 ($27,500 – $16,375).	

LIABILITIES

What types of liabilities must I focus on?

- o In accounting for liabilities, the CPA must consider numerous reporting and disclosure responsibilities:
- o Bonds payable may be issued between interest dates at a discount or premium.
- o Bonds may be amortized using the straight-line method or effective interest method.
- o Debt may be retired before its maturity date, in cases where the company can issue new debt at a lower interest rate.
- o Estimated liabilities must be booked when it is *probable* that an asset has been impaired or liability has been incurred by year-end, and the amount of loss is subject to reasonable estimation.
- o An accrued liability may also be made for future absences, for example, sick leave or vacation time.
- o Special termination benefits such as early retirement may also be offered to and accepted by employees.
- o Short-term debt may be rolled over to long-term debt, requiring special reporting.
- o A callable obligation by the creditor may also exist.
- o Long-term purchase obligations must be disclosed.

Bonds Payable

What is the effective cost of a bond?

The cost of a corporate bond is expressed in terms of yield. Two types of yield calculations are:

$$\text{Simple Yield} = \frac{\text{Nominal Interest}}{\text{Present Value of Bond}}$$

Yield to maturity

$$= \frac{\text{Nominal Interest} + \dfrac{\text{Discount}}{\text{Years}} - \dfrac{\text{Premium}}{\text{Years}}}{\dfrac{\text{Present Value} + \text{Maturity value}}{2}}$$

Simple yield is not as accurate as yield to maturity.

EXAMPLE 2.20

A \$100,000, 10 percent, 5-year bond is issued at 96. The simple yield is:

$$\frac{\text{Nominal Interest}}{\text{Present Value of Bond}} = \frac{\$10,000}{\$96,000} = \underline{10.42\%}$$

The yield to maturity is:

$$\frac{\text{Nominal Interest} + \dfrac{\text{Discount}}{\text{Years}} - \dfrac{\text{Premium}}{\text{Years}}}{\dfrac{\text{Present Value} + \text{Maturity Value}}{2}}$$

$$= \frac{\$10,000 + \dfrac{\$4,000}{5}}{\dfrac{\$96,000 + \$100,000}{2}} = \frac{\$10,800}{\$98,000} = \underline{11.02\%}$$

What is a discount or premium?

o When a bond is issued at a discount, the yield is greater than the nominal interest rate.

o When a bond is issued at a *premium*, the yield is less than the nominal interest rate.

How is a discount or premium amortized?

The two methods of amortizing bond discount or bond premium are:

1. *Straight-line method.* This results in a constant dollar amount of amortization but a different effective rate each period.

2. *Effective interest method.* This results in a constant rate of interest but different dollar amounts each period.

RECOMMENDATION
The effective interest method is preferred over the straight-line method.

The amortization entry is:

Interest Expense (Yield x Carrying Value of Bond at the beginning of the year)

    Discount

    Cash (Nominal Interest x Face Value of Bond)

In the early years, the amortization amount under the effective interest method is lower relative to the straight-line method (either for discount or premium).

EXAMPLE 2.21

On 1/1/20X1, a $100,000 bond is issued at $95,624. The yield rate is 7 Percent and the nominal interest rate is 6 Percent. The following schedule is the basis for the journal entries to be made:

Date	Debit Interest Expense	Credit Cash	Credit Discount	Carrying Value
1/1/20X1				$95,624
12/31/20X1	$6,694	$6,000	$694	96,318
12/31/20X2	6,742	$6,000	742	97,060

The entry on 12/31/20X1 is:

Interest Expense	6694	
Cash		6000
Discount		694

At maturity, the bond will be worth its face value of $100,000.

How is a discount or premium amortized when bonds are issued between interest dates?

The entry is:

Cash	
Bonds Payable	
Premium (or debit Discount)	
Interest Expense	

EXAMPLE 2.22

A $100,000, 5 percent bond having a life of five years is issued at 110 on 4/1/20X0. The bonds are dated 1/1/20X0. Interest is payable on 1/1 and 7/1. Straight-line amortization is used. The journal entries are:

4/1/20X0 Cash (110,000 + 1,250)	111,250	
Bonds Payable		100,000
Premium on Bonds Payable		10,000
Bond Interest Expense		
(100,000 × 5% × 3/12)		1,250
7/1/20X0 Bond Interest Expense	2,500	
Cash		2,500
100,000 × 5% × 6/12		
Premium on Bonds Payable	526.50	
Bond Interest Expense		526.50
4/1/20X0–1/1/20X5 4 years,		
9 months = 57 months		

$$\frac{\$10,000}{57} = \$175.50 \text{ per month}$$

EXAMPLE 2.22 *(continued)*		
175.50 × 3 months = $526.50		
12/31/20X0 Bond Interest		
Expense	2,500	
Interest Payable		2,500
Premium on Bonds Payable	1,053	
Bond Interest Expense		1,053
1/1/20X1 Interest Payable	2,500	
Cash		2,500

How is bonds payable recorded?

Bonds Payable is shown on the balance sheet at its present value this way:

Bonds Payable
Add: Premium
Less: Discount
Carrying Value

Bond issue costs are the expenditures incurred in issuing the bonds such as legal, registration, and printing fees.

RECOMMENDATION
Preferably, bond issue costs are deferred and amortized over the life of the bond. They are shown as a Deferred Charge.

How do I compute the price of a bond?

The price of a bond is determined as follows:

o The face amount is discounted using the present value of $1 table.
o The interest payments are discounted using the present value of annuity of $1 table.
o The yield rate is used as the discount rate.

EXAMPLE 2.23	
A $50,000, 10-year bond is issued with interest payable semiannually at an 8 percent nominal interest rate. The yield rate is 10 percent. The present value of $1 table factor for n = 20, i = 5% is 0.37689. The present value of annuity of $1 table factor for n = 20, i = 5% is 12.46221. The price of the bond should be:	
Present Value of Principal	
$50,000 × 0.37689	$18,844.50
Present Value of Interest	
Payments $20,000 × 12.46221	24,924.42
	$43,768.92

How do I handle a bond conversion?

In converting a bond into stock, three methods may be used:

1. Book value of bond
2. Market value of bond
3. Market value of stock

Book Value of Bond Method: No gain or loss on bond conversion will result because the book value of the bond is the basis to credit equity. This is the preferred method.

Market Value Methods: Gain or loss will result because the book value of the bond will be different from the market value of bond or market value of stock which is the basis to credit the equity accounts.

EXAMPLE 2.24

A $100,000 bond with unamortized premium of $8,420.50 is converted to common stock. There are 100 bonds ($100,000/$1,000). Each bond is converted into 50 shares of stock. Thus, 5,000 shares of common stock are involved. Par value is $15 per share. The market value of the stock is $25 per share. The market value of the bond is 120. When the book value method is used, the entry for the conversion is:

Bonds Payable	100,000.00	
Premium on Bonds Payable	8,420.50	
Common Stock (5,000 × 15)		75,000.00
Premium on Common Stock		33,420.50

When the market value of stock method is used, the entry is:

Bonds Payable	100,000.00	
Premium on Bonds Payable	8,420.50	
Loss on Conversion	16,579.50	
Common Stock		75,000.00
Premium on Common Stock		50,000.00
5,000 × $25 = $125,000		

When the market value of the bond method is used the entry is:

Bonds Payable	100,000.00	
Premium on Bonds Payable	8,420.50	
Loss on Conversion	11,579.50	
Common Stock		75,000.00
Premium on Common Stock		45,000.00
$100,000 × 120% = $120,000		

Extinguishment of Debt

When can debt be retired early?

Long-term debt may be called back early when new debt can be issued at a lower interest rate. Or when the company has excess cash and wants to avoid paying interest charges and having the debt on its balance sheet.

How is early extinguishment handled?

The gain or loss on the early extinguishment of debt is an ordinary item that should be shown in the income statement. Ordinary classification occurs whether the extinguishment is early, at scheduled maturity, or later.

NOTE
Serial bonds do not have characteristics of sinking fund requirements.

Debt may be construed as being extinguished in the case where the debtor is relieved of the principal liability and will probably not have to make future payments.

EXAMPLE 2.25

A $100,000 bond payable with an unamortized premium of $10,000 is called at 85. The entry is:

Bonds Payable	100,000	
Premium on Bonds Payable	10,000	
Cash (85% × 100,000)		85,000
Ordinary Gain		25,000

Footnote disclosures regarding extinguishment of debt includes a description of extinguishment transaction, including the source of funds used.

How do I record the conversion of debt to equity?

If convertible debt is converted to stock in connection with an "inducement offer" where the debtor alters conversion privileges, the debtor recognizes an expense. The amount is the fair value of the securities transferred in excess of the fair value of securities issuable according to the original conversion terms. This fair market value is measured at the earlier of the conversion date or date of the agreement.

An inducement offer may be accomplished by giving debt holders:

o A higher conversion ratio
o Payment of additional consideration
o Other favorable changes in terms

What if a trust is set up for payment of interest and principal?

According to FASB 76, if the debtor puts cash or other assets in an irrevocable trust to be used only for paying interest and principal on debt, disclosure should be made of the particulars, including a description of the transaction and the amount of debt considered to be extinguished.

Estimated Liabilities

How is a probable loss contingency defined?

A loss contingency should be accrued if *both* of the following criteria exist:

○ At year-end, it is *probable* (likely to occur) that an asset was impaired or a liability was incurred.

○ The amount of loss is subject to reasonable estimation.

What are some typical loss contingencies?

Examples of probable loss contingencies may be:

○ Warranties

○ Lawsuits

○ Claims and assessments

○ Expropriation of property by a foreign government

○ Casualties and catastrophes (e.g., fire)

How is a probable loss contingency booked?

The loss contingency is booked because of the principle of conservatism. The entry for a probable loss is:

Expense (Loss)	
Estimated Liability	

EXAMPLE 2.26

On 12/31/20X6, warranty expenses are estimated at $20,000. On 3/15/20X7, actual warranty costs paid for were $16,000. The journal entries are:

12/31/20X6	Warranty Expense	20,000	
	Estimated Liability		20,000
3/15/20X7	Estimated Liability	16,000	
	Cash		16,000

NOTES

A probable loss that cannot be estimated should be footnoted.

If a loss contingency exists at year-end but no asset impairment or liability incurrence exists (e.g., uninsured equipment), footnote disclosure may be made.

A probable loss occurring after year-end but before the audit report date requires only subsequent event disclosure.

If the amount of loss is within a range, the accrual is based on the best estimate within that range. However, if no amount within the range is better than any other amount, the *minimum amount* (not maximum amount) of the range is booked. The exposure to additional losses should be disclosed.

Are there any other requirements on loss contingencies?

○ In the case of a *reasonably possible loss* (more than remote but less than likely) no accrual is made, but footnote disclosure is required. The disclosure includes the nature of the contingency and the estimate of probable loss or range of loss. If an estimate of loss is not possible, that fact should be stated.

○ A *remote contingency* (slight chance of occurring) is usually ignored and no disclosure is made.

EXCEPTIONS

Guarantees of indebtedness, standby letters of credit, and agreements to repurchase receivables or properties are disclosed.

○ *General (unspecified) contingencies* are not accrued. EXAMPLES: Self-insurance and possible hurricane losses. Disclosure and/or an appropriation of retained earnings can be made for general contingencies. To be booked as an estimated liability, the future loss must be specific and measurable, such as parcel post and freight losses.

○ *Gain contingencies* cannot be booked. This violates conservatism. However, footnote disclosure can be made.

Accounting for Compensated Absences

What are compensated absences?

Compensated absences include:

- o Sick leave
- o Holiday
- o Vacation time

FASB 43 is not applicable to:

- o Severance or termination pay
- o Deferred compensation
- o Post retirement benefits
- o Stock option plans
- o Other long-term fringe benefits (e.g., insurance, disability)

When should there be an accrual for compensated absences?

The employer shall accrue a liability for employee's compensation for future absences when *all* of these criteria are met:

- o Employee services have already been performed.
- o Employee rights have vested.
- o Probable payment exists.
- o Amount of estimated liability can reasonably be determined.

NOTE
If the criteria are satisfied except that the amount is not determinable, only a footnote can be made, since an accrual is not possible.

Accrual for sick leave is required only when the employer permits employees to take accumulated sick leave days off regardless of actual illness. No accrual is required if employees may only take accumulated days off for actual illness, since losses for these are typically immaterial.

EXAMPLE 2.27

Estimated compensation for future absences is $30,000. The entry is:

Expense	30,000	
Estimated Liability		30,000

If at a later date a payment of $28,000 is made, the entry is:

Estimated Liability	28,000	
Cash		28,000

Accounting for Special Termination Benefits to Employees

What if employees leave early and take special benefits?

An expense should be accrued when an employer offers special termination benefits to an employee, he accepts the offer, and the amount is subject to reasonable estimation. The amount equals the current payment plus the discounted value of future payments.

When it can be objectively measured, the effect of changes on the employer's previously accrued expenses applicable to other employee benefits directly associated with employee termination should be included in measuring termination expense.

EXAMPLE 2.28

On 1/1/20X1, as an incentive for early retirement, the employee receives a lump-sum payment of $50,000 today, plus payments of $10,000 for each of the next 10 years. The discount rate is 10 percent. The journal entry is:

Expense	111,450	
Estimated Liability		111,450
Present value $10,000 × 6.145 =	$61,450	
Current payment	50,000	
Total	$111,450	

*Present value factor for $n = 10$, $i = 10\%$ is 6.145.

Refinancing of Short-term Debt to Long-term Debt

When can a short-term obligation be considered long-term?

A short-term obligation shall be reclassified as a long-term obligation when *either* of the following two conditions applies:

1. After the year-end of the financial statements but before the audit report is issued, the short-term debt is rolled over into a long-term obligation, or an equity security is issued in substitution.

2. Prior to the audit report date, the company enters into a contract for refinancing of the current obligation on a long-term basis and *all* of the following three conditions are met:

   - Agreement does not expire within one year
   - No violation of the agreement exists
   - The parties are financially capable of meeting the requirements of the agreement

How do I show the reclassification of debt from short- to long-term?

The proper classification of the refinanced item is under long-term debt and *not* stockholders' equity, even if equity securities were issued in substitution of the debt.

RECOMMENDATION
When short-term debt is excluded from current liabilities, a footnote should describe the financing agreement and the terms of any new obligation to be incurred.

If the amounts under the agreement for refinancing vary, the amount of short-term debt excluded from current liabilities will be the *minimum* amount expected to be refinanced based on conservatism.

CAUTION
The exclusion from current liabilities cannot be greater than the net proceeds of debt or security issuances, or amounts available under the refinancing agreement.

Once cash is paid for the short-term debt, even if long-term debt of a similar amount is issued the next day, the short-term debt shall be shown under current liabilities since cash was disbursed.

Callable Obligations by the Creditor

What if the debtor violates the debt agreement?

If the debtor violates the debt agreement, and long-term debt therefore becomes callable, include the debt as a current liability, except if *one* of the following two conditions exists:

○ The creditor waives or loses his right to require repayment for a period in excess of one year from the balance sheet date.

○ There is a grace period in the terms of the long-term debt issue during which the debtor may cure the violation and it is probable that the violation will be rectified within such grace period.

Disclosure of Long-term Purchase Obligations

What are unconditional purchase obligations?

An unconditional purchase obligation is an obligation to provide *funds* for goods or services at a determinable future date. EXAMPLE: A take-or-pay contract obligating the buyer to periodically pay specified amounts for products or services. Even in the case where the buyer does not take delivery of the goods, periodic payments must still be made.

How are unconditional purchase obligations disclosed?

When unconditional purchase obligations are recorded in the balance sheet, disclosure is still made of:

- Payments made for recorded unconditional purchase obligations.
- Maturities and sinking fund requirements for long-term borrowings.

Unconditional purchase obligations that are not reflected in the balance sheet should usually be disclosed if they meet these criteria:

- Noncancellable, except upon a remote contingency
- Negotiated to arrange financing to provide contracted goods or services
- A term in excess of one year

The disclosure needed for unconditional purchase obligations when not recorded in the accounts are:

- Nature and term
- Fixed and variable amounts
- Total amount for the current year and for the next five years
- Purchases made under the obligation for each year presented

Disclosure is optional for the amount of imputed interest required to reduce the unconditional purchase obligation to present value.

Exit or Disposal Activities

How do we account for the costs and obligation associated with exit or disposal activities?

FASB Statement No. 146 (Accounting for Costs Associated with Exit or Disposal Activities) applies to costs (e.g., costs to consolidate facilities or relocate workers, one-time termination benefits to current workers, operating lease termination costs) applicable to a restructuring, plant closing, discontinued operation, or other exit or disposal activity. These costs are recognized as incurred (*not* at the commitment date to an exit plan) based on fair value along with the related liability. The best indication of fair value is the quoted market prices in active markets. If fair value cannot reasonably be estimated, we must postpone recognizing the liability to such time.

The initiation date of an exit or disposal activity is when management obligates itself to a plan to do so or otherwise dispose of a long-lived asset and, if the activity includes worker termination.

What footnote disclosures are made for exit or disposal activities?

The following should be footnoted:

○ Description of exit or disposal activity and the anticipated completion date

○ For each major type of cost applicable to the exit activity, the total anticipated cost, the amount incurred in the current year, and the cumulative amount to date

○ If a liability for a cost is not recorded because fair value is not reasonably estimated, that should be noted along with the reasons why

○ Where exit or disposal costs are presented in the income statement

 ## STOCKHOLDERS' EQUITY

In accounting for stockholders' equity, consideration is given to:

○ Preferred stock characteristics
○ Preferred stock conversion to common stock
○ Stock retirement
○ Appropriation of retained earnings
○ Treasury stock
○ Quasi-reorganization
○ Dividends
○ Fractional share warrants
○ Stock options
○ Stock warrants
○ Stock splits

The stockholders' equity section of the balance sheet includes major categories for:

○ Capital stock (stock issued and stock to be issued)
○ Paid-in-capital
○ Retained earnings
○ Accumulated other comprehensive income
○ Treasury stock

Preferred Stock

What are some characteristics of preferred stock?

Preferred stock may be fully or partially participating. *Participating preferred stock* is entitled to share in dividend distributions in excess of the preferred stock dividend rate on a proportionate basis using the total par value of the preferred stock and common stock.

Cumulative preferred stock means that if no dividends are paid in a given year, the dividends accumulate and must be paid before any dividends can be paid to noncumulative stock.

The *liquidation value of preferred stock* means that in corporate liquidation, preferred stockholders will receive the liquidation value (sometimes stated as par value) before any funds may be distributed to common stockholders.

How is preferred stock accounted for?

When preferred stock is converted to common stock, the preferred stock and paid-in-capital account are eliminated, and the common stock and paid-in-capital accounts are credited. If a deficit results, retained earnings would be charged.

Stock Retirement

What do I do if stock is retired?

A company may decide to retire its stock. If common stock is retired *at par value*, the entry is:

| Common Stock | Par Value |
| Cash | |

If common stock is retired for *less than par value*, the entry is:

Common Stock	
Cash	
Paid-in-capital	

If common stock is retired for *more than par value*, the entry is:

Common Stock
Paid-in-capital (original premium per share)
Retained Earnings (excess over original premium per share)
Cash

NOTE
In retirement of stock, retained earnings can only be debited, not credited.

Appropriation of Retained Earnings (Reserve)

What is a retained earnings appropriation?

Appropriation of retained earnings means setting aside retained earnings and making them unavailable for dividends. It indicates the need to stockholders to restrict asset disbursements because of expected major uses or contingencies. EXAMPLES: Appropriations for plant expansion, sinking fund, and contingencies.

How are retained earnings appropriations booked?

The entry to record an appropriation is:

Retained Earnings
Appropriation of Retained Earnings

When the contingency occurs, the above entry is reversed.

Treasury Stock

How is treasury stock accounted for?

Treasury stock is issued shares that have been bought back by the company. There are two methods to account for treasury stock: the cost method and par value method.

COST METHOD

Treasury stock is recorded at the purchase cost and is shown as a reduction from total stockholders' equity.

If treasury stock is later *sold above cost*, the entry is:

Cash
Treasury Stock
Paid-in-capital

If treasury stock is sold below cost, the entry is:

Cash
Paid-in-capital—Treasury Stock (up to amount available)
Retained Earnings (if paid-in-capital is unavailable)
Treasury Stock

If treasury stock is *donated*, only a memo entry is needed. When the treasury shares are later sold the entry based on the market price at that time is:

Cash
   Paid-in-capital—Donation

	NOTE
An appropriation of retained earnings equal to the cost of treasury stock on hand is required.	

PAR VALUE METHOD

Treasury stock is recorded at its par value when bought. An appropriation of retained earnings equal to the cost of the treasury stock on hand is required. Treasury stock is shown as a contra account to the common stock it applies to under the capital stock section of stockholders' equity.

If treasury stock is *purchased at more than par value*, the entry is:

Treasury Stock—Par Value
Paid-in-capital—original premium per share
Retained Earnings—if necessary
   Cash

If treasury stock is *purchased at less than par value*, the entry is:

Treasury Stock—Par Value
   Cash
   Paid-in-capital

If treasury stock is sold *above par value*, the entry is:

Cash
   Treasury Stock
   Paid-in-capital

If treasury stock is sold *under par value*, the entry is:

Cash
Paid-in-capital (amount available)
Retained Earnings (if paid-in-capital is insufficient)
   Treasury Stock

Quasi-Reorganization

What is a quasi-reorganization?

A quasi-reorganization gives a financially troubled company with a deficit in retained earnings a "fresh start." A quasi-reorganization is undertaken to avoid formal bankruptcy. There is a revaluation of assets and an elimination of the deficit by reducing paid-in-capital.

How do I handle a quasi-reorganization?

- o Stockholders and creditors must agree to the quasi-reorganization.
- o Net assets are written down to fair market value. If fair value is not readily available, then conservative estimates of such value may be made.
- o Paid-in-capital is reduced to eliminate the deficit in retained earnings. If paid-in-capital is insufficient, then capital stock is charged.
- o Retained earnings becomes a zero balance. Retained earnings will bear the date of the quasi-reorganization for 10 years subsequent to the reorganization.

The retained earnings account consists of the following components:

Retained Earnings—Unappropriated

Dividends	Net Income
Appropriations	
Prior Period Adjustments	
Quasi-reorganization	

The entry for the quasi-reorganization is:

Paid-in-capital
Capital Stock (if necessary)
Assets
Retained Earnings

CAUTION

If potential losses exist at the readjustment date but the amounts of losses cannot be determined, there should be a provision for the maximum probable loss. If estimates used are subsequently shown to be incorrect, the difference goes to the paid-in-capital account.

NOTE

New or additional common stock or preferred stock may be issued in exchange for existing *indebtedness*. Thus, the current liability account would be debited for the indebtedness and the capital account credited.

EXAMPLE 2.29

ABC Company shows the following balances before a quasi-reorganization:

Current Assets $100,000	Capital Stock (80,000 shares, $10 par)	$800,000
Fixed Assets <u>400,000</u>	Paid-in-capital	200,000

EXAMPLE 2.29 (continued)

	Retained Earnings	(500,000)
	Total Liabilities and	
Total Assets $500,000	Capital	$500,000

Current assets are overvalued by $20,000 and fixed assets are overvalued by $100,000.

The entries for the quasi-reorganization are:

Quasi-reorganization	120,000	
Current Assets		20,000
Fixed Assets		100,000
Quasi-reorganization	500,000	
Retained Earnings		500,000
Paid-in-capital	200,000	
Quasi-reorganization		200,000
Common Stock	420,000	
Quasi-reorganization		420,000

Quasi-reorganization

120,000	200,000
500,000	420,000
620,000	620,000

Dividends

How is a cash dividend recognized?

A cash dividend is based on the outstanding shares (issued shares less treasury shares).

EXAMPLE 2.30

There are 5,000 issued shares and 1,000 treasury shares, a total of 4,000 outstanding shares. The par value of the stock is $10 per share. If a $0.30 dividend per share is declared, the dividend is:

$$4,000 \times \$0.30 = \$1,200$$

If the dividend rate is 6 percent, the dividend is:

$$4,000 \text{ shares} \times 10 \text{ par value} = \$40,000$$
$$\times 0.06$$
$$\$2,400$$

Assuming a cash dividend of $2,400 is declared, the entry is:

Retained Earnings	2,400	
Cash Dividend Payable		2,400

No entry is made at the record date.
The entry at the payment date is:

Cash Dividend Payable	2,400	
Cash		2,400

Is a property dividend handled like a cash dividend?

Yes, but in the case of a property dividend, the entry at the declaration date at the fair market value of the asset is:

Retained Earnings	
Asset	

Gain or loss arising between the carrying value and fair market value of the asset is recorded at the time of transfer.

How is a stock dividend handled?

A stock dividend is issued in the form of stock. Stock dividend distributable is shown in the capital stock section of stockholders' equity. It is *not* a liability.

- o If the stock dividend is *less than 20 to 25 percent of outstanding shares* at the declaration date, retained earnings is reduced at the market price of the shares.

- o If the stock dividend is *in excess of 20 to 25 percent of outstanding shares*, retained earnings is charged at par value. Between 20 and 25 percent is a gray area.

EXAMPLE 2.31

A stock dividend of 10 percent is declared on 5,000 shares of $10 par value common stock having a market price of $12. The entry at the declaration and issuance dates follows:

Retained Earnings (500 shares × $12)	6,000	
Stock Dividend Distributable (500 shares × $10)		5,000
Paid-in-Capital		1,000
Stock Dividend Distributable	5,000	
Common Stock		5,000

Assume instead that the stock dividend was 30 percent. The entries would be:

Retained Earnings (500 × $10)	5,000	
Stock Dividend Distributable		5,000
Stock Dividend Distributable	5,000	
Common Stock		5,000

How is a liability dividend accounted for?

A liability dividend (scrip dividend) is payable in the form of a liability (e.g., notes payable). A liability dividend sometimes occurs when a company has financial problems.

EXAMPLE 2.32		
On 1/1/20X2, a liability dividend of $20,000 is declared in the form of a one-year, 8 percent note. The entry at the declaration date is:		
Retained Earnings	20,000	
Scrip Dividend Payable		20,000
When the scrip dividend is paid, the entry is:		
Scrip Dividend Payable	20,000	
Interest Expense	1,600	
Cash		21,600

Stock Split

What is a stock split?

In a stock split, the shares are *increased* and the par value per share is *decreased*. However, total par value is the same.

How do I handle a stock split?

Only a memo entry is needed.

EXAMPLE 2.33
Before: 1,000 shares, $10 par value——— $10,000 total par value
2 for 1 stock split declared.
After: 2,000 shares, $5 par value——— $10,000 total par value
A reverse split would have the opposite effect.

Stock Options

As per FASB Statement No. 123 (Accounting for Stock-Based Compensation), employers may account for stock options by either the *intrinsic value* method or the *fair value* method.

What are noncompensatory and compensatory stock option plans?

Characteristics of noncompensatory plans are:

o Employees are offered stock on some basis (e.g., equally, percent of salary).
o Full-time employees may participate.
o A reasonable period of time exists to exercise the options.
o The price discount for employees on the stock is not better than that afforded to corporate stockholders if there was an additional issuance to the stockholders.

A compensatory plan exists if any one of the above four criteria is *not* met. Consideration received by the firm for the stock equals the cash, assets, or employee services obtained.

What is the purpose of a noncompensatory plan?

The purpose of a *noncompensatory plan* is to obtain funds and to reduce greater widespread ownership in the company among employees. It is not primarily designed to provide compensation for services rendered. Therefore, no compensation expense is recognized.

How are stock option plans recognized under the intrinsic method?

In a *compensatory* stock option plan for executives, compensation expense should be recognized in the year in which the services are performed. The deferred compensation is determined at the measurement date as the difference between the market price of the stock at that date and the option price. When more than one option plan exists, compensation cost should be computed separately for each. If treasury stock is used in the stock option plan, its market value, *not* its cost, should be used in measuring the compensation.

Deferred compensation is a contra account against stock options to derive the net amount under the capital stock section of the balance sheet.

EXAMPLE 2.34

On 1/1/20X1, 1,000 shares are granted under a stock option plan. At the measurement date, the market price of the stock is $10 and the option price is $6. The amount of the deferred compensation is:

Market price	$10
Option price	6
Deferred compensation	$ 4

Deferred compensation equals:
1,000 shares × 4 = $4,000

Assume the employees must perform services for four years before they can exercise the option.

On 1/1/20X1, the journal entry to record total deferred compensation cost is:

Deferred Compensation Cost	4,000	
Paid-in-capital—Stock Options		4,000

On 12/31/20X1, the entry to record the expense is:

Compensation Expense	1,000	
Deferred Compensation		1,000

$4,000/4 years = $1,000

The capital stock section on 12/31/20X1 would show stock options as follows:

Stock options	$4,000
Less Deferred compensation	1,000
Balance	$3,000

EXAMPLE 2.34 *(continued)*

Compensation expense of $1,000 would be reflected for each of the next three years as well.

At the time the options are exercised when the market price of the stock at the exercise date exceeds the option price, an entry must be made for stock issuance.

Assuming a par value of $5 and a market price of $22, the journal entry for the exercise is:

Cash ($6 × 1,000)	6,000	
Paid-in-capital—Stock Options	4,000	
Common Stock ($5 × 1,000)		5,000
Paid-in-capital		5,000

If the market price of the stock was below the option price, the options would lapse, requiring the following entry:

Paid-in-capital—Stock Options	4,000	
Paid-in-capital		4,000

NOTES

When an employee *leaves after finishing the required service years*, no effect is given to recorded compensation and the nonexercised options are transferred to paid-in-capital.

When the employee *leaves before the exercise period*, previously recognized compensation is adjusted currently.

If the *grant date is prior to the measurement date*, estimate the deferred compensation costs until the measurement date so that compensation expense is recognized when services are performed.

RECOMMENDATION: The difference between the actual figures and estimates is treated as a change in estimate during the year in which the actual cost is determined.

When the *measurement date comes after the grant date*, compensation expense for each period from the date of award to the measurement date should be based on the market price of the stock at the close of the accounting period.

In a *variable plan* granted for previous services, compensation should be expensed in the period the award is granted.

When the *employee performs services for several years prior to the stock being issued*, an accrual should be made during these periods for compensation expense applicable to the stock issuance related thereto.

When *employees receive cash in settlement* of a previous option, the cash paid is used to measure the compensation. If the ultimate compensation differs from the

NOTES

amount initially recorded, an adjustment should be made to the original compensation. It is accounted for as a change in estimate.

The *accrual of compensation expense* may necessitate estimates which must later be revised.

EXAMPLE: An employee resigns from the company and does not exercise his stock option. Compensation expense should be reduced when employee termination occurs. The adjustment is accounted for as a change in estimate.

Footnote disclosure for a stock option plan includes the number of shares under option, option price, number of shares exercisable, and number of shares issued under the option during the year.

Compensation expense is deductible for tax purposes when paid but deducted for book purposes when accrued. This results in interperiod income tax allocation involving a deferred income tax credit. If for some reason reversal of the temporary difference does not occur, a permanent difference exists which does not affect profit. The difference should adjust paid-in-capital in the period the accrual takes place.

How is the measurement date determined?

The measurement date is the date upon which the number of shares to be issued and the option price are known.

- o The measurement date cannot be changed by provisions that reduce the number of shares under option in the case of employee termination.
- o A new measurement date occurs when an option renewal takes place.
- o The measurement date is not altered when stock is transferred to a trustee or agent.

In the case of convertible stock being awarded to employees, the measurement date is the one upon which the conversion rate is known. Compensation is measured by the higher of the market price of the convertible stock or the market price of the securities into which the convertible stock is to be converted.

The measurement date may be postponed to the end of the reporting year if *all* of these three conditions exist:

1. A formal plan exists for the award.
2. The factors determining the total dollar award are designated.
3. The award relates to services performed by employees in the current year.

How are stock option plans recognized under the fair value method?

The FASB considers the fair value method to be preferable to account for stock option plans. Fair value is computed by using an option-pricing model that considers several factors. One popular option-pricing model is the Black-Scholes model. Under the fair value method, stock options are accounted for the same way as the journal entries under the intrinsic method, except the fair value of the options at the date of grant would be amortized as compensation expense over the compensatory period (from the date of grant to the date the options are initially exercisable).

Debt Issued with Stock Warrants

How do I distinguish between detachable and undetachable warrants?

If bonds are issued along with *detachable* stock warrants, the portion of the proceeds applicable to the warrants is credited to paid-in-capital. The basis for allocation is the relative values of the securities at the time of issuance.

In the event that the warrants are *not detachable*, the bonds are accounted for solely as convertible debt. There is *no* allocation of the proceeds to the conversion feature.

EXAMPLE 2.35

A $20,000 convertible bond is issued at $21,000 with $1,000 applicable to stock warrants. If the warrants are not detachable, the entry is:

Cash	21,000	
Bonds Payable		20,000
Premium on Bonds Payable		1,000

If the warrants are detachable, the entry is:

Cash	21,000	
Bonds Payable		20,000
Paid-in-capital—Stock Warrants		1,000

In the event that the proceeds of the bond issue were only $20,000 instead of $21,000, and $1,000 could be attributable to the warrants, the entry is:

Cash	20,000	
Discount	1,000	
Bonds Payable		20,000
Paid-in-capital—Stock Warrants		1,000

Fractional Share Warrants

What recognition is given to fractional share warrants?

Let's see how fractional share warrants are handled in an example.

EXAMPLE 2.36

There are 1,000 shares of $10 par value common stock. The common stock has a market price of $15. A 20 percent dividend is declared resulting in 200 shares (20% × 1,000). Included in the 200 shares are fractional share warrants. Each warrant equals one-fifth of a share of stock. There are 100 warrants resulting in 20 shares of stock (100/5). Thus, 180 regular shares and 20 fractional shares are involved.

At the declaration date, the journal entries are:

Retained Earnings		
(200 shares × 15)	3,000	
Stock Dividends Distributable		
(180 shares × 10)		1,800
Fractional Share Warrants		
(20 shares × 10)		200
Paid-in-capital		1,000

At time of issuance, the journal entries are:

Stock Dividend Distributable	1,800	
Common Stock		1,800
Fractional Share Warrants	200	
Common Stock		200

If instead of all the fractional share warrants being turned in, only 80 percent were turned in, the entry is:

Fractional Share Warrants	200	
Common Stock		160
Paid-in-capital		40

Disclosure

What footnote disclosures are made for stockholders' equity?

Footnote disclosures for stockholders' equity include:

- o Agreements to issue additional shares
- o Unusual voting rights
- o Participation rights
- o Dividend and liquidation preferences
- o Dividends in arrears
- o Conversion features
- o Call features
- o Sinking fund provisions

CHAPTER 3

FINANCIAL STATEMENT REPORTING: STATEMENT OF CASH FLOWS AND OTHER DISCLOSURES

*I*n addition to the income statement and balance sheet, the CPA must be conversant with:

- o Statement of cash flows
- o Interim reporting
- o Personal financial statements
- o Partnerships

STATEMENT OF CASH FLOWS

According to FASB 95, a statement of cash flows is required in the annual report. In addition, separate reporting is mandated for certain information applicable to noncash investments and financing transactions.

What is the purpose of the statement of cash flows?

The statement of cash flows:

- o Furnishes useful data regarding a company's cash receipts and cash payments for a period
- o Reflects a reconciliation between net income and net cash flow from operations
- o Shows the net effects of operating transactions on earnings and operating cash flow in different periods
- o Explains the change in *cash and cash-equivalents* for the period

What is a cash-equivalent?

A cash-equivalent is a short-term very liquid investment satisfying these two criteria:

1. Easily convertible into cash
2. Very near the maturity date so there is hardly any chance of change in market value due to interest rate

changes. (Typically, this criterion applies only to investments with original maturities of three months or less.) **EXAMPLES: commercial paper; money market fund; treasury bills.**

How are cash-equivalents disclosed?

The company's policy for determining which items represent cash equivalents should be disclosed. A change in such policy is accounted for as a change in accounting principle, which requires the restatement of previous years' financial statements for comparative purposes.

How is the statement of cash flows structured?

The statement of cash flows classifies cash receipts and cash payments as arising from:

- Investing activities
- Financing activities
- Operating activities

The statement of cash flows presents the net source or application of cash by operating, investing, and financing activities. The net effect of these flows on cash and cash equivalents for the period shall be reported so that the beginning and ending balances of cash and cash equivalents may be reconciled.

What are investing activities?

Investing activities include making and collecting loans, buying and selling fixed assets, and purchasing debt and equity securities in other entities.

Cash inflows from investing include:

- Collections or sales of loans made by a company and of another firm's debt instruments that were purchased by the company
- Receipts from sales of equity securities of other companies

Amount received from disposing of fixed assets Cash outflows for investing activities include:

- Disbursements for loans made by the company and payments to buy debt securities of other entities
- Disbursements to buy equity securities of other companies
- Payments to buy fixed assets

What are financing activities?

Financing activities include receiving equity funds and furnishing owners with a return on their investment, debt financing and repayment or settlement of debt, and obtaining and paying for other resources derived from creditors on noncurrent credit.

Cash inflows from financing activities are:

- o Funds received from the sale of stock
- o Funds obtained from the incurrence of debt

Cash outflows for financing activities are:

- o Dividend payments
- o Repurchase of stock
- o Paying off debt
- o Other principal payments to long-term creditors

What are operating activities?

Operating activities relate to manufacturing and selling goods or the rendering of services, not to investing or financing functions. Cash flow derived from operating activities typically applies to the cash effects of transactions entering into profit computation.

Cash inflows from operating activities are:

- o Cash sales or collections on receivables arising from the initial sale of merchandise or rendering of service
- o Cash receipts from returns on loans, debt securities, or equity securities of other entities (including interest and dividends received)
- o Receipt of a litigation settlement
- o Reimbursement under an insurance policy

Cash outflows for operating activities are:

- o Cash paid for raw material or merchandise for resale
- o Principal payments on accounts payable arising from the initial purchase of goods
- o Cash payments to suppliers
- o Employee payroll expenditures
- o Payments to governmental agencies (e.g., taxes, penalties, fees)
- o Interest payments to lenders and other creditors
- o Lawsuit payment

NOTES

If a cash receipt or cash payment *applies to more than one classification* (investing, financing, operating), classification is made as to the activity which is the main source of that cash flow.

EXAMPLE: The purchase and sale of equipment to be used by the company is typically construed as an investing activity.

o Charitable contributions
o Cash refund to customers for defective merchandise

In the case of *foreign currency cash flows*, use the exchange rate at the time of the cash flow in reporting its currency equivalent. The impact of changes in the exchange rate on cash balances held in foreign currencies is shown as a separate element of the reconciliation of the change in cash and cash equivalents for the period.

How are cash flows reconciled in the statement of cash flows?

Reconciliation is achieved by either the direct or indirect method.

The direct method is preferred, in that companies should report cash flows from operating activities by major classes of gross cash receipts and gross cash payments and the resulting net amount. A company using the direct method should present the following types of operating cash receipts and cash payments separately:

o Cash received from customers, licensees, and lessees
o Receipts from dividends and interest
o Other operating cash receipts
o Cash paid to employees and suppliers for goods or services
o Cash paid to advertising agencies and insurance companies
o Payment of interest
o Tax payments
o Other operating cash payments

Additional breakdowns of operating cash receipts and disbursements may be made to enhance financial reporting. **EXAMPLE: A manufacturing company may divide cash paid to suppliers into payments applicable to inventory acquisition and payments for selling expenses.**

The indirect reconciliation method may be used, although this is not the preferred practice. Under this method, the company reports net cash flow from operating activities indirectly, by adjusting profit to reconcile it to net cash from operating activities. The adjustment to reported earnings involves effects of:

o Deferrals of past operating cash receipts and cash payments (e.g., changes in inventory and deferred revenue)
o Accumulations of anticipated future operating cash receipts and cash payments (e.g., changes in receivables and payables)
o Items whose cash impact relates to investing or financing cash flows (e.g., depreciation expense, amortization expense, gain and loss on the sale of fixed assets, and gain or loss on the retirement of debt)

> **NOTES**
>
> Whether the direct or indirect method is used, there should be a reconciliation of net income to net cash flow from operating activities. The reconciliation shall identify the principal types of reconciling items.
>
> **EXAMPLE: Major classes of deferrals and accruals affecting cash flows should be reported, including changes in receivables, inventory, and payables that apply to operating activities.**

If the indirect method is employed, interest and income taxes paid during the period should be disclosed.

How are operating, financing, and investing activities distinguished on the statement of cash flows?

When the *direct method* of reporting cash flows from operating activities is used, the reconciliation of profit to cash flow from operations should be disclosed in a separate schedule. When the *indirect method* is followed, the reconciliation may appear within the body of the statement of cash flows or may be shown in a schedule.

There should be separate presentation within the statement of cash flows of cash inflows and cash outflows from investing and financing activities. EXAMPLE: The purchase of fixed assets is an application of cash, while the sale of a fixed asset is a source of cash. Both are shown separately to aid analysis by readers of the financial statements. Debt incurrence would be a source of cash, while debt payment would be an application of cash. Thus, cash received of $800,000 from debt incurrence would be shown as a source, while the payment of debt of $250,000 would be presented as an application. The net effect is $550,000.

> **NOTE**
>
> Separate disclosure shall be made of investing and financing activities that affect assets or liabilities but do *not* affect cash flow. This disclosure may be footnoted or shown in a schedule. Furthermore, a transaction having cash and noncash elements should be discussed, but only the cash aspect will be shown in the statement of cash flows.
>
> **EXAMPLES: Noncash activities of an investing and financing nature include:**
>
> o Bond conversion
> o Purchase of a fixed asset by the incurrence of a mortgage payable
> o Capital lease
> o Nonmonetary exchange of assets

Cash flow per share shall *not* be shown in the financial statements, since it will detract from the importance of the earnings-per-share statistic.

Who uses the statement of cash flows and why?

An analysis of the statement of cash flows helps creditors and investors:

- Evaluate the entity's ability to obtain positive future net cash flows
- Appraise the company's ability to satisfy debt
- Analyze the firm's dividend-paying ability
- Establish an opinion regarding the company's capability to derive outside financing
- Notice a difference between net income and cash flow
- Evaluate the impact on the firm's financial position of cash and noncash investing and financing transactions

What financial information do I need to construct a statement of cash flows?

EXAMPLE 3.1

Financial Information Necessary to Construct a Statement of Cash Flows

Summarized on pages 84 and 85 is financial information for the current year for Company M, which provides the basis for the statements of cash flows.

COMPANY M
CONSOLIDATED STATEMENT
OF FINANCIAL POSITION

	1/1/X1	12/31/X1	Change
Assets:			
Cash and cash equivalents	$ 600	$ 1,665	$1,065
Accounts receivable (net of allowance for losses of $600 and $450)	1,770	1,940	170
Notes receivable	400	150	(250)
Inventory	1,230	1,375	145
Prepaid expenses	110	135	25
Investments	250	275	25
Property, plant, and equipment, at cost	6,460	8,460	2,000
Accumulated depreciation	(2,100)	(2,300)	(200)
Property, plant, and equipment, net	4,360	6,160	1,800
Intangible assets	40	175	135
Total assets	$8,760	$11,875	$3,115

	1/1/X1	12/31/X1	Change
EXAMPLE 3.1 *(continued)*			

	1/1/X1	12/31/X1	Change
Liabilities:			
Accounts payable and accrued expenses	$1,085	$ 1,090	$ 5
Interest payable	30	45	15
Income taxes payable	50	85	35
Short-term debt	450	750	300
Lease obligation	—	725	725
Long-term debt	2,150	2,425	275
Deferred taxes	375	525	150
Other liabilities	225	275	50
Total liabilities	4,365	5,920	1,555
Stockholders' equity:			
Capital stock	2,000	3,000	1,000
Retained earnings	2,395	2,955	560
Total stockholders' equity	4,395	5,955	1,560
Total liabilities and stockholders' equity	$8,760	$11,875	$3,115

Source: Statement of Financial Accounting Standards No. 95, *Statement of Cash Flows,* 1987, Appendix C, Example 1, pp. 44–51. Reprinted with permission of the Financial Accounting Standards Board.

COMPANY M
CONSOLIDATED STATEMENT OF INCOME
FOR THE YEAR ENDED DECEMBER 31, 20X1

Sales	$13,965
Cost of sales	(10,290)
Depreciation and amortization	(445)
Selling, general, and administrative expenses	(1,890)
Interest expense	(235)
Equity in earnings of affiliate	45
Gain on sale of facility	80
Interest income	55
Insurance proceeds	15
Loss from patent infringement lawsuit	(30)
Income before income taxes	1,270
Provision for income taxes	(510)
Net income	$ 760

Company M entered into the following transactions during 20X1 and are reflected in the above financial statements:

(a) Company M wrote off $350 of accounts receivable when a customer filed for bankruptcy. A provision for losses on accounts receivable of $200 was included in Company M's selling, general, and administrative expenses.

EXAMPLE 3.1   (continued)

(b) Company M collected the third and final annual installment payment of $100 on a note receivable for the sale of inventory and collected the third of four annual installment payments of $150 each on a note receivable for the sale of a plant. Interest on these notes through December 31 totaling $55 was also collected.

(c) Company M received a dividend of $20 from an affiliate accounted for under the equity method of accounting.

(d) Company M sold a facility with a book value of $520 and an original cost of $750 for $600 cash.

(e) Company M constructed a new facility for its own use and placed it in service. Accumulated expenditures during the year of $1,000 included capitalized interest of $10.

(f) Company M entered into a capital lease for new equipment with a fair value of $850. Principal payments under the lease obligation totaled $125.

(g) Company M purchased all of the capital stock of Company S for $950. The acquisition was recorded under the purchase method of accounting. The fair values of Company S's assets and liabilities at the date of acquisition are:

Cash	$ 25
Accounts receivable	155
Inventory	350
Property, plant, and equipment	900
Patents	80
Goodwill	70
Accounts payable and accrued expenses	(255)
Long-term note payable	(375)
Net assets acquired	$ 950

(h) Company M borrowed and repaid various amounts under a line-of-credit agreement in which borrowings are payable 30 days after demand. The net increase during the year in the amount borrowed against the line-of-credit totaled $300.

(i) Company M issued $400 of long-term debt securities.

(j) Company M's provision for income taxes included a deferred provision of $150.

(k) Company M's depreciation totaled $430, and amortization of intangible assets totaled $15.

(l) Company M's selling, general, and administrative expenses included an accrual for incentive compensation of $50 that has been deferred by executives until their retirement. The related obligation was included in other liabilities.

EXAMPLE 3.1 *(continued)*

(m) Company M collected insurance proceeds of $15 from a business interruption claim that resulted when a storm precluded shipment of inventory for one week.

(n) Company M paid $30 to settle a lawsuit for patent infringement.

(o) Company M issued $1,000 of additional common stock, of which $500 was issued for cash and $500 was issued upon conversion of long-term debt.

(p) Company M paid dividends of $200.

Based on the financial data from the preceding example, the following computations illustrate a method of indirectly determining cash received from customers and cash paid to suppliers and employees for use in a statement of cash flows under the direct method:

Cash received from customers during the year

Customer sales		$13,965
Collection of installment payment for sale of inventory		100
Gross accounts receivable at beginning of year	$2,370	
Accounts receivable acquired in purchase of Company S	155	
Accounts receivable written off	(350)	
Gross accounts receivable at end of year	(2,390)	
Excess of new accounts receivable over collections from customers		(215)
Cash received from customers during the year		$13,850

Cash paid to suppliers and employees during the year

Cost of sales		$10,290
General and administrative expenses	$1,890	
Expenses not requiring cash outlay (provision for uncollectible accounts receivable)	(200)	
Net expenses requiring cash payments		$1,690
Inventory at beginning of year	(1,230)	
Inventory acquired in purchase of Company S	(350)	
Inventory at end of year	1,375	
Net decrease in inventory from Company M's operations		(205)
Adjustments for changes in related accruals:		
Account balances at beginning of year		
Accounts payable and accrued expenses	$1,085	
Other liabilities	225	

EXAMPLE 3.1 (continued)		
Prepaid expenses	(110)	
Total	1,200	
Accounts payable and accrued expenses acquired in purchase of Company S	255	
Account balances at end of year		
Accounts payable and accrued expenses	1,090	
Other liabilities	275	
Prepaid expenses	(135)	
Total	(1,230)	
Additional cash payments not included in expense		225
Cash paid to suppliers and employees during the year		$12,000

Presented below is a statement of cash flows for the year ended December 31, 20X1 for Company M. This statement of cash flows illustrates the direct method of presenting cash flows from operating activities.

COMPANY M
CONSOLIDATED STATEMENT OF CASH FLOWS
FOR THE YEAR ENDED DECEMBER 31, 20X1 INCREASE
(DECREASE) IN CASH AND CASH EQUIVALENTS

Cash flows from operating activities:		
Cash received from customers	$13,850	
Cash paid to suppliers and employees	(12,000)	
Dividend received from affiliate	20	
Interest received	55	
Interest paid (net of amount capitalized)	(220)	
Income taxes paid	(325)	
Insurance proceeds received	15	
Cash paid to settle lawsuit for patent infringement	(30)	
Net cash provided by operating activities		$1,365
Cash flows from investing activities:		
Proceeds from sale of facility	600	
Payment received on note for sale of plant	150	
Capital expenditures	(1,000)	
Payment for purchase of Company S, net of cash acquired	(925)	
Net cash used in investing activities		(1,175)
Cash flows from financing activities:		
Net borrowing under line-of-credit agreement	300	
Principal payments under capital lease obligation	(125)	
Proceeds from issuance of long-term debt	400	
Proceeds from issuance of common stock	500	
Dividends paid	(200)	
New cash provided by financing activities		875
Net increase in cash and cash equivalents		1,065
Cash and cash equivalents at beginning of year		600
Cash and cash equivalents at end of year		$1,665

EXAMPLE 3.1 *(continued)*

RECONCILIATION OF NET INCOME TO NET CASH PROVIDED
BY OPERATING ACTIVITIES:

Net income		$ 760
Adjustments to reconcile net income to net cash provided by operating activities:		
Depreciation and amortization	445	
Provision for losses on accounts receivable	200	
Gain on sale of facility	(80)	
Undistributed earnings of affiliate	(25)	
Payment received on installment note receivable for sale of inventory	100	
Change in assets and liabilities net of effects from purchase of Company S:		
Increase in accounts receivable	(215)	
Decrease in inventory	205	
Increase in prepaid expenses	(25)	
Decrease in accounts payable and accrued expenses	(250)	
Increase in interest and income taxes payable	50	
Increase in deferred taxes	150	
Increase in other liabilities	50	
Total adjustments		605
Net cash provided by operating activities		$1,365

SUPPLEMENTAL SCHEDULE OF NONCASH INVESTING AND FINANCING ACTIVITIES:

The Company purchased all of the capital stock of
Company S for $950. In conjunction with the acquisi-
tion, liabilities were assumed as follows:

Fair value of assets acquired	$1,580
Cash paid for the capital stock	(950)
Liabilities assumed	$ 630

A capital lease obligation of $850 was incurred when
the Company entered into a lease for new equipment.

Additional common stock was issued upon the conversion of $500 of long-term debt.

DISCLOSURE OF ACCOUNTING POLICY

For purposes of the statement of cash flows, the Company considers all highly liquid debt instruments purchased with a maturity of three months or less to be cash
equivalents.

Presented next is Company M's statement of cash
flows for the year ended December 31, 20X1 prepared
using the indirect method.

COMPANY M
CONSOLIDATED STATEMENT OF CASH FLOWS
FOR THE YEAR ENDED DECEMBER 31, 20X1
INCREASE (DECREASE) IN CASH AND CASH EQUIVALENTS

Cash flows from operating activities:	
Net Income	$ 760

EXAMPLE 3.1 *(continued)*

Adjustments to reconcile net income to net cash provided by operating activities:		
Depreciation and amortization	$ 445	
Provision for losses on accounts receivable	200	
Gain on sale of facility	(80)	
Undistributed earnings of affiliate	(25)	
Payment received on installment note receivable for sale of inventory	100	
Change in assets and liabilities net of effects from purchase of Company S:		
Increase in accounts receivable	(215)	
Decrease in inventory	205	
Increase in prepaid expenses	(25)	
Decrease in accounts payable and accrued expenses	(250)	
Increase in interest and income payable	50	
Increase in deferred taxes	150	
Increase in other liabilities	50	
Total adjustments		605
Net cash provided by operating activities		1,365
Cash flows from investing activities:		
Proceeds from sale of facility	600	
Payment received on note for sale of plant	150	
Capital expenditures	(1,000)	
Payment for purchase of Company S, net of cash acquired	(925)	
Net cash used in investing activities		(1,175)
Cash flows from financing activities:		
Net borrowings under line-of-credit agreement	300	
Principal payments under capital lease obligation	(125)	
Proceeds from issuance of long-term debt	400	
Proceeds from issuance of common stock	500	
Dividends paid	(200)	
Net cash provided by financing activities		875
Net increase in cash and cash equivalents		1,065
Cash and cash equivalents at beginning of year		600
Cash and cash equivalents at end of year		$1,665

SUPPLEMENTAL DISCLOSURES OF CASH FLOW INFORMATION:

Cash paid during the year for:	
Interest (net of amount capitalized)	$ 220
Income taxes	325

EXAMPLE 3.1 *(continued)*

SUPPLEMENTAL SCHEDULE OF NONCASH INVESTING AND FINANCING ACTIVITIES:

The Company purchased all of the capital stock of Company S for $950. In conjunction with the acquisition, liabilities were assumed as follows:

Fair value of assets acquired	$1,580
Cash paid for the capital stock	(950)
Liabilities assumed	$ 630

A capital lease obligation of $850 was incurred when the Company entered into a lease for new equipment.

Additional common stock was issued upon the conversion of $500 of long-term debt.

DISCLOSURE OF ACCOUNTING POLICY:

For purposes of the statement of cash flows, the Company considers all highly liquid debt instruments purchased with a maturity of three months or less to be cash equivalents.

INTERIM REPORTING

How often should interim reports be given?

Interim reports may be issued at appropriate reporting intervals, for example, quarterly or monthly. Complete financial statements or summarized data may be given, but interim financial statements do not have to be certified.

What type of report is appropriate for an interim period?

Interim balance sheets and cash flow data should be provided. If these statements are not presented, material changes in liquid assets, cash, long-term debt, and stockholders' equity should be disclosed. Interim reports usually include results of the current interim period and the cumulative year-to-date figures. Typically, comparisons are made to results of comparable interim periods for the prior year.

What are some guidelines in preparing interim reports?

o Interim results should be based on the accounting principles used in the last year's annual report unless a change has been made in the current year.

o A gain or loss cannot be deferred to a later interim period unless such deferral has been permissible for annual reporting.

o Revenue from merchandise sold and services performed should be accounted for as earned in the interim period in the same way as accounted for in annual reporting. If an advance is received in the first quarter and benefits the entire year, it should be allocated ratably to the interim periods affected.

o Costs and expenses should be matched to related revenue in the interim period. If a cost cannot be associated with revenue in a future interim period, it should be expensed in the current period. Yearly expenses such as administrative salaries, insurance, pension plan expense, and year-end bonuses should be allocated to the quarters. The allocation basis may be based on such factors as time expired, benefit obtained, and activity.

o The gross profit method can be used to estimate interim inventory and cost of sales. Disclosure should be made of the method, assumptions made, and material adjustments by reconciliations with the annual physical inventory.

o A permanent inventory loss should be reflected in the interim period during which it occurs. A subsequent recovery is treated as a gain in the later interim period. However, if the change in inventory value is temporary, no recognition is given in the accounts.

o When there is a temporary liquidation of the LIFO base with replacement expected by year-end, cost of sales should be based on replacement cost.

EXAMPLE 3.2

The historical cost of an inventory item is $10,000 with replacement cost expected at $15,000. The entry is:

Cost of Sales	15,000	
Inventory		10,000
Reserve for Liquidation of LIFO Base		5,000

NOTE

The Reserve for Liquidation of LIFO Base account is shown as a current liability.

When replenishment is made at year-end the entry is:

Reserve for Liquidation of LIFO Base	5,000	
Inventory	10,000	
Cash		15,000

Volume discounts given to customers tied into annual purchases should be apportioned to the interim period based on the ratio of:

$$\frac{\text{Purchases for the interim period}}{\text{Total estimated purchases for the year}}$$

o When a standard cost system is used, variances expected to be reversed by year-end may be deferred to an asset or liability account.

How are taxes reflected in interim reports?

The income tax provision includes current and deferred taxes, both federal and local. The tax provision for an interim period should be cumulative. EXAMPLE: Total tax expense for a nine-month period is shown in the third quarter based on nine-month income.

The tax expense for the three-month period based on three months' income may also be presented. EXAMPLE: Third quarter tax expense based on only the third quarter.

What tax rate do I use?

In computing tax expense, the estimated annual effective tax rate should be used. The effective tax rate should be based on income from continuing operations. If a reliable estimate is not practical, the actual year-to-date effective tax rate should be used.

SUGGESTION
At the end of each interim period, a revision to the effective tax rate may be necessary, employing the best current estimates of the annual effective tax rate. The projected tax rate includes adjustment for net deferred credits. Adjustments should be contained in deriving the maximum tax benefit for year-to-date figures.

The estimated effective tax rate should incorporate:

- o All available tax credits (e.g., foreign tax credit)
- o All available alternative tax methods in determining ordinary earnings

NOTE
A change in tax legislation is only reflected in the interim period affected.

How are income and losses accounted for on interim reports?

Income statement items after income from continuing operations (e.g., income from discontinued operations, extraordinary items, cumulative effect of a change in accounting principle) should be presented net of the tax effect. The tax effect on these unusual line items should be reflected *only* in the interim period when they actually occur.

CAUTION
Do not predict items before they occur. Prior period adjustments in the retained earnings statement are also shown net of tax when they take place.

What do I do about a change in principle?

When a change in principle is made *in the first interim period,* the cumulative effect of a change in principle account should be shown net of tax in the first interim period.

If a change in principle is made *in a quarter other than the first* (e.g., third quarter), we assume the change was made at the beginning of the first quarter showing the cumulative effect in the first quarter. The interim periods will have to be *restated* using the new principle (e.g., first, second, and third quarters).

When *interim data for previous years* are presented for comparative purposes, data should be restated to conform with newly adopted policies. Alternatively, disclosure can be made of the effect on prior data, if the new practice had been applied to that period.

For a change in principle, disclosure should be made of the nature and justification in the interim period of change. The effect of the change on per share amounts should be given.

What other factors affect interim results?

o Disclosure should be made of seasonality aspects affecting interim results and contingencies.
o A change in the estimated effective tax rate should be disclosed.
o If a fourth quarter is not presented, any material adjustments to that quarter must be commented upon in the footnotes to the annual report.
o If an event is immaterial on an annual basis but material in the interim period, it should be disclosed.
o Purchase transactions should be noted.

How do I present prior period adjustments?

The financial statement presentation for prior period adjustments:

o Net income for the current period should include the portion of the effect related to current operations.
o Earnings of impacted prior interim periods of the current year should be restated to include the portion related thereto.
o If the prior period adjustment affects prior years, it should be included in the earnings of the first interim period of the current year.

Criteria to be met for prior period adjustments in interim periods:

o Materiality
o Estimable
o Identified to a prior interim period

EXAMPLES: Prior period adjustments for interim reporting include:

- Error corrections
- Settlement of litigation or claims
- Adjustment of income taxes
- Renegotiation proceedings
- Utility revenue under rate-making processes

	NOTES

Earnings per share is computed for interim purposes the same way as for annual purposes.

Segmental disposal is shown separately in the interim period during which it occurs.

PERSONAL FINANCIAL STATEMENTS

What are personal financial statements used for?

Personal financial statements may be prepared for an individual or family to show financial status. The accrual basis is followed. Some uses include:

- Obtaining credit
- Financial planning
- Compliance with disclosure requirements (for public officials)

What information should personal financial statements contain?

Disclosures in personal financial statements include:

- Individuals covered by the statement
- Methods used in determining current values
- Nature of joint ownership in property
- Identification of major investments
- Percentage of ownership in an identified closely held business, including the nature of business activities consummated, and summarized financial data for the entity
- Identification of intangibles including estimated lives
- Amount of life insurance taken out
- Pension rights
- Methods and estimates employed in computing income taxes
- Particulars of receivables and payables (e.g., interest rates, pledged items, and maturities)
- Noncapitalized commitments (e.g., rental agreements)

What are the guidelines for preparing the statement of financial condition?

In the statement of financial condition:

○ Assets are reflected at the estimated current value and are listed in the order of liquidity (maturity). Current value may be determined based on recent transactions of similar items, appraisals, present value of future cash flows from the asset, adjusting historical cost for inflation, and so on.

○ There is no breakdown between current and noncurrent classifications.

○ Material business interests should be shown separately. EXAMPLE: A material interest in a closely held company should be shown separately from the equity investment in other companies.

○ If assets are jointly owned, only the individual's beneficial interest should be reported.

○ Liabilities should be shown at current amounts by order of maturity.

○ Estimated current amounts is the lesser of the present value of the debt payments or the amount the liability could be currently paid off for. Usually, the liability equals the principal plus accrued interest due.

○ Estimated taxes payable is shown as a liability, including provision for unpaid taxes of previous years and the estimated tax for the current year. The estimated tax for the present year should be based on the relationship of year-to-date taxable income to estimated taxable income for the year. The amount is reduced by any withholding and estimated tax payments.

○ Net worth is the difference between assets and liabilities.

EXAMPLE 3.3

An illustrative statement of financial condition follows:

Mr. and Mrs. J. Smith
STATEMENT OF FINANCIAL CONDITION
DECEMBER 31, 20X5

Assets

Cash	$ 5,000
Interest and Dividends Receivable	200
Marketable Securities	10,000
Interest in Closely Held Company	6,000
Cash Surrender Value of Life Insurance	1,000
Real Estate	100,000
Personal Property	30,000
Total	$152,200

Liabilities

Credit cards	$ 6,000

EXAMPLE 3.3 *(continued)*	
Income Taxes Payable	3,000
Loans Payable	10,000
Mortgage Payable	60,000
	$ 79,000
Estimated taxes on the differences between the estimated current values of assets, the current amounts of liabilities and their tax bases	40,000
Net Worth	33,200
Total	$152,200

What role does cost basis play in the statement of financial condition?

The statement of financial condition includes another element for the tax provision based on the difference between the current estimated amounts of assets and liabilities and their respective bases.

EXAMPLE 3.4
An individual owns ABC stock that was bought five years ago for $8,000. The stock is currently worth $17,000. The individual is in the 38 percent tax bracket. If the individual sold the stock today, there would be a $9,000 gain, which would result in $3,420 in taxes. The $3,420 should be included in the "provision for estimated taxes on the difference between carrying amounts and tax bases of assets and liabilities." Since the $3,420 constitutes an amount of taxes that would be payable upon sale of the stock, it should be presented as a credit in the Statement of Financial Condition reducing the individual's net worth.

Is there another statement that can be prepared?

As an option, a statement of changes in net worth may be prepared. It is useful in showing the mix of business and personal items in personal financial statements. Increases and decreases in net worth are shown.

Items increasing net worth include:

- Income
- Increases in current value of assets
- Decreases in the current amounts of liabilities
- Decreases in estimated taxes on the difference between estimated current asset values and liability amounts and their tax bases

Items decreasing net worth include:

o Expenses
o Decreases in current values of assets
o Increases in current amounts of liabilities
o Increases in estimated taxes on the difference between the current amount and the tax bases of assets and liabilities

Also optional are comparative financial statements.

INCORPORATION OF A BUSINESS

What accounting is needed when forming a corporation?

When an unincorporated entity (e.g., sole proprietorship, partnership) incorporates and issues stock or debt securities in exchange for the assets of the unincorporated business:

o The new corporation does not recognize the gain or loss on the issuance of stock in exchange for the unincorporated entity's assets.
o Assets acquired are recorded at fair market value.
o Current liabilities are recorded at face value.
o Long-term liabilities are recorded at present value.
o Stock issued is recorded at par value.
o The excess of net fair market value of assets acquired over par value is credited to paid-in-capital.

The journal entry is:

Cash	
Current Assets	
Fixed Assets	
Current Liabilities	
Long-term Liabilities	
Common Stock	
Paid-in-capital	

PARTNERSHIPS

How do I account for a partnership?

When a partnership is formed:

o Assets are debited at fair market value.
o Liabilities are credited for debt assumed, usually at the present value of future payments or fair value.
o Capital is credited for the net difference.

What accounting changes are needed when a new partner is admitted?

A new partner may be admitted to the partnership by:

o *Buying the interest of an existing partner.* When an interest is purchased from an existing partner, it is a private

> ### EXAMPLE 3.5
>
> X and Y form a partnership. X transfers $10,000 cash, and Y provides $30,000 of furniture with a loan thereon of $5,000. The journal entry is:
>
> | | | |
> |---|---|---|
> | Cash | 10,000 | |
> | Furniture | 30,000 | |
> | Loans Payable | | 5,000 |
> | X Capital | | 10,000 |
> | Y Capital | | 25,000 |

transaction between the two parties not affecting the partnership's financial records. The new partner's capital account is recorded simply by relabeling the old partner's capital account.

○ *Contributing assets to the partnership* (e.g., new capital). In this case, the new partner may receive an interest in exchange for the contributed assets and/or goodwill (e.g., client following).

How is the new partner's admission accounted for?

The new partner's admission may be accounted for under either the bonus method or the goodwill method.

Bonus Method

The new partner's capital account is credited for an amount equal to his purchased share of the partnership's total capital. The total capital equals the net book value of assets before the new partner's contribution plus the fair value of net assets contributed by the new partner. A bonus arises for the difference between the fair market value of contributed assets and the credit to the new partner's capital account.

○ If fair value of contributed assets *exceeds* the credit to the new partner's capital account, the excess increases the capital accounts of the old partners based on the profit and loss ratio.

○ If fair value of contributed assets is less than the new partner's capital account, the new partner recognizes the bonus. RESULT: The bonus reduces the old partners' capital accounts based on the profit and loss ratio.

Goodwill Method

If the new partner's contribution *exceeds* the ownership interest he has obtained, the excess assets represent goodwill applicable to the old partners.

○ When the new partner's asset contribution *is less than* the ownership interest received, the excess capital allowed to the new partner is construed as goodwill attributable to him.

How are profits and losses accounted for in a partnership?

Profit and loss of the partnership are divided equally unless stated otherwise in the partnership agreement. In dividing profits, the partnership may consider:

- o Salary provision and interest on capital balances (interest based on the beginning, ending, or average capital)
- o Time spent or capital invested

When interest and salary exceed profit, the resulting loss will be allocated based on the profit and loss ratio.

Partner drawing accounts exist to reflect cash withdrawals from the business. The drawing accounts are periodically closed to the capital accounts.

How do I treat partner withdrawals and liquidation of the partnership?

When the amount paid to a withdrawing or retiring partner exceeds his capital balance, the excess is either attributed to goodwill or charged against the remaining partners' capital balances based on the profit and loss ratio.

When a partnership is liquidated, gains or losses on sales of assets are divided among the partners based on the profit and loss ratio. The initial cash received is used to satisfy the liabilities.

NOTE
Before the cash can be distributed to a partner, liquidation losses and expenses must have been charged to the capital accounts.

CHAPTER 4

ACCOUNTING AND DISCLOSURES

Accounting changes include a change in:

- *Principle*, which requires a "cumulative effect of a change in principle" account to be shown in the current year's income statement.
- *Estimate*, which is accounted for prospectively over current and future years.
- *Reporting entity*, which mandates the restatement of previous years' financial statements as if both companies were always combined.

Corrections of errors adjust the beginning balance of retained earnings.

NOTE
Significant accounting policies must be disclosed.

Development stage companies must follow the same generally accepted accounting principles as established companies.

In a *troubled debt restructuring*, the debtor recognizes an extraordinary gain while the creditor recognizes an ordinary loss.

Segmental disclosures are required when a business segment comprises 10 percent or more of revenue, operating profit, or total assets of the entire company.

In the case of a noninterest-bearing note, interest must be imputed based on the interest rate the borrower would normally pay for a note in an arms-length transaction.

Accounting for futures contracts and oil and gas accounting problems are also addressed.

 ACCOUNTING CHANGES

APB 20 provides for accounting changes in principle, estimate, and reporting entity. Correction of an error in a prior year is also briefly mentioned. Proper disclosure of accounting changes is necessary.

Change in Accounting Principle

May accounting principles be changed?

A change in principle should be made *only when necessary.* Once adopted, it is presumed that an accounting principle should not be changed for events or transactions of a similar nature. A method used for a transaction that is being terminated or was a single, nonrecurring event in the past should not be changed.

How is a change in accounting principle reflected?

A change in accounting principle is accounted for in the current year's income statement in an account called "cumulative effect of a change in accounting principle."

- o The amount equals the difference between retained earnings at the beginning of the year with the old method, versus what retained earnings would have been at the beginning of the year if the new method had been used in prior years.
- o The account is shown net of tax with EPS on it.
- o The cumulative effect account is shown after extraordinary items and before net income in the income statement.
- o The new principle is used in the current and future years. Consistency is needed for accurate user comparisons.

NOTE

A change in depreciation method for a *new* fixed asset is not a change in principle.

NOTE

Footnote disclosure should be made of the nature of and justification for a change in principle, including an explanation of why the new principle is preferred.

What justifies a change in principle?

A change in principle is justified by:

- o A new FASB pronouncement
- o A new tax law

o A new AICPA recommended practice

o A change in circumstances

o The need to more readily conform to industry practice

NOTES

According to FASB 32, specialized accounting practices and principles included in the AICPA Statements of Position (SOPs) and Guides are "preferable accounting principles" for the application of APB 20. Where summaries of financial data for several years are present in financial reports, APB 20 applies.

Indirect effects are included in the cumulative effect only if they are to be recorded on the books as a result of a change in accounting principle. The cumulative effect does *not* include nondiscretionary adjustments based on earnings (e.g., employee bonuses), which would have been recognized if the new principle had been used in prior years.

What about comparative financial statements?

If comparative financial statements are not shown, pro forma disclosures (recalculated figures) should be made between the body of the financial statements and the footnotes. Disclosures should show:

o What earnings would have been in prior years if the new principle was used in those prior years

o The actual amounts for those years

If income statements are presented for comparative purposes, they should reflect the change on a pro forma basis as if the change had been in effect in each of such years.

How do I present comparative financial statements?

Financial statements of prior years, presented for comparative purposes, are presented *as previously reported*. Income before extraordinary items, net income, and earnings per share for previous years presented are *recalculated* and disclosed on the face of the prior periods' income statements as if the new principle had been in use in those periods. This information may be presented in separate schedules showing both the original and recalculated figures.

NOTES

If only the current period's income statement is presented, the actual and pro forma figures for the immediately preceding period should be disclosed.

In exceptional cases, pro forma amounts are not determinable for prior years, even though the cumulative effect on the opening retained earnings balance can be computed. The cumulative effect of a change in principle is presented in the usual fashion, with reasons given for omitting pro forma figures.

Similarly, when the cumulative effect of a change in principle is impossible to calculate, disclosure is given for the effect of the change on income data of the current period and explaining the reason for omitting the cumulative effect and pro forma amounts for prior periods.

EXAMPLE: A switch from the FIFO to LIFO inventory pricing method.

If an accounting change in principle is deemed immaterial in the current year but is anticipated to be material in later years, disclosure is necessary.

When do I have to restate prior years after a change in principle?

Certain types of changes in accounting principle, instead of being shown in a cumulative effect account, require the restatement of prior years as if the new principle had been used in those years. These changes are:

- Change from LIFO to another inventory method
- Change in accounting for long-term construction contracts (e.g., changing from the completed contract method to the percentage of completion method)
- Change to or from the full cost method used in the extractive industry. (In the full cost method both successful and unsuccessful exploration costs are deferred to the asset account and amortized. In the alternative successful efforts method only successful costs are deferred and unsuccessful ones are immediately expensed.)

Who is exempt from restating prior years after a change in principle?

A *closely held* business which for the *first time* registers securities, obtains equity capital, or effects a business combination is *exempt from the requirements of this opinion.* Such a company *may* restate prior year financial statements.

Not considered a change in accounting principle are:

- A principle adopted for the first time on new or previously immaterial events or transactions.

o A principle adopted or changed due to events or transactions clearly different in substance.

What if I were to change a method, not a principle?

An *accounting principle* is not only an accounting principle
or practice, but also includes the methods used to apply
such principles and practices.

EXAMPLE: *Changing the composition* of the cost elements (e.g., material, labor, and overhead) of inventory
qualifies as an accounting change. Changing the composition must be reported and justified as preferable.

The basis of preferability among the different accounting
principles is established in terms of whether the new principle improves the financial reporting function. Preferability
is not determinable by considering income tax effect alone.

EXAMPLE 4.1

X Company changed from double declining balance to
straight-line depreciation in 20X5. It uses MACRS depreciation for tax purposes. This results in depreciation
higher than the double declining balance method for
each of the three years. The tax rate is 34 percent. Relevant data follow:

Year	Double Declining Balance Depreciation	Straight-Line Depreciation	Difference
20X3	$250,000	$150,000	$100,000
20X4	200,000	150,000	50,000
20X5	185,000	150,000	35,000

The entries to reflect the change in depreciation in
20X5 follow:

Depreciation	150,000	
Accumulated Depreciation		150,000
For current year depreciation under the straight-line method.		
Accumulated Depreciation (100,000 + 50,000)	150,000	
Deferred Income Tax Credit (150,000 × 0.34)		51,000
Cumulative Effect of a Change in Accounting Principle		99,000

Change in Accounting Estimate

When do I change an accounting estimate?

A change in accounting estimate is caused by new circumstances or events requiring a revision in the estimates, such
as a change in salvage value or in the life of an asset.

How is a change in estimate disclosed?

- ○ A change in accounting estimate is accounted for prospectively over current and future years. There is *no* restatement of prior years.
- ○ A footnote should describe the nature of the change.
- ○ Disclosure is required in the period of the change for the effect on income before extraordinary items, net income, and earnings per share. Disclosure is *not* required for estimate changes in the ordinary course of business when immaterial. EXAMPLE: Revising estimates of uncollectible accounts or inventory obsolescence.

How is a change in estimate accounted for?

If a change in estimate is coupled with a change in principle and the effects cannot be distinguished, it is accounted for as a change in estimate. EXAMPLE: A change made from deferring and amortizing a cost to expensing it as incurred because of doubtful future benefits. This should be accounted for as a change in estimate.

EXAMPLE 4.2

Equipment was bought on 1/1/20X2 for $40,000, having an original estimated life of 10 years with a salvage value of $4,000. On 1/1/20X6, the estimated life was revised to eight more years remaining with a new salvage value of $3,200. The journal entry on 12/31/20X6 for depreciation expense is:

Depreciation	2,800	
Accumulated Depreciation		2,800

Computations follow:
Book value on 1/1/20X6:

Original cost		$40,000
Less: Accumulated Depreciation		

$$\frac{\$40,000 - \$4,000}{10} = \$3,600 \times 4$$

		$14,400
Book value		$25,600

Depreciation for 20X6:

Book value	$25,600
Less: New Salvage value	3,200
Depreciable cost	$22,400

$$\frac{\text{Depreciable cost}}{\text{New life}} \quad \frac{\$22,400}{8} = \$2,800$$

Change in Reporting Entity

How is a change in reporting entity treated?

A change in reporting entity (e.g., two previously separate companies combine) is accounted for by restating prior years' financial statements as if both companies were always combined.

o Restatement for a change in reporting entity is necessary to show proper trends in comparative financial statements and historical summaries.

o The effect of the change on income before extraordinary items, net income, and per share amounts is reported for all periods presented. The restatement process does not have to go back more than five years.

o Footnote disclosure should be made of the nature of and reason for the change in reporting entity only in the year of change.

EXAMPLES:

o Presenting consolidated statements instead of statements of individual companies

o Change in subsidiaries included in consolidated statements or those included in combined statements

Correction of an Error

What do I do about a mistake?

A correction of an error is accounted for as a prior period adjustment. The retained earnings account absorbs the difference related to the error for previous years.

EXAMPLE 4.3

On 1/1/20X3, B Company received $13,000 on account from a customer. It improperly credited revenue. The correcting entry on 12/31/20X5 is:

Retained Earnings	13,000	
Accounts Receivable		13,000

EXAMPLE 4.4

At the end of 20X2, a company failed to accrue telephone expense which was paid at the beginning of 20X3.
The correcting entry on 12/31/20X3 is:

Retained Earnings	16,000	
Telephone Expense		16,000

EXAMPLE 4.5

At the beginning of 20X5, a company bought equipment
for $300,000, with a salvage value of $20,000 and an
expected life of 10 years. Straight-line depreciation is
used. In error, salvage value was not deducted in computing depreciation. The correcting journal entries on
12/31/20X7 are:

		20X5 and 20X6
Depreciation taken		
$300,000/10 × 2 years		$60,000
Depreciation correctly		
stated $280,000/10 × 2 years		$56,000
		$ 4,000
Depreciation	$28,000	
Accumulated Depreciation		28,000
Depreciation for current year		
Accumulated Depreciation	4,000	
Retained Earnings		4,000
Correct prior year depreciation		
misstatement		

PRIOR PERIOD ADJUSTMENTS

What are prior period adjustments?

The two types of prior period adjustments are:

- Recognition of a tax loss carryforward benefit arising
  from a purchased subsidiary.
- Correction of an error that was made in a prior year.

Errors may be due to mathematical mistakes, errors in
applying accounting principles, or misuse of facts existing
when the financial statements were prepared. Furthermore
a change in principle from one that is not GAAP to one that
is GAAP is an error correction.

Disclosure should be made of the nature of the error and
the effect of correction on earnings.

How are prior period adjustments made?

When a single year is presented, prior period adjustments adjust the beginning balance of retained earnings. The presentation follows:

Retained Earnings—1/1 Unadjusted
Prior Period Adjustments (net of tax)
Retained Earnings—1/1 Adjusted
Add: Net Income
Less: Dividends
Retained Earnings—12/31

When comparative statements are prepared, a retroactive adjustment for the error is made insofar as it affects the prior years. The retroactive adjustment is disclosed by showing the effects of the adjustment on previous years' earnings and component items of net income.

EXAMPLE 4.6

On 1/1/20X2, an advance retainer fee of $50,000 was received covering a five-year period. In error, revenue was credited for the full amount. The error was discovered on 12/31/20X4, before closing the books. The correcting entry is:

12/31/20X4 Retained Earnings	30,000	
Revenue		10,000
Deferred Revenue		20,000

EXAMPLE 4.7

A company bought a machine on January 1, 20X4, for $32,000 with a $2,000 salvage value and a five-year life. The repairs expense was charged in error. The mistake was discovered on December 31, 20X7, before closing the books. The correcting entry is:

Depreciation Expense	6,000	
Machine	32,000	
Accumulated Depreciation		24,000
Retained Earnings		14,000

Accumulated depreciation of $24,000 is calculated below:

$$\frac{\$32,000 - \$2,000}{5} = \$6,000 \text{ per year} \times 4 \text{ years} = \$24,000$$

The credit to retained earnings reflects the difference between the erroneous repairs expense of $32,000 in 20X4 versus showing depreciation expense of $18,000 for three years (20X4–20X6).

DISCLOSURE OF ACCOUNTING POLICIES

What are accounting policies?

Accounting policies include accounting principles and methods of application in the presentation of financial statements, including:

- A selection from generally accepted accounting principles
- Practices unique to the given industry
- Unusual applications of generally accepted accounting principles

What should be described regarding accounting policies?

The first footnote or section preceding the notes to the financial statements should be a description of the accounting policies followed by the company.

EXAMPLES:

- The depreciation method used
- Consolidation bases
- Amortization period for a patent
- Construction contract method
- Inventory pricing method

NOTES

Financial statement classification methods and qualitative data (e.g., litigation) are *not* accounting policies.

Non-profit entities should also disclose the accounting policies followed.

The application of GAAP requires the use of *judgment* where alternative acceptable principles exist and where varying methods of applying a principle to a given set of facts exist.

Disclosure of these principles and methods *is vital* to the full presentation of financial position and operations, so that rational economic decisions can be made.

Is disclosure of accounting policies always necessary?

Some types of financial statements do not need a description of the accounting policies followed.

EXAMPLES:

- Quarterly unaudited statements when there has not been a policy change since the last year-end
- Statements solely for internal use

DEVELOPMENT STAGE COMPANIES

What are development stage entities?

A development stage entity is one that concentrates on establishing a new business, where major operations have not begun or operations have started but no significant revenue has been derived. Some activities of a development stage enterprise are:

- Establishing sources of supply
- Developing markets
- Obtaining financing
- Financial and production planning
- Research and development
- Buying capital assets
- Recruiting staff

What are the requirements for a development stage company?

The *same* generally accepted accounting principles for an established company must be followed by a development stage enterprise. A balance sheet, income statement, and statement of cash flows are prepared.

- The balance sheet shows the accumulated net losses as a deficit.
- The income statement presents cumulative amounts of revenues and expenses since inception of the business.
- Similarly, the statement of cash flows presents the operating, investing, and financing cash receipts and cash payments.
- The stockholders' equity statement shows for each equity security from inception the date and number of shares issued and dollar figures per share applicable to cash and noncash consideration.

The nature and basis for determining amounts of noncash consideration must also be provided.

NOTES
Financial statements must be headed "development stage enterprise."
A footnote should describe the development stage activities.
In the first year that the entity is no longer in the development stage, it should disclose that in previous years it was in the development stage.

TROUBLED DEBT RESTRUCTURING

What is a troubled debt restructuring?

In a troubled debt restructuring, a debtor in financial difficulty receives partial or complete forgiveness of the obligation by the creditor. The concession may be:

- By debtor-creditor agreement
- Imposed by law
- By foreclosure and repossession

Some types of troubled debt restructurings are:

- Debtor transfers to creditor receivables from third parties or other assets in part or full satisfaction of the debt.
- Debtor gives creditor equity securities to satisfy the debt.
- Modification of the debt terms including downwardly
  adjusting the interest rate, lengthening the maturity
  date, or reducing the face amount of the obligation.

The debtor recognizes an extraordinary gain (net of tax)
on the restructuring, while the creditor recognizes a loss.
The loss may be ordinary or extraordinary, depending on
whether such arrangement by the creditor is unusual and
infrequent. Typically, the loss is ordinary.

Debtor

How is the debtor's gain disclosed?

The gain to the debtor equals the difference between the fair
value of assets exchanged and the book value of the debt,
including accrued interest. Furthermore, there may be a gain
on disposal of assets exchanged in the transaction equal to the
difference between the fair market value and the book value of
the transferred assets. The latter gain or loss is *not* a gain or loss
on restructuring, but rather an ordinary gain or loss in connection with asset disposal.

EXAMPLE 4.8
A debtor transferred assets having a fair value of $80 and a book value of $60 in settlement of a payable with a carrying value of $90. The gain on restructuring is $10 ($90 – $80). The ordinary gain is $20 ($80 – $60).

What if the debtor transfers stock to the creditor?

A debtor may transfer an equity interest to the creditor:
The debtor enters the equity securities issued on the basis
of fair market value rather than the recorded value of the
debt satisfied. The excess of the recorded payable satisfied

over the fair market value of the securities issued is an extraordinary gain.

What must I do if the original debt agreement is changed?

When a modification in terms of an initial debt agreement exists, it is *accounted for prospectively.* There is a new interest rate computed based on the new terms. This interest rate is then employed to allocate future payments to reduce principal and interest. When the new terms of the agreement cause the sum of all the future payments to be *less* than the book value of the payable, the payable is reduced, and a restructuring gain is recognized for the difference. Future payments are construed as a reduction of principal only. No interest expense is recognized.

Is a transfer of assets the only way to restructure a debt?

A troubled debt restructuring may result in a *combination* of concessions to the debtor. This may occur when assets or an equity interest are transferred for *partial* satisfaction of the debt, and the balance is subject to a modification of terms. Two steps are involved:

o The payable is reduced by the fair market value of the assets or equity transferred.

o The remaining part of the debt is accounted for as a "modification of terms" type restructuring.

Direct costs (e.g., legal fees) incurred by the debtor in an equity transfer lower the fair value of the equity interest. All other costs reduce the gain on restructuring. If there is no gain involved, they are expensed.

Footnote disclosure by the debtor includes:

o Explaining the particulars of the restructuring agreement

o The aggregate and per share amounts of the gain on restructuring

o Amounts that are contingently payable including the contingency terms

Creditor

What is done if the creditor cannot collect?

The creditor's loss is the difference between the fair market value of assets received and the book value of the investment. In a modification of terms situation:

o The creditor recognizes interest income to the extent total future payments exceed the carrying value of the investment. Interest income is recognized using the effective interest method.

o Assets received are recorded at fair market value.
o When the carrying value of the receivable is greater than the aggregate payments, an ordinary loss is booked for the difference.
o All cash received in the future is accounted for as a recovery of the investment.
o Direct costs incurred by the creditor are expensed.

NOTES
The creditor does not recognize contingent interest until the contingency is removed and interest has been earned.
Future changes in the interest rate are accounted for as a change in estimate.

Footnote disclosure by the creditor includes:

o Commitments to lend additional funds to financially troubled debtors
o Loans and/or receivables by major class
o Debt agreements where the interest rate has been modified, explaining the particulars
o Description of terms of the restructuring

EXAMPLE 4.9
The debtor owes the creditor $100,000 and has indicated that because of financial problems there may be difficulty in meeting future payments. Footnote disclosure by the creditor and debtor are needed surrounding the financial problems.

EXAMPLE 4.10

The debtor owes the creditor $100,000. The creditor relieves the debtor of $20,000. The balance of the obligation will be paid at a later date. The journal entries are:

Debtor		Creditor	
Accounts Payable	20,000	Ordinary Loss	20,000
Extraordinary Gain	20,000	Accounts Receivable	20,000

EXAMPLE 4.11

The debtor owes the creditor $50,000. The creditor agrees to accept $45,000 in payment in full satisfaction of the debt. The journal entries are:

Debtor			Creditor		
Accounts Payable	5,000		Ordinary Loss	5,000	
Extraordinary Gain		5,000	Accounts		
			Receivable		5,000

SEGMENTAL REPORTING

What is segmental reporting?

Segmental data occurs when a company prepares a full set of financial statements (balance sheet, income statement, statement of cash flows, and related footnotes). The data are shown for each year presented. Information reported is a disaggregation of consolidated financial information.

Segmental information assists financial statement users in analyzing financial statements by allowing improved assessment of an enterprise's past performance and future prospects.

Financial reporting for business segments is useful in evaluating segmental performance, earning potential, and risk.

Segmental reporting may be by:

- Industry
- Foreign geographic area
- Export sales
- Major customers
- Governmental contracts

An industry segment sells merchandise or renders services to outside customers.

EXCEPTION

Segmental information is not required for nonpublic companies.

What does FASB Statement No. 131 (Disclosures about Segments of an Enterprise and Related Information) require?

FASB Statement No. 131 requires that the amount reported for each segment item be based on what the *chief operating decision maker* (e.g., chief executive officer, chief operating officer) uses in making a determination as to the amount of resources to assign to a segment and how to evaluate the performance of that segment.

NOTE
The term *chief operating decision maker* may relate to a function and not necessarily a specific person. This is a management approach instead of an industry approach in identifying segments. The segments are based on the company's organizational structure, income sources, nature of activities, existence of managers, and information presented to the board of directors.

Revenues, gains, expenses, losses, and assets should be allocated to a segment only if the chief operating decision maker considers doing so in measuring a segment's earnings for purposes of making a financial or operating decision.

NOTE
A start-up operation would qualify as an operating segment even though revenue is not being earned.

Do special principles apply to segmental reporting?

Accounting principles employed in preparing financial statements should be used for segment information, except that numerous intercompany transactions eliminated in consolidation are included in segmental reporting on a gross basis. The financial statement presentation for segments may appear in the body, footnotes, or in a separate schedule to the financial statements.

When must a segment be reported?

A segment must be reported if any of these criteria are met:

- Revenue is 10 percent or more of total revenue
- Operating income or loss is 10 percent or more of the combined operating profit
- Identifiable assets are 10 percent or more of the total identifiable assets

How are reportable segments established?

Reportable segments are determined by:

- Identifying specific products and services
- Grouping those products and services into segments by industry line
- Selecting material segments to the company as a whole

A number of approaches are possible in grouping products and services by industry lines. In many cases, management judgment is necessary to determine the industry segment.

A starting point in deriving the industry segment is by *profit center*. When the profit center crosses industry lines, it should be broken down into smaller groups. A company in an industry not accumulating financial information on a segregated basis must disaggregate its operations by industry line.

Although worldwide industry segmentation is recommended, it may not be practical. If foreign operations cannot be disaggregated, the firm should disaggregate domestic activities. Foreign operations should be disaggregated where possible and the remaining foreign operations be treated as a single segment.

How do I determine whether a segment is significant?

A segment that was significant in the past, even though not meeting the 10 percent test in the current year, should still be reported if it is expected that the segment will be significant in the future.

Segments should constitute a substantial portion (75 percent or more) of the company's total revenue to outside customers. The 75 percent test is applied separately each year.

In order to derive 75 percent, no more than 10 segments should be shown for practical purposes. If more than 10 are identified, similar segments may be combined.

NOTES
Even though intersegment transfers are eliminated in the preparation of consolidated financial statements, they are includable for segmental disclosure in determining the 10 percent and 75 percent rules.
Disclosures are not required for 90 percent enterprises (i.e., a company that derives 90 percent or more of its revenue, operating profit, and total assets from one segment). In effect, that segment *is* the business. The dominant industry segment should be identified.

How is the 10 percent criterion applied?

In applying the 10 percent criterion, the accountant should note the following:

o *Revenue*. Revenue to unaffiliated customers and revenue to other business segments should be separated. Transfer prices are used for intersegmental transfers. Accounting bases followed should be disclosed.

○ *Operating Profit or Loss.* Operating earnings of a segment excludes:

- General corporate revenue and expenses that are not allocable
- Interest expense (unless the segment is a financial type, such as one involved in banking)
- Domestic and foreign income taxes
- Income from unconsolidated subsidiaries or investees
- Income from discontinued operations
- Extraordinary items
- Cumulative effect of a change in accounting principles
- Minority interest

NOTE

Directly traceable and allocable costs should be charged to segments when applicable thereto.

○ *Identifiable Assets.* Assets of a segment include those directly in it and general corporate assets that can rationally be allocated to it. Allocation methods should be consistently applied. Identifiable assets include those consisting of a part of the company's investment in the segment (e.g., goodwill). Identifiable assets do not include advances or loans to other segments except for income therefrom that is used to compute the results of operations (e.g., a segment of a financial nature).

What disclosures do segments have to make?

Disclosures to be made by segments include:

○ Measurement or valuation basis, and change therein
○ Aggregate depreciation, depletion, and amortization expense
○ Capital expenditures
○ Company's equity in vertically integrated, unconsolidated subsidiaries and equity method investees (Note the geographic location of equity method investees.)
○ Effect of an accounting principle change on the operating profit of the reportable segment, including its effect on the company
○ Material segmental accounting policies not already disclosed in the regular financial statements
○ Unusual items included in segmental earnings
○ Transfer price used
○ Allocation method for costs
○ Unusual items affecting segmental profit

- Type of products
- Sales to unaffiliated customers
- Tax effects

How does consolidation affect segmental reporting?

If a segment includes a *purchase method* consolidated subsidiary, the required segmental information is based on the consolidated value of the subsidiary (i.e., fair market value and goodwill recognized), *not* on the values recorded in the subsidiary's own financial statements. However, transactions between the segment and other segments, which are eliminated in consolidation, *are* reportable.

Segmental data are *not* required for *unconsolidated subsidiaries* or other *unconsolidated investees*.

NOTE
Each subsidiary or investee is subject to the rules requiring that segment information be reported.

Some types of typical consolidation eliminations are *not* eliminated when reporting for segments.

EXAMPLE: Revenue of a segment includes intersegmental sales and sales to unrelated customers.

A full set of financial statements for a foreign investee that is *not* a subsidiary does not have to disclose segmental information when presented in the same financial report of a primary reporting entity.

EXCEPTION
The foreign investee's separately issued statements already disclose the required segmental data.

Are there other requirements that apply to segmental reporting?

The source of the segmental revenue should be disclosed, along with the percent so derived, when:

- 10 percent or more of revenue or assets is associated with a foreign area. Presentation must be made of revenue, operating profit or loss, and assets for foreign operations in the aggregate or by geographic area. (A foreign geographic area is a foreign country or group of homogeneous countries. Factors considered are geographical proximity, economic affinity, and similar business environments.)
- 10 percent or more of sales is to one customer. A group of customers under common control is construed as one customer.

o 10 percent or more of revenue is obtained from either domestic or foreign government contracts.

In some instances, *restatement* of prior period information is required for *comparative* reasons when:

o Financial statements of the company as a whole have been restated.
o A change has occurred in grouping products or services for segment determination.
o A change has taken place in grouping of foreign activities into geographic segments.

The nature and effect of restatement should be disclosed.

NOTE

Segmental data that are presented in another company's financial report are not required in financial statements if those statements are:

---

o Combined in a complete set of statements, and both sets are presented in the same report
o Presented for a foreign investee (not a subsidiary of the primary enterprise) unless the financial statements disclose segment information (e.g., foreign investees for which such information is already required by the SEC)
o Presented in the report of a nonpublic company

NOTE

If an investee uses the market value or equity method and is not exempted by one of the above provisions, its full set of financial statements presented in another enterprise's report must present segment information if such data are significant to statements of the primary enterprise. Significance is determined by applying the percentage tests (i.e., 10 percent tests) to the financial statements of the primary enterprise without adjustment for the investee's revenue, operating results, or identifiable assets.

IMPUTING INTEREST ON NOTES

What if a noninterest-bearing note exists?

If the face amount of a note does not represent the present value of the consideration given or received in the exchange, imputation of interest is needed to avoid the misstatement of profit. Interest is imputed:

o On noninterest-bearing notes
o On notes that provide for an unrealistically low interest rate

o When the face value of the note is significantly different from the "going" selling price of the property or
market value of the note

NOTES

If a note is issued only for cash, the note should be
recorded at the cash exchanged, regardless of
whether the interest rate is reasonable or of the amount
of the face value of the note. The note has a present
value at issuance equal to the cash transacted.

When a note is exchanged for property, goods, or
services, a presumption exists that the interest rate is
fair and reasonable. Where the stipulated interest rate
is not fair and adequate, the note has to be recorded
at the fair value of the merchandise or services or at an
amount that approximates fair value. If fair value is not
determinable for the goods or services, the discounted
present value of the note has to be used.

How do I determine the imputed interest rate?

The imputed interest rate is the one that would have
resulted if an independent borrower or lender had negotiated a similar transaction. EXAMPLE: It is the prevailing
interest rate the borrower would have paid for financing.

Factors to consider in deriving an appropriate discount
rate are:

o Prime interest rate
o "Going" market rate for similar quality instruments
o Issuer's credit standing
o Collateral
o Restrictive covenants and other terms in the note
agreement
o Tax effects of the arrangement

For what kinds of instruments does imputed interest have to be determined?

APB 21 applies to long-term payables and receivables.
Short-term payables and receivables are typically recorded
at face value since the extra work of amortizing a discount
or premium on a short-term note is not worth the information benefit obtained.

APB 21 is *not* applicable to:

o Security deposits
o Usual lending activities of banks
o Amounts that do not mandate repayment

○ Receivables or payables occurring within the ordinary course of business

○ Transactions between parent and subsidiary

How are premiums and discounts determined and handled?

The difference between the face value of the note and the present value of the note represents discount or premium. This must be accounted for as an element of interest over the life of the note Present value of the payments of the note is based on an imputed interest rate.

The interest method is used to amortize the discount or premium on the note. The interest method results in a constant rate of interest.

Amortization = Interest Rate × Present Value of the Liability/Receivable at the beginning of the year

Interest expense is recorded for the borrower while interest revenue is recorded for the lender. Issuance costs are treated as a deferred charge.

The note payable and note receivable are presented in the balance sheet this way:

Notes Payable (principal plus interest)
Less: Discount (interest)
Present Value (principal)
Notes Receivable (principal plus interest)
Less: Premium (interest)
Present Value (principal)

EXAMPLE 4.12

On 1/1/20X4, a machine is bought for $10,000 cash and the incurrence of a $30,000, five-year, noninterest-bearing note payable. The imputed interest rate is 10 percent. The present value factor for $n = 5$, $i = 10\%$ is 0.62. Appropriate journal entries are:

1/1/20X4

Machine (10,000 + 18,600)	28,600	
Discount	11,400	
Notes Payable		30,000
Cash		10,000

Present value of note equals $30,000 × 0.62 = $18,600. On 1/1/20X4, the balance sheet shows:

Notes Payable	$30,000
Less: Discount	11,400
Present Value	$18,600

12/31/20X4

Interest Expense	1,860	
Discount		
10% × $18,600 = $1,860		1,860

EXAMPLE 4.12 *(continued)*		
On 1/1/20X5 the balance sheet shows:		
Notes Payable	$30,000	
Less: Discount (11,400 – 1,860)	9,540	
Present Value	$20,460	
12/31/20X5		
Interest Expense	2,046	
Discount		
10% × $20,460 = $2,046		2,046

ACCOUNTING FOR FUTURES CONTRACTS

What are futures contracts?

A futures contract is a legal arrangement entered into by the purchaser or seller and a regulated futures exchange in the United States or overseas. FASB 80 does not apply to foreign currencies futures, which are dealt with in FASB 82. Futures contracts involve:

- A buyer or seller receiving or making a delivery of a commodity or financial instrument (e.g., stocks, bonds, commercial paper, mortgages) at a given date. Cash settlement rather than delivery often exists (e.g., stock index future).

- A futures contract may be eliminated prior to the delivery date by engaging in an offsetting contract for the particular commodity or financial instrument involved. EXAMPLE: A futures contract to buy 100,000 pounds of a commodity by December 31, 20X4, may be canceled by entering into another contract to sell 100,000 pounds of that same commodity on December 31, 20X4.

- Changes in value of open contracts are settled regularly (e.g., daily). The usual contract provides that when a decrease in the contract value occurs, the contract holder has to make a cash deposit for such decline with the clearinghouse. If the contract increases in value, the holder may withdraw the increased value.

When does a futures position constitute a hedge?

A *hedge* exists when both of the following criteria are met:

- The hedged item places price and interest rate risk on the firm. Risk means the sensitivity of corporate earnings to market price changes or rates of return of existing assets, liabilities, commitments, and expected transactions.

NOTE
This criterion is *not* met where other assets, liabilities, commitments, and anticipated transactions *already* offset the risk.

○ The contract lowers risk exposure and is entered into as a hedge. High correlation exists between the change in market value of the contract and the fair value of the hedged item. In effect, the market price change of the contract offsets the price and interest rate changes on the exposed item. EXAMPLE: When a futures contract exists to sell silver that offsets the changes in the price of silver.

How do I handle a change in the market value of the futures contract?

The change in market value of a futures contract involves a gain or loss that should be recognized in earnings.

EXCEPTION
For certain contracts the timing of income statement recognition relates to the accounting for the applicable asset, liability, commitment, or transaction. This accounting exception applies when the contract is designed as a hedge against price and interest rate fluctuation. When the above criteria are met, the accounting for the contract relates to the accounting for the hedged item. Thus, a change in market value is recognized in the same accounting period during which the effects of related changes in price or interest rate of the hedged item are reflected in income.

What are the requirements for a "hedge-type" futures contract?

○ A change in the market value of a futures contract that meets the hedging criteria of the related asset or liability should adjust the carrying value of the hedged item. EXAMPLE: A company has an investment in a government bond that it anticipates selling at a later date. The company can reduce its susceptibility to changes in fair value of the bonds by engaging in a futures contract. The changes in the market value of the futures contract adjust the book value of the bonds.

○ A change in the market value of a futures contract for the purpose of hedging a firm commitment is included in measuring the transaction satisfying the commitment. When the company hedges a firm purchase commitment by using a futures contract and the acquisition takes place thus satisfying the purchase commitment, the gain or loss on the futures contract is an element of the cost of the acquired item. EXAMPLE: Assume ABC Company has a purchase commitment for 30,000 pounds of a commodity at $2 per pound, totaling $60,000. At the time of the consummation of the transaction, the $60,000 cost is decreased by any gain (e.g., $5,000) arising from the hedged futures contract. The net cost is shown as the carrying value ($55,000).

o The accounting applicable for a hedged futures contract related to an expected asset acquisition or liability incurrence should be consistent with the company's accounting method employed for those assets and liabilities. EXAMPLE: The firm should book a loss for a futures contract that is a hedge of an expected inventory acquisition, if the amount will not be recovered from the sale of inventory.

o If a hedged futures contract is closed prior to the expected transaction, the accumulated value change in the contract should be carried forward to be included in measuring the related transaction. If it is probable that the quantity of an expected transaction will be less than the amount initially hedged, recognize a gain or loss for a pro rata portion of futures results that would have been included in the measurement of the subsequent transaction.

NOTE

A "hedged" futures contract requires disclosure of:

o Firm commitments
o Nature of assets and liabilities
o Accounting method used for the contract, including a description of events or transactions resulting in recognizing changes in contract values
o Transactions expected to be hedged with futures contracts

How do I account for an anticipatory hedge contract?

A futures contract may apply to transactions the company *expects* to conduct in the ordinary course of business but is not obligated to. These expected transactions do not involve existing assets or liabilities or transactions applicable to *existing* firm commitments. EXAMPLE: A company may *anticipate* buying a certain commodity in the future but has not made a formal purchase commitment. The company may minimize risk exposure to price changes by entering into a futures contract. The change in market value of this "anticipatory hedge" contract is included in measuring the subsequent transaction. The change in market value of the futures contract adjusts the cost of the acquired item.

Four criteria must be met for "anticipatory hedge" accounting:

- ○ The first two are the same as the criteria for regular hedge contracts related to *existing* assets, liabilities, or firm commitments.

- ○ Identification exists of the major terms of the contemplated transaction. Included are the type of commodity or financial instrument, quantity, and expected transaction date. If the financial instrument carries interest, the maturity date should be given.

- ○ It is probable that the expected transaction will take place. Probability of occurrence depends on

  - Time period involved
  - Monetary commitment for the activity
  - Financial capability to conduct the transaction
  - Frequency of previous transactions of a similar nature
  - Possibility that other types of transactions may be undertaken to accomplish the desired goal
  - Adverse operational effects of not engaging in the transaction

OIL- AND GAS-PRODUCING COMPANIES

What should I know about oil and gas accounting?

Under the successful efforts method used by oil and gas companies, *successful costs* of exploration are deferred and amortized. *unsuccessful costs* of exploration are immediately expensed.

Capitalization should be made of these expenditures:

- ○ Mineral interests in properties classified as proved or unproved
- ○ Wells and related equipment
- ○ Support equipment and facilities used in oil- and gas-producing activities
- ○ Uncompleted wells, equipment, and facilities

These capitalized costs should be amortized as the oil and gas reserves are produced. Unproved properties should be assessed on a periodic basis and losses recognized. Costs not resulting in the acquisition of an asset should be expensed.

Disclosures include:

- o Net quantities of proved reserves and changes during the year
- o Capitalized costs
- o Property acquisitions
- o Exploration and development costs
- o Results of operations
- o A measure of discounted future net cash flows
- o Production (lifting) costs

CHAPTER 5

KEY FINANCIAL
ACCOUNTING AREAS

CONSOLIDATIONS

What is a consolidation?

Consolidation occurs when the parent owns more than 50 percent of the voting common stock of the subsidiary. The objective of consolidation is to present as one economic unit the financial position and operating results of a parent and subsidiaries. It shows the group as a single company with one or more branches or divisions rather than as separate companies.

The companies making up the consolidated group keep their individual legal identities. Adjustments and eliminations are for the sole purpose of financial statement reporting.

NOTE
Consolidation is still appropriate even if the subsidiary has a material amount of debt. Disclosure should be made of the firm's consolidation policy in footnotes or by explanatory headings.

When is a consolidation not valid?

A consolidation is negated, even if more than 50 percent of voting common stock is owned by the parent, in these instances:

- ○ Parent is not in actual control of subsidiary. EXAMPLE: Subsidiary is in receivership or in a politically unstable foreign country.
- ○ Parent has sold or contracted to sell subsidiary shortly after year-end. The subsidiary is a temporary investment.
- ○ Minority interest is very large in comparison to the parent's interest; individual financial statements are more appropriate.

How is a consolidation accounted for?

Intercompany eliminations include those for intercompany payables and receivables, advances, and profits. For certain regulated companies, intercompany profit does not have to be eliminated to the extent the profit represents a reasonable return on investment. Subsidiary investment in the parent's shares is not consolidated outstanding stock in the consolidated balance sheet.

NOTE
Consolidated statements *do not* reflect capitalized earnings in the form of stock dividends by subsidiaries subsequent to acquisition.

Minority interest in a subsidiary is the stockholders' equity in the partially owned subsidiaries outside of the parent's controlling interest. It should be shown as a separate component of stockholders' equity. When losses applicable to the minority interest in a subsidiary exceed the minority interest's equity capital, the excess and any subsequent losses related to the minority interest are charged to the parent. If profit subsequently occurs, the parent's interest is credited to the degree of prior losses absorbed.

NOTE
If a parent acquires a subsidiary in more than one block of stock, each purchase is on a step-by-step basis, and consolidation does not occur until control exists.

- o *When the subsidiary is acquired within the year,* the subsidiary should be included in consolidation as if it had been bought at the beginning of the year with a subtraction for the preacquisition part of earnings applicable to each block of stock.

ALTERNATIVE APPROACH
Include in consolidation the subsidiary's earnings subsequent to the acquisition date.

- o *The retained earnings of a subsidiary* at the acquisition date are not included in the consolidated financial statements.
- o When the *subsidiary is disposed of during the year,* the parent should present its equity in the subsidiary's

earnings prior to the sale date as a separate line item consistent with the equity method.

o A subsidiary whose *major business activity is leasing* to a parent should always be consolidated.

o Consolidation is still permissible without adjustments when the fiscal year-ends of the parent and subsidiary are three months or less apart. Footnote disclosure of material events occurring during the intervening period is needed.

What methods of accounting may be used?

The *equity method* of accounting is used for unconsolidated subsidiaries, unless there is a foreign investment or a temporary investment.

When the equity method is not used, the *cost method* is followed. The cost method recognizes the difference between the cost of the subsidiary and the equity in net assets at the acquisition date. Depreciation is adjusted for the difference as if consolidation of the subsidiary was made. There is an elimination of intercompany gain or loss for unconsolidated subsidiaries to the extent the gain or loss exceeds the unrecorded equity in undistributed earnings.

REQUIREMENT

Unconsolidated subsidiaries accounted for with the cost method should have adequate disclosure of assets, liabilities, and earnings. Such disclosure may be in footnote or supplementary schedule form.

Wouldn't combined statements sometimes be valid?

Combined financial statements are sometimes more appropriate than consolidated statements. EXAMPLE: A person owns a controlling interest in several related operating companies (brother-sister corporation).

NOTE

In some cases parent company statements are required in addition to consolidated statements, in order to properly provide information to creditors and preferred stockholders. In this event, *dual columns* are needed—one column for the parent and other columns for subsidiaries.

BUSINESS COMBINATIONS

Purchase Method

What is the purchase method?

A business combination occurs before a consolidation. Business combinations must be accounted for under the purchase method. Accounting and reporting requirements, and disclosures must be considered for the purchase method as required by FASB Statement No. 141 (Accounting for Business Combinations).

When is there a purchase?

A purchase typically involves either the payment of assets or incurrence of liabilities for the other business. To effect a purchase, more than 50 percent of voting common stock has to be acquired.

How do I account for a purchase?

The accounting followed for a purchase is:

1. Net assets of the acquired company are brought forth at fair market value. Guidelines in assigning values to individual assets acquired and liabilities assumed (except goodwill) follow:

   - *Marketable securities*—Current net realizable values
   - *Receivables*—Present value of net receivables using present interest rates
   - *Inventories*—*Finished goods* at estimated net realizable value less a reasonable profit allowance (lower limit). *Work-in-process* at estimated net realizable value of finished goods less costs to complete and profit allowance. *Raw materials* at current replacement cost
   - *Plants and equipment*—If to be employed in operations, show at replacement cost. If to be sold, reflect at net realizable value. If to be used temporarily, show at net realizable value, recognizing depreciation for the period
   - *Identifiable intangibles*—At appraisal value
   - *Other assets* (including land and noncurrent securities)—At appraised values
   - *Payables*—At estimated present value
   - *Liabilities and accruals*—At estimated present value

- *Other liabilities and commitments*—At estimated present value. However, a deferred income tax credit account of the acquired company is not brought forth.

2. The excess of cost paid over book value of assets acquired is attributed to the identifiable net assets. The remaining balance not attributable to specific assets is of an unidentifiable nature and is assigned to goodwill. The identifiable assets are depreciated. Goodwill is subject to an annual impairment test.

REQUIREMENTS

- Goodwill of the acquired company is not brought forth.
- None of the equity accounts of the acquired business (e.g., retained earnings) appear on the acquirer's books. Ownership interests of the acquired company stockholders are not continued subsequent to the merger.
- Net income of the acquired company is brought forth from the date of acquisition to year-end.
- Direct costs of the purchase are a deduction from the fair value of the securities issued; indirect costs are expensed as incurred.

  - When stock is issued in a purchase transaction, the quoted market price of stock is typically a clear indication of asset cost. Consideration should be given to price fluctuations, volume, and issue price of stock.
  - If liabilities are assumed in a purchase, the difference between the fixed rate of the debt securities and the present yield rate for comparable securities is reflected as a premium or discount.

What if control is not established on the initial purchase?

The following step-by-step acquisition procedure is followed:

- If control is not accomplished on the initial purchase, the subsidiary cannot be included in consolidation until control has been accomplished.
- Once the parent owns in excess of 50 percent of the subsidiary, a retroactive restatement should be made including all of the subsidiary's earnings in consolidated retained earnings in a "step-by-step" fashion commencing with the initial investment.
- The subsidiary's earnings are included for the ownership years at the appropriate ownership percentage.

○ After control is accomplished, fair value and adjustments for goodwill will be applied retroactively on a "step-by-step" basis. Each acquisition is separately determined.

The acquiring company generally cannot record a net operating loss carryforward of the acquired company, since there is no assurance of realization. However, if realized in a later year, recognition will be a retroactive adjustment of the purchase transaction allocation, causing the residual purchase cost to be reallocated to the other assets acquired. In effect, there will be a reduction of goodwill or the other assets.

What are preacquisition contingencies?

A preacquisition contingency is a contingency of a business that is acquired with the purchase method and that exists prior to the consummation date. EXAMPLES: A contingent asset, a contingent liability, or a contingent impairment of an asset.

How do I account for a preacquisition contingency?

FASB 38 provides guidelines for recording "preacquisition contingencies" during the "allocation period" as a part of allocating the cost of an investment in an enterprise acquired under the purchase method. The allocation period is the one required to identify and quantify the acquired assets and liabilities assumed. This period ceases when the acquiring company no longer needs information it has arranged to obtain and that is known to be available. Hence, the existence of a preacquisition contingency for which an asset, a liability, or an impairment of an asset cannot be estimated does not, of itself, extend the allocation period. Although the time required depends on the circumstances, the allocation period typically is not greater than one year from the consummation date.

Preacquisition contingencies (except for tax benefits of net operating loss carryforwards) must be included in the allocation of purchase cost. The allocation basis is determined by the *fair value* of the preacquisition contingency, assuming a fair value can be determined during the allocation period.

If *fair value is not determinable*, the following criteria are used:

○ Information available before the termination of the *allocation* period indicates that it is probable that an asset existed, a liability had been incurred, or an asset had been impaired at the consummation date. It must be probable that one or more future events will occur confirming the existence of the asset, liability, or impairment.

o The amount of the asset or liability can be reasonably estimated.

Adjustments necessitated by a preacquisition contingency occurring after the end of the allocation period must be included in income in the year the adjustment is made.

What should I mention about a purchase in the footnotes?

Footnote disclosures under the purchase method include:

o Name and description of companies combined
o A statement that the purchase method is being used
o The period in which the earnings of the acquired company are included
o Cost of the acquired company including the number and value of shares issued, if any
o Contingencies arising under the acquisition agreement
o Earnings for the current and prior periods as if the companies were combined at the beginning of the period
o Major reasons for the acquisition
o Percentage of voting interest acquired
o Amount of purchase price assigned to each major intangible asset class
o Amount of any significant residual value, in total and by major intangible asset class
o Total goodwill and the amount of goodwill by reportable segment
o Impairment information with respect to goodwill
o Amount of goodwill deductible on the tax return
o Unresolved issues
o Commitments made
o Summarized financial data about the acquired company
o Description of the exit plan, including exit costs (e.g., relocation, employee termination)

What are the advantages and disadvantages of the purchase method?

ADVANTAGE

Fair value is used to recognize the acquired company's assets just as in the case of acquiring a separate asset.

DISADVANTAGES

Difficulty in determining fair value; mixing fair value of acquired company's assets and historical cost for the acquiring company's assets.

INVESTMENTS IN SECURITIES

Stock Investments

Investments in stock may be accounted for and reported under FASB 115 or APB 18, depending on the percentage of ownership involved in voting common stock.

MARKET VALUE ADJUSTED (FASB 115)

Securities are defined as either held-to-maturity, trading, or available-for-sale.

How are held-to-maturity securities reported?

Held-to-maturity treatment applies just to debt securities because stock does not have a maturity date. Held-to-maturity debt securities are reported at amortized cost, which equals the purchase price adjusted for the amortization of discount or premium. These securities are not adjusted to market value. Held-to-maturity categorization applies to debt securities only if the company has the intent and ability to hold the securities to the maturity date.

How are trading securities reported?

Trading securities can be either debt or equity. The intent is to sell them in a short time period. Trading securities are often bought and sold to earn short-term gain. Trading securities are recorded at market value with the unrealized (holding) loss or gain presented separately in the income statement. Trading securities should be reported as current assets in the balance sheet.

EXAMPLE 5.1

On 12/31/X8, the trading securities portfolio had a cost and market value of $500,000 and $520,000, respectively. The journal entry to account for this portfolio at market value is:

Market Adjustment	20,000	
Unrealized Gain		20,000

The Market Adjustment account has a debit balance and is added to the cost of the portfolio in the current asset section of the balance sheet as follows:

Trading securities (cost)	$500,000
Add: Market adjustment	20,000
Trading securities (market value)	$520,000

The unrealized (holding) gain is presented in the income statement under "other income."

How are available-for-sale securities reported?

Available-for-sale securities may be either debt or equity. These securities are not held for trading reasons, nor is the intent to hold them to maturity. They are reported at market value with the accumulated unrealized loss or gain shown as a separate item in the stockholders' equity section of the balance sheet. The portfolio of available-for-sale securities may be presented in the current asset or in the noncurrent asset sections of the balance sheet depending on how long these securities are intended to be held.

EXAMPLE 5.2

On 12/31/X5, the available-for-sale securities portfolio had a cost and market value of $300,000 and $285,000, respectively. The journal entry to recognize the portfolio at market value is:

Unrealized Loss	15,000	
Market Adjustment		15,000

The portfolio is presented in the balance sheet at $285,000 net of the Market Adjustment account of $15,000. The unrealized loss is presented separately in the stockholders' equity section of the balance sheet.

How is the sale of securities reported?

When securities are sold, regardless of the type, the realized gain or loss is reported in the income statement. If the decline in market value of either available-for-sale or held-to-maturity securities is deemed permanent, a realized loss is presented in the income statement. When the security is written down, market value at that date becomes the new cost basis.

EXAMPLE 5.3

On 12/31/X3, a company presented the following accounts before adjustment:

Available-for-Sale	
Securities	$300,000
Market Adjustment	25,000

It was determined on 12/31/X3 that the portfolio's market value is $290,000. The journal entry needed to bring the portfolio up to date is:

Market Adjustment	15,000	
Unrealized Gain		15,000

What if there is an exchange of stock?

If two or more securities are purchased at one price, the cost is allocated among the securities based on their relative fair market value. In the exchange of one security for another, the new security received in the exchange is valued at its fair market value.

EXAMPLE 5.4

Preferred stock costing $10,000 is exchanged for 1,000 shares of common stock having a market value of $15,000. The entry is:

Investment in Common Stock	15,000	
Investment in Preferred		
Stock		10,000
Gain		5,000

How is a stock dividend handled?

A stock dividend involves a memo entry reflecting more shares at no additional cost. As a result, the cost per share decreases.

EXAMPLE 5.5

Fifty shares at $12 per share for a total cost of $600 is owned. A 20 percent stock dividend is declared amounting to 10 shares. A memo entry is made reflecting the additional shares as follows:

	Investment	
50	$12	$600
10		0
60	($10)	$600

If 10 shares are later sold at $15, the entry is:

Cash	150	
Long-term Investment		100
Gain		50

What effect does a stock split have?

A stock split has the effect of increasing the shares and reducing the cost basis on a proportionate basis. A memo entry is made.

EXAMPLE 5.6

One hundred shares costing $20 per share was owned. A 2 for 1 split would result in 200 shares at a cost per share of $10. Total par value remains at $2,000.

EQUITY METHOD

When is the equity method used?

The investor company is the owner and the investee company is being owned. The equity method is used if:

- ○ An investor owns between 20 and 50 percent of the voting common stock of an investee.
- ○ The holder owns less than 20 percent of the voting common stock but possesses significant influence (effective control)
- ○ More than 50 percent of the voting common stock is owned but one of the negating factors for consolidation exists.

NOTE
Investments in joint ventures have to be accounted for under the equity method.

How do I account when using the equity method?

The accounting under the equity method as per APB 18 is illustrated by the "T-accounts" shown in Exhibit 5.1.

- ○ The cost of the investment includes brokerage fees. The investor recognizes his percentage ownership interest in the ordinary profit of the investee by debiting investment in investee and crediting equity in earnings of investee.
- ○ The investor's share in investee's earnings is computed after deducting cumulative preferred dividends, whether or not declared. Investor's share of investee's profit should be based on the investee's most recent income statement applied on a consistent basis.

Investment in Investee	
Cost	Dividends
Ordinary Profit	Depreciation on Excess of Fair
Extraordinary Gain	Market Value less Book Value
	of Specific Assets
	Permanent Decline

Equity in Earnings of Investee	
Depreciation	Ordinary Profit

Extraordinary Gain	
	Extraordinary Gain

Exhibit 5.1   "T-ACCOUNTS"

- o Extraordinary gains or losses as well as prior period adjustments are also picked up as shown on the investee's books.
- o Dividends reduce the carrying value of the investment account.
- o The excess paid by the investor for the investee's net assets is first assigned to the specific assets and liabilities and is depreciated. The unidentifiable portion of the excess is considered goodwill which is subject to an annual impairment test, depreciation on excess value of assets reduce the investment account and is charged to equity in earnings.
- o *Temporary decline* in price of the investment in the investee is ignored. *Permanent decline* in value of the investment is reflected by debiting loss and crediting investment in investee.
- o When the investor's share of the investee's losses is greater than the balance in the investment account, the equity method should be discontinued at the zero amount.

EXCEPTIONS
The investor has guaranteed the investee's obligations or immediate profitability is assured. A return to the equity method is made only after offsetting subsequent profits against losses not recorded.

- o When the investee's stock is sold, a realized gain or loss will arise for the difference between selling price and the cost of the investment account.

Isn't the equity method like a consolidation?

The mechanics of consolidation essentially apply to the equity method: For example, intercompany profits and losses are eliminated. Investee capital transactions impacting the investor's share of equity should be accounted for as in a consolidation. The investee's capital transactions should be accounted for as if the investee was a consolidated subsidiary. EXAMPLE: When the investee issues its common stock to third parties at a price in excess of book value, there will be an increase in the value of the investment and a related increase in the investor's paid-in-capital.

What else should I know about the equity method?

Interperiod income tax allocation will occur because the investor shows the investee's *profits* for book reporting but *dividends* for tax reporting. This results in a deferred income tax credit account.

If the ownership goes below 20 percent, or if the investor is unable to control the investee, the investor should cease recognizing the investee's earnings. The equity method is discontinued, but the balance in the investment account is maintained. The market value method should then be applied.

If the investor increases his ownership in the investee to 20 percent or more, the equity method should be used for current and future years. Furthermore, the effect of using the equity method rather than the market value method on prior years at the old percentage (e.g., 15 percent) should be recognized as an adjustment to retained earnings and other accounts so affected (e.g., investment in investee). The retroactive adjustment on the investment, earnings, and retained earnings should be applied in the same manner as a step-by-step acquisition of a subsidiary.

What disclosures are necessary?

The investor should make disclosures of the following in footnotes, separate schedules, or parenthetically:

o Percent owned
o Name of investee
o Investor's accounting policies
o Material effects of possible conversions and exercises of investee common stock
o Quoted market price (for investees not qualifying as subsidiaries)
o Summarized financial data as to assets, liabilities, and earnings for material investments in unconsolidated subsidiaries
o Material realized and unrealized gains and losses relating to the subsidiary's portfolio occurring between the dates of the financial statements of the subsidiary and parent

EXAMPLE 5.7

On 1/1/20X5, X Company bought 30,000 shares for a 40 percent interest in the common stock of AB Company at $25 per share. Brokerage commissions were $10,000. During 20X5, AB's net income was $140,000 and dividends received were $30,000. On 1/1/20X6, X Company received 15,000 shares of common stock as a result of a stock split by AB Company. On 1/4/20X6, X Company sold 2,000 shares at $16 per share of AB stock. The journal entries follow:

1/1/20X5 Investment in
  Investee   760,000
    Cash   760,000

EXAMPLE 5.7 *(continued)*		
12/31/20X5 Investment in		
Investee	56,000	
Equity in Earnings of		
Investee		56,000
40% × \$140,000 = \$56,000		
Cash	30,000	
Investment in Investee		30,000
1/1/20X6 Memo entry for		
stock split		
1/4/20X6 Cash (2,000 × \$16)	32,000	
Loss on Sale of Investment	2,940	
Investment in Investee		
(2,000 × \$17.47)		34,940

$$\frac{\$786,000}{45,000} = \$17.47 \text{ per share}$$

Investment in Investee

1/1/20X5	760,000	12/31/20X5	30,000
12/31/20X5	56,000		
	816,000		
	786,000		

EXAMPLE 5.8

On 1/1/20X6, the investor purchased 100,000 shares of the investee's 400,000 shares outstanding for \$3,000,000. The book value of net assets acquired was \$2,500,000. The \$500,000 excess paid over book value is attributable to undervalued tangible assets. The depreciation period is 20 years. In 20X6, the investee's net income was \$800,000, including an extraordinary loss of \$200,000. Dividends of \$75,000 were paid on June 1, 20X6. The following journal entries are necessary for the acquisition of investee by investor accounted for under the equity method.

1/1/20X6 Investment in		
Investee	3,000,000	
Cash		3,000,000
6/1/20X6 Cash	18,750	
Investment in Investee		18,750
25% × \$75,000 = \$18,750		
12/31/20X6		
Investment in Investee	250,000	
Equity in Earnings of		
Investee		250,000
\$1,000,000 × 25% = \$250,000		

EXAMPLE 5.8 *(continued)*		
Extraordinary Loss from Investment	50,000	
Investment in Investee		
$200,000 × 25% = $50,000		50,000
Equity in Earnings of Investee	25,000	
Investment in Investee		25,000
Computation follows:		
Undervalued depreciable assets/years $500,000/20		$25,000

LEASES

How are leases defined?

Leases are typically long-term, noncancellable commitments. In a lease, the lessee acquires the right to use property owned by the lessor. Even though no legal transfer of title occurs, many leases transfer substantially all the risks and benefits of ownership. Theoretical substance governs over legal form in accounting, resulting in the lessee recording an asset and a liability for a capital lease.

NOTES
A lease may be between related parties. This occurs when one entity has significant influence over operating and financial policies of another entity.

The *date of inception* of a lease is the time of lease *agreement, or commitment,* whichever occurs first.

REQUIREMENT
A commitment must be in writing, signed, and provide principal provisions. If any major provisions are to be negotiated later, there is no committed agreement.

Lessee

How does the lessee account for leases?

The two methods of accounting for a lease by the lessee are the operating method and capital method.

What is an operating lease?

An operating lease is a regular rental of property.

How is recognition given to an operating lease?

- As rental payments become payable, rent expense is debited and cash and/or payables are credited.
- The lessee does not show anything on his balance sheet.
- Rent expense is reflected on a straight-line basis unless another method is more appropriate.
- Accrual basis accounting is followed.

What is a capital lease?

The lessee uses the capital lease method if any *one* of the following four criteria is met:

1. The lessee obtains ownership to the property at the end of the lease term.
2. There is a bargain purchase option where the lessee can either acquire the property at a nominal amount or renew the lease at nominal rental payments.
3. The life of the lease is 75 percent or more of the life of the property.
4. The present value of minimum lease payments at the inception of the lease equals or is greater than 90 percent of the fair market value of the property. Minimum lease payments exclude executory costs to be paid by the lessor such as maintenance, insurance, and property taxes.

NOTES

If the first or second criterion is met, the depreciation period is the life of the property. If the third or fourth criterion is satisfied, the depreciation period is the life of the lease.

The third and fourth criteria do not apply where the beginning of the lease term falls within the last 25 percent of the total economic life of the property, including earlier years of use.

What is the accounting and reporting for a capital lease?

The asset and liability are recorded at the present value of the minimum lease payments plus the present value of the bargain purchase option. The expectation is that the lessee will take advantage of the nominal purchase price.

If the present value of the minimum lease payments plus the bargain purchase option is greater than the fair value of the leased property at the time of lease inception, the asset should be capitalized at the fair market value of the property.

The discount rate used by the lessee is the *lower* of the lessee's incremental borrowing rate (the rate at which the lessee would have to borrow to be able to buy the asset) or the lessor's implicit interest rate (the rate implicit in the recovery of the fair value of the property at lease inception through the present value of minimum lease payments including the lessee's guarantee of salvage value).

The liability is broken down between current and noncurrent.

What is the MLP?

The lessee's minimum lease payments (MLP) usually includes:

o MLP over the lease term plus any residual value guaranteed by the lessee. The guarantee is the determinable amount for which the lessor has the right to require the lessee to buy the property at the lease termination. It is the stated amount when the lessee agrees to satisfy any dollar deficiency below a stated amount in the lessor's realization of the residual value.

o Any payment lessee must pay due to failure to extend or renew the lease at expiration.

NOTES

MLP includes only MLP over the lease term and exercise option payment, if a bargain purchase option exists.

MLP does not include:

o Contingent rentals
o Lessee's guarantee of lessor's debt
o Lessee's obligation for executory costs

Each minimum lease payment is allocated as a reduction of principal (debiting the liability) and as interest (debiting interest expense). The interest method is used to result in a constant periodic rate of interest. Interest expense equals the interest rate times the carrying value of the liability at the beginning of the year.

How is a capital lease shown on the balance sheet and income statement?

o BALANCE SHEET: Show the "Asset Under Lease" less "Accumulated Depreciation."
o INCOME STATEMENT: Show interest expense and depreciation expense. In the first year, the expenses under a capital lease (interest expense and depreciation) are greater than the expenses under an operating lease (rent expense).

What if the lessee buys a leased asset that has been capitalized?

Per Interpretation 26, when a lessee buys a leased asset during the lease term which has been originally capitalized, the transaction is considered an *extension* of a capital lease, not a termination. The difference between the purchase price and the carrying amount of the lease obligation recorded is an *adjustment* of the carrying amount of the asset.

NOTE
No loss recognition is required on an extension of a capital lease.

EXAMPLE 5.9

On 1/1/20X1, the lessee enters into a capital lease for property. The minimum rental payment is $20,000 a year for six years to be made at year-end. The interest rate is 5 percent. The present value of an ordinary annuity factor for $n = 6$, $i = 5$ percent is 5.0757. The journal entries for the first two years are:

1/1/20X1 Asset	101,514	
Liability		101,514
12/31/20X1		
Interest Expense	5,076	
Liability	14,924	
Cash		20,000
5% × $101,514 = $5,076		
Depreciation	16,919	
Accumulated Depreciation		16,919

$$\frac{\$101,514}{6} = \$16,919$$

The liability as of 12/31/20X1 is:

Liability			
12/31/20X1	14,924	1/1/120X1	101,514
		12/31/20X1	86,590

12/31/20X2		
Interest Expense	4,330	
Liability	15,670	
Cash		20,000
5% × $86,590 = $4,330		
Depreciation	16,919	
Accumulated Depreciation		16,919

What footnote disclosures are necessary for leases?

Footnote disclosures under a capital lease include:

- o Assets under lease by class
- o Future minimum lease payments in total and for each of the next five years
- o Contingent rentals (rentals based on terms other than time, e.g., sales)
- o Total future sublease rentals
- o Description of leasing arrangement including renewal terms, purchase options, escalation options, and restrictions in the lease agreement

Lessor

How does the lessor account for leases?

The three methods of accounting for leases by the lessor are:

- o Operating method
- o Direct-financing method
- o Sales-type method

What is the operating method?

The operating method is a regular rental by the lessor. **EXAMPLE: Avis rents automobiles.**

How do I account for the operating method?

Under the operating method, the lessor records rental revenue less related expenses, including depreciation and maintenance expense.

INCOME STATEMENT

Show rental revenue less expenses to obtain profit.

BALANCE SHEET

Present the asset under lease less accumulated depreciation to derive book value.

How is rental income recognized in the operating method?

Rental income is recognized as earned using the *straight-line* basis over the lease term, except if there is another preferable method.

Initial direct costs are deferred and amortized over the lease term on a pro rata basis based on rental income recognized. However, the initial direct costs may be expensed if immaterial relative to the allocation amount.

EXAMPLE 5.10

Hall Corporation produced machinery costing $5,000,000 which it held for resale from January 1, 20X1 to June 30, 20X1, at a price to Travis Company under an operating lease. The lease is for four years, with equal monthly payments of $85,000 due on the first of the month. The initial payment was made on July 1, 20X1. The depreciation period is 10 years with no salvage value.

Lessee's rental expense for 20X1: 85,000 × 6	$510,000
Lessor's income before taxes for 19X1:	
Rental income	$510,000
Less: Depreciation	
$$\frac{\$5,000,000}{10} \times \frac{6}{12}$$	250,000
Income before taxes	$260,000

What is the direct financing method?

The direct financing method satisfies one of the four criteria for a capital lease by the lessee *plus* both of the following two criteria for the lessor:

○ Collectibility of lease payments is assured
○ No important uncertainties exist regarding future costs to be incurred

The lessor is *not* a manufacturer or dealer. The lessor acquires the property for the sole purpose of leasing it out. EXAMPLE: A bank leasing computers.

How do I account for the direct financing method?

The carrying value and fair value of the leased property are the same at the inception of the lease.

The lessor uses as the discount rate the interest rate implicit in the lease.

Interest revenue equals the interest rate times the carrying value of the receivable at the beginning of the year. Interest income is recognized only in the financial statements over the life of the lease using the interest method. Unearned interest income is amortized as income over the lease term resulting in a constant rate of interest.

Contingent rentals are recognized in earnings as earned. The lessor's MLP includes:

○ The MLP made by the lessee (net of any executory costs together with any profit thereon) o Any guarantee of the salvage value of the leased property, or of rental payments after the lease term, made by a third party unrelated to either party in the lease, provided the third party is financially able to satisfy the commitment.

NOTE

A guarantee by a third party related to the lessor makes the residual value unguaranteed. A guarantee by a third party related to the lessee infers a guaranteed residual value by the lessee.

What if there is a change in lease provisions?

A change in lease provisions that would have resulted in a different classification had it taken place at the beginning of the lease mandates that the lease be considered a new agreement and be classified under the new terms.

EXCEPTIONS

o Exercise of existing renewal options are not deemed lease changes.
o A change in estimate does not result in a new lease.

NOTE

A provision for escalation of the MLP during a construction or preacquisition period may exist. The resulting increase in MLP is considered in determining the fair value of the leased property at the lease inception. A salvage value increase resulting from an escalation clause may also exist.

What do initial direct costs include?

Initial direct costs are incurred by the lessor directly applicable to negotiating and consummating *completed* leasing transactions such as:

o Legal fees
o Commissions
o Document preparation and processing for new leases
o Credit investigation
o Relevant portion of salespersons' and other employees' compensation

Not Included

o Costs for *unconsummated leases* and
o Supervisory, administrative, or other indirect expenses.

Initial direct costs of the lease are expensed as incurred. A portion of the unearned income equal to the initial direct costs is recognized as income in the same accounting period.

What if the lease is terminated?

If the lease agreement contains a penalty for failure to renew and the penalty becomes inoperative due to lease renewal or other extension of time, the unearned interest income account must be adjusted for the difference between the present values of the old and revised agreements. The present value of the future MLP under the new agreement should be computed using the original rate for the initial lease.

Lease termination is accounted for by the lessor through eliminating the net investment and recording the leased property at the lower of cost or fair value. The net adjustment is then charged against earnings.

BALANCE SHEET

The lessor shows the total minimum lease payments plus salvage value of the property accruing to the lessor as the gross investment in the lease. This represents lease payments receivable. Deducted from lease payments receivable is unearned interest revenue. The balance sheet presentation follows:

Lease Payments Receivable (Principal + Interest)
Less: Unearned Interest Revenue (Interest)
Net Receivable Balance (Principal)
The income statement shows:
Interest Revenue
Less: Initial Direct Costs
Less: Executory Costs
Net Income

What footnote disclosure is necessary for the direct financing method?

Footnote disclosure should include:

o Assets leased out by category
o Future lease payments in total and for each of the next five years
o Contingent rentals
o The terms of the lease

What is the sales-type method?

The sales-type method must satisfy the same criteria as the direct financing method. The only difference is that the sales-type method involves a lessor who is a manufacturer or dealer in the leased item. Thus, a manufacturer or dealer profit results. Although legally there is no sale of the item, theoretical substance governs over legal form, and a sale is assumed to have taken place.

NOTE
The distinction between a sales-type lease and a direct financing lease affects only the lessor; as to the lessee, either type would be a capital lease.

If there is a renewal or extension of an existing sales-type or financing lease, it shall *not* be classified as a sales-type lease.

EXCEPTION
It may sometimes be so classified when the renewal occurs toward the end of the lease term.

How do I account for a sales-type lease?

- ○ In a sales-type lease, profit on the assumed sale of the item is recognized in the year of lease as well as interest income over the life of the lease. The cost and fair value of the leased property are different at the inception of the lease.
- ○ An annual appraisal should be made of the salvage value. Where necessary, reduce the net investment and recognize a loss. Do not adjust the salvage value.
- ○ The cost of the leased property is matched against the selling price in determining the assumed profit in the year of lease. Initial direct costs of the lease are expensed.
- ○ Except for the initial entry to record the lease, the entries are the same for the direct financing and sales-type methods.

EXAMPLE 5.11

Assume the same facts as in the capital lease example. The accounting by the lessor assuming a direct financing lease and a sales-type lease follows:

Direct Financing		Sales Type		
1/1/20X1				
Receivable	120,000	Receivable	120,000	
Asset	101,514	Cost of Sales	85,000	
Unearned		Inventory		85,000
Interest		Sales		101,514
Revenue	18,486			

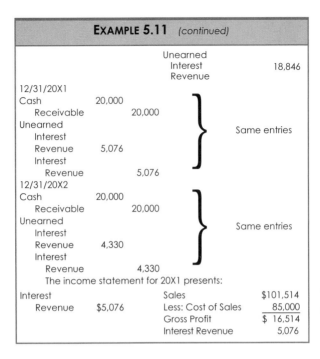

| **EXAMPLE 5.11** | *(continued)* |

			Unearned Interest Revenue	18,846
12/31/20X1				
Cash	20,000			
Receivable		20,000		
Unearned Interest Revenue	5,076		Same entries	
Interest Revenue		5,076		
12/31/20X2				
Cash	20,000			
Receivable		20,000		
Unearned Interest Revenue	4,330		Same entries	
Interest Revenue		4,330		

The income statement for 20X1 presents:

Interest Revenue	$5,076	Sales	$101,514
		Less: Cost of Sales	85,000
		Gross Profit	$ 16,514
		Interest Revenue	5,076

EXAMPLE 5.12

Jones leased equipment to Tape Company on October 1, 20X1. It is a capital lease to the lessee and a sales-type lease to the lessor. The lease is for eight years, with equal annual payments of $500,000 due on October 1 each period. The first payment was made on October 1, 20X1. The cost of the equipment to Tape Company is $2,500,000. The equipment has a life of ten years with no salvage value. The appropriate interest rate is ten percent.

Tape reports the following in its income statement for 20X1:

Asset Cost ($500,000 × 5.868 = 2,934,000)
Depreciation

$$\left(\frac{\$2,934,000}{10} \times \frac{3}{12} \right)$$ $ 73,350

Interest Expense:		
Present value of lease payments	$2,934,000	
Less: Initial payment	500,000	
Balance	$2,434,000	
Interest Expense		60,850
$2,434,000 × 10% × 3/12		
Total Expenses		**$134,200**

EXAMPLE 5.12 *(continued)*		
Jones's income before tax is:		
Interest revenue		$ 60,850
Gross profit on assumed sale of property:		
Selling price	$2,934,000	
Less: Cost	2,500,000	
Gross Profit		434,000
Income before tax		$494,850

Sales-Leaseback Arrangement

What is a sales-leaseback situation?

A sales-leaseback occurs when the lessor sells the property and then leases it back. The lessor may do this when he is in need of funds.

What is the accounting for a sales-leaseback arrangement?

The profit or loss on the sale is deferred and amortized as an adjustment in proportion to depreciation expense in the case of a capital lease, or in proportion to rental expense in the case of an operating lease. However, if the fair value of the property at the time of the sales-leaseback is below its book value, a loss is immediately recognized for the difference between book value and fair value.

EXAMPLE 5.13	
The deferred profit on a sales-leaseback is $50,000. An operating lease is involved, where rental expense in the current year is $10,000, and total rental expense is $150,000. Rental expense is adjusted as follows:	
Rental Expense	$10,000
Less: Amortization of deferred gross profit	
$50,000 \times \dfrac{\$10,000}{\$150,000}$	3,333
	$ 6,667

Subleases and Similar Transactions

What is a sublease?

There are three types of *subleases:*

- The original lessee leases the property to a third party. The lease agreement of the original parties remains intact.

- o A new lessee is substituted under the original agreement. The original lessee may still be secondarily liable.
- o The new lessee is substituted in a new agreement. There is a cancellation of the original lease.

What accounting is necessary by the lessor?

The original lessor continues his present accounting method if the original lessee subleases or sells to a third party. If the original lease is replaced by a new agreement with a new lessee, the lessor terminates the initial lease and accounts for the new lease in a separate transaction.

What accounting does the original lessee have to do?

In accounting by the original lessee, if the original lessee is relieved of primary obligation by a transaction other than a sublease, terminate the original lease.

- o If the original lease was a capital lease, remove the asset and liability, recognize a gain or loss for the difference, including any additional consideration paid or received, and accrue a loss contingency where secondary liability exists.
- o If the original lease was an operating lease and the initial lessee is secondarily liable, recognize a loss contingency accrual.

If the original lessee is not relieved of *primary* obligation under a sublease, the original lessee (now sublessor) accounts in the following manner:

- o If the original lease met lessee criterion 1 or 2, (see, What is a capital lease?, page 143) classify the new lease per normal classification criteria by lessor. If the sublease is a sales-type or direct financing lease, the unamortized asset balance becomes the cost of the leased property. Otherwise, it is an operating lease. Continue to account for the original lease obligation as before.
- o If the original lease met only lessee criterion 3 or 4, classify the new lease using lessee criterion 3 and lessor criteria 1 and 2. Classify as a direct financing lease. The unamortized balance of the asset becomes the cost of the leased property. Otherwise, it is an operating lease. Continue to account for original lease obligation as before.

NOTE
If the original lease was an operating lease, account for old and new leases as operating leases.

Leveraged Leases

What is a leveraged lease?

A leveraged lease occurs when the lessor (equity participant) finances a small part of the acquisition, retaining total equity ownership. A third party (debt participant) finances the balance. The lessor maximizes his leveraged return by recognizing lease revenue and income tax shelter (e.g., interest deduction, rapid depreciation).

A leveraged lease must meet *all* of these criteria:

- ○ It satisfies the tests for a direct financing lease. Sales-type leases are not leveraged leases.
- ○ It involves at least three parties: lessee, long-term creditor (debt participant), and lessor (equity participant).
- ○ The long-term creditor provides nonrecourse financing as to the general credit of the lessor: The financing is adequate to give the lessor significant leverage.
- ○ The lessor's net investment (see below) decreases during the initial lease years, then increases in the subsequent years just before its liquidation by sale. These increases and decreases in the net investment balance may take place more than once during the lease life.

How does the lessee account for leveraged leases?

The lessee classifies and accounts for leveraged leases in the same way as for non-leveraged leases.

How does the lessor account for leveraged leases?

The lessor records investment in the leveraged lease net of the nonrecourse debt. The net of the following balances represents the initial and continuing investment:

- ○ Rentals receivable (net of the amount applicable to principal and interest on the nonrecourse debt)
- ○ Estimated residual value
- ○ Unearned and deferred income

The initial entry to record the leveraged lease is:

Lease receivable	
Residual value of asset	
Cash investment in asset	
Unearned income	

○ The lessor's *net investment in the leveraged lease* for computing net income is the investment in the leveraged lease less deferred income taxes.

Periodic net income is determined in the following manner employing the *net investment in the leveraged* lease:

○ Determine annual cash flow equal to the following:

Gross lease rental (plus residual value of asset in last year of lease term)
Less: Loan interest payments
Less: Income tax charges (or add income tax credits)
Less: Loan principal payments
Annual Cash Flow

○ Determine the return rate on the net investment in the leveraged lease. The rate of return is the one that when applied to the net investment in the years when it is positive will distribute the net income (cash flow) to those positive years.

The *net investment* will be:

○ Positive in the early years (but declining rapidly due to accelerated depreciation and interest expense)
○ Negative during the middle years
○ Again positive in the later years (because of the declining tax shelter)

PENSION PLANS

How is a pension plan defined?

The pension plan relationship between the employer, trustee, and employee is depicted in Exhibit 5.2.

The two types of pension plans are:

○ *Defined Contribution:* In a defined contribution plan, the employer's annual contribution amount is specified, not the benefits to be paid.
○ *Defined Benefit:* In a defined benefit plan, the determinable pension benefit to be received by participants upon retirement is specified. The employer has

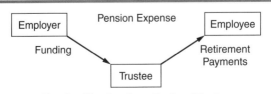

Exhibit 5.2 PENSION PLAN RELATIONSHIP

to provide plan contributions so that sufficient assets are accumulated to pay for the benefits when due. Typically, an annuity of payments is made.

NOTES

Pension expense applicable to administrative staff is expensed. Pension expense related to factory personnel can be inventoried.

What terminology is important for understanding pension plans?

○ *Actuarial Assumptions:* Actuaries make assumptions as to variables in determining pension expense and related funding. EXAMPLES: Mortality rate, employee turnover, compensation levels, and rate of return.

○ *Actuarial Cost (Funding) Method:* The method used by actuaries in determining the employer contribution to assure that sufficient funds will be available at employee retirement. The method used determines the pension expense and related liability.

○ *Actuarial Present Value of Accumulated Plan Benefits:* The discounted amount of money that would be required to satisfy retirement obligations for active and retired employees.

○ *Benefit Information Date:* The date the actuarial present value of accumulated benefits is presented.

○ *Vested Benefits:* Employee vests when she has accumulated pension rights to receive benefits upon retirement. The employee no longer has to remain in the company to receive pension benefits.

○ *Projected Benefit Obligation:* The year-end pension obligation based on *future* salaries. It is the actuarial present value of vested and nonvested benefits for services performed before a particular actuarial valuation date based on expected *future* salaries.

○ *Accumulated Benefit Obligation:* The year-end obligation based on *current* salaries. It is the actuarial present value of benefits (vested and nonvested) attributable to the pension plan based on services performed before a specified date, based on *current* salary levels.

NOTE

The accumulated and projected benefit obligation figures will be the same in the case of plans having flat-benefit or non-pay-related pension benefit formulas.

o *Net Assets Available for Pension Benefits:* Net assets represents plan assets less plan liabilities. The plan's liabilities *exclude* participants' accumulated benefits.

In general, what are the accounting requirements for pension plans?

A company does not have to have a pension plan. If it does, the firm must conform to FASB and governmental rules regarding the accounting and reporting for the pension plan. FASB 87 requires accounting for pension costs on the accrual basis.

Pension expense is reflected in the service periods using a method that considers the benefit formula of the plan. On the income statement, pension expense is presented as a single amount.

Defined Contribution Pension Plan

How do I account for a defined contribution plan?

o Pension expense equals the employer's cash contribution for the year. There is no deferred charge or deferred credit arising.
o If the defined contribution plan stipulates that contributions are to be made for years subsequent to an employee's rendering of services (e.g., after retirement), there should be an accrual of costs during the employee's service period.

Footnote disclosure includes:

o Description of plan including employee groups covered
o Basis of determining contributions
o Nature and effect of items affecting interperiod comparability
o Cost recognized for the period

Defined Benefit Pension Plan

What is the accounting for a defined benefit plan?

The components of pension expense in a defined benefit pension plan are:

o Service cost
o Prior service cost
o Return on plan assets (reduces pension expense)
o Interest on projected benefit obligation
o Actuarial gain or loss

Service cost is based on the present value of future payments under the benefit formula for employee services of the current period. It is recognized in full in the current year. The calculation involves actuarial assumptions.

Prior service cost is the pension expense applicable to services rendered before the adoption or amendment date of a pension plan. The cost of the retroactive benefits is the increase in the projected benefit obligation at the date of amendment. It involves the allocation of amounts of cost to future service years. Prior service cost determination involves actuarial considerations.

NOTE

The total pension cost is not booked. Rather, there are periodic charges based on actuarial determinations.

Amortization is accomplished by assigning an equal amount to each service year of active employees as of the amendment date who are expected to receive plan benefits. The amortization of prior service takes into account:

○ Future service years
○ Change in the projected benefit obligation
○ Period employees will receive benefits
○ Decrement in employees receiving benefits each year

EXAMPLE 5.14

X Company changes its pension formula from 2 to 5 percent of the last three years of pay multiplied by the service years on January 1, 20X1. This results in the projected benefit obligation being increased by $500,000. Employees are anticipated to receive benefits over the next ten years.

Total Future Service Years Equals:

$$\frac{n(n+1)}{2} \times P$$

where:
n is the number of years services are to be made
P is the population decrement each year

$$\frac{10(10+1)}{2} \times 9 = 495$$

Amortization of prior service cost in 20X1 equals:

$$\$500,000 \times \frac{10 \times 9}{495} = \underline{\$90,909}$$

The *return on plan assets* (e.g., stocks, bonds) reduces pension expense. Plan assets are valued at the moving average of asset values for the accounting period.

Interest is on the projected benefit obligation at the beginning of the year. The settlement rate, representing the rate that pension benefits could be settled for, is employed.

Interest = Interest Rate × Projected Benefit
Obligation at the
beginning of the year

Actuarial gain and loss represents the difference between estimates and actual experience. **EXAMPLE: If the assumed interest rate is 10 percent and the actual interest rate is 12 percent, an actuarial gain results.**

There may also be a change in actuarial assumptions regarding the future. Actuarial gains and losses are deferred and amortized as an adjustment to pension expense over future years. Actuarial gains and losses related to a single event *not* related to the pension plan and not in the ordinary course of business are immediately recognized in the current year's income statement. **EXAMPLES: Plant closing and segment disposal.**

NOTE

Pension expense will not usually equal the employer's funding amount. Pension expense is typically based on the unit credit method. Under this approach, pension expense and related liability are based on estimating future salaries for total benefits to be paid.

If Pension Expense > Cash Paid = Deferred
Pension Liability

If Pension Expense < Cash Paid = Deferred
Pension
Charge

The *unit credit* method is used for flat-benefit plans (benefits are stated as a constant amount per year of service). In the case of final-pay plans, the projected unit credit method is used.

What does minimum pension liability involve?

A minimum pension liability must be recognized when the accumulated benefit obligation exceeds the fair value of pension plan assets.

CAUTION

No minimum pension asset is recognized because it violates conservatism.

When there is an accrued pension liability, an additional liability is booked up to the minimum pension liability. When an additional liability is recorded, the debit is to an intangible asset under the pension plan.

> **NOTE**
>
> The intangible asset cannot exceed the unamortized prior service cost. If it does, the excess is reported as a separate component of stockholders' equity shown net of tax. Although these items may be adjusted periodically, they are not amortized.

EXAMPLE 5.15

Accumulated Benefit Obligation	$500,000
Less: Fair Value of Pension Plan Assets	200,000
Minimum Pension Liability	$300,000
Less: Accrued Pension Liability	120,000
Additional Liability	$180,000

> **NOTE**
>
> If instead of there being an accrued pension liability, there was an accrued pension asset of $120,000, the additional liability would be $420,000.

Assume unamortized prior service cost is $100,000. The entry is:

Intangible Asset Under Pension Plan	100,000	
Stockholders' Equity	80,000	
Additional Liability		180,000

EXAMPLE 5.16

Mr: A has 6 years prior to retirement. The estimated salary at retirement is $50,000. The pension benefit is 3 percent of final salary for each service year payable at retirement. The retirement benefit is computed below:

Final Annual Salary	$50,000
Formula Rate	× 3%
	$ 1,500
Years of Service	× 6
Retirement Benefit	$ 9,000

EXAMPLE 5.17

On 1/1/20X1, a company adopts a defined benefit pension plan. Return rate and interest rate are both 10 percent. Service costs for 20X1 and 20X2 are $100,000 and $120,000, respectively. The funding amounts for 20X1 and 20X2 are $80,000 and $110,000, respectively.

EXAMPLE 5.17 (continued)

The entry for 20X1 is:

Pension Expense	100,000	
Cash		80,000
Pension Liability		20,000

The entry in 20X2 is:

Pension Expense	122,000	
Cash		110,000
Pension Liability		12,000

Computation:

Service Cost	120,000	
Interest on Projected Benefit Obligation (10% × $100,000)	10,000	
Return on Plan Assets (10% × $80,000)	(8,000)	
	$122,000	

At 12/31/20X2:

Projected Benefit Obligation = $230,000
($100,000 + $120,000 + $10,000)
Pension Plan Assets = $198,000 ($80,000 + $110,000 + 8,000)

EXAMPLE 5.18

Company X has a defined benefit pension plan for its 100 employees. On 1/1/20X1, pension plan assets have a fair value of $230,000, accumulated benefit obligation is $285,000, and the projected benefit obligation is $420,000. Ten employees are expected to resign each year for the next 10 years. They will be eligible to receive benefits. Service cost for 20X1 is $40,000. On 12/31/20X1, the projected benefit obligation is $490,000, fair value of plan assets is $265,000, and accumulated benefit obligation is $340,000. The return on plan assets and the interest rate are both 8 percent. No actuarial gains or losses occurred during the year. Cash funded for the year is $75,000.

Pension expense equals:

Service Cost		$40,000
Interest on Projected Benefit Obligation (8% × $420,000)	33,600	
Return on Plan Assets (8% × $230,000)	(18,400)	
Amortization of Actuarial Gains and Losses	—	
Amortization of Unamortized Prior Service Cost	34,545*	
Pension Expense		$89,745
Obligation		$420,000
Fair Value of Pension Plan Assets		230,000
Initial Net Obligation		$190,000

EXAMPLE 5.18 *(continued)*

Amortization $\dfrac{\$190,000}{5.5 \text{ years}^{**}} = \underline{\$34,545}$

The journal entries at 12/31/20X1 follow:

Pension Expense	89,745	
Cash		75,000
Deferred Pension Liability		14,745
Intangible Asset—Pension		
Plan	60,255	
Additional Pension Liability		60,255
Computation follows:		
Accumulated Benefit		$340,000
Obligation—12/31/20X1		
Fair Value of Plan		
Assets—12/31/20X1		265,000
Minimum Liability		$ 75,000
Deferred Pension Liability		14,745
Additional Pension Liability		$ 60,255

*Projected Benefit

$**\dfrac{n(n+1)}{2} \times P = \dfrac{10(10+1)}{2} \times 10 = 550$

$\dfrac{550}{100} = 5.5$ years (average remaining service period)

What information should be disclosed in the footnotes?

Footnote disclosure for a pension plan as required by FASB statement No. 132 (Employers' Disclosures about Pension and other Postretirement Benefits) includes:

○ Description of plan including benefit formula, funding policy, employee groups covered, and retirement age
○ Components of pension expense
○ Pension assumptions (e.g., interest rate, mortality rate, employee turnover)
○ Reconciliation of funded status of plan with employer amounts recognized on the balance sheet (e.g., fair value of plan assets, projected benefit obligation, unrecognized prior service cost)
○ Present value of vested and nonvested benefits
○ Weighted-average assumed discount rate involved in measuring the projected benefit obligation
○ Weighted-average return rate on pension plan assets
○ Amounts and types of securities included in pension plan assets
○ Amount of approximate annuity benefits to employees
○ Investment policy, strategies, and objectives
○ Measurement dates

- ○ Risk management practices
- ○ Unallowable investments in the pension plan such as certain derivatives
- ○ Benefits expected to be paid
- ○ Expected contributions
- ○ Rates of compensation increase

NOTE
For analytical purposes, the excess of the projected benefit obligation over the accumulated benefit obligation represents an unrecorded liability.

When is there settlement in a pension plan?

Per FASB 88, a settlement is discharging some or all of the employer's pension benefit obligation. A settlement *must* satisfy all of the following criteria:

- ○ It is irrevocable.
- ○ It relieves pension benefit responsibility.
- ○ It materially curtails risk related to the pension obligation.

Excess plan assets may revert back to the employer.

How is settlement in a pension plan handled?

The amount of gain or loss recognized in the income statement when a pension obligation is settled is limited to the unrecognized net gain or loss from realized or unrealized changes in either the pension benefit obligation or plan assets. Changes arise when actual experiences deviate from the original assumptions. All or a pro rata share of the unrecognized gain or loss is recognized when a plan is settled.

- ○ If full settlement occurs, all unrecognized gains or losses are recognized.
- ○ If only a part of the plan is settled, a pro rata share of the unrecognized net gain or loss is recognized.

EXAMPLE: When the employer furnishes employees with a lump-sum amount to give up pension rights, the gain or loss resulting is included in the current year's income statement.

When does curtailment occur in a pension plan?

Per FASB 88, a curtailment occurs when an event significantly reduces the future service years of present employees or eliminates for most employees the accumulation of defined benefits for future services. EXAMPLE: A plant closing ends employee services prior to pension plan expectations.

How do I handle curtailment in a pension plan?

The gain or loss is recognized in the current year's income statement and contains these elements:

○ Unamortized prior service cost attributable to employee services no longer needed

○ Change in pension benefit obligation due to the curtailment

What is involved in a termination in a pension plan?

When termination benefits are offered by the employer, accepted by employees, and the amount can reasonably be determined:

○ An expense and liability are recognized

○ The amount of the accrual equals the down payment plus the present value of future payments to be made by the employer

○ The entry is to debit loss and credit cash (down payment) and liability (future payments)

○ Footnote disclosure of the arrangement should be made

Trustee Reporting for a Defined Benefit Pension Plan

What recognition is made by the trustee?

We discuss the reporting and disclosures by the trustee of a defined benefit pension plan. Generally Accepted Accounting Principles (GAAP) must be followed. Financial statements are *not* required to be issued by the plan. If they are issued, reporting guidelines have to be followed. The prime objective is to assess the plan's capability to meet retirement benefits.

BALANCE SHEET

Present *pension assets and liabilities* as an offset. Operating assets are at book value. In determining net assets available, accrual accounting is followed. EXAMPLE: Accruing for interest earned but not received. *Investments* are shown at fair market value. An asset shown is "contributions receivable due from employer."

○ In computing pension plan liability, the participants' accumulated benefits are *excluded*. In effect, plan participants are equity holders rather than creditors of the plan.

Disclosure is required of:

o Net assets available for benefits
o Changes in net assets available for benefits including
  net appreciation in fair value of each major class of
  investments
o Actuarial present value of accumulated plan benefits
  (i.e., benefits anticipated to be paid to retired employees, beneficiaries, and present employees)
o Changes in actuarial present value of accumulated
  plan benefits
o Description of the plan including amendments
o Accounting and funding policies

NOTE

An annuity contract may exist whereby an insurance
company agrees to give specified pension benefits in
return for receiving a premium.

OTHER POSTRETIREMENT BENEFITS

How do I handle postretirement benefits other than pensions?

FASB 106 applies to the employer's accounting and reporting
for postretirement benefits other than pensions: (1) health care
and welfare and (2) life insurance. These benefits are accrued
as employee services are rendered. Under the defined contribution plan, the amount contributed yearly is presented as
postretirement benefits expense. However, under the defined
benefit plan the amount contributed for the year will probably
differ from the expense.

The postretirement benefit cost is based on actuarial
determinations, and the benefits are allocated over the service periods of employees who will obtain them. Such benefits must be fully accrued by the date that the employee
attains full eligibility, even if the employee is expected to
continue working beyond that date.

Footnote disclosures include a description of the plan,
types of benefits provided, components of postretirement
expense, unamortized past service cost, cost trend factors in
health care, trend in compensation, fair market value of
plan assets, accumulated postretirement benefit obligations,
funding policy, return on plan assets, and the impact of a
one-percentage-point increase in trend rates.

INCOME TAX ACCOUNTING

How do I account for taxes?

FASB 109 applies to income tax allocation. Temporary differences occur between book income and taxable income.

The deferred tax liability or asset is measured at the tax rate under current law that will exist when the temporary difference reverses. Furthermore, the deferred tax liability or asset must be adjusted for changes in tax law or in tax rate. Consequently, the liability method must be used to account for deferred income taxes. Comprehensive deferred tax accounting is practiced. Tax expense equals taxes payable plus the tax effects of all temporary differences. Interperiod tax allocation is used to account for temporary differences impacting the current year's results. The tax effects of future events should be reflected in the year they occur. It is improper to anticipate them and recognize a deferred tax liability or asset in the current year.

Temporary Differences

How do I handle temporary differences?

Temporary differences arise from four kinds of transactions, as follows:

1. Revenue included on the tax return after being reported on the financial records (e.g., installment sales).
2. Expenses deductible on the tax return after being deducted on the financial records (e.g., bad debts provision).
3. Revenue included on the tax return before being recognized in the financial records (e.g., unearned revenue).
4. Expenses deductible on the tax return before being deducted on the financial records (e.g., accelerated depreciation).

Footnote reference is made to the types of temporary differences. If tax rates are graduated based on taxable income, aggregate calculations may be made using an estimated average rate.

Permanent Differences

What about permanent differences?

Permanent differences do not reverse and thus do not require tax allocation. Examples are penalties and fines, which are not tax deductible, and interest on municipal bonds, which is not taxable.

Financial Statement Presentation

How do I present financial statement information?

Deferred charges and deferred credits must be offset and presented (a) net current and (b) net noncurrent. Deferred tax assets or liabilities are classified according to the related asset or liability to which they apply. For instance, a deferred liability arising from depreciation on a fixed asset would be noncurrent. Deferred taxes not applicable to specific assets or liabilities are classified as current or noncurrent depending on the expected reversal dates of the temporary differences.

Temporary differences reversing within one year are current, but those reversing after one year are noncurrent.

Intraperiod Tax Allocation

How is intraperiod tax allocation handled?

Intraperiod tax allocation takes place when tax expense is shown in different parts of the financial statements for the current year. The income statement presents the tax effect of income from continuing operations, of income from discontinued operations, of extraordinary items, and of the cumulative effect of a change in accounting principle. In the statement of retained earnings, prior period adjustments are presented net of tax.

Loss Carrybacks and Carryforwards

What about loss carrybacks and carryforwards?

The tax effects of net operating loss carrybacks are allocated to the loss period. A business may carry back a net operating loss two years and receive a tax refund for taxes paid in those years. The loss is first applied to the earliest year; any remaining loss is carried forward up to 20 years.

A loss carryforward may be recognized to the degree that there exist net taxable amounts in the carryforward period (deferred tax liabilities) to absorb them. A loss carryforward benefit may also be recognized if there is more than a 50 percent probability of future realization. Footnote disclosure should be provided of the amount and expiration dates of operating loss carryforwards.

Deferred Tax Liability vs. Deferred Tax Asset

What about the recognition of a deferred tax liability vs. a deferred tax asset?

If book income is more than taxable income, then tax expense exceeds tax payable, causing a deferred tax credit. If book income is below taxable income, then tax expense is less than tax payable, resulting in a deferred tax charge.

EXAMPLE 5.19

Assume that book income and taxable income are both $10,000. Depreciation for book purposes is $1,000 using the straight-line method, whereas depreciation for tax purposes is $2,000 based on the modified ACRS method. If we assume a 40 percent tax rate, the entry is:

Income Tax Expenses		
($9,000 × 0.40)	3,600	
Income Tax Payable		3,200
($8,000 × 0.40)		
Deferred Tax Liability		
($1,000 × 0.40)		400

At the end of the asset's life, the deferred tax liability of $400 will be fully reversed.

A deferred tax asset may be recognized when it is more likely than not that the tax benefit will be realized in the future. The phrase "more likely than not" means at least slightly more than a 50 percent probability of occurring. The deferred tax asset must be reduced by a valuation allowance if it is more likely than not that some or all of the deferred tax asset will not be realized. The net amount is the amount likely to be realized. The deferred tax asset would be shown in the balance sheet as presented below, assuming a temporary difference of $200,000, the tax rate of 30 percent, and $140,000 of the tax benefit having a probability in excess of 50 percent of being realized.

Deferred Tax Asset (gross)	
($200,000 × 0.30)	$60,000
Less: Valuation Allowance	
($60,000 × 0.30)	$18,000
Deferred Tax Asset (net)	
($140,000 × 0.30)	$42,000

EXAMPLE 5.20

In 20X4, a business sold a fixed asset at a gain of $35,000 for book purposes, which was deferred for tax purposes (installment method) until 20X5. Furthermore, in 20X4, $20,000 of unearned revenue was received. The income was recognized for tax purposes in 20X4 but was deferred for book purposes until 20X5. The deferred tax asset may be recognized because the deductible amount in the future ($20,000) offsets the taxable amount ($35,000). Using a 40 percent tax rate and income taxes payable of $50,000, we find this the entry in 20X4 is:

Income Tax Expense	
(balancing figure)	56,000
Deferred Tax Asset	
($20,000 × 0.40)	8,000

EXAMPLE 5.20 *(continued)*	
Deferred Tax Liability	
($35,000 × 0.40)	14,000
Income Tax Payable	50,000

A deferred tax asset can also be recognized for the tax benefit of deductible amounts realizable by carrying back a loss from future years to reduce taxes paid in the current or in a previous year.

Tax Rates

How do I account for different tax rates in future years?

Deferred taxes are presented at the amounts of settlement when the temporary differences reverse.

EXAMPLE 5.21				

Assume in 20X1 a total temporary difference of $100,000 that will reverse in the future, generating the following taxable amounts and tax rate:

	20X2	20X3	20X4	Total
Reversals	$30,000	$50,000	$20,000	$100,000
Tax Rate	×0.40	×0.35	×0.33	
Deferred tax liability	$12,000	$17,500	$6,600	$36,100

On December 31, 20X4 the deferred tax liability is recorded at $36,100.

How do I account for a change in tax rate because of a new tax law?

A change in tax rate must immediately be accounted for by adjusting tax expense and deferred tax.

EXAMPLE 5.22				

Assume that at the end of 20X3 a law is passed lowering the tax rate from 34 to 32 percent beginning in 20X5. In 20X3, the company had a deferred profit of $200,000 and presented a deferred tax liability of $68,000. The gross profit is to be reflected equally in 20X4, 20X5, 20X6, and 20X7. Therefore, the deferred tax liability at the end of 20X3 is $65,000 computed below:

	20X4	20X5	20X6	20X7	Total
Reversals	$50,000	$50,000	$50,000	$50,000	$200,000
Tax rate	×0.34	×0.32	×0.32	×0.32	
Deferred tax liability	$17,000	$16,000	$16,000	$16,000	$65,000

EXAMPLE 5.22 *(continued)*		
The required journal entry in 20X3 is:		
Deferred Tax Liability	3,000	
Income Tax Expense		3,000

Footnote disclosures for income taxes include:

○ Current and deferred portions of income taxes
○ Reconciliation between tax expense per books and tax payable per the tax return
○ Reconciliation between the actual and expected tax rates
○ Adjustments to tax expense
○ Government grants that reduce tax expense
○ Tax-related balances due to or from affiliates

Indefinite Reversal

How are indefinite reversals handled?

As per APB Opinions 23 and 24, no interperiod tax allocation is needed for indefinite reversal situations. Indefinite reversal is when undistributed earnings of a foreign subsidiary will indefinitely be postponed as to remission back to the United States or when profit will be remitted in a tax-free liquidation. If a change in circumstances takes place and the assumption of indefinite reversal is no longer applicable, tax expense should be adjusted. Disclosure should be made not only of the declaration to reinvest indefinitely or to remit tax free, but also of the cumulative amount of undistributed earnings.

 ## FOREIGN CURRENCY TRANSLATION AND TRANSACTIONS

FASB 52 applies to:

○ Foreign currency transactions such as exports and imports denominated in a currency other than a company's functional currency
○ Foreign currency financial statements of branches, divisions, and other investees incorporated in the financial statements of a U.S. company by combination, consolidation, or the equity method

What are the purposes of a translation?

The purposes of translation are to:

○ Furnish data of expected impacts of rate changes on cash flow and equity

o Provide data in consolidated financial statements relative to the financial results of each individual foreign consolidated entity

FASB 52 covers the translation of foreign currency statements and gains and losses on foreign currency transactions. Translation of foreign currency statements is typically needed when the statements of a foreign subsidiary or equity-method investee having a functional currency other than the U.S. dollar are to be included in the financial statements of a domestic enterprise (e.g., through consolidation or using the equity method).

NOTES
Generally, foreign currency statements should be translated using the exchange rate at the end of the reporting year. Resulting translation gains and losses are shown as a separate item in the stockholders' equity section.   Also important is the accounting treatment of gains and losses emanating from transactions denominated in a foreign currency. These are presented in the current year's income statement.

What are important terms in foreign currency?

o *Conversion:* An exchange of one currency for another

o *Currency Swap:* An exchange between two companies of the currencies of two different countries per an agreement to re-exchange the two currencies at the same rate of exchange at a specified future date.

o *Denominate:* Pay or receive in that *same* foreign currency. It can only be denominated in one currency (e.g., pounds). It is a real account (asset or liability) fixed in terms of a foreign currency regardless of exchange rate.

o *Exchange Rate:* Ratio between a unit of one currency and that of another at a particular time. If there is a *temporary lack of exchangeability* between two currencies at the transaction date or balance sheet date, the *first rate available* thereafter at which exchanges could be made is used.

o *Foreign Currency:* A currency other than the functional currency of a business (for instance, the dollar could be a foreign currency for a foreign entity).

o *Foreign Currency Statements:* Financial statements using as the unit of measure a functional currency that is not the reporting currency of the business.

o *Foreign Currency Transactions:* Transactions whose terms are denominated in a currency other than the entity's functional currency. Foreign currency transactions take place when a business:

- Buys or sells on credit goods or services the prices of which are denominated in foreign currency
- Borrows or lends funds, and the amounts payable or receivable are denominated in foreign currency
- Is a party to an unperformed forward exchange contract
- Acquires or disposes of assets, or incurs or settles liabilities denominated in foreign currency

○ *Foreign Currency Translation:* Expressing in the reporting currency of the company those amounts that are denominated or measured in a different currency.

○ *Foreign Entity:* An operation (e.g., subsidiary, division, branch, joint venture) whose financial statements are prepared in a currency other than the reporting currency of the reporting entity.

○ *Functional Currency:* An entity's functional currency is the currency of the *primary economic environment* in which the business operates. It is typically the currency of the environment in which the business primarily obtains and uses cash. The functional currency of a foreign operation may be the same as that of a related affiliate in the case where the foreign activity is an essential component or extension of the related affiliate.

○ *Local Currency:* The currency of a particular foreign country.

○ *Measure:* Translation into a currency other than the original reporting currency. Foreign financial statements are measured in U.S. dollars by using the applicable exchange rate.

○ *Reporting Currency:* The currency in which the business prepares its financial statements in, usually U.S. dollars.

○ *Spot Rate:* Exchange rate for immediate delivery of currencies exchanged.

○ *Transaction Gain or Loss:* Transaction gains or losses occur due to a change in exchange rates between the functional currency and the currency in which a foreign currency transaction is denominated. They represent an increase or a decrease in (a) the actual functional currency cash flows realized upon settlement of foreign currency transactions and (b) the expected functional currency cash flows on unsettled foreign currency transactions.

○ *Translation Adjustments:* Adjustments arising from translating financial statements from the entity's functional currency into the reporting one.

What are the steps in a translation?

Four steps in translating the foreign country's financial statements into U.S. reporting requirements are:

- ○ Conform the foreign country's financial statements to U.S. GAAP.
- ○ Determine the functional currency of the foreign entity.
- ○ Remeasure the financial statements in the functional currency, if necessary. Gains or losses from remeasurement are includable in remeasured current net income.
- ○ Convert from the foreign currency into U.S. dollars (reporting currency).

What accounting recognition is given to foreign currency?

Prior to translation, the foreign country figures are remeasured in the functional currency. EXAMPLE: If a company in Italy is an independent entity and received cash and incurred expenses in Italy, the Italian currency is the functional currency. However, if the Italian company is an extension of a Canadian parent, the functional currency is the Canadian currency.

The functional currency should be consistently used except if material economic changes necessitate a change.

EXCEPTION
Previously issued financial statements are not restated for an alternation in the functional currency.

Consistent use of the functional currency of the foreign entity must exist over the years except if changes in circumstances occur warranting a change. If a change in the functional currency takes place, it is accounted for as a change in estimate.

If a company's books are *not* kept in its functional currency, remeasurement into the functional currency is mandated. The remeasurement process occurs before translation into the reporting currency takes place. When a foreign entity's functional currency is the reporting currency, remeasurement into the reporting currency obviates translation. The remeasurement process is intended to generate the same result as if the entity's books had been kept in the functional currency.

How do I determine the functional currency?

Guidelines are referred to in determining the functional currency of a foreign operation.

- *Selling price.* The functional currency is the foreign currency when the foreign operation's selling prices of products or services are due primarily to local factors (e.g., government law and competition). It is *not* due to changes in exchange rate. The functional currency is the parent's currency when the foreign operation's sales prices mostly apply in the short run to fluctuation in the exchange rate resulting from international factors (e.g., worldwide competition).

- *Market.* The functional currency is the foreign currency when the foreign activity has a strong local sales market for products or services, even though a significant amount of exports may exist. The functional currency is the parent's currency when the foreign operation's sales market is mostly in the parent's country.

- *Cash flow.* The functional currency is the foreign currency when the foreign operation's cash flows are primarily in foreign currency not directly affecting the parent's cash flow. The functional currency is the parent's currency when the foreign operation's cash flows directly impact the parent's cash flows. They are usually available for remittance via intercompany accounting settlement.

- *Financing.* The functional currency is the foreign currency if financing the foreign activity is in foreign currency and funds obtained by the foreign activity are sufficient to meet debt obligations. The functional currency is the parent's currency when financing of foreign activity is provided by the parent or occurs in U.S. dollars. Funds obtained by the foreign activity are insufficient to satisfy debt requirements.

- *Expenses.* The functional currency is the foreign currency when the foreign operation's production costs or services are usually incurred locally. However, some foreign imports may exist. The functional currency is the parent's currency when the foreign operation's production and service costs are primarily component costs obtained from the parent's country.

- *Intercompany transactions.* If there is a restricted number of intercompany transactions, the functional currency is the foreign currency—that is, when minor interrelationship occurs between the activities of the foreign entity and parent except for competitive advantages (e.g., patents). If many intercompany transactions exist, the functional currency is the parent's currency—that is, when a material interrelationship exists between the foreign entity and parent.

Translation Process

What currency is used in a translation of foreign currency statements when the U.S. dollar is the functional currency?

The foreign entity's financial statement in a highly *inflationary* economy is not stable enough and should be remeasured as if the functional currency were the reporting currency. In effect, the reporting currency is used directly.

A *highly inflationary environment* is one that has cumulative inflation of about *100 percent or more over a three-year period*. In other words, the inflation rate must be increasing at a rate of about 35 percent a year for three consecutive years.

NOTE
The International Monetary Fund in Washington, D.C., publishes monthly figures on international inflation rates.

What currency is used in a translation of foreign currency statements when the foreign currency is the functional currency?

BALANCE SHEET

Items are translated via the *current exchange rate*. For assets and liabilities, use the rate at the balance sheet date. If a current exchange rate is not available at the balance sheet date, use the first exchange rate available after that date. The *current exchange rate* is also used to translate the statement of cash flows, except for those items found in the income statement which are translated using the weighted-average rate.

INCOME STATEMENT

For these items (revenues, expenses, gains, and losses), use the exchange rate at the dates those items are recognized.

RECOMMENDATION
Since translation at the exchange rates at the dates the many revenues, expenses, gains, and losses are recognized is almost always impractical, use a weighted-average exchange rate for the period in translating income statement items.

Disclosure should consist of:

o A material change occurring between the date of the financial statements and the audit report date should be disclosed as a subsequent event.
o The effects on unsettled balances pertaining to foreign currency transactions.

Translation Adjustments

What are translation adjustments?

If a company's functional currency is a foreign currency, *translation adjustments* arise from translating that company's financial statements into the reporting currency. Translation adjustments are unrealized and the *current year* foreign translation gain or loss should be presented in the income statement under "other comprehensive income." However, the **total** foreign translation gain or loss for all the years should be presented in the stockholders' equity section of the balance sheet under "accumulated other comprehensive income."

How do I handle the sale or liquidation of an investment in a foreign entity?

Upon sale or liquidation of an investment in a foreign entity, the amount attributable to that entity and accumulated in the translation adjustment component of equity is removed from the stockholders' equity section. It is considered a part of the gain or loss on sale or liquidation of the investment in the income statement for the period during which the sale or liquidation occurs.

According to Interpretation 37, sale of an investment in a foreign entity may include a partial sale of an ownership interest. In that case, a pro rata amount of the cumulative translation adjustment reflected as a stockholders' equity component can be included in arriving at the gain or loss on sale. **EXAMPLE: If a business sells a 40 percent ownership interest in a foreign investment, 40 percent of the translation adjustment applicable to it is included in calculating gain or loss on sale of that ownership interest.**

Foreign Currency Transactions

What are foreign currency transactions?

Foreign currency transactions may result in receivables or payables fixed in terms of the amount of foreign currency to be received or paid.

A foreign currency transaction requires settlement in a currency other than the functional currency. A change in exchange rates between the functional currency and the currency in which a transaction is denominated increases or decreases the expected amount of functional currency cash flows upon settlement of the transaction.

How are foreign currency transactions accounted for?

The change in expected functional currency cash flows is a *foreign currency transaction gain or loss* that is typically included in arriving at earnings in the *income statement* for the period in which the exchange rate is altered. **EXAMPLE: A transaction may result in a gain or loss when a British subsidiary has a receivable denominated in pounds from a French customer.**

Similarly, a transaction gain or loss (measured from the *transaction date* or the most recent intervening balance sheet date, whichever is later) realized upon settlement of a foreign currency transaction should usually be included in determining net income for the period in which the transaction is settled.

EXAMPLE 5.23

An exchange gain or loss occurs when the exchange rate changes between the purchase date and sale date.

Merchandise is bought for 100,000 lira. The exchange rate is 4 lira to 1 dollar. The journal entry is:

Purchases	$25,000	
Accounts Payable		$25,000
100,000/4 = $25,000		

When the merchandise is paid for, the exchange rate is 5 to 1. The journal entry is:

Accounts Payable	$25,000	
Cash		$20,000
Foreign exchange gain		5,000
100,000/5 = $20,000		

The $20,000, using an exchange rate of 5 to 1, can buy 100,000 lira. The transaction gain is the difference between the cash required of $20,000 and the initial liability of $25,000.

NOTE

A foreign transaction gain or loss has to be determined at each balance sheet date on all recorded foreign transactions that have not been settled.

EXAMPLE 5.24

A U.S. company sells goods to a customer in England on 11/15/X7 for 10,000 pounds. The exchange rate is 1 pound to $0.75. Thus, the transaction is worth $7,500 (10,000 pounds × 0.75). Payment is due two months later. The entry on 11/15/X7 is:

Accounts Receivable— England	$7,500	
Sales		$7,500

Accounts receivable and sales are measured in U.S. dollars at the transaction date employing the spot rate. Even though the accounts receivable are measured and reported in U.S. dollars, the receivable is fixed in pounds. Thus, a transaction gain or loss can occur if the exchange rate changes between the transaction date (11/15/X7) and the settlement date (1/15/X8).

Since the financial statements are prepared between the transaction date and settlement date, receivables denominated in a currency other than the functional currency (U.S. dollar) must be restated to reflect the spot rate on the balance sheet date. On December 31, 19X7 the exchange rate is 1 pound equals $0.80. Hence, the 10,000 pounds are now valued at $8,000 (10,000 × $0.80). Therefore, the accounts receivable denominated in pounds should be upwardly adjusted by $500. The required journal entry on 12/31/X7 is:

Accounts Receivable— England	$500	
Foreign Exchange Gain		$500

The income statement for the year ended 12/31/X7 shows an exchange gain of $500. Note that sales is not affected by the exchange gain since sales relates to operational activity.

On 1/15/X8, the spot rate is 1 pound = $0.78. The journal entry is:

Cash	$7,800	
Foreign Exchange Loss	200	
Accounts Receivable— England		$8,000

The 20X8 income statement shows an exchange loss of $200.

What transaction gains and losses may be excluded from determination of net income?

Gains and losses on these foreign currency transactions are not included in earnings but rather reported as translation adjustments:

○ Foreign currency transactions designated as *economic hedges* of a net investment in a foreign entity, beginning as of the designation date

○ Intercompany foreign currency transactions of a *long-term investment* nature (settlement is not planned or expected in the foreseeable future), when the entities to the transaction are consolidated, combined, or accounted for by the equity method in the reporting company's financial statements

A gain or loss on a forward contract or other foreign currency transaction that is intended to *hedge* an identifiable foreign currency commitment (e.g., an agreement to buy or sell machinery) should be deferred and included in the measurement of the related foreign currency transaction.

NOTE
Losses should not be deferred if it is anticipated that deferral would cause losses to be recognized in subsequent periods.

A foreign currency transaction is considered a hedge of an identifiable foreign currency commitment provided both of these criteria are satisfied:

○ The foreign currency transaction is designated as a hedge of a foreign currency commitment.

○ The foreign currency commitment is firm.

Forward Exchange Contracts

What is a forward exchange contract?

A forward exchange contract is an agreement to exchange different currencies at a given future date and at a specified rate (forward rate). A forward contract is a foreign currency transaction.

How do I handle forward contracts?

A gain or loss on a forward contract that does not meet the conditions described below are included in net income.

NOTE
Currency swaps are accounted for in a similar fashion.

○ A *gain or loss on a forward contract*, except a speculative forward contract, should be computed by multiplying the foreign currency amount of the forward
contract by the difference between the *spot rate* at the
balance sheet date and the spot rate at the date of
inception of the forward contract.

○ The *discount or premium on a forward contract* (the foreign currency amount of the contract multiplied by
the difference between the contracted forward rate
and the spot rate at the date of inception of the contract) should be accounted for separately from the
gain or loss on the contract. It should be included in
computing net income over the life of the forward
contract.

○ A *gain or loss on a speculative forward contract* (a contract
that does not hedge an exposure) should be computed
by multiplying the foreign currency amount of the forward contract by the difference between the forward
rate available from the remaining maturity of the contract and the contracted forward rate (or the forward
rate last used to measure a gain or loss on that contract
for an earlier period).

NOTE
No separate accounting recognition is given to the dis-count or premium on a speculative forward contract.

Hedging

How can foreign currency transactions be hedged?

Foreign currency transactions gains and losses on assets
and liabilities, denominated in a currency other than the
functional currency, can be hedged if the U.S. company
enters into a forward exchange contract.

A hedge can occur even if a forward exchange contract
does not exist. **EXAMPLE: A foreign currency transaction
can serve as an economic hedge offsetting a parent's net
investment in a foreign entity when the transaction is
entered into for hedging purposes and is effective.**

EXAMPLE 5.25

A U.S. parent completely owns a French subsidiary having net assets of $3 million in francs. The U.S. parent can
borrow $3 million francs to hedge its net investment in
the French subsidiary. Also assume that the French franc
is the functional currency and that the $3 million
obligation is denominated in francs. Variability in the

EXAMPLE 5.25 *(continued)*

exchange rate for francs does not have a net impact on the parent's consolidated balance sheet, since increases in the translation adjustments balance arising from translation of the net investment will be netted against decreases in this balance emanating from the adjustment of the liability denominated in francs.

Derivative Products

What are derivatives?

A derivative is defined as a contract whose value is tied to the return in stocks, bonds, currencies, or commodities. Derivatives may also be contracts derived from an indicator such as interest rates or from a stock market or other index. For example, swaps are usually designed to track the interest rates or currencies.

What disclosures are necessary for derivatives?

FASB 133 covers accounting and disclosures of derivative financial instruments. Disclosure is required of the amount, type, and terms of derivative financial products, including option contracts (calls and puts), futures, forwards, and swaps. If derivative financial instruments are held or issued for trading purposes, disclosure must be made of average fair values along with the net trading gains or losses. If derivatives are for other than trading purposes, disclosures should be made about why they are being held or issued and how such products are being presented in the balance sheet and income statement. The pronouncement recommends (not requires) quantitative data concerning market risks associated with derivatives.

If the derivative products are for hedging purposes, disclosures include nature of the transaction, categorization of such instruments, deferred hedging gains or losses, and gains or losses recognized for the current year.

Disclosures are required of derivatives with off-balance-sheet risk of accounting loss by category, terms of the instruments, business activity, significant concentrations of credit risk, contract (face) amount, accounting policy followed, and description of any collateral.

If the estimation of fair value of a financial instrument is not practical, disclosure should be made of descriptive information relevant to estimating fair value of the instrument.

PART 2

ANALYZING FINANCIAL STATEMENTS

CHAPTER 6

FINANCIAL STATEMENT ANALYSIS

*F*inancial statement analysis is an appraisal of a company's previous financial performance and its future potential. The CPA is often involved in analyzing the financial statements of an existing client, prospective client, or targeted company for a potential acquisition. Financial statement analysis aids the CPA in determining what areas to audit and in appraising the overall health of the business. A "going-concern" problem may be identified. After the CPA completes his financial statement analysis, he should consult with management to discuss their plans and prospects, identify problem areas, and offer possible solutions.

This chapter covers:

○ Analytical techniques to be followed in appraising the balance sheet and income statement
○ Indicators of prospective business failure

Why analyze financial statements?

The CPA analyzes the financial statement of a client for a number of important reasons:

○ It indicates areas requiring audit attention. The CPA can look at the percentage change in an account over the years or relative to some base year to identify inconsistencies. EXAMPLE: If promotion and entertainment expense to sales was 2 percent last year and shot up to 16 percent this year, the auditor would want to uncover the reasons. This would be especially disturbing if other companies in the industry still had a percentage relationship of 2 percent. The auditor might suspect that the promotion and entertainment expense account contained some personal rather than business charges. Supporting documentation for the charges would be requested and carefully reviewed by the CPA.

o It indicates the financial health of the client which is of interest to the CPA for the following reasons:
   • A determination has to be made if the client is financially sound enough to pay the accounting fees.
   • The CPA must ascertain whether poor financial conditions exist which may cause a going-concern problem.
   • The CPA wants to know his potential legal exposure. If the client has a poor financial condition, corporate failure may occur resulting in lawsuits by creditors and others. If financial problems exist, the auditor would have to take proper audit and reporting steps including suitable references in the audit report.
o It provides vital information to be included in the management letter.
o It assists in identifying areas of financial problems and means of corrective action for the client.
o It aids the client in determining the appropriateness of mergers and acquisitions.

A company's financial health has a bearing upon its price-earnings ratio, bond rating, cost of financing, and availability of financing. CPAs should especially watch out for "high accounting risk" companies:

o "Glamour" companies known for earnings growth
o Companies in the public eye
o Companies having difficulty obtaining financing
o Companies whose management previously committed dishonest acts

How does the CPA draw conclusions from financial analysis?

To obtain worthwhile conclusions from financial ratios, the CPA has to make two comparisons: industry comparison and trend analysis.

INDUSTRY COMPARISON

The CPA should compare the company's ratios to those of competing companies in the industry or with industry standards. Industry norms can be obtained from such services as:

o Dun and Bradstreet
o Robert Morris Associates
o Standard and Poor's
o Value Line

EXAMPLES: Dun and Bradstreet computes 14 ratios for each of 125 lines of business. They are published annually in *Dun's Review and Key Business Ratios*. Robert Morris Associates publishes *Annual Statement Studies*. Sixteen ratios are computed for more than 300 lines of business, as is a percentage distribution of items on the balance sheet and income statement (common size financial statements).

In analyzing a company, the CPA should appraise the trends in its particular industry. What is the pattern of expansion or contraction in the industry? The profit dollar is worth more if earned in a healthy, expanding industry than in a declining one.

TREND ANALYSIS

A company's ratio may be compared over several years to identify direction of financial health or operational performance.

The optimum value for any given ratio usually varies across industry lines, through time, and within different companies in the same industry. In other words, a ratio deemed optimum for one company may be inadequate for another. A particular ratio is typically deemed optimum within a given range of values. An increase or decrease beyond this range points to weakness or inefficiency. EXAMPLE: whereas a low current ratio may indicate poor liquidity, a very high current ratio may indicate inefficient utilization of assets (e.g., excessive inventory) or inability to use short-term credit to the firm's advantage.

NOTE

In appraising a seasonal business, the CPA may find that year-end financial data are not representative. Thus, averages based on quarterly or monthly information may be used to level out seasonality effects.

HORIZONTAL AND VERTICAL ANALYSIS

How do horizontal and vertical analysis work?

Horizontal analysis looks at the trend in accounts over the years and aids in identifying areas of wide divergence mandating further attention. Horizontal analysis may also be presented by showing trends relative to a base year.

In *vertical analysis*, a significant item on a financial statement is used as a base value, and all other items on the financial statement are compared to it. In performing vertical analysis for the balance sheet, total assets is assigned 100 percent. Each asset is expressed as a percentage of total assets. Total liabilities and stockholders' equity is also assigned 100 percent. Each liability and stockholders' equity account is then expressed as a percentage of total liabilities and stockholders' equity. In the income statement, net sales is given the value of 100 percent, and all other accounts are appraised in comparison to net sales. The resulting figures are then given in a common size statement.

Vertical analysis is helpful in disclosing the internal structure of the business. It shows the relationship between each income statement account and revenue. It indicates the mix of assets that produces the income and the mix of the sources of capital, whether by current or long-term liabilities or by equity funding. Besides making internal evaluation possible, the results of vertical analysis are also employed to appraise the company's relative position in the industry. Horizontal and vertical analysis point to possible problem areas to be evaluated by the CPA.

BALANCE SHEET ANALYSIS

In analyzing the balance sheet, the CPA is primarily concerned with the realizability of the assets, turnover, and earning potential. The evaluation of liabilities considers arbitrary adjustments and understatement.

Assets

How do I appraise the quality of assets?

If assets are overstated, net income will be overstated since the earnings do not include necessary charges to reduce earnings to their proper valuations. Asset quality depends on the amount and timing of the realization of assets. Therefore, assets should be categorized by risk category.

○ Useful ratios are the percentage of high-risk assets to total assets and high-risk assets to sales. High asset realization risk points to poor quality of earnings due to possible future write-offs. EXAMPLE: The future realization of accounts receivable is better than that of goodwill.

○ Multipurpose assets are of better quality than single-purpose ones resulting from readier salability.

○ Assets lacking separable value cannot be sold easily and as such have low realizability. EXAMPLES: Work-in-process and intangibles.

NOTES
In appraising realization risk in assets, the effect of changing government policies on the entity has to be taken into account. Risk may exist with chemicals and other products deemed hazardous to health. Huge inventory losses may have to be taken.

EXAMPLE 6.1

Company A presents total assets of $6 million and sales of $10 million. Included in total assets are the following high-risk assets as perceived by the CPA:

Deferred plant rearrangement costs	$400,000
Receivables for claims under a government contract	200,000
Goodwill	150,000

Applicable ratios are:

$$\frac{\text{High-risk Assets}}{\text{Total Assets}} = \frac{\$750,000}{\$6,000,000} = \underline{12.5\%}$$

$$\frac{\text{High-risk Assets}}{\text{Sales}} = \frac{\$750,000}{\$10,000,000} = \underline{7.5\%}$$

 ## CASH
Is cash proper and unrestricted?

A high ratio of sales to cash may indicate inadequate cash. This may lead to financial problems if additional financing is not available at reasonable interest rates. A low turnover ratio indicates excessive cash being held.

The CPA should determine whether part of the cash is restricted and unavailable for use. EXAMPLES: A compensating balance that does not constitute "free" cash. Cash in a politically unstable foreign country that may have remission restrictions.

Accounts Receivable
Are accounts receivable realizable?

Realization risk in receivables can be appraised by studying the nature of the receivable balance. EXAMPLES: High-risk receivables include:

o Amounts from economically unstable foreign countries
o Receivables subject to offset provisions
o Receivables due from a company experiencing severe financial problems

Companies dependent on a few customers have greater risk than those with a large number of important accounts. Receivables due from industry are usually safer than those arising from consumers. Fair trade laws are more protective of consumers.

What do increases in accounts receivable mean?

A significant increase in accounts receivable compared to the prior year may indicate increased realization risk. The firm may be selling to riskier customers. The trends in accounts receivable to total assets and accounts receivable to sales should be evaluated.

The CPA should appraise the trends in the ratios of bad debts to accounts receivable and bad debts to sales. An unwarranted decrease in bad debts lowers the quality of earnings. This may happen when there is a decline in bad debts even though the company is selling to less creditworthy customers and/or actual bad debt losses are increasing.

A company may purposely overstate bad debts to provide accounting cushions for reporting understated profits. Also, companies may have substantial bad debt provisions in the current period because improper provisions were made in prior years, distorting the earnings trend. A sudden write-off of accounts receivable may arise from prior understated bad debt provisions. Earnings may be managed by initially increasing and then lowering the bad debt provision.

Receivables are of low quality if they arose from loading customers with unneeded merchandise by giving generous credit terms. Be alert for these "red-flagged" items:

○ A significant increase in sales in the final quarter of the year

○ A substantial amount of sales returns in the first quarter of the next year

○ A material decrease in sales for the first quarter of the next year

In a *seasonal* business, the accounts receivable turnover (credit sales/average accounts receivable) may be based on monthly or quarterly sales figures so that a proper averaging takes place.

How significant are sales returns and allowances?

The trend in sales returns and allowances is often a good reflection of the quality of merchandise sold to customers. A significant decrease in a firm's sales allowance account as a percentage of sales is not in conformity with reality when a greater liability for dealer returns exist. This will result in lower earnings quality.

EXAMPLE 6.2			
Company X's sales and sales returns for the period 20X3 to 20X5 follow:			
	20X5	**20X4**	**20X3**
Balance in sales returns account at year-end	$2,000	$3,800	$1,550

EXAMPLE 6.2 *(continued)*		
Sales	$240,000	$215,000	$100,000
Percentage of sales returns to sales	0.0083	0.0177	0.0155

The reduction in the ratio of sales returns to sales from 20X4 to 20X5 indicates that the company is making less of a provision for returns. This is unrealistic if there is a greater liability for dealer returns and credits on an expanded sales base.

Inventory

What does an inventory buildup mean?

An inventory buildup may point to:

○ *Greater realization risk.* The buildup may be at the plant, wholesaler, or retailer. A sign of buildup is when the inventory increases at a faster rate than sales.

○ *A production slowdown,* when there is a reduction in raw materials coupled with an increase in work-in-process and finished goods. Furthermore, greater obsolescence risk exists with work-in-process and finished goods due to major buildups. Raw materials have the best realizability because of greater universality and their multipurpose nature.

What should I do in the event of inventory buildup?

Computation of the turnover rate should be made by each major inventory category and by department.

○ A *low turnover rate* may indicate overstocking, obsolescence, or problems with the product line or marketing effectiveness. There are cases where a low inventory rate is appropriate. EXAMPLE: A higher inventory level may arise because of expected future increases in price.

○ A *high turnover rate* may point to inadequate inventory, possibly leading to a loss in business. At the "natural year-end," the turnover rate may be unusually high because at that time the inventory balance may be very low.
   The number of days inventory is held should be computed. The age of inventory should be compared to industry averages and to prior years of the company.

- *High realization risk* applies with specialized, techno-logical, "fad," luxurious, perishable, and price-sensi-tive merchandise. The CPA must be sure that the company has not assigned values to unsalable and obsolete merchandise. If there is a sudden inventory write-off, the CPA may be suspicious of the firm's deferral policy.

- *Low realization risk* applies to standard, staple, and necessity goods, owing to their better salability.

- *Collateralized inventory* has a greater risk, because cred-itors can retain it in the event of nonpayment of an obligation.

- Inventory can have *political risk* associated with it.

EXAMPLE: Increased gas prices due to a shortage situ-ation making it infeasible to purchase large cars.

Look for inventory that is overstated due to mistakes in:

- Quantities
- Costing
- Pricing
- Valuation of work-in-process

The more technical the product and the more depen-dence on internally developed cost records, the greater the susceptibility of the cost estimates to misstatement.

NOTES
If adequate insurance cannot be obtained at reason-able rates due to unfavorable geographic location of the merchandise (e.g., high crime area, flood suscepti-bility), a problem exists. The CPA should note the appropriateness of a change in inventory. Is it required by a new FASB pro-nouncement, SEC Release, or IRS tax ruling?

Investments

Are securities properly stated?

An indication of the fair value of investments may be the rev-enue (dividend income, interest income) obtained from them. Have decreases in portfolio market values been recognized in the accounts? Higher realization risk exists where there is a declining trend in the percentage of earnings derived from investments to their carrying value. Also check subsequent event disclosures for unrealized losses in the portfolio occur-ring after year-end.

EXAMPLE 6.3		
Company X presents the following information:		
	20X4	**20X5**
Investments	$50,000	$60,000
Investment Income	$ 7,000	$ 5,000

The percent of investment income to total investments decreased from 14 percent in 20X4 to 8.3 percent in 20X5, pointing to higher realization risk in the portfolio.

If a company is buying securities in other companies for diversification purposes, this will reduce overall risk. Risk in an investment portfolio can be ascertained by computing the standard deviation of its rate of return.

An investment portfolio of securities fluctuating widely in price is of higher realization risk than a portfolio that is diversified by industry and economic sector. But the former portfolio will show greater profitability in a bull market.

RECOMMENDATIONS
Appraise the extent of diversification and stability of the investment portfolio. There is less risk when securities are negatively correlated (price goes in opposite directions) or not correlated compared to a portfolio of positively correlated securities (price goes in same direction).
Note cases where held-to-maturity securities have a cost in excess of market value.

Fixed Assets

Are property, plant, and equipment properly maintained?

Inadequate provision for the maintenance of property, plant, and equipment detracts from the long-term earning power of the firm. If obsolete assets are not replaced and repairs not properly made, breakdowns and detracted operational efficiency will result. Failure to write down obsolete fixed assets results in overstated earnings.

RECOMMENDATIONS
o Determine the age and condition of each major asset along with its replacement cost.
o Review the trend in fixed asset acquisitions to total gross assets. This trend is particularly revealing for a technological company that has to keep up-to-date.

RECOMMENDATIONS
A decrease in the trend points to the failure to replace older assets on a timely basis. Inactive and unproductive assets are a drain on the firm. ○ Review asset efficiency by evaluating production levels, downtime, and discontinuances. Assets that have not been used for a long period of time may have to be written down.

NOTE
Pollution-causing equipment may necessitate replacement or modification to meet governmental ecology requirements.

EXAMPLE 6.4

Company T presents the following information regarding its fixed assets:

	20X4	20X5
Fixed Assets	$120,000	$105,000
Repairs and Maintenance	6,000	4,500
Replacement Cost	205,000	250,000

The company has inadequately maintained its assets as indicated by:

○ The reduction in the ratio of repairs and maintenance to fixed assets from 5 percent in 20×4 to 4.3 percent in 20×5

○ The material variation between replacement cost and historical cost

○ The reduction in fixed assets over the year

What does the fixed asset turnover ratio mean?

The fixed asset turnover ratio (net sales to average fixed assets) aids in appraising a company's ability to use its asset base efficiently to obtain revenue. A low ratio may mean that investment in fixed assets is excessive relative to the output generated.

When a company's rate of return on assets (e.g., net income to fixed assets) is poor, the firm may be justified in not maintaining fixed assets. If the industry is declining, fixed asset replacement and repairs may have been restricted.

A company having specialized or risky fixed assets has greater vulnerability to asset obsolescence. **EXAMPLE: Machinery used to manufacture specialized products and "fad" items.**

RECOMMENDATIONS
A depreciation method should be used that most realistically measures the expiration in asset usefulness. **EXAMPLE: The units-of-production method may result in a realistic charge for machinery. Unrealistic book depreciation may be indicated when depreciation for stockholder reporting is materially less than depreciation for tax return purposes.**

Examine the trend in depreciation expense as a percent of both fixed assets and net sales. A reduction in the trend may point to inadequate depreciation charges for the potential obsolescence of fixed assets. Another indication of inadequate depreciation charges is a concurrent moderate rise in depreciation coupled with a material increase in capital spending.

EXAMPLE 6.5		
The following information applies to X Company:		
	20X4	**20X5**
Depreciation expense to fixed assets	5.3%	4.4%
Depreciation expense to sales	4.0%	3.3%

The above declining ratios indicate improper provision for the deterioration of assets.

NOTES
A change in classification of newly acquired fixed assets to depreciation categories different from the older assets (e.g., accelerated depreciation to straight-line) will result in lower earnings quality.
A vacillating depreciation policy will distort continuity in earnings.
If there is a reduction in depreciation expense caused by an unrealistic change in the lives and salvage values of property, plant, and equipment, there will be overstated earnings.
An inconsistency exists when there is a material decline in revenue coupled with a major increase in capital expenditures. It may be indicative of overexpansion and later write-offs of fixed assets.

Intangibles

When is there a high realization risk for intangible assets?

High realization risk is indicated when there are high ratios of:

o Intangible assets to total assets
o Intangible assets to net worth

Intangibles may be overstated compared to their market value or future earning potential. EXAMPLE: A firm's goodwill may be overstated or worthless in a recessionary environment.

An unwarranted lengthening in the amortization period for intangibles overstates earnings. EXAMPLE: An unjustified change is when the company's reputation has been worsened due to political bribes or environmental violations.

The change in intangible assets to the change in net income should also be examined. A rising trend may mean this net income has been relieved of appropriate charges.

How do leasehold improvements affect intangibles?

Leasehold improvements are improvements made to rented property, (e.g., paneling and fixtures). Leasehold improvements are amortized over the life of the rented property or the life of the improvement, whichever is shorter. Leasehold improvements have no cash realizability.

What about the goodwill value of an acquired company?

A company's goodwill account should be appraised to determine whether the acquired firm has superior earning potential to justify the excess of cost over fair market value of net assets paid for it. If the acquired company does not have superior profit potential, the goodwill has no value because excess earnings do not exist relative to other companies in the industry. However, internally developed goodwill is expensed and not capitalized. It represents an undervalued asset (e.g., the good reputation of McDonald's).

Are patents properly valued?

Patents may be undervalued. They are recorded at the registration cost plus legal fees to defend them. These costs may be far below the present value of future cash flows derived from the patents.

Patents are less valuable when they may easily be infringed upon by minor alteration or when they apply to high-technology items. The company's financial condition must also be considered, since it may incur significant legal costs in defending patents. What are the expiration dates of the patents and the degree to which new patents are coming on stream?

Deferred Charges

Are deferred charges of poor quality?

Deferred expenses depend to a greater extent on estimates of future probabilities than do other assets. The estimates may be overly optimistic. Is the company deferring an item having no future benefit only to defer costs in order not to burden net income? Deferred charges are not cash realizable assets and cannot be used to meet creditor claims. **EXAMPLES: Questionable deferred charges are:**

o Deferred exploration costs under the full cost method

o Deferred interest on borrowed funds for self-constructed assets

RECOMMENDATIONS
A company may try to hide declining profitability by deferring costs that were expensed in prior years. Be on the lookout for such a situation. Examine the trend in deferred charges to sales, deferred charges to net income, and deferred charges (e.g., deferred promotion costs) to total expenditures. Increasing trends may be indicative of a more liberal accounting policy.

EXAMPLE 6.6		
Company G presents the following information:		
	20X4	**20X5**
Deferred charges	$ 70,000	$150,000
Total assets	500,000	590,000
Sales	800,000	845,000
Net income	200,000	215,000
Computed ratios are:		
Deferred costs to total assets	14%	25.4%
Deferred costs to sales	8.8%	17.8%
Deferred costs to net income	35%	69.8%

The higher ratios of deferred charges to total assets, to sales, and to net income indicate more realization risk in assets. Furthermore, 20X5's earnings quality may be lower because deferred costs may include in it items that should have been expensed.

NOTE
A high ratio of intangible assets and deferred charges to total assets points to an asset structure of greater real-ization risk. Overstated assets in terms of realizability may necessitate later write-off.

Unrecorded Assets

Do off-balance sheet assets exist?

Unrecorded assets are positive aspects of financial position even though they are not shown on the balance sheet. EXAMPLE: Unrecorded assets include tax loss carryfor-ward benefit and a purchase commitment where the com-pany has a contract to buy an item at a price materially less than the going rate.

RECOMMENDATION
Note the existence of unrecorded assets representing resources of the business or items expected to have future economic benefit.

Liabilities

What is the quality of liabilities?

If liabilities are understated, net income is overstated because it does not include necessary charges to reflect the proper val-uation of liabilities.

RECOMMENDATIONS
Examine trends in current liabilities to total liabilities, to stockholders' equity, and to sales. Rising trends may point to liquidity problems.
Determine whether liabilities are "patient" or "press-ing." A "patient" supplier with a long relationship may postpone or modify the debt payable for a financially troubled company. "Pressing debt" includes taxes and loans payable. These have to be paid without excuse. A high ratio of "pressing liabilities" to "patient liabilities" points to greater liquidity risk.

EXAMPLE 6.7		

Company A reports the following information:

Current Liabilities	20X4	20X5
Accounts payable	$ 30,000	$ 26,000
Short-term loans payable	50,000	80,000
Commercial paper	40,000	60,000
Total current liabilities	$ 120,000	$ 166,000
Total noncurrent liabilities	300,000	308,000
Total liabilities	$ 420,000	$ 468,000
Sales	$1,000,000	$1,030,000
Relevant ratios follow:		
Current liabilities to total liabilities	28.6%	35.5%
Current liabilities to sales	12.0%	16.1%
"Pressing" current liabilities to "patient" current liabilities (short-term loans payable plus commercial paper/ accounts payable)	3.01	5.4

The company has greater liquidity risk in 20X5 as reflected by the higher ratios of current liabilities to total liabilities, current liabilities to sales, and "pressing" current liabilities to "patient" current liabilities.

How do adjustments of estimated liabilities affect earnings?

Arbitrary adjustments of estimated liabilities should be eliminated in deriving corporate earning power. Estimated liability provisions should be realistic given the nature of the circumstances. EXAMPLE: Profits derived from a recoupment of prior year reserves may necessitate elimination.

RECOMMENDATION

If you find that reserves are used to manage earnings, add back the amounts charged to earnings and deduct the amounts credited to earnings.

A firm having an unrealistically low provision for future costs has understated earnings. EXAMPLE: It is inconsistent for a company to have a lower warranty provision when prior experience points to a deficiency in product quality.

An overprovision in estimated liabilities is sometimes made. In effect, the company is providing a reserve for a "rainy day." EXAMPLE: Profits are too high, and management wants to bring them down.

	NOTE

Poor earnings quality is indicated when more operating expenses and losses are being charged to reserve accounts compared to prior years.

Are some liabilities off the balance sheet?

○ Unrecorded liabilities are not reported on the financial statements but do require future payment or services. **EXAMPLES: Lawsuits and noncapitalized leases.**

○ Useful disclosures of long-term obligations are mandated by FASB 47.

	RECOMMENDATION

Review commitments applicable to unconditional purchase obligations and future payments on long-term debt and redeemable stock.

○ FASB Interpretation 34 requires disclosure of indirect guarantees of indebtedness. Included are contracts in which a company promises to advance funds to another if financial problems occur, as when sales drop below a stipulated level.

○ Preferred stock with a maturity date or subject to sinking fund requirements is more like debt than equity. However, convertible bonds with an attractive conversion feature are more like equity than debt since there is an expectation of conversion.

Evaluation of Liquidity

How do I analyze a firm's liquidity?

In appraising a company's liquidity, sufficient funds flow is necessary so that current assets are sufficient to meet short-term debt. Measures of funds flow include:

○ *Current Ratio* equals current assets divided by current liabilities.

○ *Quick Ratio* equals cash plus marketable securities plus receivables divided by current liabilities. It is a stringent test of liquidity.

○ *Working Capital* equals current assets less current liabilities. A high working capital is needed when the company may have difficulty borrowing on short notice. Working capital should be compared to other financial statement items such as sales and total assets.

EXAMPLE: Working capital to sales indicates if the company is optimally employing its liquid balance. To identify changes in the composition of working capital, ascertain the trend in the percentage of each current asset to total current assets. A movement from cash to inventory, for instance, points to less liquidity.

o *Sales to Current Assets.* A high turnover rate indicates inadequate working capital. Current liabilities may be due prior to inventories and receivables turning into cash.

o *Working Capital Provided from Operations to Net Income* (net income plus nonworking capital expenses minus nonworking capital revenue). Liquidity is enhanced when net income is backed up by liquid funds.

o *Working Capital Provided from Operations to Total Liabilities.* This indicates the extent to which internally generated working capital is available to meet debt.

o *Cash Plus Marketable Securities to Current Liabilities.* This indicates the immediate amount of cash available to satisfy short-term obligations.

o *Cost of Sales, Operating Expenses, and Taxes to Average Total Current Assets.* The trend in this ratio indicates the adequacy of current assets in meeting ongoing business-related expenses.

o *Quick Assets to Year's Cash Expenses.* This indicates the days of expenses the highly liquid assets could support.

o *Sales to Short-term Trade Liabilities.* This indicates whether the firm can partly finance by cost-free funds. A decline in trade credit means creditors have less faith in the financial strength of the business.

o *Net Income to Sales.* A decline in the profit margin of the business indicates financial deterioration.

o *Fixed Assets to Short-term Debt.* A company financing long-term assets with short-term obligations has a problem satisfying debt when due, because the return and proceeds from the fixed asset will not be realized prior to the maturity date of the current liabilities.

o *Short-term Debt to Long-term Debt.* A higher ratio points to greater liquidity risk because debt is of a current nature.

o *Accounts Payable to Average Daily Purchases.* This indicates the number of days required for the company to pay creditors.

o *Liquidity Index.* This indicates the days in which current assets are removed from cash.

EXAMPLE 6.8

	Amount	Days Removed from Cash	Total
Cash	$10,000 ×	—	—
Accounts receivable	40,000 ×	25	$1,000,000
Inventory	60,000 ×	40	2,400,000
	$110,000 ×		$3,400,000

$$\text{Index} = \frac{\$3,400,000}{\$110,000} = 30.9 \text{ days}$$

EXAMPLE 6.9

Company B provides the following financial information:

Current assets	$400,000
Fixed assets	800,000
Current liabilities	500,000
Noncurrent liabilities	600,000
Sales	5,000,000
Working capital provided from operations	100,000
Industry norms are:	
Fixed assets to current liabilities	4.0 times
Current liabilities to noncurrent liabilities	45.0%
Sales to current assets	8.3 times
Working capital provided from operations to total liabilities	30.5%

Company B's ratios are:

Fixed assets to current liabilities	1.6 times
Current liabilities to noncurrent liabilities	83.3%
Sales to current assets	12.5 times
Working capital provided from operations to total liabilities	9.1%

Company B's liquidity ratios are all unfavorable compared to industry standards. There is a high level of short-term debt, as well as deficiency in current assets. Also, working capital provided from operations to satisfy total debt is inadequate.

How does taking cash discounts affect a company financially?

A company's failure to take cash discounts raises a question as to management's financial astuteness because a high opportunity cost is involved.

EXAMPLE 6.10

Company C bought goods for $300,000 on terms of 2/10, net/60. It failed to take advantage of the discount. The opportunity cost is:

$$\frac{\text{Discount foregone}}{\text{Proceeds use of}} \times \frac{360}{\text{Days Delayed}}$$

$$\frac{\$6,000}{\$294,000} \times \frac{360}{50} = \underline{14.7\%}$$

The firm would have been better off financially paying within the discount period by taking out a loan, since the prime interest rate is below 14.7 percent.

Appraising Corporate Solvency

How do I evaluate a firm's solvency?

Corporate solvency depends on:

- The long-term debt-paying ability of the entity to ascertain whether the firm can meet long-term principal and interest payments
- Whether long-term funds are forthcoming to meet noncurrent debt
- The long-term financial and operating structure of the business
- The magnitude of noncurrent liabilities and the realization risk in noncurrent assets
- Earning power—a company will not be able to satisfy its obligations unless it is profitable

NOTE
When practical to do so, use the market value of assets instead of book value in ratio computations; it is more representative of true worth.

Measures of long-term debt paying ability are:

- *Long-term Debt to Stockholders' Equity.* High leverage indicates risk because it may be difficult for the company to meet interest and principal payments as well as obtain further reasonable financing. The problem is particularly acute when a company has cash problems. Excessive debt means less financial flexibility because the entity will have more problems obtaining funds during a tight money market.

○ *Cash Flow to Long-term Debt.* This evaluates the adequacy of available funds to satisfy noncurrent obligations.

○ *Net Income Before Taxes and Interest to Interest (Interest Coverage Ratio).* This indicates the number of times interest expense is covered. It is a safety margin indicator that shows the degree of decline in income a company can tolerate.

○ *Cash Flow Generated from Operations Plus Interest to Interest.* This ratio indicates available cash to meet interest charges. Cash *not* profit pays interest.

○ *Net Income Before Taxes Plus Fixed Charges to Fixed Charges.* This ratio helps in appraising a firm's ability to meet fixed costs. A low ratio points to risk—when corporate activity falls, the company is unable to meet its fixed charges.

○ *Cash Flow from Operations Plus Fixed Charges to Fixed Charges.* A high ratio indicates the ability of the company to meet its fixed charges. Furthermore, a company with stability in operations is better able to meet fixed costs.

○ *Noncurrent Assets to Noncurrent Liabilities.* Long-term debt is ultimately paid from long-term assets. A high ratio affords more protection for long-term creditors.

○ *Retained Earnings to Total Assets.* The trend in this ratio reflects the firm's profitability over the years.

EXAMPLE 6.11

The following partial balance sheet and income statement data are provided for Company D:

Long-term assets	$700,000
Long-term liabilities	500,000
Stockholders' equity	300,000
Net income before tax	80,000
Cash flow provided from operations	100,000
Interest expense	20,000

Average norms taken from competitors:

Long-term assets to long-term liabilities	2.0
Long-term debt to stockholders' equity	0.8
Cash flow to long-term liabilities	0.3
Net income before tax plus interest to interest	7.0

Company D's ratios are:

Long-term assets to long-term liabilities	1.4
Long-term debt to stockholders' equity	1.67
Cash flow to long-term liabilities	0.2
Net income before tax plus interest to interest	5.0

After comparing the company's ratios with the industry norms, it is evident that the firm's solvency is worse than its competitors' due to the greater degree of long-term liabilities in the capital structure and lower interest coverage.

What can financial management do to avoid solvency problems?

Ways for management to avoid solvency difficulties include:

o Avoid heavy debt
o Lengthen the maturity date of debt
o Assure that there is a "buffer" between actual status and compliance requirements (e.g., working capital) in connection with loan agreements
o Divest of unprofitable segments and assets
o Have adequate insurance
o Avoid operations in risky foreign areas
o Finance assets with liabilities of similar maturity
o Adjust to changes in technology
o Diversify horizontally and vertically
o Avoid long-term "fixed fee" commitments

 INCOME STATEMENT ANALYSIS

The analysis of the income statement indicates a company's earning power, quality of earnings, and operating performance.

NOTES
Net income backed up by cash is important for corporate liquidity.
The accounting policies employed should be realistic in reflecting the substance of the transactions.
Accounting changes should only be made for proper reasons.
A high degree of estimation in the income measurement process results in uncertainty in reported figures.
Earnings stability enhances the predictability of future results based on currently reported profits.

Cash Flow from Operations

How does proximity to cash realization affect the quality of earnings?

The closer a transaction is to cash, the more objective is the evidence supporting revenue and expense recognition. As the proximity to cash becomes less, the transaction becomes less objective and the interpretations become more subjective. Higher earnings quality relates to recording transactions close to cash realization.

How is cash flow from operations treated?

Cash flow from operations equals net income plus noncash expenses less noncash revenue. Net income is of higher quality if it is backed up by cash. The trend in the ratio of cash flow from operations to net income should be evaluated.

In appraising the cash adequacy of a company, compute the following:

○ Cash flow generated from operations before interest expense

○ Cash flow generated from operations less cash payments to meet debt principal, dividends, and capital expenditures

---

EXAMPLE 6.12

A condensed income statement for Company A follows:

Sales		$1,000,000
Less: Cost of sales		300,000
Gross margin		$ 700,000
Less: Operating expenses		
Salary	$100,000	
Rent	200,000	
Telephone	50,000	
Depreciation	80,000	
Amortization expense	60,000	
Total operating expenses		490,000
Income before other items		$210,000
Other revenue and expense		
Interest expense	$70,000	
Amortization of deferred credit	40,000	
Total other revenue and expense		30,000
Net income		$ 180,000

The ratio of cash flow from operations to net income is 1.55, calculated as follows:

Cash flow from operations		$180,000
Add: Noncash expenses		
Depreciation	$80,000	
Amortization expense	60,000	140,000
Less: Noncash revenue		
Amortization of deferred credit		(40,000)
Cash flow from operations		$280,000

$$\frac{\text{Cash flow from operations}}{\text{Net income}} = \frac{\$280,000}{\$180,000} = 1.55$$

Discretionary Costs

What are discretionary costs?

Discretionary costs include:

- Advertising
- Repairs and maintenance
- Research and development

Discretionary costs may be easily changed by management. They may be decreased when a company is having problems or wants to show a stable earnings trend.

What are the effects of a change in discretionary costs?

A pullback in discretionary costs results in overstated earnings. It has long-term negative effect because management is starving the company of needed expenses. Cost reduction programs may lower earnings quality when material cutbacks are made in discretionary costs.

NOTE
The CPA cannot always conclude that any reduction in discretionary costs is improper. The reduction may be necessary when the prior corporate strategy is deficient or ill-conceived.

RECOMMENDATIONS
Determine whether the present level of discretionary costs is in conformity with the company's prior trends and with current and future requirements. Index numbers may be used in comparing current discretionary expenditures with base-year expenditures. A vacillating trend in discretionary costs to revenue may indicate the company is smoothing earnings by altering its discretionary costs. A substantial increase in discretionary costs may have a positive impact on corporate earning power and future growth.   A declining trend in discretionary costs to net sales may indicate lower earnings quality. Review the relationship of discretionary costs to the assets they apply to.

EXAMPLE 6.13
The following relationship exists between advertising and sales:

	20X4	20X5	20X6
Sales	$120,000	$150,000	$100,000
Advertising	11,000	16,000	8,000

EXAMPLE 6.13   *(continued)*

20X4 is the most typical year.
Increasing competition is expected in 20X7.

Advertising to sales equals:

20X4	20X5	20X6
9.2%	10.7%	8%

In terms of base dollars, 20X4 is assigned 100. In 20X5, the index number is 145.5 ($16,000/$11,000), and in 20X6 it is 72.7 ($8,000/$11,000).

The above are negative indicators regarding 20X6. Advertising is of a lower level than in previous years. In fact, advertising should have risen due to expected increased competition.

Accounting Policies

What is the nature of the company's accounting principles and estimates?

Conservatively determined net income is of higher quality than liberally determined net income. Conservatism applies to the accounting methods and estimates used.

RECOMMENDATIONS
Compare the company's accounting policies with the prevailing accounting policies in the industry. If the firm's policies are more liberal, earnings quality may be lower. Take into account the company's timing of revenue recognition and the deferral of costs relative to prevailing industry practices.

The accounting policies employed should be realistic in reflecting the economic substance of the firm's transactions. The underlying business and financial realities of the company and industry have to be taken into account. EXAMPLE: The depreciation method should most approximately measure the decline in usefulness of the asset.

The CPA may question the reasonableness of a company's accounting estimates when prior estimates have been materially different from what actually occurred. Examples of realistic accounting policies are cited in AICPA Industry Audit Guides and in accounting policy guides published by various CPA firms. If the use of realistic policies results in substantially lower earnings than the policies used, earnings quality is lower.

The artificial shifting of earnings from one year to another results in poor earnings quality. This encompasses:

o Bringing future revenue into the current year (or its converse)

○ Shifting earnings from good years to bad years
○ Shifting expenses and losses among the years

It is a questionable practice when a company immediately recognizes revenue even though services still have to be performed. EXAMPLE: A magazine publisher recognizes subscription income immediately when payment is received, even though the subscription period may be three years.

The unrealistic deferral of revenue recognition results in poor earnings quality because profits are unjustifiably understated. When there is a reversal of previously recorded profits, the company's revenue recognition policies should be questioned.

If expenses are underaccrued or overaccrued, lower earnings quality results. EXAMPLES: An *underaccrued expense* is the failure of a computer manufacturer to provide for normal maintenance service for rented computers because they are being used by lessees.

An *overadorned expense* is a company with high earnings deciding to accrue for possible sales returns that are highly unlikely to materialize. Try to ascertain what these normal charges are and adjust reported earnings accordingly.

Accounting changes made to conform with new FASB Statements, AICPA Industry Audit Guides, and IRS Regulations are justifiable. However, an unjustified accounting change causes an earnings increment of low quality. Unwarranted changes may be made in accounting principles, estimates, and assumptions.

RECOMMENDATION

Question whether accounting changes are being made in order to create artificial earnings growth. If there are numerous accounting changes, it will be more difficult to use current profits as a predictor for future earnings.

Degree of Certainty in Accounting Estimates

How are the estimates?

The more subjective accounting estimates and judgments are in arriving at earnings, the more uncertain is the net income figure. EXAMPLE: A firm engaged in long-term activity (e.g., a shipbuilder using the percentage of completion contract method) has more uncertainty regarding earnings due to the material estimates involved. A higher percentage of assets subject to accounting estimates (intangibles) to total assets means uncertain earnings.

RECOMMENDATIONS
Determine the difference between estimated reserves and actual losses for previous years. A significant difference between the two may point to lower earnings quality. Further, substantial gains and losses on the sale of assets may point to inaccurate depreciation estimates being originally used.

Segregate cash expenses versus estimated expenses. Trends should be determined in:

○ Cash expenses to net sales
○ Estimated expenses to net sales
○ Estimated expenses to total expenses
○ Estimated expenses to net income

EXAMPLE 6.14

The CPA assembles the following information for Company B for the period 20X4 and 20X5

	20X4	20X5
Cash and near-cash (conversion period to cash is short) revenue items	$100,000	$110,000
Noncash revenue items (long-term receivables arising from credit sales to the government, revenue recognized under the percentage of completion method)	150,000	200,000
Total revenue	$250,000	$310,000

	20X4	20X5
Cash and near-cash expenses (salaries, rent, telephone)	$ 40,000	$ 60,000
Noncash expenses (depreciation, depletion, amortization, bad debts)	70,000	120,000
Total expenses	$110,000	$180,000
Net income	$140,000	$130,000

Estimated revenue items to total revenue was 60 percent ($150,000/$250,000) in 20X4 and 65 percent ($200,000/$310,000) in 20X5. Estimated revenue to net income was 107 percent ($150,000/$140,000) in 20X4 and 154 percent ($200,000/$130,000) in 20X5.

EXAMPLE 6.14 *(continued)*

Estimated expense items to total expenses was 64 percent ($70,000/$110,000) in 20X4 and 67 percent ($120,000/$180,000) in 20X5. Estimated expenses to total revenue was 28 percent ($70,000/$250,000) in 20X4 and 39 percent ($120,000/$310,000) in 20X5. Estimated expenses to net income was 50 percent ($70,000/$140,000) in 20X4 and 92 percent ($120,000/$130,000) in 20X5.

Uncertainty exists with respect to the earnings of 20X4 and 20X5, arising from the high percentages of estimated income statement items. Also, a greater degree of estimation exists with regard to 20X5's income measurement process.

Residual Income

What are the implications of residual income?

An increasing trend in residual income to net income points to a strong degree of corporate profitability because the company is earning enough to meet its imputed cost of capital. (Residual income is discussed in more detail in Chapter 7.)

Taxable Income

What about the discrepancy between taxable income and book income?

A company that has a significant deferred income tax credit account will have book profits in excess of taxable earnings. An increase in the deferred tax credit account may indicate the company is moving toward more liberal accounting policies. This is because a widening gap in the deferred tax credit account indicates a greater disparity between book earnings and taxable earnings.

A decline in the effective tax rate because of a nonrecurring source (e.g., a loss carryforward that will shortly expire) results in an earnings increment of low quality. The tax benefits will not continue in the future. However, the effective tax rate may be stable when it results from a recurring source (e.g., foreign tax credit, interest on municipal bonds).

Lower earnings quality exists if there is a high percentage of foreign earnings that will not be repatriated to the U.S. for a long time.

RECOMMENDATION

If a company reports significant stockholder earnings and a substantial tax loss, evaluate the quality of reported results.

Foreign Operations

How about foreign activities?

An erratic foreign exchange rate results in instability.

- ○ To measure the degree of vacillation of the foreign exchange rate, determine its percentage change over time and/or its standard deviation
- ○ To evaluate the degree of stability, look at the trend in the ratio of foreign translation gains and losses to net income.

In evaluating the effect of foreign operations on the company's financial health, consider:

- ○ Degree of intercountry transactions
- ○ Different year-ends of foreign subsidiaries
- ○ Foreign restrictions on the transfer of funds
- ○ Tax structure of the foreign country
- ○ Economic and political stability of the foreign country

Discontinued Operations

What is the analytical implication of discontinuing an operation?

Income from discontinued operations is usually of a one-time nature and should be ignored when forecasting future earnings. Furthermore, a discontinued operation implies that a company is in a state of decline or that a poor management decision was the cause for the firm's having entered the discontinued line of business in the first place.

Stability of Earnings

Are profits of a recurring nature?

A company with an unstable earnings trend has more risk associated with it. Measures of earnings stability are:

- ○ *Average net income* (e.g., five years).
- ○ *Average pessimistic earnings.* This represents the average earnings based on the *worst* possible scenario for the company's operational activities. The average minimum earnings is useful in appraising a risky company.
- ○ *Standard deviation.*

$$SD = \sqrt{\frac{\Sigma(y - \bar{y})^2}{n}}$$

where

y = reported earnings for period t
$\bar{y}$ = average earnings
n = number of years

A high standard deviation means instability in profit.

○ *Coefficient of variation.*

$$CV = \frac{SD}{\bar{y}}$$

The coefficient of variation is useful in appraising relative instability in earnings among companies. A high coefficient indicates greater risk in the earnings stream.

○ *Instability index of earnings.*

$$I = \sqrt{\frac{\Sigma(y - y^T)^2}{n}}$$

where y^T = trend earnings for period t and is computed by:

$$y^T = a + bt$$

where

a = dollar intercept
b = slope of trend line
t = time period

A simple trend equation solved by computer is used to determine trend income. The index reflects the deviation between actual profit and trend income. A high index is indicative of instability.

○ *Beta.* Beta is computed via a computer run with the use of the following equation:

$$r_{jt} = a_j + B_j r_{Mt} + E_{jt}$$

where

r_{jt} = return on security j for period t
a_j = constant
B_j = beta for security j
r_{Mt} = return on a market index such as the New York Stock Exchange Index
E_{jt} = error term

Beta is a measure of systematic or undiversifiable risk of a stock. A high beta means that the firm's stock price has vacillated more than a market index, indicating that it is a risky security.

EXAMPLE 6.15

A beta of 1.7 means that the company's stock price can rise or fall 70 percent faster than the market. Beta values for particular stocks may be obtained from various financial services such as Standard & Poor's.

Operating Leverage

What is operating leverage?

Operating leverage applies to the degree to which fixed costs exist in a company's cost structure.

How do I gauge operating leverage?

Measures of operating leverage are:

1. Fixed costs to total costs
2. Percentage change in operating income to the percentage change in sales volume
3. Net income to fixed costs

	NOTES
An increase in (1) and (2) or a decrease in (3) may point to lower earnings quality because higher fixed charges may result in greater earnings instability. A high percentage of variable costs to total costs indicates greater earnings stability. Variable costs can be adjusted more easily than fixed costs in meeting a decline in product demand. A high breakeven company is very susceptible to economic declines.	

Profitability Measures

What about profitability?

Absolute dollar profit by itself has little meaning unless it is related to its source. A company's profit margin (net income to sales) indicates how well it is being managed and provides clues to a company's pricing, cost structure, and production efficiency.

A high gross profit percent (gross profit to sales) is favorable since it indicates that the company is able to control its manufacturing costs.

The return on common equity equals earnings available to common stockholders divided by average stockholders' equity. This ratio indicates the rate of return earned on common stockholders' investment.

Growth Rate

How do I compute growth rate?

Determine a company's growth rate as follows:

$$\frac{\text{EPS (end of year)} - \text{EPS (beginning of year)}}{\text{EPS (beginning of year)}}$$

Growth in dividends per share may be similarly computed:

$$\frac{\text{Change in Retained Earnings}}{\text{Stockholders' Equity (beginning of year)}}$$

Other measures of growth are the change in sales and total assets.

Market Value Measures

What indicators of market value exist?

Market value ratios apply to a comparison of the company's stock price to its earnings (or book value) per share. Also involved are dividend-related ratios. Included are:

- ○ *Earnings per share*. This equals net income less preferred dividends divided by common stock outstanding.
- ○ *Price-earnings ratio*. This equals market price per share divided by earnings per share.
- ○ *Book value per share*. This equals:

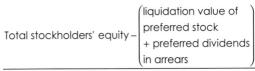

$$\frac{\text{Total stockholders' equity} - \left(\begin{array}{l}\text{liquidation value of}\\ \text{preferred stock}\\ + \text{preferred dividends}\\ \text{in arrears}\end{array}\right)}{\text{Common stock outstanding}}$$

By comparing book value per share to market price per share, the CPA can see how investors feel about the business.

- ○ *Dividend yield*. This equals dividends per share divided by market price per share.
- ○ *Dividend payout*. This equals dividends per share divided by earnings per share. The investing public looks unfavorably upon lower dividends since dividend payout is a sign of the financial health of the entity.

 ## BANKRUPTCY PREDICTION
Will the company fail?

Some key indicators to be examined by the CPA in predicting corporate bankruptcy are:

- ○ Cash flow from operations to total liabilities
- ○ Net income to total assets
- ○ Total liabilities to total assets
- ○ Quick ratio
- ○ Current ratio
- ○ Operating income to total assets

o Interest coverage (income before interest and taxes to interest)
o Retained earnings to total assets
o Common equity to total liabilities
o Working capital to total assets
o Debt to equity
o Fixed assets to stockholders' equity

What is the "Z-score"?

Edward Altman's "Z-score" can be used to predict bankruptcy within the short run (one or two years).

The "Z-score" equals:

$$\frac{\text{Working capital}}{\text{Total assets}} \times 1.2 + \frac{\text{Retained earnings}}{\text{Total assets}} \times 1.4$$

$$+ \frac{\text{Operating income}}{\text{Total assets}} \times 3.3$$

$$+ \frac{\begin{array}{c}\text{Market value of}\\\text{common stock and}\\\text{preferred stock}\end{array}}{\text{Total debt}} \times 0.6$$

$$+ \frac{\text{Sales}}{\text{Total assets}} \times 1.1$$

His scoring chart follows:

Score	Probability of short-term illiquidity
1.80 or less	Very high
1.81 to 2.7	High
2.8 to 2.9	Possible
3.0 or higher	Not likely

EXAMPLE 6.16

Company D provides the following relevant information:

Working capital	$250,000
Total assets	900,000
Total liabilities	300,000
Retained earnings	200,000
Sales	1,000,000
Operating income	150,000
Common stock:	
Book value	210,000
Market value	300,000
Preferred stock:	
Book value	100,000
Market value	160,000

EXAMPLE 6.16 *(continued)*

The "Z-score" is:

$$\frac{\$250,000}{\$900,000} \times 1.2 + \frac{\$200,000}{\$900,000} \times 1.4$$

$$+ \frac{\$150,000}{\$900,000} \times 3.3 + \frac{\$460,000}{\$300,000} \times 0.6$$

$$+ \frac{\$1,000,000}{\$900,000} \times 1.1 = 3.225$$

The score indicates that it is unlikely for business failure to occur.

Does company size bear a relationship to the probability of failure?

In a study done by Dun and Bradstreet,[1] it was found that small companies had higher failure rates than large companies. Size can be measured by total assets, sales, and age.

What are indicators of financial distress?

Financial and operating deficiencies pointing to financial distress include:

- o Significant decline in stock price
- o Reduction in dividend payments
- o Sharp increase in the cost of capital
- o Inability to obtain further financing
- o Inability to meet past-due obligations
- o Poor financial reporting system
- o Movement into business areas unrelated to the company's basic business
- o Failure to keep up-to-date
- o Failure to control costs
- o High degree of competition

LIQUIDATION VALUE

What is the expected liquidation value for a company?

J. Wilcox's "gambler's ruin prediction formula" can be used to determine a company's expected liquidation value as follows:

+ Cash and trading securities at market value
+ (Inventory, accounts receivable, and prepaid expenses) × 70%
+ (Other assets) × 50%
− Total liabilities

---

[1] *The Business Failure Record*—1975 (New York: Dun and Bradstreet, 1976).

EXAMPLE 6.17

Based on the following information, calculate A Company's liquidation value:

Cash	$200,000
Trading securities	80,000
Accounts receivable	70,000
Inventory	90,000
Prepaid expenses	20,000
All other assets	300,000
Current liabilities	100,000
Noncurrent liabilities	250,000

Liquidation value equals:

+ ($200,000 + $80,000)	= $280,000
+ ($90,000 + $70,000 + $20,000) × 70%	= 126,000
+ ($300,000) × 50%	= 150,000
− ($100,000 + $250,000)	= −350,000
Liquidation value	$206,000

PART 3

MANAGERIAL ACCOUNTING APPLICATIONS

CHAPTER 7

APPRAISING SEGMENTAL PERFORMANCE

Accountants typically look at budgeting and profit planning as tools for control of responsibility center operations and as facilitating factors in judging managerial performance. Accountants should be familiar with fundamental managerial accounting tools such as standard costing, flexible budgeting, and the contribution approach. They should have a thorough understanding of two important issues that arise frequently with decentralized operations—divisional performance and transfer pricing.

This chapter covers measures and guidelines for internally evaluating a company's performance, including:

- ○ Responsibility accounting and responsibility centers
- ○ Cost center performance and standard costs
- ○ Flexible budgets and performance reports
- ○ Profit centers and segmented reporting
- ○ Evaluation of divisional performance
- ○ Transfer pricing
- ○ Budgeting and financial planning

THE WHAT AND WHY OF RESPONSIBILITY ACCOUNTING

What is responsibility accounting?

Responsibility accounting is the system for collecting and reporting revenue and cost information by areas of responsibility. It operates on the premise that managers should be held responsible for their performance, the performance of their subordinates, and all activities within their responsibility center.

What are the benefits of responsibility accounting?

Responsibility accounting, also called *profitability accounting and activity accounting*, has the following advantages:

- ○ It facilitates delegation of decision making.
- ○ It helps management promote the concept of management by objective, in which managers agree on a set of

goals. The manager's performance is then evaluated based on his or her attainment of these goals.

○ It provides a guide to the evaluation of performance and helps establish standards of performance which are then used for comparison purposes.

○ It permits effective use of the concept of *management by exception*, which means that the manager's attention is concentrated on the important deviations from standards and budgets.

What are responsibility centers?

A well-designed responsibility accounting system establishes *responsibility centers* within the organization. A responsibility center is a unit in the organization that has control over costs, revenues, and/or investment funds. Responsibility centers may be a cost center, profit center, or investment center.

Cost Center

A cost center is the unit within the organization that is responsible only for costs. EXAMPLES: The production and maintenance departments of a manufacturing company, the admissions department of a university.

RECOMMENDATION

Variance analysis based on standard costs and flexible budgets would be a typical performance measure of a cost center.

Profit Center

A profit center is the unit that is held responsible for the revenues earned and costs incurred in that center. EXAMPLES: A sales office of a publishing company, an appliance department in a retail store, an auto repair center in a department store.

RECOMMENDATION

The contribution approach to cost allocation is widely used to measure the performance of a profit center.

Investment Center

An investment center is the unit within the organization that is held responsible for the costs, revenues, and related investments made in that center. EXAMPLES: The corporate headquarters, a division in a large decentralized organization.

RECOMMENDATION

Return on investment and residual income are two key performance measures of an investment center.

Exhibit 7.1 illustrates how responsibility accounting can be used within an organization and highlights profit and cost centers.

COST CENTER PERFORMANCE AND STANDARD COSTS

How do I measure the performance of a cost center?

One of the most important phases of responsibility accounting is establishing standard costs in order to evaluate performance by comparing actual costs with standard costs. The difference between the actual costs and the standard costs, called the *variance*, is calculated for individual cost centers. The variance analysis is a key tool for measuring the performance of a cost center.

The standard cost is based on physical and dollar measures: it is determined by multiplying the standard quantity of an input by its standard price. Two general types of variances (price and quantity) can be calculated for most cost items. The *price variance* is calculated as follows:

$$\begin{aligned}
\frac{\text{Price}}{\text{Variance}} &= \frac{\text{Actual}}{\text{Quantity}} \times \left(\frac{\text{Actual}}{\text{Price}} - \frac{\text{Standard}}{\text{Price}} \right) \\
&= \underset{}{AQ} \times (AP - SP) \\
&= \underset{(1)}{(AQ \times AP)} - \underset{(2)}{(AQ \times SP)}
\end{aligned}$$

The *quantity variance* is calculated as follows:

$$\begin{aligned}
\frac{\text{Quantity}}{\text{Variance}} &= \left(\frac{\text{Actual}}{\text{Quantity}} - \frac{\text{Standard}}{\text{Quantity}} \right) \times \frac{\text{Standard}}{\text{Price}} \\
&= (AQ - SQ) \times SP \\
&= \underset{(2)}{(AQ \times SP)} - \underset{(3)}{(SQ \times SP)}
\end{aligned}$$

Exhibit 7.2 shows a general (three-column) model for variance analysis that incorporates the items (1), (2), and (3) from the above equations.

How is standard costing useful?

Standard costing has many advantages:

○ Aids in cost control and performance evaluation

○ "Red flags" current and future problems through the "management by exception" principle

○ Improves performance by recommending paths for corrective action in cost reduction

○ Fixes responsibility

○ Constitutes a vehicle of communication between top management and supervisors

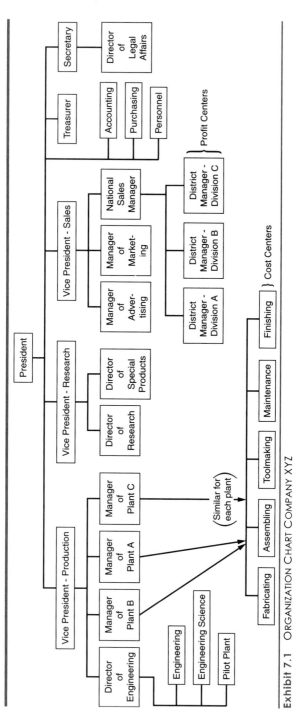

Exhibit 7.1 ORGANIZATION CHART COMPANY XYZ

224

Actual Quantity of Inputs, at Actual Price (AQ × AP) (1)	Actual Quantity of Inputs, at Standard Price (AQ × AP) (2)	Standard Quantity Allowed for Output, at Standard Price (SQ × SP) (3)
Price variance (1) – (2)		Quantity variance (2) – (3)
Total Variance		
o Materials purchase price variance o Labor rate variance o Variable overhead spending variance	o Materials quantity (usage variance) o Labor efficiency variance o Variable overhead efficiency variance	

Exhibit 7.2 A GENERAL MODEL FOR VARIANCE ANALYSIS: VARIABLE MANUFACTURING COSTS

- o Establishes selling prices and transfer prices
- o Determines bid prices on contracts
- o Sets business goals
- o Aids in the planning and decision-making processes
- o Simplifies bookkeeping procedures and saves clerical costs

Standard costing is not without some drawbacks. EXAMPLES: The possible biases involved in deriving standards and the dysfunctional effects of setting improper norms and standards.

Materials Variances

How are materials variances computed?

A *materials price variance* is isolated at the time of purchase of the material. Therefore, it is normally computed based on the actual quantity purchased. The purchasing department is responsible for any materials price variance that might occur. The *materials quantity (usage) variance* is computed based on the actual quantity used.

NOTE
The production department is responsible for any materials quantity variance that might occur.

What causes material variances?

The possible causes of *unfavorable* materials variances are:

MATERIALS PRICE VARIANCE

- o Inaccurate standard prices
- o Failure to take a discount on quantity purchases

- Failure to shop for bargains
- Inflationary cost increases
- Scarcity in raw material supplies resulting in higher prices
- Purchasing department inefficiencies

Materials Quantity (Usage) Variance

- Poorly trained workers
- Improperly adjusted machines
- Use of improper production method
- Outright waste on the production line
- Use of a lower grade material purchased in order to economize on price

EXAMPLE 7.1

ABC Corporation uses a standard cost system. The standard variable costs for Product J are:

Materials: 2 lb at $3.00 per lb
Labor: 1 hour at $5.00 per hour
Variable overhead: 1 hour at $3.00 per hour

During March, 25,000 pounds of material were purchased for $74,750, and 20,750 pounds of material were used in producing 10,000 units of finished product. Direct labor costs incurred were $49,896 (10,080 direct labor hours), and variable overhead costs incurred were $34,776. Using the general (three column) model, we find that the materials variances are:

Materials Variances

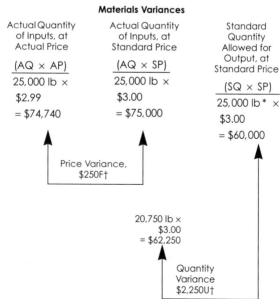

EXAMPLE 7.1 *(continued)*

Alternatively, we can compute the materials variances as follows:

Materials (purchase) price variance

$= AQ \times (AP - SP) = (AQ \times AP) - (AQ \times SP)$

$= 25{,}000 \text{ lb } (\$2.99 - \$3.00) = \$74{,}750 - \$75{,}000$

$= \$250F$

Materials quantity (usage) variance

$= (AQ - SQ) \times SP$

$= (20{,}750 \text{ lb} - 20{,}000 \text{ lb}) \times \$3.00$

$= \$62{,}250 - \$60{,}000$

$= \$2{,}250U$

---

*10,000 units actually produced × 2 lb allowed per unit = 20,000 lb.
NOTE: The amount of materials purchased (25,000 lb) differs from the amount of materials used in production (20,750 lb). The materials purchase price variance was computed using 25,000 lb purchased, whereas the material quantity (usage) variance was computed using the 20,750 lb used in production. A total variance cannot be computed because of the difference.

†A variance represents the deviation of actual cost from the standard or budgeted cost. U and F stand for "unfavorable" and "favorable," respectively.

Labor Variances

How are labor variances computed?

Labor variances are isolated when labor is used for production. They are computed in a manner similar to materials variances, except that in the three-column model the terms hours and rate are used in place of the terms quantity and price. The production department is responsible for both the prices paid for labor services and the quantity of labor services used. Therefore, the production department must explain the cause of any labor variances.

What causes labor variances?

Possible causes of unfavorable labor variances are:

- Labor price (rate) variance
  - Increase in wages
  - Poor scheduling of production resulting in over-time work
  - Use of workers commanding higher hourly rates than contemplated in the standards
- Labor efficiency variance
  - Poor supervision
  - Use of unskilled workers paid lower rates or the wrong mixture of labor for a given job
  - Use of poor quality machinery

- Improperly trained workers
- Poor quality of materials requiring more labor time in processing
- Machine breakdowns
- Employee unrest
- Production delays due to power failure

EXAMPLE 7.2

Using the same data given in Example 7.1, the labor variances can be calculated as follows:

Labor Variances

Actual Hours of Input, at the Actual Rate	Actual Hours of Input, at the Standard Rate	Standard Hours Allowed for Output, at the Standard Rate
(AH × AR)	(AH × SR)	(SH × SR)
10,080 hr × $4.95 = $49,896	10,080 hr × $5.00 = $50,400	10,000 hr *× $5.00 = $50,000

	Rate Variance, $540F		Efficiency Variance $400U
		Total Variance, $104F	

*10,000 units actually produced × 1 hour allowed per unit = 10,000 hr.

NOTE

The symbols (AQ, SO, AP, and SP) have been changed to (AH, SH, AR, and SR) to reflect the terms *hour* and *rate*.

Alternatively, we can calculate the labor variances as follows:

Labor rate variance = AH × (AR – SR) = (AH × AR) – (AH × SR)

= 10,080 hr ($4.95 – $5.00) = $49,896 – $50,400

= $504F

Labor efficiency variance = (AH – SH) × SR

= (10,080 hr – 10,000 hr) × $5.00 = $50,400 – $50,000

= $400U

Variable Overhead Variances

How are variable overhead variances determined?

Variable overhead variances are computed in a way similar to labor variances. The production department is usually responsible for any variable overhead variance that might occur. Variances for fixed overhead are of questionable usefulness for control purposes, since these variances are usually beyond the control of the production department.

What causes unfavorable variable overhead variances?

Possible causes of unfavorable variable overhead variances are:

- ○ Variable overhead spending variance
  - Increase in supplier prices
  - Increase in labor rates
  - Inaccurate standards
  - Waste
  - Theft of supplies
- ○ Variable overhead efficiency variance
  - Poorly trained workers
  - Use of poor quality materials
  - Use of faulty equipment
  - Poor supervision
  - Employee unrest
  - Work interruptions
  - Poor production scheduling
  - A lack of automation and computerization in processing

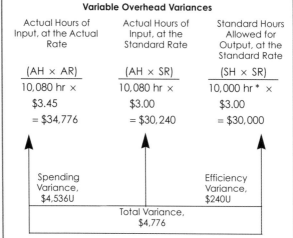

EXAMPLE 7.3

Using the same data given in Example 7.1, the variable overhead variances can be computed as follows:

Variable Overhead Variances

Actual Hours of Input, at the Actual Rate	Actual Hours of Input, at the Standard Rate	Standard Hours Allowed for Output, at the Standard Rate
(AH × AR)	(AH × SR)	(SH × SR)
10,080 hr ×	10,080 hr ×	10,000 hr * ×
$3.45	$3.00	$3.00
= $34,776	= $30,240	= $30,000

Spending Variance, $4,536U

Efficiency Variance, $240U

Total Variance, $4,776

* 10,000 units actually produced × 1 hour allowed per unit = 10,000 hr.

EXAMPLE 7.3 *(continued)*

Alternatively, we can compute the variable overhead variances as follows:

Variable overhead spending variance
$$= AH \times (AR - SR) = (AH \times AR) - (AH \times SR)$$
$$= 10{,}080 \text{ hr } (\$3.45 - \$3.00) = \$34{,}776 - \$30{,}240$$
$$= \$4{,}536U$$

Variable overhead efficiency variance
$$= (AH - SH) \times SR$$
$$= (10{,}080 \text{ hr} - 10{,}000 \text{ hr}) \times \$3.00$$
$$= \$30{,}240 - \$30{,}000$$
$$= \$240U$$

Fixed Overhead Variances

How are fixed overhead variances determined?

By definition, fixed overhead does not change over a relevant range of activity; the amount of fixed overhead per unit varies inversely with the level of production. In order to calculate variances for fixed overhead, it is necessary to determine a standard fixed overhead rate, which requires the selection of a predetermined (denominator) level of activity. This activity should be measured on the basis of standard inputs allowed. The formula is:

$$\text{Standard fixed overhead rate} = \frac{\text{Budgeted fixed overhead}}{\text{Budgeted level of activity}}$$

Total fixed overhead variance is simply under- or over-applied overhead. It is the difference between actual fixed overhead incurred and fixed overhead applied to production (generally, on the basis of standard direct labor hours allowed for actual production). Total fixed overhead variance combines fixed overhead spending (flexible-budget) variance and fixed overhead volume (capacity) variance.

a. *Fixed overhead spending (flexible-budget) variance.* It is the difference between actual fixed overhead incurred and budgeted fixed overhead. This variance is not affected by the level of production. Fixed overhead, by definition, does not change with the level of activity. The spending (flexible-budget) variance is caused solely by events such as unexpected changes in prices and unforeseen repairs.

b. *Fixed overhead volume (capacity) variance.* This variance results when the actual level of activity differs from the denominator activity used in determining the standard fixed overhead rate. Note that the denominator used in the formula is the expected annual activity level. Fixed overhead volume variance is a measure of the cost of failure to operate at the denominator (budgeted) activity level and may be caused by such factors as failure to meet sales targets, idleness due to poor scheduling, and machine breakdowns. The volume variance is calculated as follows:

Fixed overhead volume variance
= (Budgeted fixed overhead)
– (fixed overhead applied)

or

= (Denominator activity – standard hours allowed)
× standard fixed overhead rate

When denominator activity exceeds standard hours allowed, the volume variance is unfavorable (U) because it is an index of less-than-denominator utilization of capacity.

There are no efficiency variances for fixed overhead. Fixed overhead does not change regardless of whether or not productive resources are used efficiently. For example, property taxes, insurance, and factory rents are not affected by whether production is being carried on efficiently.

Exhibit 7.3 below illustrates the relationship between the various elements of fixed overhead, and the possible variances.

	Incurred: Actual Hours x Actual Rate (1)	Flexible Budget Based on Actual Hours (2)	Flexible Budget Based on Standard Hours Allowed (3)	Applied (4)
3-way Analysis	Spending Variance (1) – (2)	Efficiency Variance (Not Applicable)	Volume Variance (3) – (4)	
2-way Analysis	Flexible Budget Variance (1) – (3)		Volume Variance (3) – (4)	
	(1) – (4) Under- or Over-applied			

Exhibit 7.3   Fixed Overhead Variances

Example 7.4

The Doubtfire Manufacturing Company has the following standard cost of factory overhead at a normal monthly production (denominator) volume of 1,300 direct labor hours:

Variable overhead (1 hour @ $2)
Fixed overhead (1 hour @ $5)

> **EXAMPLE 7.4** *(continued)*
>
> Fixed overhead budgeted is $6,500 per month. During the month of March, the following events occurred:
>
> a. Actual overhead costs incurred (for 1,350 hours) were:
>
> | | |
> |---|---|
> | Variable | $2,853 |
> | Fixed | $6,725 |
>
> b. Standard hours allowed, 1,250 hours (1 hour × 1,250 units of output)
>
> Note that:
>
> a. Flexible budget formula:
>
> | | |
> |---|---|
> | Variable overhead rate | $2 per direct labor hour |
> | Fixed overhead budgeted | $6,500 |
>
> b. Standard overhead applied rates:
>
> | | |
> |---|---|
> | Variable | $2 per direct labor hour |
> | Fixed | $5 per direct labor hour |
>
> Exhibit 7.4 shows all the variances for variable overhead as well as fixed overhead.

Alternatively, fixed overhead volume variance can be calculated as follows:

$$\text{Fixed overhead} = \text{(Denominator activity}$$
$$- \text{standard hours allowed)}$$
$$\times \text{volume variance}$$
$$\times \text{standard fixed overhead rate}$$
$$= (1{,}300 \text{ hours} - 1{,}250 \text{ hours}) \times \$5$$
$$= 50 \text{ hours} \times \$5 = \$250 \text{ U}$$

Incurred: Actual Hours x Actual Rate (1,350 hr) **(1)**	Flexible Budget Based on Actual Hours (1,250 hr) **(2)**	Flexible Budget Based on Standard Hours Allowed (1,250 hr) **(3)**	Applied (1,350 hr) **(4)**
V $2,853	$2,700 (1,350 X $2)	$2,500 (1,250 X $2)	$2,500
F 6,725	6,500	6,500	6,250
$9,578	$9,200	$9,000	$8,750

3-way	Spending Variance (1) – (2) V $153 U F 225 U $378 U	Efficiency Variance (Not Applicable) $200 U Not Applicable $200 U	Volume Variance (3) – (4) Not Applicable $250 U $250 U
2-way	Flexible Budget Variance (1) – (3) V $353 U F 225 U $578 U		Volume Variance (3) – (4) Not Applicable $250 U $250 U
	Under- or Overapplied (1) – (4) V $353 U F 475 U $828 U		

Exhibit 7.4   VARIANCE ANALYSIS FOR VARIABLE OVERHEAD AND FIXED OVERHEAD

What are the methods of variance analysis for factory overhead?

Variance analysis for factory overhead consists of a two-, three-, or four-way method of computation, depending on the significance of the variance amounts compared to the cost of analysis. These methods are indicated in the two previous figures.

The two-way analysis computes two variances: budget variance (sometimes called the flexible-budget or controllable variance) and volume variances, which means:

a. Budget variance = Variable spending variance
                    + Fixed spending (budget) variance
                    + Variable efficiency variance

b. Volume variance = Fixed volume variance

The three-way analysis computes three variances: spending, efficiency, and volume variances.
Therefore,

a. Spending variance = Variable spending variance
                     + Fixed spending (budget) variance

b. Efficiency variance = Variable efficiency variance

c. Volume variance = Fixed volume variance

The four-way analysis includes the following:

a. Variable spending variance
b. Fixed spending (budget) variance
c. Variable efficiency variance
d. Fixed volume variance

Mix and Yield Variances

What about the computation of mix and yield variances?

The *material mix variance* measures the impact of the deviation from the standard mix on material costs. The *material yield variance* measures the impact on material costs of the deviation from the standard input material allowed for actual production. The *material quantity variance* is divided into a material mix variance and a material yield variance.

o Compute the material mix variance by holding the total input units constant at their actual amount.

o Compute the material yield variance by holding the mix constant at the standard amount.

The computations for labor mix and yield variances are the same as those for materials. If there is no mix, the yield variance is the same as the quantity (or usage) variance.

What causes mix and yield variances?

Possible causes of unfavorable mix variances are:

- o When capacity restraints force substitution
- o Poor production scheduling
- o Lack of certain types of labor
- o Short supply of certain materials

Possible causes of unfavorable yield variances are:

- o Low quality materials and/or labor
- o Faulty equipment
- o Improper production methods
- o Improper or costly mix of materials and/or labor

EXAMPLE 7.5

J Company produces a compound composed of Materials Alpha and Beta which is marketed in 20-lb bags. Material Alpha can be substituted for Material Beta. Standard cost and mix data have been determined as follows:

	Unit Price	Standard Unit	Standard Mix Proportions
Material Alpha	$3	5 lb	25%
Material Beta	4	15	75
		20 lb	100%

Processing each 20 lb of material requires 10 hr. of labor. The company employs two types of labor—skilled and unskilled—working on two processes, assembly and finishing. The following standard labor cost has been set for a 20-lb bag.

	Standard Hours	Standard Wage Rate	Total	Standard Mix Proportions
Unskilled	4	$2	$8	40%
Skilled	6	3	18	60
	10	$2.60	26	100%

At standard cost, labor averages $2.60 per unit. During the month of December 100 20-lb bags were completed with the following labor costs:

	Actual Hours	Actual Rate	Actual Wages
Unskilled	380	$2.50	$950
Skilled	600	3.25	1,950
	980	$2.96	$2,900

We now want to determine the following variances from standard costs.

a. Material purchase price
b. Material mix
c. Material quantity
d. Labor rate

EXAMPLE 7.5 *(continued)*

e. Labor mix

f. Labor efficiency

Material records show:

	Beginning Inventory	Purchase	Ending Inventory
Material Alpha	100 lb	800 @ $3.10	200 lb
Material beta	225	1,350 @ $3.90	175

We will also prepare appropriate journal entries. We will show how to compute these variance in a tabular form as follows:

a. Material Purchase Price Variance

	Material Price per Unit			Actual Quantity Purchased	Variance ($)
	Standard	Actual	Difference		
Material Alpha	$3	$3.10	$0.10 U	800 lb	$ 80 U
Material Beta	4	3.90	0.10 F	1,350	135 F
					$55 F

b. Material Mix Variance

	Unit Which Should Have Been Used at Standard Mix*	Actual Unit at Actual Mix**	Diff.	Standard Unit Price	Variance ($)
Material Alpha	525 lb	700 lb	175 U	$3	$525 U
Material Beta	1,575	1,400	175 F	4	700 F
	2,100 lb	2,100 lb			$175 F

The material mix variance measures the impact of the deviation from the standard mix on material costs. Therefore, it is computed holding the total quantity used constant at its actual amount and allowing the material mix to vary between actual and standard. As shown above, because of a favorable change in mix, we ended up with a favorable material mix variance of $175.

c. Material Quantity Variance

	Should Have Been Used at Standard Mix*	Standard Units at Standard Mix	Diff.	Standard Unit Price	Variance ($)
Material Alpha	525 lb	500 lb	25 U	$3	$75 U
Material Beta	1,575	1,500	75 U	4	300 U
	2,100 lb	2,000 lb			$375 U

*This is the standard mix proportion of 25% and 75% applied to the actual material units used of 2,100 lb

**Actual units used = beginning inventory + purchases − ending inventory. Therefore,

Material Alpha: 700 lb = 100 + 800 − 200

Material Beta: 1,400 lb = 225 + 1,350 − 175

EXAMPLE 7.5 *(continued)*

The total material variance is the sum of the three variances:

Purchase price variance	$55 F
Mix variance	175 F
Quantity variance	375 U
	$145 U

The increase of $145 in material costs was due solely to an unfavorable quantity variance of 100 lb of material Alpha and Beta. The unfavorable quantity variance, however, was compensated largely by favorable mix and price variances. J Company must look for ways to cut down waste and spoilage.

The labor cost increase of $300 ($2,900 – $2,600) is attributable to three causes:

1. An increase of $0.50 per hour in the rate paid to skilled labor and $0.25 per hour in the rate paid to unskilled labor.
2. An unfavorable mix of skilled and unskilled labor.
3. A favorable labor efficiency variance of 20 hours.

Three labor variances are computed below.

d. Labor Rate Variance

	Labor Rate per Hour			Actual Hour	variance
	Standard	Actual	Diff.	Used	($)
Unskilled	$2	$2.50	$0.5 U	380 U	$190 U
Skilled	3	3.25	0.25 U	600 U	150 U
					$340 U

e. Labor Mix Variance

	Actual Hours at Standard Mix*	Actual Hours at Actual Mix	Diff.	Standard Rate	Variance ($)
Unskilled	392 hr	380 hr	12 F	$2	$24 F
Skilled	588	600	12 U	3	36 U
	980 hr	980 hr			$12 U

*This is the standard proportions of 40% and 60% applied to the actual total labor hrs. used of 980.

f. Labor Efficiency Variance

	Actual Hours at Standard Mix	Standard Hours at Standard Mix	Diff.	Standard Rate	Variance ($)
Unskilled	392 hr	400 hr	8 F	$2	$16 F
Skilled	588	600	12 F	3	36 F
	980 hr	1,000 hr			$52 F

The total labor variance is the sum of these three variances:

Rate variance	$340 U
Mix variance	12 U
Efficiency variance	52 F
	$300 U

which is proved to be:

EXAMPLE 7.5 *(continued)*

Total Labor Variance

	Actual Hours Used	Actual Rate	Total Actual Cost	Standard Hours Allowed	Standard Hours Rate	Total Cost	Variance ($)
Unskilled	380 hr	$2.50	$950	400	$2	$800	$150 U
Skilled	600	3.25	1,950	600	3	1,800	150 U
			$2,900			$2,600	$300 U

EXAMPLE 7.5 *(continued)*

The unfavorable labor variance, as evidenced by the cost increase of $300, may be due to:

1. Overtime necessary because of poor production scheduling resulting in a higher average labor cost per hour; and/or
2. Unnecessary use of more expensive skilled labor. J Company should put more effort into better production scheduling.

EXAMPLE 7.6

A company uses a standard cost system for its production of a chemical product. This chemical is produced by mixing three major raw materials, A, B, and C. The company has the following standards:

36 lb of Material A	@1.00	= $36.00
48 lb of Material B	@2.00	= $96.00
36 lb of Material C	@1.75	= $63.00
120 lb of standard mix	@1.625	= $195.00

The company should produce 100 lb of finished product at a standard cost of $1.625 per lb ($195/120 lb). To convert 120 lb of materials into 100 lb of finished chemical requires 400 direct labor hours at $3.50 per hour, or $14 per lb. During the month of December, the company completed 4,250 lb of output with the following labor: direct labor 15,250 hours @$3.50. Material records show:

	Materials Purchased during the Month	Materials Used during the Month
Material A	1,200 @ $1.00	1,160 lb
Material B	1,800 @ 1.95	1,820
Material C	1,500 @ 1.80	1,480

The material *price variance is isolated at the time of purchase.* We want to compute the material purchase price, quantity, mix, and yield variances. We also want to prepare appropriate journal entries.

We will show the computations of variances in a tabular form as follows.

Material Variances

Material Purchase Price Variance.

	Material Price per unit			Actual Quantity Purchased	Variance ($)
	Standard	Actual	Diff.		
Material A	$1.00	$1.10	$0.10 U	1,200 lb	$120 U
Material B	2.00	1.95	0.05 F	1,800	90 F
Material C	1.75	1.80	0.05 U	1,500	75 U
					$105 U

EXAMPLE 7.6 (continued)

The material quantity variance computed below results from the change in the mix of materials as well as from changes in the total quantity of materials. The standard input allowed for actual production consists of 1,275 lb of Material A, 1,700 lb of Material B, and 1,275 lb of Material C, a total of 4,250 lb. The actual input consisted of 1,160 lb of Material A, 1,820 lb of Material B, and 1,480 lb of Material C. The total of variance is subdivided into a material mix variance and a material yield variance, as shown below.

Material Quantity Variance

	Actual Units Used at Actual Mix	Should Have Been Inputs Based Upon Actual Output	Diff.	Standard Unit Price	Variance ($)
Material A	1,160 lb	1,275 lb	115 F	$1.00	$115 F
Material B	1,820	1,700	120 U	2.00	240 U
Material C	1,480	1,275			358.75 U
	4,460 lb	4,250 lb			$483,75 U

The computation of the material mix variance and the material yield variance for the Giffen Manufacturing Company is given below.

Material Mix Variance

	Actual Units Used at Actual Output*	Should Have Been Individual Input Based Upon Total Actual Throughput*	Diff.	Standard Unit Price	Variance ($)
Material A	1,338 lb	1,160 lb	178 F	$1.00	$178 F
Material B	1,784	1,820	36 U	2.00	72 U
Material C	1,338	1,480	142 U	1.79	248.5 U
	4,460 lb	4,460 lb			$142.5 U

*This is the standard mix proportions of 30%, 40%, and 30% applied to the actual material units used of 4,460 lb.

Material Yield Variance

	Expected Input Units at Standard Mix	Should Have Been Inputs Based Upon Actual Output*	Diff.	Standard Unit Price	Variance ($)
Material A	1,338 lb	1,275 lb	63 U	$1.00	$63 U
Material B	1,784	1,700	84 U	2.00	168 U
Material C	1,338	1,275	63 U	1.75	110.25 U
	4,460 lb	4,420 lb			$341.25 U

EXAMPLE 7.6 (continued)

*This is the standard mix proportions of 30%, 40%, and 30% applied to the actual throughput of 4,460 lb or output of 4,250 lb.

**The material yield variance of $341.25 U can be computed alternatively as follows.

Actual input quantity at standard prices
Material A 1,338 lb @ $1.00 = $1,338
Material B 1,784 lb @   2.00 = 3,568
Material C 1,338 lb @   1.75 = 2,341.5 $7,247.50
Hence, $7,247.5 – $4,906.25= $341.25 U

The material mix and material yield variances are unfavorable, indicating that a shift was made to a more expensive (at standard) input mix and that an excessive quantity of material was used. Poor production scheduling requiring an unnecessarily excessive use of input material and an undesirable mix of Material A, B, and C was responsible for this result. To remedy the situation, the company must ensure that:

a. The material mix is adhered to in terms of the least cost combination without affecting product quality;

b. The proper production methods are being implemented; Inefficiencies, waste, and spoilage are within the standard allowance; and

c. Quality materials, consistent with established standards are being used.

Journal Entries

To Record Material Purchases

Material and Supplies	7,425*	
Material Purchase Price Variance	105 U	
Cash (or Accounts Payable)		7,530**

*Actual quantities purchased at standard prices:

Material A (1,200 lb	@	$1.00)	$1,200	
Material B (1,800	@	2.00)	3,600	
Material C (1,500	@	1.75)	2,625	7,425

**Actual quantities purchased at actual prices:

Material A (1,200 lb	@	$1.10)	$1,320	
Material B (1,800	@	1.95)	3,510	
Material C (1,500	@	1.80)	2,700	7,530

To Charge Materials into Production

Work-in-Process	$7,247.50*	
Material Mix Variance	42.50 U	
Material and Supplies		7,390**

* Actual quantities used at standard mix at standard prices:

EXAMPLE 7.6 *(continued)*

Material A (1,338 lb @	$1.00)	$1,338.00	
Material B (1,784 @	2.00)	3,568.00	
Material C (1,480 @	1.75)	2,341.50	7,247.50

** Actual quantities used at standard prices:

Material A (1,160 lb @	$1.00)	$1,160	
Material B (1,820 @	2.00)	3,640	
Material C (1,480 @	1.75)	2,590	7,390.00

To Transfer Material Costs to Finished Goods

Finished Goods	$6,906.25*	
Material Yield Variance	341.25 U	
Work-in-Process		7,240.50*

*See the previous page for the numerical computations.

Employees seldom complete their operations according to standard times. Two factors should be considered in computing labor variances if the analysis and computation are to be used to fix responsibility:

1. The change in labor cost resulting from the efficiency of the workers, measured by a labor efficiency variance. (In finding the change, allowed hours are determined through the material input.)
2. The change in labor cost due to a difference in the yield, measured by a labor yield variance. (In computing the change, actual output is converted to allowed input hours.)

For the Giffen Manufacturing Company, more efficient workers resulted in a savings of 383.33 hours (15,250 hr - 14,866.67 hr). Priced at the standard rate per hour, this produced an unfavorable labor efficiency variance of $1,341.66 as shown below:

Labor Efficiency Variance
Actual hrs. at standard rate	$53,375
Actual hrs. at expected output	52,033.3
(4,460 hr x 400/120) = 14,866.67 hr @ $3.5	$ 1,341.6

With a standard yield of 83 1/3% (=100/120), 4,250 lb of finished material should have required 17,000 hr of direct labor (4,250 lb x 400 DLH/100). Comparing the hours allowed for the actual input 14,866.67 hr with the hours allowed for actual output, 17,000 hr, we find a favorable labor yield variance of $7,466.66, as shown below.

Labor Yield Variance
Actual hr at expected output	$52,033.3
Actual output (4,250 lb x 400/100	
= 17,000 hrs. @ $3.5 or 4,250 lb @ $14.00)	59,500
	$ 7,466.6

EXAMPLE 7.6   *(continued)*

The labor efficiency variance can be combined with the yield variance to give us the *traditional* labor efficiency variance, which turns out to be favorable as follows.

Labor efficiency variance	$1,341.66 U
Labor yield variance	7,466.66 F
	$6,125.00 F

This division is necessary when there is a difference between the actual yield and standard yield, if responsibility is to be fixed. The producing department cannot be rightfully credited with a favorable efficiency variance of $6,125. Note, however, that a favorable yield variance, which is a factor most likely outside the control of the producing department, more than offsets the *unfavorable* labor efficiency variance of $1,341.66, for which the producing department rightfully should have been responsible.

Journal Entries
To Transfer Labor Costs to Work-in-Process

Work-in-Process	52,033.34	
Labor Efficiency Variance	1,341.66 U	
Payroll		53,375.00

To Transfer Labor Costs to Finished Goods

Finished Goods	59,500	
Labor Yield Variance		7,466.66 F
Work-in-Process		52,033.34

FLEXIBLE BUDGETS AND PERFORMANCE REPORTS

What are the implications of a flexible budget?

A flexible budget is an extremely useful tool in cost control. In contrast to a *static budget*, the flexible budget is:

○ Geared toward a range of activity rather than a single level of activity.

○ Dynamic in nature rather than static.

The static (fixed) budget is geared to only one level of activity and has problems in cost control. Flexible budgeting distinguishes between fixed and variable costs, thus allowing for a budget that can be automatically adjusted (via changes in variable cost totals) to the particular level of activity *actually* attained. By using the *cost-volume formula* (or *flexible budget formula*), a series of budgets can be easily developed for various levels of activity. Thus, variances between actual costs and budgeted costs are adjusted for volume ups and downs before differences due to price and quantity factors are computed.

NOTE
The primary use of the flexible budget is for accurate measure of performance by comparing actual costs for a given output with the budgeted costs for the same level of output.

EXAMPLE 7.7

To illustrate the difference between the static budget and the flexible budget, assume that the fabricating department of Company X is budgeted to produce 6,000 units during June. Assume further that the company was able to produce only 5,800 units. The budget for direct labor and variable overhead costs is as follows:

COMPANY X
DIRECT LABOR AND VARIABLE OVERHEAD BUDGET
FABRICATING DEPARTMENT
FOR THE MONTH OF JUNE

Budgeted production	6,000 units
Actual production	5,800 units
Direct labor	
Variable overhead costs:	$39,000
Indirect labor	6,000
Supplies	900
Repairs	300
	$46,200

If a static budget approach is used, the performance report will appear as follows:

COMPANY X
DIRECT LABOR AND VARIABLE OVERHEAD BUDGET
FABRICATING DEPARTMENT
FOR THE MONTH OF JUNE

	Budget	Actual*	Variance (U or F)
Production in units	6,000	5,800	200U
Direct labor	$39,000	$38,500	$500F
Variance overhead costs:	6,000	5,950	50F
Indirect labor	900	870	30F
Supplies	300	295	5F
Repairs	$46,200	$45,615	$585F

* Provided by accounting record

These given cost variances are useless; they compare oranges with apples. The problem is that the budget costs are based on an activity level of 6,000 units, whereas the actual costs were incurred at an activity level below this (5,800 units). From a control standpoint, it makes no sense

EXAMPLE 7.7 *(continued)*

to try to compare costs at one activity level with costs at a different activity level. Such comparisons would make a production manager look good as long as the actual production is less than the budgeted production. Using the cost-volume formula and generating the budget based on the 5,800 actual units give the following performance report:

COMPANY X PERFORMANCE REPORT
FABRICATING DEPARTMENT
FOR THE MONTH OF JUNE

Budgeted production		6,000 units		
Actual production		5,800 units		
	Cost-volume formula	Budget 5,800 units	Actual 5,800 units	Variance (U or F)
Direct labor	$6.50 per unit	$37,700	$38,500	$800U
Variable overhead:				
Indirect labor	1.00	5,800	5,950	150U
Supplies	0.15	870	870	0
Repairs	0.05	290	295	5U
	$7.70	$44,660	$45,615	$955U

Note: All cost variances are unfavorable (U), as compared to the favorable (F) cost variance on the performance report based on the static budget approach.

PROFIT CENTERS AND SEGMENTED REPORTING

How do I evaluate business segments?

Segmented reporting is the process of reporting activities of *profit centers* of an organization such as divisions, product lines, or sales territories. The *contribution approach* is valuable for segmented reporting. It emphasizes the cost behavior patterns and the controllability of costs that are generally useful for profitability analysis of various segments of an organization. The *contribution approach* is based on the theses that:

○ Fixed costs are much less controllable than variable.

○ *Direct fixed costs* and *common fixed costs* must be clearly distinguished. Direct fixed costs are those fixed costs that can be identified directly with a particular segment of an organization. Common fixed costs are those costs that cannot be identified directly with the segment.

○ Common fixed costs should be clearly identified as *unallocated* in the contribution income statement by segments. Any attempt to allocate these types of costs arbitrarily to the segments of the organization can destroy the value of responsibility accounting. It would lead to unfair evaluation of performance and misleading managerial decisions.

The following concepts are highlighted in the contribution approach:

○ *Contribution margin*—Sales minus variable costs
○ *Contribution controllable by segment managers*—Contribution margin minus direct fixed costs controllable by segment managers. Direct fixed costs include discretionary fixed costs, (e.g., certain advertising, R&D, sales promotion, and engineering).
○ *Segment margin*—Contribution controllable by segment managers minus fixed costs controllable by others. Fixed costs controllable by others include traceable and committed fixed costs, (e.g., depreciation, property taxes, insurance, and the segment managers' salaries).
○ *Net income*—Segment margin minus unallocated common fixed costs.

EXAMPLE 7.8

Exhibit 7.5 illustrates two levels of segmental reporting:

○ By segments defined as divisions
○ By segments defined as product lines of a division

The segment margin is the best measure of the profitability of a segment. Unallocated fixed costs are common to the segments being evaluated and should be left unallocated in order not to distort the performance results of segments.

PROFIT VARIANCE ANALYSIS

What is profit variance analysis?

Profit variance analysis, often called *gross profit analysis*, deals with how to analyze the profit variance which constitutes the departure between actual profit and the previous year's income or the budgeted figure. The primary goal of profit variance analysis is to improve performance and profitability in the future.

Profit, whether it is gross profit in absorption costing or contribution margin in direct costing, is affected by at least three basic items: sales price, sales volume, and costs. In addition, in a multi-product firm, if not all products are equally profitable, profit is affected by the mix of products sold.

The difference between budgeted and actual profits are due to one or more of the following:

1. Changes in unit sales price and cost, called *sales price* and *cost price variances*, respectively. The difference between sales price variance and cost price variance

is often called a contribution-margin-per-unit variance or a gross-profit-per-unit variance, depending upon what type of costing system is being referred to, that is, absorption costing or direct costing. Contribution margin, however, is considered a better measure of product profitability because it deducts from sales revenue only the variable costs that are controllable in terms of fixing responsibility. Gross profit does not reflect cost–volume–profit relationships. Nor does it consider directly traceable marketing costs.

2. Changes in the volume of products sold summarized as the sales volume variance and the cost volume variance. The difference between the two is called the *total volume variance*.

3. Changes in the volume of the more profitable or less profitable items referred to as the *sales mix variance*.

Detailed analysis is critical to management when multi-products exist. The volume variances may be used to measure a change in volume (while holding the mix constant) and the mix may be employed to evaluate the effect of a change in sales mix (while holding the quantity constant). This type of variance analysis is useful when the products are substituted for each other, or when products which are not necessarily substitutes for each are marketed through the same channel.

Types of Standards in Profit Variance Analysis

To determine the various causes for a favorable variance (an increase) or an unfavorable variance (a decrease) in profit, we need some kind of yardsticks to compare against the actual results. The yardsticks may be based on the prices and costs of the previous year, or any year selected as the base periods. Some companies are summarizing profit variance analysis data in their annual report by showing departures from the previous year's reported income. However, one can establish a more effective control and budgetary method rather than the previous year's data. Standard or budgeted mix can be determined using such sophisticated techniques as linear and goal programming.

Single-Product Firms

Profit variance analysis is simplest in a single product firm, for there is only one sales price, one set of costs (or cost price), and a unitary sales volume. An unfavorable profit variance can be broken down into four components: a sales price variance, a cost price variance, a sales volume variance, and a cost volume variance.

The sales price variance measures the impact on the firm's contribution margin (or gross profit) of changes in the unit selling price. It is computed as:

Sales price variance
= (actual price − budget price)
× actual sales

If the actual price is lower than the budgeted price, for example, this variance is unfavorable; it tends to reduce profit. The cost price variance, on the other hand, is simply the summary of price variances for materials, labor and overhead. (This is the sum of material price, labor rate, and factory overhead spending variances). It is computed as:

Cost price variance
= (actual cost − budget cost)
× actual sales

If the actual unit cost is lower than budgeted cost, for example, this variance is favorable; it tends to increase profit. We simplify the computation of price variances by taking the sales price variance less the cost price variance and call it the gross-profit-per-unit variance or contribution-margin-per-unit variance.

The sales volume variance indicates the impact on the firm's profit of changes in the unit sales volume. This is the amount by which sales would have varied from the budget if nothing but sales volume had changed. It is computed as:

Sales volume variance
= (actual sales − budget sales)
× budget price

If actual sales volume is greater than budgeted sales volume, this is favorable; it tends to increase profit. The cost volume variance has the same interpretation. It is:

(Actual sales − budget sales) × budget cost per unit

The difference between the sales volume variance and the cost volume variance is called the total volume variance.

Multiproduct Firms

When a firm produces more than one product, there is a fourth component of the profit variance. This is the sales mix variance, the effect on profit of selling a different proportionate mix of products than that which has been budgeted. This variance arises when different products have different contribution margins. In a multiproduct firm, actual sales volume can differ from that budgeted in two ways. The total number of units sold could differ from the target aggregate sales. In addition, the mix of the products actually sold may not be proportionate to the target mix. Each of these two different types of changes in volume is reflected in a separate variance.

The total volume variance is divided into the two variances: the sales mix variance and the sales quantity variance. These two variances should be used to evaluate the marketing department of the firm. The sales mix variance shows how well the department has done in terms of selling the more profitable products while the sales quantity variance measures how well the firm has done in terms of its overall sales volume. They are computed as:

Sales Mix Variance
= (Actual Sales at budget mix – Actual Sales at actual mix)
× Budget CM (or gross profit / unit)

Sales Quantity Variance
= (Actual Sales at budget mix – Budget Sales at budget mix)
× Budget CM (or gross profit / unit)

Sales Volume Variance
= (Actual Sales at actual mix – Budget Sales at budget mix)
× Budget CM (or gross profit / unit)

EXAMPLE 7.9 PROFIT VARIANCE ANALYSIS

The Lake Tahoe Ski Store sells two ski models: Model X and Model Y. For the years 20×1 and 20×2, the store realized a gross profit of $246,640 and only $211,650, respectively. The owner of the store was astounded since the total sales volume in dollars and in units was higher for 20×2 than for 20×1, yet the gross profit achieved actually declined. Given below are the store's unaudited operating results for 20×1 and 20×2. No fixed costs were included in the cost of goods sold per unit.

	Model X				Model Y			
		Costs of				Costs of		
	Selling	Goods Sold	Sales in	Sales	Selling	Goods Sold	Sales in	Sales
Year	Price	per unit	Units	Revenue	Price	per unit	Units	Revenue
1	$150	$110	2,800	$420,000	$172	$121	2,640	$454,080
2	160	125	2,650	424,000	176	135	2,900	510,400

Explain why the gross profit declined by $34,990. Include a detailed variance analysis of price changes and changes in volume for both sales and cost. Also subdivide the total volume variance into change in price and changes in quantity.

Sales price and sales volume variances measure the impact on the firm's CM (or GM) of changes in the unit selling price and sales volume. In computing these variances, all costs are held constant in order to stress changes in price and volume. Cost price and cost volume

EXAMPLE 7.9 PROFIT VARIANCE ANALYSIS *(continued)*

variances are computed in the same manner, holding price and volume constant. All these variances for the Tahoe Ski Store are computed below.

Sales Price Variance

Actual sales for 20×2:	$896,300
Model X 2,650 × $160 = $424,000	
Model Y 2,900 × $179 = $510,400	$934,400
Actual 20×2 sales at 20×1 prices:	
Model X 2,650 × $150 = $397,500	
Model Y 2,900 × $172 = $498,800	896,300
	$38,100F

Sales Volume Variance

Actual 20×2 sales at 20×1 prices:	$896,300
Actual 20×1 sales (at 20×1 prices):	
Model X 2,800 × $150 = $420,000	
Model Y 2,640 × 172 = 454,080	874,080
	$22,220F

Cost Price Variance

Actual cost of goods sold for 20×2:	$896,300
Model X 2,650 × $125 = $331,250	
Model Y 2,900 × $135 = $391,500	
Actual 20×2 sales at 20×1 costs:	
Model X 2,650 × $110 = $291,500	
Model Y 2,900 × $121 = $350,900	$642,400
	$80,350U

Cost Volume Variance

Actual 20×2 sales at 20×1 costs:	$642,400
Actual 20×1 sales (at 20×1 costs):	
Model X 2,800 × $110 = $308,000	
Model Y 2,640 × 121 = 319,440	627,440
	$14,960U

Total volume variance = sales volume variance – cost volume variance

= $22,220 F – $14,960 U = $7,260 F

$80,350 U

EXAMPLE 7.9 PROFIT VARIANCE ANALYSIS *(continued)*

The total volume variance is computed as the sum of a sales mix variance and a sales quantity variance as follows:

Sales Mix Variance

	20X2 Actual Sale at 20X1 Mix*	20X2 Actual Sale at 20X2 Mix	Diff.	20X1 Gross Profit per Unit	Variance ($)
Model X	2,857	2,650	207 U	$40	$8,280U
Model Y	2,693	2,900	207 F	51	10,557F
	5,500	5,550			$2,277F

*This is the 20X1 mix (used as standard or budget) proportions of 51.47% (or 2,800/5,440 = 51.47%) and 48.53% (or 2,640/5,440 = 48.53%) applied to the actual 20×2 sales figure of 5,550 units.

Sales Quantity Variance

	20X2 Actual Sale at 20X1Mix*	20X2 Actual Sale at 20X1 Mix	Diff.	20X1 Gross Profit per Unit	Variance ($)
Model X	2,857	2,800	57 F	$40	$2,280F
Model Y	2,693	2,640	52 F	51	2,703F
	5,550	5,440			$4,983F

A favorable total volume variance is due to a favorable shift is the sales mix (that is from Model X to Model Y) and also to a favorable increase in sales volume (by 110 units) which is shown as follows.

Sale mix variance	$2,277F
Sales quantity	4,983F
	$7,260

However, there remains the decrease in gross profit. The decrease in gross profit of $34,990 can be explained as follows.

	Gains	Losses
Gain due to increased sales price	$38,100F	
Loss due to increased cost		80,350
Gain due to increase in units sold	4,983F	
Gain due to shift in sales mix	2,277F	
	$45,360F	$80,350

Hence, net decrease in gross profit = $80,350 − $45,360
= $34,990U

Despite the increase in sales price and volume and the favorable shift in sales mix, the Lake Tahoe Ski Store ended up losing $34,990 compared to 20×1. The major reason for this comparative loss was the tremendous increase in cost of goods sold, as costs for both Model X and Model Y went up quite significantly over 20×1. The

EXAMPLE 7.9 PROFIT VARIANCE ANALYSIS (continued)

store has to take a close look at the cost picture, even though only variable and fixed costs should be analyzed in an effort to cut down on controllable costs. In doing that, it is essential that responsibility be clearly fixed to given individuals. In a retail business like the Lake Tahoe Ski Store, operating expenses such as advertising and of store payroll employees must also be closely scrutinized.

EXAMPLE 7.10 SALES MIX ANALYSIS

Shim and Siegel, Inc. sells two products, C and D. Product C has a budgeted unit CM (contribution margin) of $3 and Product D has a budgeted Unit CM of $6. The budget for a recent month called for sales of 3,000 units of C and 9,000 units of D, for a total of 12,000 units. Actual sales totaled 12,200 units: 4,700 of C and 7,500 of D. Compute the sales volume variance and break this variance down into the sales quantity variance and sales mix variance.

Shim and Siegel's sales volume variance is computed below. As we can see, while total unit sales increased by 200 units, the shift in sales mix resulted in a $3,900 unfavorable sales volume variance.

Sales Volume Variance

	Actual Sales at Actual Mix	Standard Sales at Budgeted Mix	Difference	Budgeted CM per Unit	Variance ($)
Product C	4,700	3,000	1,700F	$3	$5,100F
Product D	7,500	9,000	1,500U	6	9,000U
	12,200	12,000			$3,900U

In multiproduct firms, the sales volumes variance is further divided into a sales quantity variance and a sales mix variance. The computations of these variances are shown below.

Sales Quantity Variance

Product C	3,050	3,000	50F	$3	$ 150F
Product D	9,150	9,000	150F	6	900F
	12,200	12,000			$1,050F

Sale Mix Variance

	Actual Sales at Actual Budgeted Mix	Standard Sales at Actual Mix	Difference	Standard CM per Unit	Variance ($)
Product C	3,050	4,700	1,650F	$3	$4,950F
Product D	9,150	7,500	1,650U	6	9,900U
	12,200	12,200			$4,950U

> ## EXAMPLE 7.10 SALES MIX ANALYSIS *(continued)*
>
> The sales quantity variance reflects the impact of deviations from the standard sales volume on the CM or GM (gross margin), whereas the sales mix variance measures the impact on the CM of deviations from the budgeted mix. In the case of Shim and Siegel, Inc., the sales quantity variance came out to be favorable, (i.e., $1,050 F), and the sales mix variance came out to be unfavorable, (i.e., $4,950 U). These variances indicate that while there was a favorable increase in sales volume by 200 units, it was obtained by an unfavorable shift in the sales mix, that is, a shift from Product D, with a high margin, to Product C, with a low margin.
>
> Note that the sales volume variance of $3,900 U is the algebraic sum of the following two variances.
>
> | | |
> |---|---|
> | Sales quantity variance | $1,050F |
> | Sales mix variance | 4,950U |
> | | $3,900U |
>
> In conclusion, the product emphasis on high margin sales is often a key to success for multiproduct firms. Increasing sales volume is one side of the story; selling the more profitable products is another.

Managerial Planning and Decision Making

In view of the fact that Shim and Siegel, Inc. experienced an unfavorable sales volume variance of $3,900 due to an unfavorable (or less profitable) mix in the sales volume, the company is advised to put more emphasis on increasing the sales of Product D.

In doing that the company might wish to:

1. Increase the advertising budget for succeeding periods to boost Product D sales.
2. Set up a bonus plan in such a way that the commission is based on quantities sold rather than higher rates for higher margin items such as Product D or revise the bonus plan to consider the sale of product D.
3. Offer a more lenient credit term for Product D to encourage its sale.
4. Reduce the price of Product D enough to maintain the present profitable mix while increasing the sale of the product. This strategy must take into account the price elasticity of demand for Product D.

SALES MIX ANALYSIS

Many product lines include a lower-margin price leader model, and often a high-margin deluxe model. For example, the automobile industry includes in its product line low-margin energy-efficient small cars and higher-margin deluxe models. In an attempt to increase overall profitability, management would wish to emphasize the higher-margin expensive items, but salesmen might find it easier to sell lower-margin cheaper models. Thus, a salesman might meet his unit sales quota with each item at its budgeted price, but because of mix shifts he could be far short of contributing his share of budgeted profit.

Management should realize that

1. Greater proportions of more profitable products mean higher profits.
2. Higher proportions of lower margin sales reduce overall profit despite the increase in overall sales volume. That is to say that an unfavorable mix may easily offset a favorable increase in volume, and vice versa.

PERFORMANCE REPORTS

Profit variance analysis aids in fixing responsibility by separating the causes of the change in profit into price, volume, and mix factors. With responsibility resting in different places, the segregation of the total profit variance is essential. The performance reports based on the analysis of profit variances must be prepared for each responsibility center, indicating the following:

1. Is it controllable?
2. Is it favorable or unfavorable?
3. If it is unfavorable, is it significant enough for further investigation?
4. Who is responsible for what portion of the total profit variance?
5. What are the causes of an unfavorable variance?
6. What remedial action can be taken?

The performance report must address such questions. The report is useful in two ways: (1) in focusing attention on situations in need of management action and (2) in increasing the precision of planning and control of sales and costs. The report should be produced as part of the overall standard costing and responsibility accounting system.

HOW TO MEASURE THE PERFORMANCE OF INVESTMENT CENTERS

Is the investment center healthy?

Two measurements of performance are widely used for the investment center, for example, division of a decentralized firm: *rate of return on investment* (ROI) and *residual income* (RI).

SEGMENTS DEFINED AS DIVISIONS			
	Total	**Segments**	
	Company	**Division 1**	**Division 2**
Sales	$150,000	$90,000	$60,000
Variable costs:			
Manufacturing	40,000	30,000	10,000
Selling and admin.	20,000	14,000	6,000
Total variable costs	60,000	44,000	16,000
Contribution margin	$90,000	$46,000	$44,000
Less: Direct fixed costs controllable by division managers	55,000	33,000	22,000
Contribution controllable by division managers	$35,000	$13,000	$22,000
Less: Direct fixed costs controllable by others	15,000	10,000	5,000
Divisional segment margin	$20,000	$ 3,000	$17,000
Less: Unallocated common fixed costs	$10,000		
Net income	$10,000		

SEGMENTS DEFINED AS PRODUCT LINES OF DIVISION 2			
	Division	**Segments**	
	2	**Deluxe Model**	**Regular Model**
Sales	$60,000	$20,000	$40,000
Variable costs:			
Manufacturing	10,000	5,000	5,000
Selling and admin.	6,000	2,000	4,000
Total variable costs	16,000	7,000	9,000
Contribution margin	$44,000	$13,000	$31,000
Less: Direct fixed costs controllable by product line managers	22,000	8,000	14,000
Contribution controllable by product line managers	$22,000	$ 5,000	$17,000
Less: Direct fixed costs controllable by others	4,500	1,500	3,000
Product line margin	$17,500	$ 3,500	$14,000
Less: Unallocated common fixed costs	$ 500		
Divisional segment margin	$17,000		

Exhibit 7.5   SEGMENTAL INCOME STATEMENT

RATE OF RETURN ON INVESTMENT (ROI)

How do I calculate ROI?

ROI relates operating income to operating assets, Specifically,

$$ROI = \frac{\text{Operating Income}}{\text{Operating Assets}}$$

ROI can be expressed as a product of the following two important factors:

$$
\begin{aligned}
ROI &= \text{Margin} \times \text{Turnover} \\
&= \frac{\text{Operating Income}}{\text{Sales}} \times \frac{\text{Sales}}{\text{Operating Assets}} \\
&= \frac{\text{Operating Income}}{\text{Operating Assets}}
\end{aligned}
$$

Margin is a measure of profitability or operating efficiency, whereas turnover measures how well a division manages its assets.

EXAMPLE 7.11

Consider the following financial data for a division:

Operating Assets	$100,000
Operating Income	$ 18,000
Sales	$200,000

$$ROI = \frac{\text{Operating Income}}{\text{Operating Assets}} = \frac{\$18,000}{\$100,000} = \underline{\underline{18\%}}$$

Alternatively,

$$\text{Margin} = \frac{\text{Operating Income}}{\text{Sales}} = \frac{\$18,000}{\$200,000} = \underline{\underline{9\%}}$$

$$\text{Turnover} = \frac{\text{Sales}}{\text{Operating Assets}} = \frac{\$200,000}{\$100,000} = \underline{\underline{2 \text{ times}}}$$

Therefore,

$$
\begin{aligned}
ROI &= \text{Margin} \times \text{Turnover} = 9\% \times 2 \text{ times} \\
&= \underline{\underline{18\%}}
\end{aligned}
$$

What are the benefits of breaking down ROI (the Du Pont formula)?

The breakdown of ROI into margin and turnover (often called the Du Pont formula) has several advantages over the original formula in terms of profit planning:

- o The importance of turnover as a key to overall return on investment is emphasized in the breakdown. In fact, turnover is just as important as profit margin.

○ The importance of sales is explicitly recognized. It is not reflected in the regular formula.
○ The breakdown stresses the possibility of trading one off for the other in an attempt to improve the overall performance of a division.

What effect does ROI have on the bottom line?

The breakdown of ROI into turnover and margin gives the manager of a division insight into planning for profit improvement. Generally speaking, a division manager can improve margin and/or turnover.

○ *Improving margin* is a popular way of improving performance. Margins may be increased by reducing expenses, by raising selling prices, or by increasing sales faster than expenses.
○ *Improving turnover* can be achieved by increasing sales while holding the investment in assets relatively constant, or by reducing assets.
○ *Improving both* margin and turnover may be achieved by increasing sales revenue or by any combination of the first two.

EXAMPLE 7.12

Assume that management sets a 20 percent ROI as a profit target. It is currently making an 18 percent return on its investment.

$$\text{ROI} = \frac{\text{Operating Income}}{\text{Sales}} \times \frac{\text{Sales}}{\text{Operating Assets}}$$

$$\text{Present: } 18\% = \frac{18,000}{200,000} \times \frac{200,000}{100,000}$$

Increase margin by reducing expenses:

$$20\% = \frac{20,000}{200,000} \times \frac{200,000}{100,000}$$

Increase turnover by reducing investment in assets:

$$20\% = \frac{18,000}{200,000} \times \frac{200,000}{90,000}$$

Increase both margin and turnover by disposing of obsolete and redundant inventories:

$$20\% = \frac{19,000}{200,000} \times \frac{200,000}{95,000}$$

Excessive investment in assets is just as much of a drag on profitability as excessive expenses. In this case, cutting unnecessary inventories also helps cut down the expenses of carrying those inventories, so that both margin and turnover are improved at the same time. In practice, improving both margin and turnover is much more common than improving only one or the other.

Residual Income (RI)

What is residual income?

Residual income (RI) is the operating income that an investment center is able to earn above some minimum rate of return on its operating assets. RI, unlike ROI, is an absolute amount of income rather than a specific rate of return.

$$RI = \text{Operating income} - (\text{Minimum required rate of return} \times \text{Operating assets})$$

What are the benefits of RI?

When RI is used to evaluate divisional performance, the objective is to maximize the total amount of residual income, not to maximize the overall ROI figure.

RI is regarded as a better measure of performance than ROI because it encourages investment in projects that would be rejected under ROI. Other advantages of RI are as follows:

o The incorporation of risk by varying the minimum rate of return based on the division's risk

o Varying the minimum return depending on the riskiness of a specific asset

A major disadvantage of RI is that it can't be used to compare divisions of different sizes.

NOTE
RI tends to favor larger divisions due to the larger amount of dollars involved.

EXAMPLE 7.13
Using the numbers in Example 7.11, assume the minimum required rate of return is 13 percent. Then the residual income of the division is $\$18,000 - (13\% \times \$100,000)$ $= \$18,000 - \$13,000 = \underline{\underline{\$5,000}}$

RI is regarded as a better measure of performance than ROI because it encourages investment in projects that would be rejected under ROI. A major disadvantage of RI, however, is that it cannot be used to compare divisions of different sizes. RI tends to favor the larger divisions owing to the larger amount of dollars involved.

Residual Income and Economic Value Added

Residual income is better known as *economic value added* (EVA). Many firms are addressing the issue of aligning division managers' incentives with those of the firm by using EVA as a measure of performance. EVA encourages managers to focus on increasing the value of the company to shareholders, because EVA is the value created by a company in excess of the cost of capital for the investment base. Improving EVA can be achieved in three ways:

1. Invest capital in high-performing projects.
2. Use less capital.
3. Increase profit without using more capital.

INVESTMENT DECISIONS UNDER ROI AND RI

How can I use ROI and RI?

The decision of whether to use ROI or RI as a measure of divisional performance affects the manager's investment decisions.

○ Under the *ROI method*, division managers tend to accept only the investments whose returns exceed the division's ROI. Otherwise, the division's overall ROI would decrease if the investment were accepted.

○ Under the *RI method*, division managers would accept an investment as long as it earns a rate in excess of the minimum required rate of return. The addition of such an investment would increase the division's overall RI.

EXAMPLE 7.14

Consider the same data given in Examples 7.11 and 7.13.

Operating Assets	$100,000
Operating Income	$18,000
Minimum required rate of return	13%

ROI = 18% and RI = $5,000.

Assume that the division is presented with a project that would yield 15 percent on a $10,000 investment. The division manager would not accept this project under the ROI approach since the division is already earning 18 percent. Acquiring this project will bring down the present ROI to 17.73 percent, as shown below:

EXAMPLE 7.14 *(continued)*

	Present	New Project	Overall
Operating assets (a)	$100,000	10,000*	110,000
Operating income (b)	$18,000	1,500*	19,500
ROI (b) ÷ (a)	18%	15%	17.73%

*$10,000 × 15% = $1,500

Under the RI approach, the manager would accept the new project since it provides a higher rate than the minimum required rate of return (15 percent vs. 13 percent). Accepting the new project will increase the overall residual income to $5,200, as shown below:

	Present	New Project	Overall
Operating assets (a)	$100,000	$10,000	$110,000
Operating income (b)	18,000	1,500	19,500
Minimum required income at 13% (c)	13,000	1,300*	14,300
RI (b) - (c)	$5,000	$200	$5,200

*$10,000 × 13% = $1,300

THE CORPORATE BALANCED SCORECARD

What is the corporate balanced scorecard?

A problem with just assessing performance with financial measures like profit, ROI and Economic Value Added (EVA) is that the financial measures are "backward looking." ' In other words, today's financial measures tell you about the accomplishments and failures of the past. An approach to performance measurement that also focuses on what managers are doing today to create future shareholder value is the Balanced Scorecard.

Essentially, a Balanced Scorecard is a set of performance measures constructed for four dimensions of performance. As indicated in Exhibit 7.3, the dimensions are financial, customer, internal processes, and learning and growth. Having financial measures is critical even if they are backward looking. After all, they have a great affect on the evaluation of the company by shareholders and creditors. Customer measures examine the company's success in meeting customer expectations. Internal process measures examine the company's success in improving critical business processes. And learning and growth measures examine the company's success in improving its ability to adapt, innovate, and grow. The customer, internal processes, and learning and growth measures are generally thought to be predictive of *future* success (i.e., they are not backward-looking).

A variety of potential measures for each dimension of a Balanced Scorecard are indicated in Exhibit 7.6. After reviewing these measures, note how "balance" is achieved:

o Performance is assessed across a *balanced set of dimensions* (financial, customer, internal processes, and innovation).

o *Quantitative* measures (e.g., number of defects) are balanced with *qualitative* measures (e.g., ratings of customer satisfaction).

o There is a balance of *backward-looking* measures (e.g., financial measures like growth in sales) and *forward-looking* measures (e.g., number of new patents as an innovation measure).

		Measures
Financial	Is the company achieving its financial goals?	Operating income
		Return on assets
		Sales growth
		Cash flow from operations
		Reduction of administrative expense
Customer	Is the company meeting customer expectations?	Customer satisfaction
		Customer retention
		New customer acquisition
		Market share
		On-time delivery
		Time to fill orders
Internal Processes	Is the company improving critical internal processes?	Defect rate
		Lead time
		Number of suppliers
		Material turnover
		Percent of practical capacity
Learning and Growth	Is the company improving its ability to innovate?	Amount spent on employee training
		Employee satisfaction
		Employee retention
		Number of new products
		New product sales as a percent of total sales
		Number of patents

Exhibit 7.6 BALANCED SCORECARD

HOW TO PRICE GOODS AND SERVICES TRANSFERRED

How are transfer prices determined?

Goods and services are often exchanged between various divisions of a decentralized organization. The question then is: what monetary values should be assigned to these exchanges or transfers? Market price?

Some kind of cost? Some version of either? Single transfer price will please everybody—that is, top management, the selling division, and the buying division—involved in the transfer.

The choice of a transfer pricing policy (i.e., which type of transfer price to use) is normally decided by top management. The decision will typically include consideration of:

○ *Goal congruence*. Will the transfer price promote the goals of the company as a whole? Will it harmonize the divisional goals with organizational goals?

○ *Performance evaluation*. Will the selling division receive enough credit for its transfer of goods and services to the buying division? Will the transfer price hurt the performance of the selling division?

○ *Autonomy*. Will the transfer price preserve autonomy, the freedom of the selling and buying division managers to operate their divisions as decentralized entities?

○ *Other factors* such as minimization of tariffs and income taxes and observance of legal restrictions must be taken into account.

ALTERNATIVE TRANSFER PRICING SCHEMES

What other factors may determine transfer prices?

Transfer prices can also be based on:

○ Market price
○ Cost-based price—variable or full cost
○ Negotiated price
○ General formula that is usually the sum of variable costs per unit and opportunity cost for the company as a whole (lost revenue per unit on outside sales)

How suitable is market price for transfers?

Market price is the best transfer price in the sense that it will maximize the profits of the company as a whole, if it meets the following two conditions:

○ A competitive market price exists
○ Divisions are independent of each other

If any one of these is violated, market price will not lead to an optimal economic decision for the company.

What are the pros and cons of cost-based prices?

Cost-based transfer price, another alternative transfer pricing scheme, is easy to understand and convenient to use. But there are some disadvantages:

○ Inefficiencies of the selling divisions are passed on to the buying divisions with little incentive to control costs. The use of standard costs is recommended in such a case.

○ The cost-based method treats the divisions as cost centers rather than profit or investment centers. Therefore, measures such as ROI and RI cannot be used for evaluation purposes.

The variable cost-based transfer price has an advantage over the full cost method because it may tend to insure the best use of the company's overall resources. The reason is that, in the short run, fixed costs do not change. Any use of facilities, without incurrence of additional fixed costs, will increase the company's overall profits.

When is a negotiated transfer price used?

A negotiated price is generally used when there is no clear outside market. A negotiated price is one agreed upon between the buying and selling divisions that reflects unusual or mitigating circumstances.

NOTE
This method is widely used when no intermediate market price exists for the product transferred and the selling division is assured of a normal profit.

EXAMPLE 7.15 NEGOTIATED TRANSFER PRICE

Company X just purchased a small company that specializes in the manufacture of Part 323. Company X is a decentralized organization. It will treat the newly acquired company as an autonomous division called Division B with full profit responsibility. Division B's fixed costs total $30,000 per month, and variable costs per unit are $18. Division B's operating capacity is 5,000 units. The selling price per unit is $30. Division A of Company X is currently purchasing 2,500 units of Part

EXAMPLE 7.15 NEGOTIATED TRANSFER
PRICE (continued)

323 per month from an outside supplier at $29 per unit, which represents the normal $30 price less a quantity discount. Top management of the company wishes to decide what transfer price should be used.

Top management may consider the following alternative prices:

o $30 market price
o $29, the price that Division A is currently paying to the outside supplier
o $23.50 negotiated price, which is $18 variable cost plus 1/2 of the benefits of an internal transfer (($29 – $18) × 1/2)
o $24 full cost, which is $18 variable cost plus $6 ($30,000 ÷ 5,000 units) fixed cost per unit
o $18 variable cost

We will discuss each of these prices:

o $30 would not be an appropriate transfer price. Division B cannot charge a price more than the price Division A is paying now ($29).
o $29 would be an appropriate transfer price if top management wishes to treat them as autonomous investment centers. This price would cause all of the benefits of internal transfers to accrue to the selling division, with the buying division's position remaining unchanged.
o $23.50 would be an appropriate transfer price if top management wishes to treat them as investment centers, but wishes to share the benefits of an internal transfer *equally* between them, as follows:

Variable Costs of Division B	$18.00
1/2 of the difference between the variable costs of Division B and the price Division A is paying ($29 – $18) × 1/2	5.50
Transfer price	$23.50

NOTE

$23.50 is just one example of a negotiated transfer price. The exact price depends on how they divide the benefits.

o $24[$24 = $18 + ($30,000/5,000 units)] would be an appropriate transfer price if top management treats them like cost centers with no profit responsibility.

All benefits from both divisions will accrue to the buying division. This will maximize the profits

**EXAMPLE 7.15 NEGOTIATED TRANSFER
PRICE** *(continued)*

of the company as a whole, but adversely affect
the performance of the selling division. Another
disadvantage of this cost-based approach is that
inefficiencies (if any) of the selling division are
being passed on to the buying division.

o $18 would be an appropriate transfer price for
guiding top management in deciding whether
transfers between the two divisions should take
place. Since $18 is less than the outside pur-
chase price of the buying division, and the selling division has excess capacity, the transfer
should take place, because it will maximize the
profits of the company as a whole. However, if
$18 is used as a transfer price, then all of the
benefits of the internal transfer accrue to the
buying division, and the performance of the
selling division will be hurt.

BUDGETING AND FINANCIAL PLANNING

What is a budget?

A budget is:

o A formal statement of management's expectation
regarding sales, expenses, volume, and other financial transactions of an organization for the coming
period

o A set of *pro forma (projected* or *planned)* financial statements—income statement, balance sheet, and cash
budget

o A tool for both planning and control

o At the beginning of the period, a plan or standard

o At the end of the period, a control device to help
management measure its performance against the
plan so that future performance may be improved

Exhibit 7.7 shows a simplified diagram of the various parts of
the comprehensive budget, the master plan of the company.

What are the types of budgets?

Budgets are classified into two broad categories:

o *Operating budget*, reflecting the results of operating
decisions

o *Financial budget*, reflecting the financial decisions of
the firm

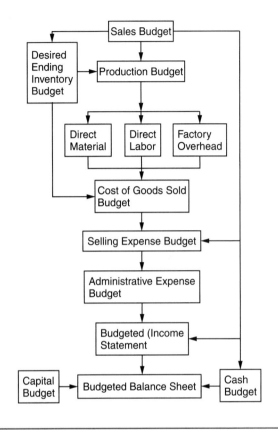

Exhibit 7.7 COMPREHENSIVE BUDGET

What is an operating budget?

The operating budget consists of:

- ○ Sales budget
- ○ Production budget
- ○ Direct materials budget
- ○ Direct labor budget
- ○ Factory overhead budget
- ○ Selling and administrative expense budget
- ○ Pro forma income statement

What does a financial budget contain?

The financial budget consists of:

- ○ Cash budget
- ○ Pro forma balance sheet

How do I prepare a budget?

The major steps in preparing the budget are:

o Prepare a sales forecast
o Determine expected production volume
o Estimate manufacturing costs and operating expenses
o Determine cash flow and other financial effects
o Formulate projected financial statements

How can I prepare a budget quickly?

In actual practice, use of a shortcut approach is widely used in formulating a budget. The approach can be summarized as follows:

Step 1. A pro forma income statement is developed using past percentage relationships between certain expense and cost items and the firm's sales. These percentages are then applied to the firm's projected sales. The income statement can be set up in a traditional or contribution format.

Step 2. A pro forma balance sheet is estimated, using the *percentage of sales method*. This involves the following steps:

- Express balance sheet items that *vary directly with sales* as a percentage of sales. Any item that does not vary with sales (such as long-term debt) is designated *not applicable* (n.a.). Multiply these percentages by the sales projected to obtain the amounts for the future period.

- Where no percentage applies (such as long-term debt, common stock, and paid-in-capital), simply insert the figures from the present balance sheet or their "desired" level in the column for the future period.

- Compute the projected retained earnings as follows:

  Projected retained earnings
  = present retained earnings
  + projected net income
  − cash dividend to be paid

- Sum the asset accounts and the liability and equity accounts to see if there is any difference. The difference, if any, is a *shortfall*, which is the amount of financing the firm has to raise externally.

Should I use a computer to prepare budgets and do financial planning?

More and more companies are developing computer-based models for financial planning and budgeting, using powerful, yet easy-to-use, financial modeling languages such as *Comshare's Interactive Financial Planning System (IFPS)* and *Up Your*

Cash Flow. The models help not only build a budget for profit planning but answer a variety of "what-if" scenarios. The resultant calculations provide a basis for choice among alternatives under conditions of uncertainty. Furthermore, budget modeling can also be accomplished using spreadsheet programs such as *Microsoft's Excel*.

In this section we will illustrate the use of *Excel* to develop a financial model. For illustrative purposes, we will present three examples of projecting an income statement.

CASE 1

> Sales for 1st month = $60,000
>
> Cost of sales = 42% of sales, all variable
>
> Operating expenses = $10,000 fixed plus 5% of sales
>
> Taxes = 30% of net income
>
> Sales increase by 5% each month

1. Based on this information, Exhibit 7.8 presents a spreadsheet for the contribution income statement for the next 12 months and in total.
2. Exhibit 7.9 shows the same in (1) assuming that sales increase by 10 percent and operating expenses = $10,000 plus 10 percent of sales. This is an example of "what-if" scenarios.

CASE 2

Delta Gamma Company wishes to prepare a three-year projection of net income using the following information:

1. 2004 base-year amounts are as follows:

Sales revenues	$4,500,000
Cost of sales	2,900,000
Selling and administrative expenses	800,000
Net income before taxes	800,000

2. Use the following assumptions:

o Sales revenues increase by 6 percent in 2005, 7 percent in 2006, and 8 percent in 2007.
o Cost of sales increase by 5 percent each year.
o Selling and administrative expenses increase only 1 percent in 2005 and will remain at the 2005 level thereafter.
o Income tax rate = 46 percent

Exhibit 7.10 presents a spreadsheet for the income statement for the next three years.

	1	2	3	4	5	6	7	8	9	10	11	12	TOTAL	PERCENT
Sales	$60,000	$63,000	$66,150	$69,458	$72,930	$76,577	$80,406	$84,426	$88,647	$93,080	$97,734	$102,620	$955,028	100%
Less: VC														
Cost of sales	$25,200	$26,460	$27,783	$29,172	$30,631	$32,162	$33,770	$35,459	$37,232	$39,093	$41,048	$43,101	$401,112	42%
Operating ex.	$3,000	$3,150	$3,308	$3,473	$3,647	$3,829	$4,020	$4,221	$4,432	$4,654	$4,887	$5,131	$47,751	5%
CM	$31,800	$33,390	$35,060	$36,812	$38,653	$40,586	$42,615	$44,746	$46,983	$49,332	$51,799	$54,389	$506,165	53%
Less: FC														
Op. expenses	$10,000	$10,000	$10,000	$10,000	$10,000	$10,000	$10,000	$10,000	$10,000	$10,000	$10,000	$10,000	$120,000	13%
Net income	$21,800	$23,390	$25,060	$26,812	$28,653	$30,586	$32,615	$34,746	$36,983	$39,332	$41,799	$44,389	$386,165	40%
Less: Tax	$6,540	$7,017	$7,518	$8,044	$8,596	$9,176	$9,785	$10,424	$11,095	$11,800	$12,540	$13,317	$115,849	12%
NI after tax	$15,260	$16,373	$17,542	$18,769	$20,057	$21,410	$22,831	$24,322	$25,888	$27,533	$29,259	$31,072	$270,315	28%

Exhibit 7.8 PROJECTED INCOME STATEMENT

268

269

	1	2	3	4	5	6	7	8	9	10	11	12	TOTAL	PERCENT
Sales	$60,000	$66,000	$72,600	$79,860	$87,846	$96,631	$106,294	$116,923	$128,615	$141,477	$155,625	$171,187	$1,283,057	134%
Less: VC														
Cost of sales	$25,200	$27,720	$30,492	$33,541	$36,895	$40,585	$44,643	$49,108	$54,018	$59,420	$65,362	$71,899	$538,884	56%
Operating ex.	$6,000	$6,600	$7,260	$7,986	$8,785	$9,663	$10,629	$11,692	$12,862	$14,148	$15,562	$17,119	$64,153	7%
CM	$28,800	$31,680	$34,848	$38,333	$42,166	$46,383	$51,021	$56,123	$61,735	$67,909	$74,700	$82,170	$615,867	64%
Less: FC														
Op. expenses	$10,000	$10,000	$10,000	$10,000	$10,000	$10,000	$10,000	$10,000	$10,000	$10,000	$10,000	$10,000	$120,000	$13%
Net income	$18,800	$21,680	$24,848	$28,333	$32,166	$36,383	$41,021	$46,123	$51,735	$57,909	$64,700	$72,170	$495,867	52%
Less: Tax	$5,640	$6,504	$7,454	$8,500	$9,650	$10,915	$12,306	$13,837	$15,521	$17,373	$19,410	$21,651	$148,760	$16%
NI after tax	$13,160	$15,176	$17,394	$19,833	$22,516	$25,468	$28,715	$32,286	$36,215	$40,536	$45,290	$50,519	$347,107	$36%

Exhibit 7.9 PROJECTING INCOME STATEMENT

	2004	2005	2006	2007
DELTA GAMMA COMPANY				
THREE-YEAR INCOME PROJECTIONS (2005-2007)				
Sales	$4,500,000	$4,770,000	$5,103,900	$5,512,212
Cost of sales	2,900,000	3,045,000	3,197,250	3,357,113
Gross margin	1,600,000	1,725,000	1,906,650	2,155,100
Selling & adm. exp.	800,000	808,000	808,000	808,000
Net income before tax	800,000	917,000	1,098,650	1,347,100
Tax	368,000	421,820	505,379	619,666
Net income after tax	$ 432,000	$ 495,180	$ 593,271	$ 727,434

Exhibit 7.10

BUDGETING SOFTWARE

There are many user-oriented software packages specifically designed for corporate planners, treasurers, budget preparers, managerial accountants, CFOs, and business analysts. These languages do not require any knowledge of programming languages (such as BASIC and COBOL) on the part of the user; they are all English-like languages. Several popular ones are described briefly.

Adaytum Planning

Adaytum Planning by Adaytum Software (*www.adaytum .com*; 1-800-262-4445) is a multiuser budgeting, planning, and forecasting system. It gives you the flexibility to:

- Update hierarchies directly from the General Ledger (G/L).
- Combine top-down planning with bottom-up budgeting
- Make last minute changes to model structure
- Empower end-users to do ad hoc modeling without information system (IS) support.

Comshare's Interactive Financial Planning System (IFPS/Plus) and BudgetPLUS

Comshare's IFPS/Plus is a multipurpose, interactive financial modeling that supports and facilitates the building, solving, and asking of "what-if" questions of financial models. It is a powerful modeling and analysis tool designed to handle large complicated problems with lots of data. It is unsurpassed for large corporatewide applications—especially those that get their data directly from the enterprise relational database. Originally marketed by Execucom in the 1970's, IFPS is currently used by more than 600 businesses. The data and models created through IFPS/PLUS can be shared throughout the organization because the model logic is self-documenting. The capabilities of the program include the ability to explain, perform spreadsheet type editing, produce reports, and provide built-in business functions. Some of the capabilities of the system are forecasting, linear regression, and automatic extrapolation. The most current version of IFPF/PLUS is 5.1.1, which introduces Visual IFPS. This is a Microsoft Windows application that acts as the "client in the client-server application." The application runs on the PC and is connected to the IFPS/PLUS running on the server. In other words, IFPS/PLUS can access and take the data from the organization's main database and send the results directly to the user. The user is not inundated with all of the data, but is just presented with the results. This keeps the network from getting bogged down. Thus, the user has the power of the server on a PC and all the benefits of IFPS/ PLUS. *Comshare BudgetPLUS* is a Web-architectured budgeting software that runs in Web or client/server environments, with a relational or multidimensional database. For more information on this system, log on to the Comshare Web site (*www.comshare.com*; 1-800-922-7979, 3001 S. State St., P.O. Box 1588, Ann Arbor, Michigan 48106).

Encore Plus

This package was developed by Ferox Microsystems. The analytical functions are similar to IFPS, but Encore has more model-building capability. For example, it is stronger in its risk analysis than IFPS, and it even includes a Monte Carlo Simulator. Since Encore Plus is more powerful at the application development level than, say, IFPS, it requires a higher level of programming ability.

Budget Maestro

Planet's Budget Maestro is probably the best answer to distributed budgeting, strategic planning and financial control. Budget Maestro shortens your budgeting cycle and puts you into control of the process. Its information-driven environment guides you through budgeting, planning, modeling, forecasting, resource management, consolidation, analysis, and reporting. CFOs and budget managers can plan, analyze and manage, in ways never before possible. Look at a user's screen and make changes directly without ever being there. Deliver budget models and deploy reconfigured software updates to many users at once. Plus manage budgetary information, even enterprise wide information systems, with a single consistent interface. Planet's Budget Maestro is designed to put CFOs and financial managers in control of all aspects of managing budgets, creating financial models and building and deploying financial plans. Budget Maestro allows business managers unparalleled flexibility in analyzing cash flow and business performance throughout the enterprise. Budget Maestro significantly shortens your budgeting and planning cycles. It eliminates rekeying and formatting of data. It increases your data accuracy and integrity. It allows your time to manage and analyze your business. It is available in both Desktop and Enterprise Edition. Budget Maestro Enterprise Editions enables multiple independent budgets and plans to be consolidated into a unified enterprise model. The Desktop Edition can be upgraded to the Enterprise Edition at any time.

Microsoft Business Solutions for Analytics—Forecaster

This is a Web-based budgeting and planning solution from FRx Software (*www.frxsoftware.com*). Many organizations find it difficult to perform the ongoing budgeting and planning processes necessary to keep business performance on target. Financial "surprises" are met with panic, and more often than not, companies are forced to make sacrifices in places they cannot afford. The result is a direct, negative impact on their strategic objectives. But it's not for lack of trying—finance departments simply don't have the time it takes to combine multiple spreadsheets submitted from across the company (let alone the resources to make sure all line managers understand the importance of the budgeting and planning process, and of submitting well-planned information on time!). *Forecaster* puts the systems and processes in place to help you immediately realize the benefits of an effective budgeting and planning process, and make it an ongoing part of your business strategy.

THE LATEST GENERATION OF BUDGETING AND PLANNING (B&P) SOFTWARE

The new budgeting and planning (B&P) software represents a giant step forward for accountants. Finance managers can use these robust, Web-enabled programs to scan a wide range of data, radically speed up the planning process, and identify managers who have failed to submit budgets. More often known as *active financial planning software*, this software includes applications and the new level of functionality that combine budgeting, forecasting analytics, business intelligence, and collaboration. Exhibit 7.11 lists popular B&P software.

Companies	Web sites	Software
ABC Technologies	www.abctech.com	Oros
ActiveStrategy	www.activestrategy.com	ActiveStrategy Enterprise

Exhibit 7.11 Active Financial Planning Software—Next Generation Budgeting and Planning (B & P) Software

Actuate	www.actuate.com	e.Reporting Suite
Adaytum Software	www.adaytum.com	e.Planning
Applix	www.applix.com	iPlanning, iTM1
Brio Technology	www.brio.com	Brio.ONE, Brio.Impact, Brio.Inform
Business Objects	www.businessobjects.com	e-BI, BusinessObjects Auditor, BusinessObjects BW Connect, Webintelligence
Cartesis	www.cartesis.com	Cartesis Budget Planning, Cartesis Carat, Cartesis Magnitude
Closedloop Solutions	www.closedloopsolutions.com	CBizPlan Manager, SpendCap Manager, TopLine Manager
Cognos	www.cognos.com	Cognos Finance, Cognos Visualizer, Cognos Enterprise, Business Intelligence
Comshare	www.comshare.com	Management Planning and Control (MPC) Application, Comshare Decision
CorVu	www.corvu.com	CorManage, CorVu Rapid Scorecard, CorBusiness, CorPortfolio
E.Intelligence	www.eintelligence-inc.com	e.Intelligence Suite
Epicor	www.epicor.com	Epicor eintelligence Suite
Geac	www.geac.com	Geac Smartstream Financials, Enterprise Solutions Expert Series, FRx
Great Plains Software	www.greatplains.com	eEnterprise, FRx Budget Controller, Dynamics
Hyperion	www.hyperion.com	Hyperion Financial Management, Hyperion Planning, Hyperion Essbase
J.D. Edwards	www.jdedwards.com	J.D. Edwards Financial Planning and Budgeting, Business Intelligence, OneWorld Xe

Exhibit 7.11 ACTIVE FINANCIAL PLANNING SOFTWARE—NEXT GENERATION BUDGETING AND PLANNING (B & P) SOFTWARE *(continued)*

Lawson Software	www.lawson.com	Enterprise Budgeting SEA Application - including E-Scorecard; Analytic Extensions
Longview Solutions	www.longview.com	Khalix
MIS-AG	www.misag.com	MIS Alea Decisionware, MIS DelaMiner, Collaborative Analytic Processing
NextStrat	www.nextstrat.com	NextStrat Strategic Implementation Portal (NextSIP)
Oracle	www.oracle.com	Oracle Strategic Enterprise Management (SEM)
OutlookSoft	www.outlooksoft.com	OutlookSoft Financial Planning and Analysis (FPA), OutlookSoft Enterprise Analytic Portal
PeopleSoft	www.peoplesoft.com	Enterprise Performance Management (EPM), PeopleSoft Balanced Scorecard, PeopleSoft Enterprise Warehouse, PeopleSoft eBusiness Analytics, PeopleSoft Activity-Based Management
SAP	www.sap.com	SAP Strategic Enterprise Management (SEM), SAP Financial Analyzer Business Intelligence with mySAP.com
SAS Institute	www.sas.com	SAS Total Financial Management, Strategic Vision, SAS/Warehouse Administrator, SAS Enabling Technology (OLAP)
Silvon	www.silvon.com	Stratum
SRC Software	www.srcsoftware.com	Budget Advisor, Payroll Planner, Information Advisor

Exhibit 7.11   ACTIVE FINANCIAL PLANNING SOFTWARE—NEXT GENERATION BUDGETING AND PLANNING (B & P) SOFTWARE *(continued)*

CHAPTER 8

ANALYSIS OF PROJECTS, PROPOSALS, AND SPECIAL SITUATIONS

*A*ccountants need to be equipped with various tools and techniques in order to cope with short-term and long-term decisions. Cost-volume-profit (CVP) analysis is an extremely useful tool for accountants. When used in conjunction with any spreadsheet program, it can help accountants choose a wise decision by simulating a variety of "what-if" scenarios. Analysis of short-term, special decisions typically requires such simple concepts as *contribution margin* and *relevant costs*. Long-term investment decisions, commonly called *capital budgeting*, however, require not only a good understanding of the time value concept and its application, but also a working knowledge of how to analyze and evaluate investment proposals.

This chapter covers the tools and guidelines that facilitate various short-term, nonroutine decisions and long-term investment decisions. Specifically:

- Breakeven and cost–volume–profit (CVP) analysis
- Short-term decisions, For example, pricing decisions on special order and the make-or-buy decision
- Time value fundamentals
- Long-term investment decisions, commonly known as capital budgeting

COST–VOLUME–PROFIT AND BREAKEVEN ANALYSIS

What are variable and fixed costs?

Not all costs behave in the same way. Certain costs, called *variable costs*, vary in proportion to change in activity. Other costs that do not change, regardless of the volume, are called *fixed costs*.

Why analyze cost behavior?

An understanding of costs by behavior is very useful:

o For breakeven and cost-volume-profit (CVP) analysis

o For analysis of short-term, nonroutine decisions such as the make-or-buy decision and the sales mix decision

o For appraisal of profit center performance by means of the contribution approach and for flexible budgeting (see Chapter 7)

What is cost–volume–profit and breakeven analysis?

Cost-volume-profit (CVP) analysis, together with cost behavior information, helps accountants perform many useful analyses. CVP analysis deals with how profit and costs change with a change in volume. It specifically looks at the effects on profits of changes in such factors as variable costs, fixed costs, selling prices, volume, and mix of products sold. By studying the relationships of costs, sales, and net income, accountants are better able to cope with planning decisions.

Breakeven analysis, a branch of CVP analysis, determines the breakeven sales, which is the level of sales at which total costs equal total revenue.

How may I use CVP analysis in solving business problems?

CVP analysis tries to answer the following questions:

o What sales volume is required to break even?

o What sales volume is necessary in order to earn a desired profit?

o What profit can be expected on a given sales volume?

o How would changes in selling price, variable costs, fixed costs, and output affect profit?

o How would a change in the mix of products sold affect the breakeven and target income volume and profit potential?

Contribution Margin

What does contribution margin involve?

For accurate CVP analysis, a distinction must be made between variable and fixed costs. Semivariable costs (or mixed costs) must be separated into their variable and fixed components.

To compute the breakeven point and perform various CVP analyses, note the following important concepts:

o *Contribution margin (CM)*. The contribution margin is the excess of sales (S) over the variable costs (VC) of the product. It is the amount of money available to cover fixed costs (FC) and to generate profits. Symbolically, CM = S – VC.

o *Unit CM*. The unit CM is the excess of the unit selling price (p) over the unit variable cost (v). Symbolically, unit CM = p – v.

o *CM ratio*. The CM ratio is the contribution margin as a percentage of sales, that is,

$$\text{CM Ratio} = \frac{CM}{S} = \frac{S - VC}{S} = 1 - \frac{VC}{S}$$

CM ratio can also be computed using per-unit data as follows:

$$\text{CM Ratio} = \frac{\text{Unit CM}}{p} = \frac{p - v}{p} = 1 - \frac{v}{p}$$

	NOTE

The CM ratio is 1 minus the variable cost ratio.
EXAMPLE: If variable costs account for 70 percent of the price, the CM ratio is 30 percent.

EXAMPLE 8.1

To illustrate the various concepts of CM, consider the following data for Company Z:

	Per Unit	Total	Percentage
Sales (1,500 units)	$25	$37,500	100%
Less: Variable cost	10	15,000	40
Contribution margin	$15	22,500	60%
Less: Fixed costs		15,000	
Net income		$ 7,000	

From the data listed above, CM, unit CM, and the CM ratio are computed as:

$$CM = S - VC = \$37{,}500 - \$15{,}000 = \$22{,}500$$

$$\text{Unit CM} = p - v = \$25 - \$10 = \$15$$

$$\text{CM ratio} = \frac{CM}{S} = \frac{\$22{,}500}{\$37{,}500}$$

$$= 60\% \text{ or } 1 - \frac{VC}{S}$$

$$= 1 - 0.4 = 0.6 = 60\%$$

How can the breakeven point be calculated?

The breakeven point, the point of no profit and no loss, provides accountants with insights into profit planning. It can be computed in three different ways.

The *equation approach* is based on the cost–volume equation, which shows the relationships among sales, variable and fixed costs, and net income.

$$S = VC + FC + \text{Net Income}$$

At the breakeven volume, $S = VC + FC + 0$. Defining $x =$ volume in *units*, we can rewrite the above relationship in terms of x:

$$px = vx + FC$$

To find the breakeven point in units, simply solve the equation for x.

EXAMPLE 8.2

In Example 8.1, $p = \$25$, $v = \$10$, and FC = \$15,000. Thus, the equation is:

$$\$25x = \$10x + \$15,000$$
$$\$25x - \$10x = \$15,000$$
$$(\$25 - \$10)x = \$15,000$$
$$\$15x = \$15,000$$
$$x = \$15,000 / \$15 = 1,000 \text{ units}$$

Therefore, Company Z breaks even at a sales volume of 1,000 units.

The *contribution margin approach*, another technique for computing the breakeven point, is based on solving the cost-volume equation. Solving the equation $px = vx + FC$ for x yields:

$$x_{BE} = FC / (p - v)$$

where $(p - v)$ is the unit CM by definition, and $x_{BE} =$ breakeven unit sales volume.
In words,

Breakeven point in *units* = Fixed Costs/Unit CM

If the breakeven point is desired in terms of dollars, then

Breakeven point in *dollars* = breakeven point in units *times* unit sales price

Alternatively,

Breakeven point in *dollars* = Fixed Costs/CM Ratio

EXAMPLE 8.3

Using the same data given in Example 8.1, where unit CM = $25 – $10 = $15 and CM ratio = 60%, we get:

Breakeven point in units = $15,000/$15
                                                = 1,000 units

Breakeven point in dollars = 1,000 units × $25
                                                    = $25,000

Alternatively, $15,000/0.6 = $25,000

The *graphical approach* is based on the so-called *breakeven chart* shown in Exhibit 8.1. Sales revenue, variable costs, and fixed costs are plotted on the vertical axis. Volume (x) is plotted on the horizontal axis. The breakeven point is the point where the total sales revenue line intersects the total cost line. This chart can also effectively report profit potential for a wide range of activity.

The *profit-volume (P/V) chart* shown in Exhibit 8.2 focuses more directly on how profits vary with changes in volume. Profits are plotted on the vertical axis while units of output are shown on the horizontal axis.

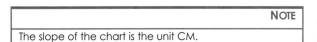

	NOTE
The slope of the chart is the unit CM.	

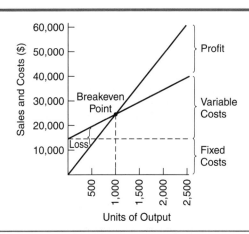

Exhibit 8.1   BREAKEVEN CHART

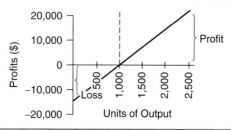

Exhibit 8.2   PROFIT–VOLUME (P/V) CHART

Target Income Volume and Margin of Safety

How do I determine target income volume?

Besides being able to determine the breakeven point, CVP analysis determines the sales required to attain a particular income level or target net income. There are two ways target net income can be expressed.

As a *specific dollar amount*, the cost–volume equation specifying target net income is:

$$px = vx + FC + \text{Target Income}$$

Solving the equation for x yields:

$$x_{TI} = \frac{FC + \text{Target Income}}{p - v}$$

where

x_{TI} = sales volume required to achieve a given target income.

In words,

$$\text{Target Income Sales Volume} = \frac{\text{Fixed Costs} + \text{Target Income}}{\text{Unit CM}}$$

Specifying target income as a *percentage of sales*, the cost-volume equation is:

$$px = vx + FC + \%(px)$$

Solving this for x yields:

$$x_{TI} = \frac{FC}{p - v - \%(p)}$$

In words,

Target Income Sales Volume
= Fixed Costs/(Unit CM –% of unit sales price)

EXAMPLE 8.4

Using the same data given in Example 8.1, assume that
Company Z wishes to attain:

As a specific dollar amount: A target income of $15,000
before tax

Target income sales volume (in units) required would
be:

$$x_{TI} = \frac{FC + \text{Target Income}}{p - v}$$

$$= \frac{\$15,000 + \$15,000}{\$25 - \$10} = 2,000 \text{ units}$$

As a percentage of sales: A target income of 20 percent
of sales

The target income volume required would be:

$$x_{TI} = \frac{FC}{p - v - \%(p)} = \frac{\$15,000}{\$15 - 20\%(\$25)}$$

$$= \frac{\$15,000}{\$15 - \$5} = 1,500 \text{ units}$$

What is the impact of income taxes on target income volume?

If target income is given on an after-tax basis, the target
income volume formula becomes:

$$\text{Target income volume} = \frac{\text{Fixed Costs} + \dfrac{\text{Target After - Tax Income}}{1 - \text{tax rate}}}{\text{Unit CM}}$$

EXAMPLE 8.5

Assume in Example 8.1 that Company Z wants to achieve
an after-tax income of $6,000. Income tax is levied at 40
percent. Then,

$$\text{Target income volume} = \frac{\$15,000 + \dfrac{\$6,000}{1 - 0.04}}{\$15}$$

$$= \frac{\$15,000 + \$10,000}{\$15}$$

$$= 1,667 \text{ units}$$

What is the margin of safety?

The margin of safety is a measure of difference between the actual level of sales and the breakeven sales. It is the amount by which sales revenue may drop before losses begin and is expressed as a percentage of budgeted sales as follows:

$$\text{Margin of safety} = \frac{\text{Budgeted sales} - \text{break-even sales}}{\text{Budgeted sales}}$$

What is the use of the margin of safety?

The margin of safety is often used as a measure of risk. The larger the ratio, the safer the situation, since there is less risk of reaching the breakeven point.

EXAMPLE 8.6

Assume Company Z projects sales of $30,000 with a breakeven sales level of $25,000. The expected margin of safety is:

$$\frac{\$30,000 - \$25,000}{\$30,000} = \underline{16.7\%}$$

How is CVP analysis used in practice?

The concepts of contribution margin have many applications in profit planning and short-term decision making. Applications are illustrated in Examples 8.7 through 8.11, using the data from Example 8.1.

EXAMPLE 8.7

Recall from Example 8.1 that Z has a CM of 60 percent and fixed costs of $15,000 per period. Assume that the company expects sales to go up by $10,000 for the next period. How much will income increase?

Using the CM concepts, we can quickly compute the impact of a change in sales on profits. The formula for computing the impact is:

Change in net income = dollar change in sales × CM ratio

Thus, the increase in net income = $10,000 X 60% = $6,000. Therefore, the income will go up by $6,000, assuming

EXAMPLE 8.7 *(continued)*

there is no change. If we are given a change in sales in *units* instead of dollars, then the formula becomes:

Change in net income = change in unit sales
× unit CM

EXAMPLE 8.8

We now compute before-tax income expected on sales of $47,500.

CM $47,500 × 60%	$28,500
Less: Fixed costs	15,000
Net income	$13,500

EXAMPLE 8.9

Company Z is considering increasing the advertising budget by $5,000, which would increase sales revenue by $8,000. Should the advertising budget be increased? The answer is no, since the increase in the CM is less than the increased cost.

Increase in CM $8,000 × 60%	$4,800
Increase in advertising	5,000
Decrease in net income	($200)

EXAMPLE 8.10

Company Z's accountant is considering a $3,000 increase in sales salaries. What additional sales are required to cover the higher cost?

The increase in fixed cost must be matched by an equal increase in CM:

Increase in CM = increase in cost
0.60 sales = $3,000
sales = $5,000

EXAMPLE 8.11

Consider the original data. Assume again that Company Z is currently selling 1,500 units per period. In an effort to increase sales, the accountant is considering cutting its unit price by $5 and increasing the advertising budget by $1,000. If these two steps are taken, the accountant feels that unit sales will go up by 60 percent. Should the two steps be taken?

EXAMPLE 8.11   (continued)

A $5 reduction in the selling price would cause the unit CM to decrease from $15 to $10. Thus,

Proposed CM 2,400 units × $10	$24,000
Present CM 1,500 units × $15	22,500
Increase in CM	1,500
Increase in advertising outlay	1,000
Increase in net income	$500

The answer is yes. Alternatively, the same answer can be obtained by developing comparative income statements in contribution margin format:

	Present (1,500 units)	Proposed (2,400 units)	Difference
Sales	$37,500 (@25)	$48,000 (@20)	$10,500
Less: Variable cost	15,000	24,000	9,000
CM	22,500	24,000	1,500
Less: Fixed costs	15,000	16,000	1,000
Net income	$7,500	$8,000	$500

Sales Mix Analysis

What effect does the sales mix have?

Breakeven and cost–volume–profit analyses require some additional computations and assumptions when a company produces and sells more than one product. Different selling prices and different variable costs result in different unit CM and CM ratios. As a result, breakeven points vary with the relative proportions of the products sold, called the *sales mix*. In breakeven and CVP analysis, it is necessary to:

○ Predetermine the sales mix and then compute a weighted average CM

○ Assume that the sales mix does not change for a specified period

The breakeven formula for the company as a whole is:

Companywide breakeven in units (or in dollars)

$$= \frac{\text{Fixed Costs}}{\textit{Average} \text{ Unit CM (or } \textit{Average} \text{ CM Ratio)}}$$

EXAMPLE 8.12

Assume that Company X has two products with the following CM data:

	A	B
Selling price	$15	$10
Variable cost	12	5
Unit CM	$3	$5
Sales mix	60%	40%
Fixed costs	$76,000	

EXAMPLE 8.12 *(continued)*

The weighted average unit CM = $3(0.6) + $5(0.4) = $3.80

Then the company's breakeven point in units is $76,000/$3.80 = 20,000 units

This is divided as follows:

A: 20,000 units × 60%= 12,000 units
B: 20,000 units × 40%   8,000
                        20,000 units

EXAMPLE 8.13

Assume that Company Y produces and sells three products with the following data:

	A	B	C	Total
Sales	$30,000	$60,000	$10,000	$100,000
Sales mix	30%	60%	10%	100%
Less: VC	24,000	40,000	5,000	69,000
CM	$ 6,000	$20,000	$ 5,000	$ 31,000
CM ratio	20%	33-1/3%	50%	31%

Total fixed costs are $18,600.

The CM ratio for Company Y is $31,000/$100,000 = 31%. Therefore the breakeven point *in dollars* is $18,600/ 0.31 = $60,000.

This will be split in the mix ratio of 3:6:1 to give us the following breakeven points for the individual products A, B, and C:

A: $60,000 × 30% = $18,000
B: $60,000 × 60% = 36,000
C: $60,000 × 10% =   6,000
                   $60,000

EXAMPLE 8.14

Assume in Example 8.13 that total sales remain unchanged at $100,000, but a shift in mix from Product B to Product C is expected:

	A	B	C	Total
Sales	$30,000	$30,000	$40,000	$100,000
Sales mix	30%	30%	40%	100%
Less: VC	24,000	20,000*	20,000	64,000
CM	$ 6,000	$10,000	$20,000	$ 36,000
CM ratio	20%	33-1/3%	50%	36%

*$20,000 = $30,000 × 66 2/3%.

NOTE: The shift in sales mix toward the more profitable line C has caused the CM ratio for the company as a whole to go from 31 percent to 36 percent. The new breakeven point will be $18,600/0.36 = $51,667. The breakeven dollar volume has decreased from $60,000 to $51,667.

What does breakeven and CVP analysis assume?

The basic breakeven and CVP models are subject to a number of limiting assumptions:

o The behavior of both sales revenue and expenses is *linear* throughout the entire *relevant* range of activity.

o All costs are classified as fixed or variable.

o There is only one product. In a multiproduct firm, the sales mix will not change during the planning period. If the sales mix changes, the breakeven point will also change.

o Inventories do not change significantly from period to period.

o Volume is the only factor affecting variable costs.

SHORT-TERM NONROUTINE DECISIONS

What nonrecurring situations do I have to consider?

When analyzing the manufacturing and selling functions, accountants are constantly faced with the problem of choosing alternative courses of action. Typical questions include:

o What to make?

o How to make it?

o Where to sell the product or service?

o What price should be charged?

In the short run, the accountant is typically confronted with the following nonroutine, nonrecurring types of decisions:

o Acceptance or rejection of a special order

o Make or buy

o Add or drop a certain product line

o Utilization of scarce resources

o Sell or process further

What are relevant costs?

In each of the above situations, the ultimate decision rests upon cost data analysis. Cost data are important in many decisions, since they are the basis for profit calculations. However, not all costs are of equal importance in decision making, and accountants must identify the costs that are relevant to a decision. Such costs are called *relevant costs*.

Which costs are relevant in a nonroutine decision?

The relevant costs are the expected future costs which differ between the decision alternatives. Therefore:

- The *sunk costs* are *not* relevant to the decision at hand, because they are past, historical costs.
- The *incremental* or *differential* costs are relevant since they are the ones that differ between the alternatives.

EXAMPLE: In a decision on whether to sell an existing business for a new one, the cost to be paid for the new venture is relevant. However, the initial cost of the old business is not relevant to the decision because it is a sunk cost.

What is incremental analysis?

The method that uses the concept of *relevant costs* is called the *incremental approach*, also known as the *differential* or *relevant cost approach*. Under this method, the decision involves the following steps:

- Gather all costs associated with each alternative
- Drop the *sunk costs*
- Drop those costs that do not differ between alternatives
- Select the best alternative based on the remaining cost data

EXAMPLE 8.15

Assume that ABC Company is planning to expand its productive capacity. The plans consist of purchasing a new machine for $50,000 and disposing of the old machine without receiving anything. The new machine has a five-year life. The old machine has a five-year remaining life and a book value of $12,500. The new machine will reduce variable operating costs from $35,000 per year to $20,000 per year. Annual sales and other operating costs are shown below.

	Present Machine	New Machine
Sales	$60,000	$60,000
Variable costs	35,000	20,000
Fixed costs:		
Depreciation (straight-line)	2,500	10,000
Insurance, taxes, etc.	4,000	4,000
Net income	$18,500	$26,000

At first glance, it appears that the new machine provides an increase in net income of $7,500 per year. The

EXAMPLE 8.15   *(continued)*

book value of the present machine, however, is a sunk cost and is irrelevant in this decision. Furthermore, sales and fixed costs such as insurance and taxes, are also irrelevant since they do not differ between the two alternatives being considered. Eliminating all the irrelevant costs leaves us with only the following incremental costs:

Savings in variable costs	$15,000
Increase in fixed costs	10,000 (a $2,500 sunk cost is irrelevant)

Net annual cash
  savings arising from
  the new machine
	$ 5,000

When should a company accept special orders?

A company often receives a short-term, special order for its products at lower prices than usual. In normal times, the company may refuse such an order since it will not yield a satisfactory profit.

RECOMMENDATION
If times are bad or when there is idle capacity, an order should be accepted if the incremental revenue exceeds the incremental costs involved. Such a price, one lower than the regular price, is called a *contribution price*. This approach to pricing is called the *contribution approach to pricing*, also called the *variable pricing model*. This approach is most appropriate when:

o There is idle capacity
o Faced with sharp competition or in a competitive bidding situation
o Operating in a distress situation

EXAMPLE 8.16

Assume that a company with 100,000-unit capacity is currently producing and selling only 90,000 units of product each year with a regular price of $2. If the variable cost per unit is $1 and the annual fixed cost is $45,000, the income statement shows:

		Per Unit
Sales (90,000 units)	$180,000	$2.00
Less: Variable cost	90,000	1.00
Contribution margin	$ 90,000	$ 1.00
Less: Fixed cost	45,000	0.50
Net income	$ 45,000	$0.50

EXAMPLE 8.16 *(continued)*

The company has just received an order that calls for 10,000 units @ $1.20, for a total of $12,000. The acceptance of this special order will not affect regular sales. Management is reluctant to accept this order because the $1.20 price is below the $1.50 factory unit cost ($1.50 = $1.00 + $0.50).

Is filling the order advisable? The answer to this question is yes. The company can add to total profits by accepting this special order even though the price offered is below the unit factory cost. At a price of $1.20, the order will contribute $0.20 (CM per unit = $1.20 – $1.00 = $0.20) toward fixed cost, and profit will increase by $2,000 (10,000 units × $0.20). Using the contribution approach to pricing, the variable cost of $1.00 will be a better guide than the full unit cost of $1.50.

NOTE

The fixed costs will not increase because of the presence of idle capacity.

What is a make-or-buy decision?

The make-or-buy decision is the decision whether to produce a component part internally or to buy it from an outside supplier. This decision involves both quantitative and qualitative factors.

- o The *qualitative* considerations include ensuring product quality and the necessity for long-run business relationships with the subcontractors.
- o The *quantitative* factors, dealing with cost, are best seen through *incremental analysis*.

EXAMPLE 8.17

Assume a firm has prepared the following cost estimates for the manufacture of a subassembly component based on an annual production of 8,000 units:

	Per Unit	Total
Direct materials	$ 5	$ 40,000
Direct labor	4	32,000
Variable overhead applied	4	32,000
Fixed overhead applied (150% of direct labor cost)	6	48,000
Total cost	$19	$152,000

The supplier has offered to provide the subassembly at a price of $16 each. Two-thirds of fixed factory overhead, which represents executive salaries, rent, depreciation, and taxes, continue regardless of the decision.

EXAMPLE 8.17 *(continued)*

Should the company buy or make the product? The key to the decision lies in the investigation of those relevant costs that change between the make-or-buy alternatives. Assuming that the productive capacity will be idle if not used to produce the subassembly, the analysis takes the following form:

	Per Unit		Total of 8,000 units	
	Make	Buy	Make	Buy
Purchase price		$16	$40,000	$128,000
Direct materials	$5		32,000	
Direct labor	4		32,000	
Variable overhead	4			
Fixed overhead that can be avoided by *not* making	2	—	16,000	
Total relevant costs	$15	$16	$120,000	$128,000
Difference in favor of making	$1		$8,000	

NOTE

The make-or-buy decision must be investigated in the broader perspective of available facilities. The alternatives are:
- Leaving facilities idle
- Buying the parts and renting out idle facilities
- Buying the parts and using unused facilities for other products

How do I decide whether to add or drop a product line?

The decision of whether to drop an old product line or add a new one must take into account both qualitative and quantitative factors. Ultimately, any final decision should be based on the impact the decision will have on contribution margin or net income.

EXAMPLE 8.18

The ABC grocery store has three major product lines: produce, meats, and canned goods. The store is considering dropping the meat line because the income statement shows it is being sold at a loss. Note the income statement for these product lines:

	Produce	Meats	Canned Food	Total
Sales	$10,000	$15,000	$25,000	$50,000
Less: Variable costs	6,000	8,000	12,000	26,000
CM	$ 4,000	$ 7,000	$13,000	$24,000

EXAMPLE 8.18 *(continued)*			

Less: Fixed costs				
Direct	2,000	6,500	4,000	12,500
Allocated	1,000	1,500	2,500	5,000
Total	$ 3,000	$ 8,000	$ 6,500	$17,500
Net income	$ 1,000	($ 1,000)	$ 6,500	$ 6,500

In this example, *direct fixed costs* are those costs that are identified directly with each of the product lines. *Allocated fixed costs* are the amount of common fixed costs allocated to the product lines using some base such as space occupied. The amount of *common fixed costs* typically continues regardless of the decision and thus cannot be saved by dropping the product line to which it is distributed.

The following calculations show the effects on the company as a whole with and without the meat line:

	Keep Meats	**Drop Meats**	**Difference**
Sales	$50,000	$35,000	($15,000)
Less:			
Variable cost	26,000	18,000	(8,000)
CM	$24,000	$17,000	($ 7,000)
Less:			
Fixed cost:			
Direct	12,500	6,000	(6,500)
Allocated	5,000	5,000	—
Total	$13,500	$11,000	($ 6,500)
Net income	$ 6,500	$ 6,000	($ 500)

From either of the two methods, we see that by dropping meats the store will lose an additional $500. Therefore, the meat product line should be kept.

CAUTION

One of the great dangers in allocating common fixed costs is that such allocations can make a product line look less profitable than it really is.

Because of such an allocation, the meat line showed a loss of $1,000. In effect it contributes $500 ($7,000 − $6,500) to the recovery of the store's common fixed costs.

How do I make the best use of scarce resources?

In general, the emphasis on products with higher contribution margin maximizes a firm's total net income, even though total sales may decrease. This is not true, however, where there are constraining factors and scarce resources. The constraining factor is the factor that restricts or limits the production or sale of a given product. EXAMPLES: machine hours, labor hours, or cubic feet of warehouse space.

	NOTE

In the presence of these constraining factors, maximizing total profits depends on getting the highest contribution margin *per unit* of the factor (rather than the highest contribution margin per unit of product output).

EXAMPLE 8.19

Assume that a company produces products A and B with the following contribution margins per unit.

	A	B
Sales	$8	$24
Variable costs	6	20
CM	$2	$ 4
Annual fixed costs		$42,000

As is indicated by CM per unit, B is more profitable than A since it contributes more to the company's total profits than A ($4 vs. $2). But assume that the firm has limited capacity of 10,000 labor hours. Further, assume that A requires two labor hours to produce and B requires five labor hours. One way to express this limited capacity is to determine the contribution margin per labor hour.

	A	B
CM/unit	$2.00	$4.00
Labor hours required per unit	2	5
CM per labor hour	$1.00	$ .80

Since A returns the higher CM per labor hour, it should be produced and B should be dropped.

	NOTE

The presence of only one limited resource is unrealistic. Virtually all firms encounter multiple constraints: restrictions on materials, labor inputs, demand for each product, warehouse space, display space, and so on. The solution of the product mix problem with multiple constraints is considerably more complex and requires a technique known as *linear programming*.

THEORY OF CONSTRAINTS

What is the theory of constraints?

A binding constraint can limit a company's profitability. For example, a manufacturing company may have a *bottleneck operation*, through which every unit of a product must pass before moving on to other operations. The *theory of constraints (TOC)* calls for identifying such limiting constraints and seeking ways to relax them. Also referred to as *managing constraints*, this management approach can significantly improve an organization's level of goal attainment. Among the ways that management can relax a constraint by expanding the capacity of a bottleneck operation are the following:

○ *Outsourcing* (subcontracting) all or part of the bottleneck operation

○ Investing in additional production equipment and employing *parallel processing*, in which multiple product units undergo the same production operation simultaneously

○ Working *overtime* at the bottleneck operation

○ *Retaining* employees and shifting them to the bottleneck

○ Eliminating any *non-value-added activities* at the bottleneck operation

LIFE-CYCLE COSTS AND TARGET COSTING

What is life-cycle costing?

Life-cycle costing tracks and accumulates all product costs in the value chain from research and development and design of products and processes through production, marketing, distribution, and customer service. The value chain is the set of activities required to design, develop, produce, market, and service a product (or service). The terms *cradle-to-grave costing* and *womb-to-tomb costing* convey the sense of fully capturing all costs associated with the product.

Life-cycle costing focuses on minimizing locked-in costs, for example, by reducing the number of parts, promoting standardization of parts, and using equipment that can make more than one kind of product. The product life cycle is simply the time a product exists—from conception to abandonment. *Life-cycle costs* are all costs associated with the product for its entire life cycle. These costs include development (planning, design, and testing), manufacturing (conversion activities), and logistics support (advertising, distribution, warranty, and so on).

Can you achieve cost reduction through life-cycle costing?

Because total customer satisfaction has become a vital issue in the new business setting, whole-life cost has emerged as the central focus of life-cycle cost management. *Whole-life cost* is the life-cycle cost of a product plus after-purchase (or postpurchase) costs that consumers incur, including operation, support, maintenance, and disposal. Since the costs a purchaser incurs after buying a product can be a significant percentage of whole-life costs and, thus, an important consideration in the purchase decision, managing activities so that whole-life costs are reduced can provide an important competitive advantage.

NOTE

Cost reduction not cost control is the emphasis. Moreover, cost reduction is achieved by judicious analysis and management of activities.

Studies show that 90 percent or more of a product's costs are committed during the development stage. Thus, it makes sense to emphasize management of activities during this phase of a product's existence. Every dollar spent on premanufacturing activities is known to save $8 to $10 on manufacturing and postmanufacturing activities. The real opportunities for cost reduction occur before manufacturing begins. Managers need to invest more in premanufacturing assets and dedicate more resources to activities in the early phases of the product life cycle so that overall whole-life costs can be reduced.

What is the role of target costing?
How does it differ from cost-plus pricing?

Life-cycle and whole-life cost concepts are associated with target costing and target pricing. A firm may determine that market conditions require that a product sell at a given target price. Hence, target cost can be determined by subtracting the desired unit profit margin from the target price. The cost reduction objectives of life-cycle and whole-life cost management can therefore be determined using target costing.

Thus, *target costing* becomes a particularly useful tool for establishing cost reduction goals. Toyota, for example, calculates the lifetime target profit for a new car model by multiplying a target profit ratio times the target sales. It then calculates the estimated profit by subtracting the estimated costs from target sales. Usually, (at this point), target profit is greater than estimated profit. The cost reduction goal is defined by the difference between the target profit and the estimated profit. Toyota then searches for cost-reduction opportunities through better design of the new model. Toyota's management recognizes that more opportunities exist for cost reduction during product planning than in actual development and production.

The Japanese developed target costing to enhance their ability to compete in the global marketplace. This approach to product pricing differs significantly from the cost-based methods just described. Instead of first determining the cost

	Formula	Implications
Cost-plus pricing	Cost base + markup = selling price	• Cost is the base (given) • Markup is added (given) • The firm puts the product on the market and hopes the selling price is accepted
Pricing based on target costing	Target selling price – Desired profit = Target cost	• Markets determine prices (given) • Desired profit must be sustained for survival (given) • Target cost is the residual, the variable to be managed

Exhibit 8.3 COST-PLUS PRICING VERSUS TARGET COSTING

of a product or service and then adding a profit factor to arrive at its price, target costing reverses the procedure. Target costing is a pricing method that involves (1) identifying the price at which a product will be competitive in the marketplace, (2) defining the desired profit to be made on the product, and (3) computing the target cost for the product by subtracting the desired profit from the competitive market price. The formula

Target Price – Desired Profit = Target Cost

Target cost is then given to the engineers and product designers, who use it as the maximum cost to be incurred for the materials and other resources needed to design and manufacture the product. It is their responsibility to create the product at or below its target cost.

Exhibit 8.3 compares the cost-plus philosophy with the target costing philosophy.

EXAMPLE 8.20

A salesperson at Sunghi Products Company has reported that a customer is seeking price quotations for two electronic components: a special-purpose battery charger (Product X101) and a small transistorized machine computer (Product Y101). Competing for the customer's order are one French company and two Japanese companies. The current market price ranges for the two products are as follows:

Product X101	$310—$370 per unit
Product Y101	$720—$820 per unit

EXAMPLE 8.20 (continued)

The salesperson feels that if Sunghi could quote prices of $325 for Product X101 and $700 for Product Y101, the company would get the order and gain a significant share of the global market for those goods. Sunghi's usual profit markup is 25 percent of total unit cost. The company's design engineers and cost accountants put together the following specifications and costs for the new products:

Activity-based cost rates:

Materials-handling activity cost	$1.30 per dollar of raw materials and purchased parts
Production activity	$3.50 per machine hour
Product delivery activity	$24.00 per unit of X101
	$30.00 per unit of Y101

	Product X101	Product Y101
Projected unit demand	26,000	18,000
Per unit data:		
Raw materials cost	$30.00	$65.00
Purchased parts cost	$15.00	$45.00
Manufacturing labor		
Hours	2.6	4.8
Hourly labor rate	$12.00	$15.00
Assembly labor		
Hours	3.4	8.2
Hourly labor rate	$14.00	$16.00
Machine hours	12.8	28.4

The company wants to address the following three questions:

1. What is the target cost for each product?
2. What is the projected total unit cost of production and delivery?
3. Using the target costing approach, should the company produce the products?

1. Target cost for each product:

Product X101 = $325.00 ÷ 1.25 = $260.00*

Product Y101 = $700.00 ÷ 1.25 = $560.00

*Target Price – Desired Profit = Target Cost

$325.00 – 0.25X = X

$325.00 = 1.25X

$$X = \frac{\$325.00}{1.25} = \$260.00$$

EXAMPLE 8.20 *(continued)*

2. Projected total unit cost of production and delivery:

	Product X101	Product Y101
Raw materials cost	$ 30.00	$ 65.00
Purchased parts cost	15.00	45.00
Total cost of raw materials and parts	$ 45.00	$110.00
Manufacturing labor		
X101 (2.6 hours X $12.00)	31.20	
Y101 (4.8 hours × $15.00)		72.00
Assembly labor		
X101 (3.4 hours X $14.00)	47.60	
Y101 (8.2 hours X $16.00)		131.20
Activity-based costs		
Materials handling activity		
X101 ($45.00 x $1.30)	58.500	
Y101 ($110.00 x $1.30)		143.00
Production activity		
X101 (12.8 machine hours x $3.50)	44.80	
Y101 (28.4 machine hours X $3.50)		99.40
Product delivery activity		
X101	24.00	
Y101		30.00
Projected total unit cost	$251.10	$585.60

3. Production decision:

	Product X101	Product Y101
Target unit cost	$260.00	$560.00
Less: projected unit cost	251.10	585.60
Difference	$8.90	($25.60)

Product X101 can be produced below its target cost, so it should be produced. As currently designed, Product Y101 cannot be produced at or below its target cost; either it needs to be redesigned, or the company should drop plans to make it.

ACTIVITY-BASED COSTING

What is activity-based costing?

Many companies use a traditional cost system such as job-order costing or process costing, or some hybrid of the two. These traditional systems may provide distorted product cost information. In fact, companies selling multiple products are making critical decisions about product pricing, making bids, or product mix based on inaccurate cost data. In all likelihood, the problem is not with assigning the costs of direct labor or direct materials. These prime costs are traceable to individual products, and most conventional cost systems are designed to ensure that this tracing takes place.

However, the assignment of overhead costs to individual products is another matter. The traditional methods of assigning overhead costs to products, using a single predetermined overhead rate based on any single activity measure, can produce distorted product costs. Activity-based costing (ABC) attempts to get around this problem. An ABC system assigns costs to products based on the product's use of activities, not on product volume. This approach has proved to produce more accurate product costing results in an environment where there is diversity in product line and services coming out of the same shop. A recent survey by the Institute of Management Accounting shows that over 30 percent of the companies that responded are using ABC systems to replace their existing traditional cost systems.

How is overhead costing handled in a single-product situation?

The accuracy of overhead cost assignment becomes an issue only when multiple products are manufactured in a single facility. If only a single product is produced, all overhead costs are traceable to it. The overhead cost per unit is simply the total overhead for the year divided by the number of hours or units produced, which was discussed in detail in the previous chapters.

The cost calculation for a single-product setting is illustrated in Exhibit 8.4. There is no question that the cost of manufacturing the product illustrated in Exhibit 8.4 is $28 per unit. All manufacturing costs were incurred specifically to make this product. Thus, one way to ensure product-costing accuracy is to focus on producing one product. For this reason, some multiple-product firms choose to dedicate entire plants to the manufacture of a single product.

By focusing on only one or two products, small manufacturers are able to calculate the cost of manufacturing the high-volume products more accurately and price them more effectively.

Manufacturing Costs		Units Produced	Unit Cost
Direct materials	$ 800,000	50,000	$ 16.00
Direct labor	200,000	50,000	4.00
Factory overhead	400,000	50,000	8.00
Total	$1,400,000	50,000	$ 28.00

Exhibit 8.4 UNIT COST COMPUTATION: SINGLE PRODUCT

How is overhead costing handled in a multiple-product or -job situation?

In a multiple-product or -job situation, manufacturing overhead costs are caused jointly by all products or jobs. The problem becomes one of identifying the amount of overhead caused or consumed by each. This is accomplished by searching for *cost drivers*, or activity measures that cause costs to be incurred.

In a traditional setting, it is normally assumed that overhead consumption is highly correlated with the volume of production activity, measured in terms of direct labor hours, machine hours, or direct labor dollars. These volume-related cost drivers are used to assign overhead to products to develop *plantwide* or *departmental* rates.

EXAMPLE 8.21

To illustrate the limitation of this traditional approach and ABC, assume that Global Metals, Inc. has established the following overhead cost pools and cost drivers for their product:

Budgeted Overhead Cost Pool	Overhead Cost	Cost Driver	Predicted Level for Cost Driver	Predetermined Overhead Rate
Machine setups	$100,000	Number of setups	100	$1,000 per setup
Material handling	100,000	Weight of raw material	50,000 pounds	$2 per pound
Waste control	50,000	Weight of hazardous chemicals used	10,000 pounds	$5 per pound
Inspection	75,000	Number of inspections	1,000	$75 per inspection
Other overhead costs	$200,000	Machine hours	20,000	$10 per machine
	$525,000			

EXAMPLE 8.21 (continued)

Job No. 107 consists of 2,000 special purpose machine tools with the following requirements:

Machine setups	2 setups
Waste materials required	2,000 pounds
Inspections	10 inspections
Machine hours	500 machine hours

The overhead assigned to Job No. 107 is computed below.

Overhead Cost Pool	Predetermined Overhead Rate	Level of Cost Driver	Assigned Overhead Cost
Machine setups	$1,000 per setup	2 setups	$ 2,000
Material handling	$2 per pound	10,000 pounds	20,000
Waste control	$5 per pound	2,000 pounds	10,000
Inspection	$75 per inspection	10 inspections	750
Other overhead costs	$10 per machine hour	500 machine hours	5,000
Total			$37,750

The total overhead cost assigned to Job No. 107 is $37,750, or $18.88 per tool ($37,750/2,000).

Compare this with the overhead cost that is assigned to the job if the firm uses a single predetermined overhead rate based on machine hours:

$$\frac{\text{Total budgeted overhead cost}}{\text{Total predicted machine hours}} = \frac{\$525,000}{20,000} = \$26.25 \text{ per machine hour}$$

> ### EXAMPLE 8.21 (continued)
>
> Under this approach, the total overhead cost assigned to Job No. 107 is $13,125 ($26.25 per machine hour × 500 machine hours). This is only $6.56 per tool ($13,125/2,000), which is about one-third of the overhead cost per tool computed when multiple-cost drivers are used.
>
> The reason for this wide discrepancy is that these special-purpose tools require a relatively large number of machine setups, a sizable amount of waste materials, and several inspections. Thus, they are relatively costly in terms of driving overhead costs. Use of a single predetermined overhead rate obscures that fact.
>
> Inaccurately calculating the overhead cost per unit to the extent illustrated above can have serious adverse consequences for the firm. For example, it can lead to poor decisions about pricing, product mix, or contract bidding.
>
> NOTE
>
> The cost accountant needs to weigh carefully such considerations in designing a product-costing system. A costing system using multiple-cost drivers is more costly to implement and use, but it may save millions through improved decisions.

How do I choose which cost drivers to use?

At least two major factors should be considered in selecting cost drivers: (1) the cost of measurement and (2) the degree of correlation between the cost driver and the actual consumption of overhead.

The Cost of Measurement

In an ABC system, a large number of cost drivers can be selected and used. It is preferable, however, to select cost drivers that use information that is readily available. Information that is not available in the existing system must be produced, which will increase the cost of the firm's information system. A homogeneous cost pool could offer a number of possible cost drivers. For this situation, any cost driver that can be used with existing information should be chosen. This choice minimizes the costs of measurement.

Indirect Measures and the Degree of Correlation

The existing information structure can be exploited in another way to minimize the costs of obtaining cost-driver quantities. It is sometimes possible to replace a cost driver that directly measures the consumption of an activity with a cost driver that indirectly measures that consumption. For example, inspection hours could be replaced by the actual

Manufacturing

Number of setups	Square footage
Weight of material	Number of vendors
Number of units reworked	Asset value
Number of orders placed	Number of labor transactions
Number of orders received	Number of units scrapped
Number of inspections	Number of parts
Number of material handling operations	Replacement cost
	Machine hours
Number of orders shipped	Direct labor hours
Design time	

Nonmanufacturing:
Number of hospital beds occupied
Number of takeoffs and landings for an airline
Number of rooms occupied in a hotel

Exhibit 8.5   COST DRIVERS

	Traditional	ABC
Cost pools:	One or a limited number	Many—to reflect different activities
Applied rate:	Volume-based, financial	Activity-based, nonfinancial
Suited for:	Labor-intensive, low-overhead companies	Capital-intensive, product-diverse, high-overhead companies
Benefits:	Simple, inexpensive	Accurate product costing, possible elimination of nonvalue-added activities

Exhibit 8.6   COST SYSTEM COMPARISON

number of inspections associated with each product; this number is more likely to be known. This replacement works, of course, only if hours used per inspection are reasonably stable for each product. *The least-squares method (regression analysis),* which will be covered in Chapter 9, can be utilized to determine the degree of correlation.

A list of potential cost drivers is given in Exhibit 8.5.

The fundamental differences in the traditional and ABC cost systems are summarized in Exhibit 8.6

JUST-IN-TIME (JIT) AND TOTAL QUALITY MANAGEMENT (TQM)

Inventory control problems occur in almost every type of organization. They exist whenever products are held to meet some expected future demand. In most industries, cost of inventory represents the largest liquid asset under the control of management. Therefore, it is very important to develop a production- and inventory-planning system that will minimize both purchasing and carrying costs.

In recent years, the Japanese have demonstrated the ability to manage their production systems effectively. Much of their success has been attributed to what is known as the *Just-In-Time (JIT)* approach to production and inventory control, which has generated a great deal of interest among practitioners. The "Kanban" system—as they call it—has been a focal point of interest, with its dramatic impact on the inventory performance and productivity of the Japanese auto industry.

What is Just-In-Time (JIT)?

JIT is a demand-pull system. Demand for customer output (not plans for using input resources) triggers production. Production activities are "pulled," not "pushed," into action. JIT production, in its purest sense, is buying and producing in very small quantities just in time for use. As a philosophy, JIT targets inventory as an evil presence that obscures problems that should be solved and maintains that by contributing significantly to costs, large inventories keep a company from being as competitive or profitable as it otherwise might be. Practically speaking, JIT has as its principal goal the elimination of waste, and the principal measure of success is how much or how little inventory there is. Virtually anything that achieves this end can be considered a JIT innovation.

Furthermore, the little inventory that exists in a JIT system must be of good quality. This requirement has led to JIT purchasing practices uniquely able to deliver high-quality materials. This ties in very closely with the principle of *Total Quality Management (TQM)*.

JIT systems integrate five functions of the production process—sourcing, storage, transportation, operations, and quality control—into one controlled manufacturing process. In manufacturing, JIT means that a company produces only the quantity needed for delivery to dealers or customers. In purchasing, it means suppliers deliver subassemblies just in time to be assembled into finished goods. In delivery, it requires selecting a transportation mode that will deliver purchased components and materials in small-lot sizes at the loading dock of the manufacturing facilities just in time to support the manufacturing process.

How does JIT compare with traditional manufacturing?

JIT manufacturing is a demand-pull, rather than the traditional "push" approach. The philosophy underlying JIT manufacturing is to produce a product when it is needed and only in the quantities demanded by customers. Demand pulls products through the manufacturing process. Each operation produces only what is necessary to satisfy the demand of the succeeding operation. No production takes place until a signal from a succeeding process indicates a need to produce. Parts and materials arrive just in time to be used in production.

What is the main objective of JIT?

The primary goal of JIT is to reduce inventories to insignificant or zero levels. In traditional manufacturing, inventories result whenever production exceeds demand. Inventories are needed as a buffer when production does not meet expected demand.

What are manufacturing cells?

In traditional manufacturing, products are moved from one group of identical machines to another. Typically, machines with identical functions are located together in an area referred to as a department or process. Workers who specialize in the operation of a specific machine are located in each department. JIT replaces this traditional pattern with a pattern of manufacturing cells or work centers. Robots supplement people to do many routine operations.

Manufacturing cells contain machines that are grouped in families, usually in a semicircle. The machines are arranged so that they can be used to perform a variety of operations in sequence. Each cell is set up to produce a particular product or product family. Products move from one machine to another from start to finish. Workers are assigned to cells and are trained to operate all machines within the cell. Thus, labor in a JIT environment is multifunction labor, not specialized labor. Each manufacturing cell is basically a minifactory or a factory within a factory.

How does JIT result in better cost management?

Cost management differs from cost accounting in that it refers to the management of cost, whether or not the cost has direct impact on inventory or the financial statements. The JIT philosophy simplifies the cost accounting procedure and helps managers manage and control their costs.

JIT recognizes that with simplification comes better management, better quality, better service, and better cost control. Traditional cost accounting systems have a tendency to be very complex, with many transactions and much reporting of data. Simplification of this process will transform a cost "accounting" system into a cost "management" system that can be used to support management's needs for better decisions about product design, pricing, marketing, and mix, and to encourage continual operating improvements.

What is total quality management (TQM)?

JIT goes hand in hand with a stronger emphasis on quality control. A defective part brings production to a grinding halt. Poor quality simply cannot be tolerated in a stockless manufacturing environment. In other words, JIT cannot be implemented without a commitment to *total quality management (TQM)*. TQM is essentially an endless quest for perfect quality. It is a *zero-defects* approach, which views the optimal level of quality costs as the level where zero defects are produced. This approach to quality is opposed to the traditional belief, called *acceptable quality level (AQL)*, which allows a predetermined level of defective units to be produced and sold. AQL is the level where the number of defects minimizes total quality costs.

Quality costs are classified into three broad categories: prevention, appraisal, and failure costs. *Prevention costs* are those incurred to prevent defects. Amounts spent on quality training programs, researching customer needs, quality circles, and improved production equipment are considered prevention costs. Expenditures made for prevention will minimize the costs that will be incurred for appraisal and failure. *Appraisal costs* are costs incurred for monitoring or inspection; these costs compensate for mistakes not eliminated through prevention. *Failure costs* may be internal (such as scrap and rework costs and reinspection) or external (such as product returns due to quality problems, warranty costs, lost sales due to poor product performance, and complaint department costs).

Quality cost reports can be used to point out the strengths and weaknesses of a quality system. Improvement teams can use them to describe the monetary benefits and ramifications of proposed changes. Return-on-investment (ROI) models and other financial analyses can be constructed directly from quality cost data to justify proposals to management. In practice, quality costs can define activities of quality programs and quality improvement efforts in a language that management can understand and act on—dollars.

The negative effect on profits, resulting from product or service of less than acceptable quality or from ineffective quality management, is almost always dynamic. Once started, it continues to mushroom until ultimately the company finds itself in serious financial difficulties due to the two-pronged impact of an unheeded increase in quality costs coupled with a declining performance image. Management that clearly understands this understands the economics of quality.

TAGUCHI METHOD OF QUALITY CONTROL

The Taguchi method of quality control is a method of controlling quality, developed by Genich Taguchi, a past winner of the Deming Award, that emphasizes robust quality design and the *quality loss function* (QLF). Taguchi claims that quality is largely determined at the design level. In addition to quality control in production, he emphasizes quality control in four other functions: (1) product planning, (2) product design, (3) process design, and (4) production service after purchase. In addition, Taguchi's QLF quantitatively measures the success or failure of quality control. The traditional view is that any product that measures within the upper and lower specification limits is "good" and a product outside the limits is "bad." In contrast, the QLF presumes that *any* deviation from the target specification is important since it means economic losses for the customer. Furthermore, the economic losses increase quadratically as the actual value deviates from the target value. The QLF can be described by the following equation: where

$$L(y) = k(y - T)^2$$

where

L = Quality loss

y = Actual value of quality characteristic

k = A proportionality constant dependent upon the firm's external failure cost structure.

T = Target value of quality characteristic

EXAMPLE 8.22

Davidson Company has decided to estimate its quality loss using the Taguchi loss function. After some study, it was determined that k = $400 and T = 10 inches in diameter. Exhibit 8.7 illustrates the computations of the quality loss for a sample of 4 units.

Note that the average loss per unit is $10. The total expected loss for, say, 1,000 units would be $10,000 (10 × 1,000 units).

Unit	Actual Diameter (y)	y − T	$(y - T)^2$	$k(y - T)^2$
1	9.9	−0.10	0.010	$4.00
2	10.1	0.10	0.010	4.00
3	10.2	0.20	0.040	16.00
4	9.8	−0.20	0.040	16.00
Total			0.100	$40.00
Average			0.025	$10.00

Exhibit 8.7 QUALITY-LOSS COMPUTATION

Is cost accounting simpler under JIT?

The cost accounting system of a company adopting JIT will be quite simple compared to job-order or processing costing. Under JIT, raw materials and workin-process (WIP) accounts are typically combined into one account called resources in process (RIP) or raw and in-process. Under JIT, the materials arrive at the receiving area and are whisked immediately to the factory area. The journal entries that accompany JIT costing are remarkably simple, as follows:

Raw and in-process	45,000	
(RIP) inventory		
Accounts payable or cash		45,000
To record purchases.		
Finished goods	40,000	
RIP inventory		40,000

To record raw materials in completed units.

As can be seen, there are no Stores Control and WIP accounts under JIT.

In summary, JIT costing can be characterized as follows:

1. There are fewer inventory accounts.
2. There are no work orders. Thus, there is no need for detailed tracking of actual raw materials.
3. With JIT, activities can be eliminated on the premise that they do not add value. Prime target for elimination are storage areas for WIP inventory and material-handling facilities.
4. Direct labor costs and factory overhead costs are not tracked to specific orders. Direct labor is now regarded as just another part of factory overhead. Virtually all of the factory overhead incurred each month, now including direct labor, flows through to cost of goods sold in the same month. Tracking overhead through WIP and finished goods inventory provides no useful information. Therefore, it makes sense to treat manufacturing overhead as an expense charged directly to cost of goods sold.

The major differences between JIT manufacturing and traditional manufacturing are summarized in Exhibit 8.8.

TIME VALUE FUNDAMENTALS

The time value of money is a critical consideration in investment decisions. EXAMPLES: Compound interest calculations are needed to appraise future sums of money resulting from an investment. Discounting, or the calculation of

JIT	Traditional
1. Pull system	1. Push system
2. Insignificant or zero inventories	2. Significant inventories
3. Manufacturing cells	3. "Process" structure
4. Multifunction labor	4. Specialized labor
5. Total quality management (TQM)	5. Acceptable quality level (AQL)
6. Decentralized services	6. Centralized services
7. Simple cost accounting	7. Complex cost accounting

Exhibit 8.8 COMPARISON OF JIT AND TRADITIONAL MANUFACTURING

present values, which is inversely related to compounding, is used to evaluate future cash flow streams associated with the investment in fixed assets, such as machinery and equipment.

What is money worth in the future?

A dollar in hand today is worth more than a dollar to be received tomorrow because of the interest it could earn from putting it into a bank account or an investment. Compounding interest means that interest earns interest. For the discussion of this and the subsequent time value concepts, let us define:

F_n = future value = the amount of money at the end of year n

P = principal

i = annual interest rate

n = number of years

To generalize, the future value of an investment if compounded annually at a rate of i for n years is:

$$F_n = P(1+i)^n = P \cdot T_1(i,n)$$

where $T_1(i,n)$ is the future value interest factor for $1 (found in Exhibit 8.9).

EXAMPLE 8.23

Your client placed $1,000 in a savings account earning 8 percent interest compounded annually.

How much money will the client have in his or her account at the end of four years?

Substituting P = $1,000, i = 0.08, and n = 4 into the formula and referring to Exhibit 8.9 gives:

$$F_4 = \$1,000(1 + 0.08)^4 = \$1,000$$
$$\text{(Exhibit 8.9 value)}$$

$$= \$1,000(1.361) = \$1,361.00$$

Periods	4%	6%	8%	10%	12%	14%	20%
1	1.040	1.060	1.080	1.100	1.120	1.140	1.200
2	1.082	1.124	1.166	1.210	1.254	1.300	1.440
3	1.125	1.191	1.260	1.331	1.405	1.482	1.728
4	1.170	1.263	1.361	1.464	1.574	1.689	2.074
5	1.217	1.338	1.469	1.611	1.762	1.925	2.488
6	1.265	1.419	1.587	1.772	1.974	2.195	2.986
7	1.316	1.504	1.714	1.949	2.211	2.502	3.583
8	1.369	1.594	1.851	2.144	2.476	2.853	4.300
9	1.423	1.690	1.999	2.359	2.773	3.252	5.160
10	1.480	1.791	2.159	2.594	3.106	3.707	6.192
11	1.540	1.898	2.332	2.853	3.479	4.226	7.430
12	1.601	2.012	2.518	3.139	3.896	4.818	8.916
13	1.665	2.133	2.720	3.452	4.364	5.492	10.699
14	1.732	2.261	2.937	3.798	4.887	6.261	12.839
15	1.801	2.397	3.172	4.177	5.474	7.138	15.407
20	2.191	3.207	4.661	6.728	9.646	13.743	38.338
30	3.243	5.744	10.063	17.450	29.960	50.950	237.380
40	4.801	10.286	21.725	45.260	93.051	188.880	1469.800

Exhibit 8.9 FUTURE VALUE OF $1

What is the future value of an annuity?

An annuity is defined as a series of equal payments (or receipts) for a specified number of periods. The future value of an annuity is a compound annuity that involves depositing or investing an equal sum of money at the end of each year for a certain number of years and allowing it to grow.

It is computed as follows:

$$F = A \; T_2(i,n)$$

where A = the amount of an annuity and $T_2(i,n)$ = the future value interest factor for an n-year annuity compounded at i percent and can be found in Exhibit 8.10.

EXAMPLE 8.24

Your client wishes to determine the sum of money he or she will have in a savings account at the end of six years by depositing $1,000 at the end of each year for the next six years. The annual interest rate is 8 percent. The amount is:

$1,000 (Exhibit 8.10 value) = $1,000(7.336)
= $7,336.00

What is present value?

Present value is the present worth of future sums of money. The process of calculating present values, or *discounting*, is actually the opposite of finding the compounded future value.

Recall from the future value formula:

$$F_n = P(1 + i)^n$$

Therefore,

$$P = F_n/(1 + i)^n = F_n \; T_3(i,n)$$

where $T_3(i,n)$ represents the present value interest factor for $1 (given in Exhibit 8.11).

Periods	4%	6%	8%	10%	12%	14%	20%
1	1.000	1.000	1.000	1.000	1.000	1.000	1.000
2	2.040	2.060	2.080	2.100	2.120	2.140	2.220
3	3.122	3.184	3.246	3.310	3.374	3.440	3.640
4	4.247	4.375	4.506	4.641	4.779	4.921	5.368
5	5.416	5.637	5.867	6.105	6.353	6.610	7.442
6	6.633	6.975	7.336	7.716	8.115	8.536	9.930
7	7.898	8.394	8.923	9.487	10.089	10.730	12.916
8	9.214	9.898	10.637	11.436	12.300	13.233	16.499
9	10.583	11.491	12.488	13.580	14.776	16.085	20.799
10	12.006	13.181	14.487	15.938	17.549	19.337	25.959
11	13.486	14.972	16.646	18.531	20.655	23.045	32.150
12	15.026	16.870	18.977	21.395	24.133	27.271	39.580
13	16.627	18.882	21.495	24.523	28.029	32.089	48.497
14	18.292	21.015	24.215	27.976	32.393	37.581	59.196
15	20.024	23.276	27.152	31.773	37.280	43.842	72.035
20	29.778	36.778	45.762	57.276	75.052	91.025	186.690
30	56.085	79.058	113.283	164.496	241.330	356.790	1181.900
40	95.026	154.762	259.057	442.597	767.090	1342.000	7343.900

Exhibit 8.10 FUTURE VALUE OF AN ANNUITY OF $1

Periods	4%	5%	6%	8%	10%	12%	14%	16%	18%	20%	22%	24%	26%	28%	30%	40%
1	0.962	0.952	0.943	0.926	0.909	0.893	0.877	0.862	0.847	0.833	0.820	0.806	0.794	0.781	0.769	0.714
2	0.925	0.907	0.890	0.857	0.826	0.797	0.769	0.743	0.718	0.694	0.672	0.650	0.630	0.610	0.592	0.510
3	0.889	0.864	0.840	0.794	0.751	0.712	0.675	0.641	0.609	0.579	0.551	0.524	0.500	0.477	0.455	0.364
4	0.855	0.823	0.792	0.735	0.683	0.636	0.592	0.552	0.516	0.482	0.451	0.423	0.397	0.373	0.350	0.260
5	0.822	0.784	0.747	0.681	0.621	0.567	0.519	0.476	0.437	0.402	0.370	0.341	0.315	0.291	0.269	0.186
6	0.790	0.746	0.705	0.630	0.564	0.507	0.456	0.410	0.370	0.335	0.303	0.275	0.250	0.227	0.207	0.133
7	0.760	0.711	0.665	0.583	0.513	0.452	0.400	0.354	0.314	0.279	0.249	0.222	0.198	0.178	0.159	0.095
8	0.731	0.677	0.627	0.540	0.467	0.404	0.351	0.305	0.266	0.233	0.204	0.179	0.157	0.139	0.123	0.068
9	0.703	0.645	0.592	0.500	0.424	0.361	0.308	0.263	0.225	0.194	0.167	0.144	0.125	0.108	0.094	0.048
10	0.676	0.614	0.558	0.463	0.386	0.322	0.270	0.227	0.191	0.162	0.137	0.116	0.099	0.085	0.073	0.035
11	0.650	0.585	0.527	0.429	0.350	0.287	0.237	0.195	0.162	0.135	0.112	0.094	0.079	0.066	0.056	0.025
12	0.625	0.557	0.497	0.397	0.319	0.257	0.208	0.168	0.137	0.112	0.092	0.076	0.062	0.052	0.043	0.018
13	0.601	0.530	0.469	0.368	0.290	0.229	0.182	0.145	0.116	0.093	0.075	0.061	0.050	0.040	0.033	0.013
14	0.577	0.505	0.442	0.340	0.263	0.205	0.160	0.125	0.099	0.078	0.062	0.049	0.039	0.032	0.025	0.009
15	0.555	0.481	0.417	0.315	0.239	0.183	0.140	0.108	0.084	0.065	0.051	0.040	0.031	0.025	0.020	0.006

Periods	4%	5%	6%	8%	10%	12%	14%	16%	18%	20%	22%	24%	26%	28%	30%	40%
16	0.534	0.458	0.394	0.292	0.218	0.163	0.123	0.093	0.071	0.054	0.042	0.032	0.025	0.019	0.015	0.005
17	0.513	0.436	0.371	0.270	0.198	0.146	0.108	0.080	0.060	0.045	0.034	0.026	0.020	0.015	0.012	0.003
18	0.494	0.416	0.350	0.250	0.180	0.130	0.095	0.069	0.051	0.038	0.028	0.021	0.016	0.012	0.009	0.002
19	0.475	0.396	0.331	0.232	0.164	0.116	0.083	0.060	0.043	0.031	0.023	0.017	0.012	0.009	0.007	0.002
20	0.456	0.377	0.312	0.215	0.149	0.104	0.073	0.051	0.037	0.026	0.019	0.014	0.010	0.007	0.005	0.001
21	0.439	0.359	0.294	0.199	0.135	0.093	0.064	0.044	0.031	0.022	0.015	0.011	0.008	0.006	0.004	0.001
22	0.422	0.342	0.278	0.184	0.123	0.083	0.056	0.038	0.026	0.018	0.013	0.009	0.006	0.004	0.003	0.001
23	0.406	0.326	0.262	0.170	0.112	0.074	0.049	0.033	0.022	0.015	0.010	0.007	0.005	0.003	0.002	
24	0.390	0.310	0.247	0.158	0.102	0.066	0.043	0.028	0.019	0.013	0.008	0.006	0.004	0.003	0.002	
25	0.375	0.295	0.233	0.146	0.092	0.059	0.038	0.024	0.016	0.010	0.007	0.005	0.003	0.002	0.001	
26	0.361	0.281	0.220	0.135	0.084	0.053	0.033	0.021	0.014	0.009	0.006	0.004	0.002	0.002	0.001	
27	0.347	0.268	0.207	0.125	0.076	0.047	0.029	0.018	0.011	0.007	0.005	0.003	0.002	0.001	0.001	
28	0.333	0.255	0.196	0.116	0.069	0.042	0.026	0.016	0.010	0.006	0.004	0.002	0.002	0.001	0.001	
29	0.321	0.243	0.185	0.107	0.063	0.037	0.022	0.014	0.008	0.005	0.003	0.002	0.001	0.001	0.001	
30	0.308	0.231	0.174	0.099	0.057	0.033	0.020	0.012	0.007	0.004	0.003	0.002	0.001	0.001		
40	0.208	0.142	0.097	0.046	0.022	0.011	0.005	0.003	0.001	0.001						

Exhibit 8.11 PRESENT VALUE OF $1

EXAMPLE 8.25

A client has been given an opportunity to receive $20,000 six years from now. If the client can earn 10 percent on the investment, what is the most he or she should pay for this opportunity?

We compute the present worth of $20,000 he or she will receive six years from now at a 10 percent rate of discount. Use Exhibit 8.11 value as follows:

> $20,000 (Exhibit 8.11 value) = $20,000(0.564)
> = $11,280.00.

This means that the client should be indifferent to the choice between receiving $11,280 now or $20,000 six years from now since the amounts are time equivalent. In other words, the client could invest $11,280 today at 10 percent and have $20,000 in six years.

What is the present value of an annuity?

Interest received from bonds, pension funds, and insurance obligations all involve annuities. To compare these financial instruments, one would like to know the present value of each of these annuities. The way to find the present value of an annuity is:

$$P = A \, T_4(i,n)$$

where A = the amount of an annuity, and $T_4(i,n)$ = the value for the present value interest factor for a $1 annuity at i percent for n years (found in Exhibit 8.12).

EXAMPLE 8.26

A client is to receive an annuity of $1,000 each year for the next three years. You are asked to compute the present value of the annuity. Use Exhibit 8.12 for this purpose as follows:

> $1,000 (Exhibit 8.12 value) = $1,000(2.673)
> = $2,673.00

CAPITAL BUDGETING

What is capital budgeting?

Capital budgeting is the process of making long-term planning decisions for investments. There are typically two types of investment decisions:

1. *Selection decisions* in terms of obtaining new facilities or expanding existing facilities.

Periods	4%	5%	6%	8%	10%	12%	14%	16%	18%	20%	22%	24%	26%	28%	30%	40%
1	0.962	0.952	0.943	0.926	0.909	0.893	0.877	0.862	0.847	0.833	0.820	0.806	0.794	0.781	0.769	0.714
2	1.886	1.859	1.833	1.783	1.736	1.690	1.647	1.605	1.566	1.528	1.492	1.457	1.424	1.392	1.361	1.224
3	2.775	2.723	2.673	2.577	2.487	2.402	2.322	2.246	2.174	2.106	2.042	1.981	1.868	1.816	1.816	1.589
4	3.630	3.546	3.465	3.312	3.170	3.037	2.914	2.798	2.690	2.589	2.494	2.404	2.320	2.241	2.166	1.879
5	4.452	4.330	4.212	3.993	3.791	3.605	3.433	3.274	3.127	2.991	2.864	2.745	2.635	2.532	2.436	2.035
6	5.242	5.076	4.917	4.623	4.355	4.111	3.889	3.685	3.498	3.326	3.167	3.020	2.885	2.759	2.643	2.168
7	6.002	5.786	5.582	5.206	4.868	4.564	4.288	4.039	3.812	3.605	3.416	3.242	3.083	2.937	2.802	2.263
8	6.733	6.463	6.210	5.747	5.335	4.968	4.639	4.344	4.078	3.837	3.619	3.421	3.241	3.076	2.925	2.331
9	7.435	7.108	6.802	6.247	5.759	5.328	4.946	4.607	4.303	4.031	3.786	3.566	3.366	3.184	3.019	2.379
10	8.111	7.722	7.360	6.710	6.145	5.650	5.216	4.833	4.494	4.192	3.923	3.682	3.465	3.269	3.092	2.414
11	8.760	8.306	7.887	7.139	6.495	5.988	5.453	5.029	4.656	4.327	4.035	3.776	3.544	3.335	3.147	2.438
12	9.385	8.863	8.384	7.536	6.814	6.194	5.660	5.197	4.793	4.439	4.127	3.851	3.606	3.387	3.190	2.456
13	9.986	9.394	8.853	7.904	7.103	6.424	5.842	5.342	4.910	4.533	4.203	3.912	3.656	3.427	3.223	2.468
14	10.563	9.899	9.295	8.244	7.367	6.628	6.002	5.468	5.008	4.611	4.265	3.962	3.695	3.459	3.249	2.477
15	11.118	10.380	9.712	8.559	7.606	6.811	6.142	5.575	5.092	4.675	4.315	4.001	3.726	3.483	3.268	2.484

Exhibit 8.12 PRESENT VALUE OF AN ANNUITY OF $1

Periods	4%	5%	6%	8%	10%	12%	14%	16%	18%	20%	22%	24%	26%	28%	30%	40%
16	11.652	10.838	10.106	8.851	7.824	6.974	6.265	5.669	5.162	4.730	4.357	4.033	3.751	3.503	3.283	2.489
17	12.166	11.274	10.477	9.122	8.022	7.120	6.373	5.749	5.222	4.775	4.391	4.059	3.771	3.518	3.295	2.492
18	12.659	11.690	10.828	9.372	8.201	7.250	6.467	5.818	5.273	4.812	4.419	4.080	3.786	3.529	3.304	2.494
19	13.134	12.085	11.158	9.604	8.365	7.366	6.550	5.877	5.316	4.844	4.442	4.097	3.799	3.539	3.311	2.496
20	13.590	12.462	11.470	9.818	8.514	7.469	6.623	5.929	5.353	4.870	4.460	4.110	3.808	3.546	3.316	2.497
21	14.029	12.821	11.764	10.017	8.649	7.562	6.687	5.973	5.384	4.891	4.476	4.121	3.816	3.551	3.320	2.498
22	14.451	13.163	12.042	10.201	8.772	7.645	6.743	6.011	5.410	4.909	4.488	4.130	3.822	3.556	3.323	2.498
23	14.857	13.489	12.303	10.371	8.883	7.718	6.792	6.044	5.432	4.925	4.499	4.137	3.827	3.559	3.325	2.499
24	15.247	13.799	12.550	10.529	8.985	7.784	6.835	6.073	5.451	4.937	4.507	4.143	3.831	3.562	3.327	2.499
25	15.622	14.094	12.783	10.675	9.077	7.843	6.873	6.097	5.467	4.948	4.514	4.147	3.834	3.564	3.329	2.499
26	15.983	14.375	13.003	10.810	9.161	7.896	6.906	6.118	5.480	4.956	4.520	4.151	3.837	3.566	3.330	2.500
27	16.330	14.643	13.211	10.935	9.237	7.943	6.935	6.136	5.492	4.964	4.525	4.154	3.839	3.567	3.331	2.500
28	16.663	14.898	13.406	11.051	9.307	7.984	6.961	6.152	5.502	4.970	4.528	4.157	3.840	3.568	3.331	2.500
29	16.984	15.141	13.591	11.158	9.370	8.022	6.983	6.166	5.510	4.975	4.531	4.159	3.841	3.569	3.332	2.500
30	17.292	15.373	13.765	11.258	9.427	8.055	7.003	6.177	5.517	4.979	4.534	4.160	3.842	3.569	3.332	2.500
40	19.793	17.159	15.046	11.925	9.779	8.244	7.105	6.234	5.548	4.997	4.544	4.166	3.846	3.571	3.333	2.500

Exhibit 8.12 PRESENT VALUE OF AN ANNUITY OF $1 (continued)

EXAMPLES:

- Investments in long-term assets such as property, plant, and equipment
- Resource commitments in the form of new product development, market research, refunding of long-term debt, introduction of a computer, and so on.

2. Replacement decisions in terms of replacing existing facilities with new facilities.

EXAMPLES:

- Replacing a manual bookkeeping system with a computerized system
- Replacing an inefficient lathe with one that is numerically controlled

What are the popular selection techniques?

There are several methods of evaluating investment projects:

o Payback period
o Accounting rate of return (ARR) (also called *simple rate of return*)
o Net present value (NPV)
o Internal rate of return (IRR) (also called *time adjusted rate of return*)
o Profitability index (also called the *excess present value index*)

NOTE

The NPV method and the IRR method are called *discounted cash flow* (DCF) methods since they both recognize the time value of money and thus discount future cash flows. Each of the methods presented above is discussed below.

Payback Period

How do I determine the payback period?

Payback period measures the length of time required to recover the amount of initial investment. The payback period is determined by dividing the amount of initial investment by the cash inflow through increased revenues or cost savings.

EXAMPLE 8.27

Assume:

Cost of investment	$18,000
Annual cash savings	$ 3,000

Then, the payback period is:

$$\frac{\$18,000}{\$3,000} = 6 \text{ years}$$

When cash inflows are not even, the payback period is determined by trial and error. When two or more projects are considered, the rule for making a selection decision is as follows:

REQUIREMENT

Choose the project with the shorter payback period. The rationale is: The shorter the payback period, the less risky the project, and the greater the liquidity.

EXAMPLE 8.28

Consider two projects whose cash inflows are not even. Assume each project costs $1,000.

Year	A	B
1	100	500
2	200	400
3	300	300
4	400	100
5	500	—
6	600	—

Based on trial and error, the payback period of project A is four years ($100 + 200 + 300 + 400 = $1,000 in four years). The payback period of project B is

$$2 \text{ years} + \frac{\$100}{\$300} = 2 \ 1/3 \text{ years}$$

Therefore, according to this method, choose project B over project A.

What are the pros and cons of the payback period method?

ADVANTAGES

- o It is simple to compute and easy to understand.
- o It handles investment risk effectively.

DISADVANTAGES

- o It does not recognize the time value of money.
- o It ignores the impact of cash inflows after the payback period. It is essentially cash flows after the payback period that determine profitability of an investment.

How do I not account for the time value of money?

To correct for the deficiency of not taking into account the time value of money, the *discounted* payback method may be used. In this case:

- o Each year's cash inflows are expressed in present value terms.
- o Each year's present value is added to determine how long it takes to recoup the initial investment.

Accounting (Simple) Rate of Return

What is the accounting rate of return?

Accounting rate of return (ARR) measures profitability from the conventional accounting standpoint by relating the required investment to the future annual net income. Sometimes, the former is the average investment.

EXAMPLE 8.29

Consider the investment:

Initial investment	$6,500
Estimated life	20 years
Cash inflows per year	$1,000
Depreciation by straight-line	$325

$$\text{Then, ARR} = \frac{\$1,000 - \$325}{\$6,500} = 10.4\%$$

Using the *average* investment which is usually assumed to be one-half of the original investment, the resulting rate of return will be doubled, as shown below.

$$\text{ARR} = \frac{\$1,000 - \$325}{1/2\ (\$6,500)} = \frac{\$675}{\$3,250} = 20.8\%$$

The justification for using the average investment is that each year the investment amount is decreased by $325 through depreciation. Therefore, the average is computed as one-half of the original cost.

RECOMMENDATION

Under the ARR method, choose the project with the higher rate of return.

What are benefits and drawbacks of the ARR method?

ADVANTAGES

- The method is easily understandable, simple to compute, and recognizes the profitability factor.

DISADVANTAGES

- It fails to recognize the time value of money.
- It uses accounting data instead of cash flow data.

Net Present Value

What is net present value?

Net present value (NPV) is the excess of the present value (PV) of cash inflows generated by the project over the amount of the initial investment (I). Simply, NPV = PV – I. The present value of future cash flows is computed using the so-called cost of capital (or minimum required rate of return) as the discount rate.

RECOMMENDATION
If NPV is positive, accept the project. Otherwise, reject.

EXAMPLE 8.30

Initial investment	$12,950	
Estimated life	10 years	
Annual cash inflows	$ 3,000	
Cost of capital (minimum required rate of return)	12%	

Present value of cash inflows (PV):
$3,000 × PV of annuity of $1 for 10 years
and 12% $3,000 (Exhibit 8.8 value) = $3,000
(5.65) = $16,950
Initial investment (I) $12,950
Net present value (NPV = PV – I) $ 4,000

Since the investment's NPV is positive, the investment should be accepted.

What are the pros and cons of the NPV method?

ADVANTAGES

- It recognizes the time value of money.
- It is easy to compute whether the cash flows form an annuity or vary from period to period.

DISADVANTAGE

- It requires detailed long-term forecasts of incremental cash flow data.

Internal Rate of Return (or Time Adjusted Rate of Return)

What is internal rate of return?

Internal rate of return (IRR) is defined as the rate of interest that equates I with the PV of future cash inflows. In other words, at IRR, I = PV, or NPV = 0.

RECOMMENDATION
Accept if IRR exceeds the cost of capital; otherwise, reject.

EXAMPLE 8.31

Assume the same data given in Example 8.30. We will set up the following equality (I = PV):

$12,950 = $3,000 × PV

PV = $12,950/$3,000 = 4.317, which stands some where between 18 percent and 20 percent in the 10-year line of Exhibit 8.8. Using interpolation, we derive the exact rate.

PV Factor (Exhibit 8.8 value)

18%	4.494	4.494
IRR		4.317
20%	4.192	
Difference	0.302	0.177

$$\text{Therefore, IRR} = 18\% + \frac{0.177}{0.302}(20\% - 18\%)$$
$$= 18\% + 0.586\,(2\%)$$
$$= 18\% + 1.17\% = 19.17\%$$

Since the investment's IRR is greater than the cost of capital (12%), the investment should be accepted.

What are the benefits and drawbacks of the IRR method?

ADVANTAGE

- o It considers the time value of money and is therefore more exact and realistic than ARR.

DISADVANTAGES

- o It is difficult to compute, especially when the cash inflows are not even.

○ It fails to recognize the varying sizes of investments in competing projects and their respective dollar profitabilities.

How is IRR computed by trial and error?

The trial-and-error method for computing IRR when cash inflows are different each year is summarized step by step, as follows:

Step 1. Compute NPV at cost of capital, denoted here as r_1.

Step 2. See if NPV is positive or negative.

Step 3. If NPV is positive, then pick another rate (r_2) much higher than r_1. If NPV is negative, then pick another rate (r_2) much smaller than r_1. The true IRR at which NPV = 0 must be somewhere in between these two rates.

Step 4. Compute NPV using r_2.

Step 5. Use interpolation for the exact rate.

EXAMPLE 8.32

Consider the following investment whose cash flows are different from year to year:

Year	Cash Inflows
1	1,000
2	2,500
3	1,500

Assume that the amount of initial investment is $3,000 and the cost of capital is 14 percent.

Step 1. NPV at 14 percent:

Year	Cash Inflows	PV Factor at 14%	Total PV
1	1,000	0.877	$ 877
2	2,500	0.769	1,923
3	1,500	0.675	$1,013
			$3,813

Thus, NPV = $3,813 − $3,000 = $813.

Step 2. We see that NPV = $813 is positive at r_1 = 14%.

Step 3. Pick, say, 30% to play safe as r_2.

Step 4. Computing NPV at r_2 = 30%:

Year	Cash Inflows	PV Factor at 30%	Total PV
1	1,000	0.769	$ 769
2	2,500	0.592	1,480
3	1,500	0.455	$ 683
			$2,932

| | **EXAMPLE 8.32** *(continued)* | |

Thus, NPV = $2,932 – $3,000 = $(68).

Step 5.   Interpolate:

		NPV	
14%		$813	$813
IRR			0
30%		–68	
Difference		$881	$813

$$\text{Therefore, IRR} = 14\% + \frac{\$813}{\$881} \ (30\% - 14\%)$$
$$= 14\% + 0.923 \ (16\%)$$
$$= 14\% + 14.76\%$$
$$= 28.76\%$$

Can a computer help?

Spreadsheet programs can be used in making IRR calculations. For example, *Excel* has a function IRR (*values, guess*). Excel considers negative numbers as cash outflows such as the initial investment, and positive numbers as cash inflows. Many financial calculators have similar features. As in Example 8.30, suppose you want to calculate the IRR of a $12,950 investment (the value — 12950 entered in year 0 that is followed by 10 monthly cash inflows of $3,000). Using a guess of 12 percent (the value of 0.12), which is in effect the cost of capital, your formula would be @IRR(values, 0.12) and Excel would return 19.15 percent, as shown below.

Year:	0	1	2	3	4	5	6	7	8	9	10
	$ (12,950)	3,000	3,000	3,000	3,000	3,000	3,000	3,000	3,000	3,000	3,000

IRR = 19.15%
NPV = $4,000.67

Note: The Excel formula for NPV is NPV (discount rate, cash inflow values) + I, where I is given as a negative number.

What are the differences between NPV and IRR?

NET PRESENT VALUE (NPV)

- o Calculate the NPV, using the cost of capital as the discount rate.
- o If the NPV is positive, accept the project; otherwise, reject.

INTERNAL RATE OF RETURN (IRR)

- o Using Present Value tables, compute the IRR by trial-and-error interpolation.
- o If this rate of return exceeds the cost of capital, accept the project; if not, reject.

Profitability Index (or Excess Present Value Index)

What is the profitability index?

The profitability index is the ratio of the total PV of future cash inflows to the initial investment, that is, PV/I. This index is used as a means of ranking projects in descending order of attractiveness.

RECOMMENDATION
If PV/I is greater than 1, then accept.

EXAMPLE 8.33
Using the data in Example 8.28, the profitability index = PV/I = $16,950/$12,950 = 1.31. Since this project generates $1.31 for each dollar invested (its profitability index is greater than 1), you should accept the project.

How do I choose between mutually exclusive investments?

A project is said to be *mutually exclusive* if the acceptance of one project automatically excludes the acceptance of one or more other projects. The conditions under which contradictory rankings can occur are:

- o Projects have different expected lives.
- o Projects have different size of investment.
- o The time of the projects' cash flow differs (e.g., the cash flows of one project increase over time, while those of the other decrease).

The contradiction results from different assumptions with respect to the reinvestment rate on cash flows released from the projects.

- o The NPV method discounts all cash flows at the cost of capital, thus implicitly assuming that these cash flows can be reinvested at this rate.
- o The IRR method implies a reinvestment rate at IRR. Thus, the implied reinvestment rate will differ from project to project.

When one must choose between mutually exclusive investments, the NPV and IRR methods may give decision results contradictory to each other. The NPV method generally gives correct ranking, since the cost of capital is a more realistic reinvestment rate.

EXAMPLE 8.34

Assume the following:

Cash Flows

	0	1	2	3	4	5
A	(100)	120	—	—	—	—
B	(100)	—	—	—	—	201.14

Computing IRR and NPV at 10 percent gives the different rankings as follows:

	IRR	NPV at 10%
A	20%	9.08
B	15%	24.91

NOTE: The general rule is to go by NPV ranking, thus choosing project B over project A.

Limited Funds for Capital Spending

How do I deal with limited funds for capital spending?

Many firms specify a limit on the overall budget for capital spending. *Capital rationing* is concerned with the problem of selecting the mix of acceptable projects that provides the *highest overall NPV* in such a case. The profitability index is used widely in ranking projects competing for limited funds.

EXAMPLE 8.35

Projects	I	PV	Profitability Index	Ranking
A	$70,000	$112,000	1.6	1
B	100,000	145,000	1.45	2
C	110,000	126,500	1.15	5
D	60,000	79,000	1.32	3
E	40,000	38,000	0.95	6
F	80,000	95,000	1.19	4

	EXAMPLE 8.35 *(continued)*	

Assume that the company's fixed budget is $250,000. Using the profitability index, we select projects A, B, and D:

	I	PV
A	$70,000	$112,000
B	100,000	145,000
D	60,000	79,000
	$230,000	$336,000

Therefore, NPV = $336,000 – $230,000 = $106,000

Effects of Income Tax Factors on Capital Budgeting Decisions

How do income tax factors affect capital budgeting decisions?

Income taxes make a difference in many capital budgeting decisions. The project that is attractive on a pretax basis may have to be rejected on an after-tax basis. Income taxes typically affect both the amount and the timing of cash flows. Since net income, not cash inflows, is subject to tax, after-tax cash inflows are not usually the same as after-tax net income.

Let us define:

S = sales

E = cash operating expenses

d = depreciation

t = tax rate

Before-tax cash inflows = $(S - E)$

Net income = $(S - E - d)$

By definition,

After-tax cash inflows = before-tax cash inflow – taxes

After-tax cash inflows = $(S - E) - (S - E - d) \times t$

Rearranging gives the *short-cut formula*:

After-tax cash inflow = $(S - E)(1 - t) + d \times t$

As can be seen, the deductibility of depreciation from sales in arriving at net income subject to taxes *reduces* income tax payments and thus serves as a *tax shield*.

Tax shield = tax savings on depreciation

$= d \times t$

EXAMPLE 8.36

Assume:

S = \$12,000

E = \$10,000

d = \$500/year by straight-line

t = 40%

Then, after-tax cash inflow

= (\$12,000 − \$10,000) (1 − 0.4) + \$500 (0.4)

= \$1,200 + \$200 = \$1,400

NOTE: A tax shield = tax savings on depreciation = $d \times t$ = \$500 (0.4) = \$200

How is after-tax outflow determined?

After-tax cash *outflow* is computed by simply dropping "S" in the previous formula. Therefore:

After-tax cash outflow = $(− E) (1 − t) + d \times t$

EXAMPLE 8.37

Assume:

E = \$6,000

d = \$800/year by straight-line

t = 4%

Then, after-tax cash *outflow*

= (−\$6,000) (1 −0.4) + \$800 (0.4)

= \$3,600 + \$320

= −\$3,280

What is the effect of accelerated depreciation on tax savings?

Since the tax shield is $d \times t$, the higher the depreciation deduction, the higher the tax savings on depreciation. Therefore, the accelerated-depreciated methods such as the double-declining balance method and the sum-of-years'-digits methods produce higher tax savings than the straight-line method. They will produce higher present values for the tax savings which greatly affect the investment decision. Let us look at the present values of tax shield effects of alternative depreciation methods.

EXAMPLE 8.38

Assume:

Initial investment	$100,000
Estimated life	4 years
Salvage value	0
Cost of capital after taxes	15%
Tax rate	40%

Method of depreciation	15% PV factor	PV of tax savings

Straight-Line Depreciation

Annual depreciation
($100,000 ÷ 4 = $25,000):

Depreciation deduction

$25,000

Multiply by 40% ...   × 40%

Income tax savings, years 1– 4 .... $10,000   2.855

$28,550

Sum-of-the-Years'-Digits Depreciation

Year	Multi-plier*	Deprecia-tion Deduc-tion	Tax Shield: Income Tax Savings at 40%	15% PV Factor	PV of tax Savings
1 . . . 4/10		$40,000	$16,000	0.870	$13,920
2 . . . 3/10		30,000	12,000	0.756	9,072
3 . . . 2/10		20,000	8,000	0.658	5,264
4 . . . 1/10		10,000	4,000	0.572	2,288
					$30,544

*The denominator for the sum-of-the-years'-digits method is: 1 + 2 + 3 + 4 = 10 or

$$S = \frac{n(n+1)}{2} \quad S = \frac{4\,(4+1)}{2} = 10$$

where S = sum of the years
n = life of the asset

EXAMPLE 8.38 (continued)

Double Declining Balance Depreciation

Year	Book Value	Rate** (%)	Depreciation Deduction	Tax Shield: Income Tax Savings at 40%		
1 . . .	$100,000	50	$50,000	$20,000	0.870	$17,400
2 . . .	50,000	50	25,000	10,000	0.756	7,560
3 . . .	25,000	50	12,500	5,000	0.658	3,290
4 . . .	12,500	50	12,500***	5,000	0.572	2,860
						$31,110

**The percentage rate for the double-declining method is: 2 × straight-line rate = 2 × 25% = 50%.

***The asset is depreciated to zero salvage value in the fourth year.

THE MACRS RULE

How does MACRS affect investment decisions?

Although the traditional methods still can be used for computing depreciation for book purposes, there is a new way of computing depreciation deductions for tax purposes, called the *Modified Accelerated Cost Recovery System* (MACRS) rule. Under this rule:

1. The concept of useful life is abandoned and depreciation deductions are accelerated by placing all depreciable assets into one of eight age property classes. MACRS calculates deductions, based on an allowable percentage of the asset's original cost (See Exhibits 8.13 and 8.14).

   Using a shorter time frame than useful life, the company can deduct depreciation more quickly and save more in income taxes in the earlier years, thereby making an investment more attractive. The rationale behind the system is that the company is encouraged to invest in facilities and increase its productive capacity and efficiency. (Remember that the higher the d, the larger the tax shield $(d)(t)$.)

2. There is no need to consider the salvage value of an asset in computing depreciation, since the allowable percentages in Exhibit 8.14 add up to 100 percent.

3. The company may elect the straight-line method, which must follow what is called the *half-year convention*. This means that the company can deduct only half of the regular straight-line depreciation amount in the first year.

4. If an asset is disposed of before the end of its class life, the half-year convention allows half the depreciation for that year (early disposal rule).

Why elect the straight-line method?

The reason for electing to use the MACRS optional straight-line method is that some firms may prefer to stretch out depreciation deductions rather than to accelerate them. Those firms may be just starting out and/or have little or no income and wish to show more income on their income statements.

Property Class

Year	3-year	5-year	7-year	10-year	15-year	20-year
1	33.3%	20.0%	14.3%	10.0%	5.0%	3.8%
2	44.5	32.0	24.5	18.0	9.5	7.2
3	14.8[a]	19.2	17.5	14.4	8.6	6.7
4	7.4	11.5[a]	12.5	11.5	7.7	6.2
5		11.5	8.9[a]	9.2	6.9	5.7
6		5.8	8.9	7.4	6.2	5.3
7			8.9	6.6[a]	5.9[a]	4.9
8			4.5	6.6	5.9	4.5[a]
9				6.5	5.9	4.5
10				6.5	5.9	4.5
11				3.3	5.9	4.5
12					5.9	4.5
13					5.9	4.5
14					5.9	4.5
15					5.9	4.5

16					4.4
17					4.4
18					4.4
19					4.4
20				3.0	4.4
21					2.2
Total	100%	100%	100%	100%	100%

aDenotes the year of changeover to straight-line depreciation.

Exhibit 8.13 MODIFIED ACCELERATED COST RECOVERY SYSTEM: CLASSIFICATION OF ASSETS

MACRS Property Class and Depreciation Method	Useful Life (ADR Midpoint Life)[a]	Examples of Assets
3-year property 200% declining balance	4 years or less	Most small tools are included; the law specifically excludes autos and light trucks from this property class.
5-year property 200% declining balance	More than 4 years to less than 10 years	Autos and light trucks, computers, typewriters, copiers, duplicating equipment, heavy general-purpose trucks, and research and experimentation equipment are included.
7-year property 200% declining balance	10 years or more to less than 16 years	Office furniture and fixtures and most items of machinery and equipment used in production are included.
10-year property 200% declining balance	16 years or more to less than 20 years	Various machinery and equipment, such as that used in petroleum distilling and refining and in the milling of grain, are included.
15-year property 150% declining balance	20 years or more to less than 25 years	Sewage treatment plants, telephone and electrical distribution facilities, and land improvements are included.
20-year property 150% declining balance	25 years or more	Service stations and other real property with an ADR mid-point[a] life of less than 27.5 years are included.
27.5-year property Straight-line	Not applicable	All residential rental property is included.
31.5-year property Straight-line	Not applicable	All nonresidential real property is included.

[a]The term ADR midpoint life means the "useful life" of an asset in a business sense; the appropriate ADR midpoint lives for assets are designated in the Tax Regulations.

Exhibit 8.14 MACRS TABLES BY PROPERTY CLASS

EXAMPLE 8.39

Assume that a machine falls under a three-year property class and costs $3,000 initially. The straight-line option under MACRS differs from the traditional straight-line method in that under this method the company would deduct only $500 depreciation in the first year and in the fourth year ($3,000/3 years = $1,000; $1,000/2 = $500). The table accompanying compares the straight-line with half-year convention with the standard MACRS rule.

Year	Straight-Line (Half-year) Depreciation	Cost MACRS%	MACRS Deduction
1	$ 500	$3,000 × 33.3%	$ 999
2	1,000	3,000 × 44.5	1,335
3	1,000	3,000 × 14.8	444
4	500	3,000 × 7.4	222
	$3,000		$3,000

EXAMPLE 8.40

A machine costs $10,000. Annual cash inflows are expected to be $5,000. The machine will be depreciated using the MACRS rule and will fall under the three-year property class. The cost of capital after taxes is 10 percent. The estimated life of the machine is four years. The salvage value of the machine at the end of the fourth year is expected to be $1,200. The tax rate is 30 percent.

The formula for computation of after-tax cash inflows $(S - E)(1 - t) + (d)(t)$ needs to be computed separately. The NPV analysis can be performed as follows:

	Present Value Factor @ 10%	Present Value
Initial investment: $10,000	1.000	$(10,000)
$(S - E)(1 - t)$:		
$5,000 (1 - 0.3) = $3,500 for 4 years	3.170(a)	$11,095

$(d)(t)$:

Year	Cost MACRS %	d	(d)(t)		
1	$10,000 × 33.3%	$3,330	$ 999	0.909(b)	908.09
2	$10,000 × 44.5	4,450	1,335	0.826(b)	1,102.71
3	$10,000 × 14.8	1,480	444	0.751(b)	333.44
4	$10,000 × 7.4	740	222	0.683(b)	151.63

Salvage value

$1,200 in year 4: $1,200 (1 - 0.3) =			
$840(c)		0.683(b)	573.72
Net present value (NPV)			
			$4,164.59

EXAMPLE 8.40 *(continued)*

a. T4(10%, 4 years) = 3.170$(from Exhibit 8.12).

b. T3 values obtained from Exhibit 8.11.

c. Any salvage value received under the MACRS rules is a *taxable gain* (the excess of the selling price over book value, $1,200 in this example), since the book value will be zero at the end of the life of the machine.

Since NPV = PV – I = $4,164.59 is positive, the machine should be bought.

What are the tax effects of disposal?

In general, gains and losses on disposal of equipment are taxed in the same way as ordinary gains and losses. Immediate disposal of the old equipment results in a loss that is fully tax deductible from current income. The loss (the excess of the book value over the disposal value) must be computed to isolate its effect on current income tax, but the total cash inflow is the selling price *plus* the current income tax benefit.

EXAMPLE 8.41

Assume that the equipment has a salvage value of $1,200, while its book (undepreciated) value is $2,000. *Two* cash inflows are connected with this sale. The tax rate is 30 percent.

1. A $1,200 cash inflow in the form of the sale price, and

2. A $240 cash inflow in the form of a reduction in income taxes, resulting from the tax shield provided by the loss sustained on the sale, just like the tax shield provided by depreciation deduction, as computed as follows:

Book value	$2,000	
Selling price	1,200	
Loss	800	
Tax shield	× 0.3	$240

Thus, the total cash inflow from the disposal is $1,440 ($1,200 + $240).

CHAPTER 9

QUANTITATIVE APPLICATIONS AND MODELING IN ACCOUNTING

Quantitative applications and modeling in accounting have been on the rise, coupled with the advent of micro-computers and wide availability of software for various quantitative decision-making tools. The accountant should make use of quantitative techniques and modeling to ana-lyze and solve the various accounting and financial prob-lems faced by the client or the business entity he or she is employed by. These quantitative tools allow for the consid-eration of a multitude of data.

STATISTICAL ANALYSIS AND EVALUATION

How do I handle large volumes of data?

In many situations, accountants have a large volume of data that needs to be analyzed. These data could be earnings, cash flows, accounts receivable balances, weights of an incoming shipment, and so on. The statistics most com-monly used to describe the characteristics of the data are the *mean* and the *standard deviation*. These statistics are also used to measure the return and risk in investment and financial decision making, in which the CPA may be asked to participate by the business entity.

Mean

What is a mean?

The *mean* gives us the average or central value of our data. Typically, there are three measures of central tendency:

- ○ Arithmetic mean
- ○ Weighted mean
- ○ Geometric mean

What is the arithmetic mean ($\bar{x}$)?

The arithmetic mean is a simple average. To find it, we sum the values in our data and divide by the number of observations. Symbolically,

$$\bar{x} = \frac{\Sigma x}{n}$$

where n = number of observations.

EXAMPLE 9.1

John Jay Lamp Company has a revolving credit agreement with a local bank. The loan showed the following ending monthly balances last year:

Jan.	$18,500
Feb.	21,000
Mar.	17,600
Apr.	23,200
May	18,600
Jun.	24,500
Jul.	60,000
Aug.	40,000
Sep.	25,850
Oct.	33,100
Nov.	41,000
Dec.	28,400

Then the mean monthly balance for the loan last year is computed as follows:

Arithmetic mean balance

$$= \frac{\begin{array}{l}\$18,500 + \$21,000 + \$17,600 \\ + \$23,200 + \$18,600 + \$24,500 \\ + \$60,000 + \$40,000 + \$25,850 \\ + \$33,100 + \$41,000 + \$28,400\end{array}}{12}$$

$$= \frac{\$351,750}{12} = \$29,312.50$$

How do I determine a weighted mean?

The arithmetic mean is an unweighted average. It assumes equal likelihood of each value in one data. When observations have different degrees of importance or frequency, use the *weighted mean*. The weighted average enables us to take into account the importance of each value in the overall total. Symbolically, the formula for calculating the weighted average is:

Weighted mean = $\Sigma\, w \cdot x$

where

w = Weight (in percentage or in relative frequency) assigned to each observation

---

EXAMPLE 9.2

Consider the company that uses three grades of labor to produce a finished product. The company wants to know the average cost of labor per hour for this product.

Grade of Labor	Labor Hours per Unit of Output	Hourly Wages (x)
Skilled	6	$10.00
Semiskilled	3	8.00
Unskilled	1	6.00

Using the arithmetic mean of the labor wage rates results in:

$$\text{Arithmetic mean} = \frac{\$10.00 + \$8.00 + \$6.00}{3}$$

$$= \frac{\$24.00}{3}$$

$$= \$8.00/\text{hour}$$

This implicitly assumes that the same amounts of each grade of labor were used to produce the output. More specifically,

$$\frac{\$10.00 + \$8.00 + \$6.00}{3} = \frac{\$10.00(1/3) + \$8.00(1/3)}{+ \ 6.00 \ (1/3)}$$

$$= \$8.00/\text{hour}$$

This is simply not true. We have to consider different amounts of each grade of labor in calculating the average cost of labor per hour. The correct way is to take a weighted average as follows:

$$\text{Weighted mean} = \$10.00(6/10) + \$8.00(3/10)$$
$$+ \ \$6.00(1/10)$$
$$= \$9.00/\text{hour}$$

NOTE: Weight the hourly wage for each grade by its proportion of the total labor required to produce the product.

When should the geometric mean be used?

Sometimes we are dealing with quantities that change over a period of time. In such a case, we need to know an average rate of change, such as an average rate of return on investment or an average rate of growth in earnings over a period of several years. The formula for finding the geometric mean over n periods is:

Geometric mean

$$= \sqrt[n]{(1+x_1)(1+x_2) \ldots (1+x_n)} - 1$$

where x represents the percentage rate of change or percentage return on investment.

Since it is cumbersome to calculate the nth root (although most scientific calculators have a key to compute this), we will only illustrate the two-period return calculation ($n = 2$).

The following example shows the inadequacy of the arithmetic mean return when the price of a stock doubles in one period and then depreciates back to the original price.

EXAMPLE 9.3

	Time Periods		
	t = 0	t = 1	t = 2
Price (end of period)	$80	$160	$80
Rate of return	—	100%	-50%

The rate of return for periods 1 and 2 are computed as follows:

$$\text{Period } 1 \, (t = 1) \quad \frac{(\$160 - \$80)}{\$80}$$

$$= \frac{\$80}{\$80} = \underline{\underline{100\%}}$$

$$\text{Period } 2 \, (t = 2) \quad \frac{(\$80 - \$160)}{\$160}$$

$$= \frac{-\$80}{\$160} = \underline{\underline{-50\%}}$$

Therefore, the arithmetic mean return over the two periods is the average of 100% and –50%, which is 25%, as shown below:

$$\frac{100\% + (-50\%)}{2} = \underline{\underline{25\%}}$$

As can be easily seen, the stock purchased for $80 and sold for the same price two periods later did not earn 25 percent. It clearly earned a *zero* return. This can be shown by computing the geometric *mean* return.

EXAMPLE 9.3   *(continued)*

Note that $n = 2$, $x_1 = 100\% = 1$, and $x_2 = -50\% = -0.5$

Geometric mean return

$$= \sqrt[2]{(1 + 1)(1 - 0.5)} - 1$$

$$= \sqrt[2]{(2)(0.5)} - 1$$

$$= \sqrt{1} - 1 = 1 - 1 = \underline{\underline{0\%}}$$

Standard Deviation

What is the standard deviation?

The standard deviation measures the tendency of data to be spread out. Accountants can make important inferences from past data with this measure. The standard deviation, denoted with and read as *sigma*, is defined as follows:

$$\sigma = \sqrt{\frac{\Sigma(x - \bar{x})^2}{n - 1}}$$

where $\bar{x}$ is the mean.

The standard deviation can be used to measure the variation of such items as the expected contribution margin (CM) or expected variable manufacturing costs. It can also be used to assess the risk associated with investment decisions.

How do I calculate standard deviation?

The standard deviation is calculated, step-by-step, as follows:

- Subtract from the mean each value of the data.
- Square each of the differences obtained in step 1.
- Add together all the squared differences.
- Divide the sum of all the squared differences by the number of values *minus* one.
- Take the square root of the quotient obtained in step 4.

EXAMPLE 9.4

One and one-half years of quarterly returns are listed for United Motors stock as follows:

Time Period	x	$(x - \bar{x})$	$(x - \bar{x})^2$
1	10%	0	0
2	15	5	25
3	20	10	100

EXAMPLE 9.4 *(continued)*			
4	5	−5	25
5	−10	−20	400
6	20	10	100
	60		650

From the above table, note that $x = 60/6 = 10\%$

$$= \sqrt{\Sigma(x - \bar{x})^2/(n - 1)} = \sqrt{650/(6 - 1)}$$
$$= \sqrt{130} = 11.40\%$$

The United Motors stock has returned on the average 10 percent over the last six quarters. The variability about its average return was 11.40 percent. The high standard deviation (11.40 percent) relative to the average return of 10 percent indicates that the stock is very risky.

REGRESSION ANALYSIS

What is regression analysis?

Regression analysis is a very popular statistical method used to project sales and earnings.

It is also used to estimate the *cost–volume formula* (also called the *flexible budget formula*), which takes the following functional form:

$$y = a + bx$$

where

y = the semivariable (mixed) costs to be broken up

x = any given measure of activity such as production volume, machine hours, or direct labor hours

a = the fixed cost component

b = the variable rate per unit of x

The regression method is a statistical procedure for estimating mathematically the average relationship between the dependent variable y and the independent variable x.

- ○ *Simple regression* involves one independent variable (e.g., direct labor hours (DLH) or machine hours alone)
- ○ *Multiple regression* involves two or more activity variables

(We will assume simple *linear* regression throughout this chapter, which means that we will maintain the $y = a + bx$ relationship.)

The Method of Least Squares

How do I use least squares in making a decision?

In estimating the values of a and b, the regression method attempts to find a line of *best fit*. To find the line of *best fit*, a technique called the *method of least squares* is used.

To explain the least squares method, we define the error as the difference between the observed value and the estimated value of some semivariable cost and denote it with u. Symbolically,

$$u = y - y'$$

where

y = observed value of a semivariable expense
y' = estimated value based on $y' = a + bx$

The least-squares criterion requires that the line of best fit be such that the sum of the squares of the errors (or the vertical distance in Exhibit 9.1 from the observed data points to the line) is a minimum, that is,

$$\text{Min } \Sigma u^2 = \Sigma (y - y')^2$$

Using differential calculus we obtain the following equations, called *normal equations*:

$$\Sigma y = n \cdot a + b \cdot \Sigma x$$
$$\Sigma xy = a \cdot \Sigma x + b \cdot \Sigma x^2$$

Solving the equations for b and a yields:

$$b = \frac{n\Sigma xy - (\Sigma x)(\Sigma y)}{n\Sigma x^2 - (\Sigma x)^2}$$
$$a = \bar{y} - b\bar{x} \text{ where } \bar{y} = \Sigma y / n \text{ and } \bar{x} = \Sigma x / n$$

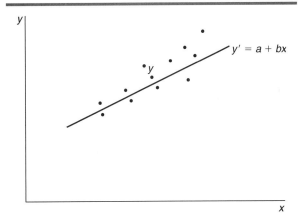

NOTE: The formula for a is a short-cut formula, which requires the computation of b first. This will save a considerable amount of time.

Exhibit 9.1   ACTUAL (Y) VERSUS ESTIMATED (Y')

EXAMPLE 9.5

To illustrate the computations of b and a, use the following data. All the sums required are computed and shown:

DLH (x)	Factory Overhead (y)	xy	x^2	y^2
9 hours	$ 15	135	81	225
19	20	380	361	400
11	14	154	121	196
14	16	224	196	256
23	25	575	529	625
12	20	240	144	400
12	20	240	144	400
22	23	506	484	529
7	14	98	49	196
13	22	286	169	484
15	18	270	225	324
17	18	306	289	324
174 hours	$225	3,414	2,792	4,359

From the table above:

$$\Sigma x = 174$$
$$\Sigma y = 225$$
$$\Sigma xy = 3,414$$
$$\Sigma x^2 = 2,792$$
$$\bar{x} = \Sigma x / n = 174 / 12 = 14.5$$
$$\bar{y} = \Sigma y / n = 225 / 12 = 18.75$$

Substituting these values into the formula for b first:

$$b = \frac{n\Sigma xy - (\Sigma x)(\Sigma y)}{n\Sigma x^2 - (\Sigma x)^2}$$
$$= \frac{(12)(3,414) - (174)(225)}{(12)(2,792) - (174)^2}$$
$$= \frac{1,818}{3,228} = \underline{0.5632}$$

$$a = \bar{y} - b\bar{x}$$
$$= (18.75) - (0.5632)(14.5) = 18.75 - 8.1664$$
$$= \underline{10.5836}$$

NOTE: Σy^2 is not used here but rather is computed for future use.

Our final regression equation is:

$$y' = \$10.5836 + \$0.5632\,x$$

where
y' = estimated factory overhead
x = DLH

USE OF A SPREADSHEET PROGRAM FOR REGRESSION

How do I use an electronic spreadsheet?

To utilize Excel for regression analysis, the following procedure needs to be followed:

1. Click the *Tools* menu.
2. Click *Add-Ins.*
3. Click *Analysis ToolPak.* (If *Analysis ToolPak* is not listed among your available add-ins, exit Excel, double-click the MS Excel Setup icon, click Add/Remove, double-click Add-Ins, and select *Analysis ToolPak.* Then restart Excel and repeat the above instruction.)

After ensuring that the Analysis ToolPak is available, you can access the regression tool by completing the following steps:

1. Click the *Tools* menu.
2. Click *Data Analysis.*
3. Click *Regression.*

NOTE
To obtain a scattergraph, use Excel's Chart Wizard.

Exhibit 9.2 captures the regression input dialog screen.

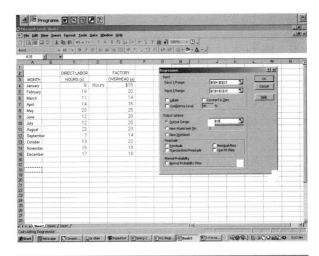

Exhibit 9.2 REGRESSION INPUT DIALOG SCREEN

SUMMARY OUTPUT

Regression Statistics	
Multiple R	0.7800
R square	0.6084
Adjusted R Square	0.5692
Standard error	2.3436
Observations	12

ANOVA

	df	SS	MS	F	Significance F
Regression	1	85.3243	85.3243	15.5345	0.0028
Residual	10	54.9257	5.4926		
Total	11	140.25			

	Coefficients	Standard Error	t Stat	P-value*	Lower 95%	Upper 95%
Intercept	10.583643	2.1796	4.8558	0.0007	5.7272	15.4401
DLH	0.563197	0.1429	3.9414	0.0028	0.2448	0.8816

*The P-value for X Variable = 0.0028 indicates that we have a 0.28% chance that the true value of the variable coefficient is equal to 0, implying a high level of accuracy about the estimated value of 0.563197.

Exhibit 9.3 EXCEL REGRESSION OUTPUT

Exhibit 9.3 shows the Excel regression output.
The result shows:

$Y' = 10.58364 + 0.563197 X$ (in the form of $Y' = a + bX$)

with: r-squared ($r^2 = 0.608373 = 60.84\%$)
All of the above are the same as the ones obtained manually.

Exhibit 9.4 shows the regression output from popular statistical software, *Minitab*.

Regression Analysis

The regression equation is
FO = 10.6 + 0.563 DLH

Predictor	Coef	Stdev	t-ratio	p
Constant	10.584	2.180	4.86	0.000
DLH	0.5632	0.1429	3.94	0.003

s = 2.344   R-sq = 60.8%   R-sq(adj) = 56.9%

Analysis of Variance

SOURCE	DF	SS	MS	F	p
Regression	1	85.324	85.324	15.53	0.003
Error	10	54.926	5.493		
Total	11				

Exhibit 9.4 MINITAB REGRESSION OUTPUT

Trend Analysis

What is trend analysis?

Another common method for forecasting sales or earnings is the use of trend analysis, a special case of regression analysis. This method involves a regression whereby a trend line is fitted to a time series of data.

How do I apply trend analysis?

The trend line equation can be shown as:

$$y = a + bx$$

The formulas for the coefficients a and b are essentially the same as the fomulas for simple regression. However, for regression purposes, a time period can be given a number so that $\Sigma x = 0$. When there is an *odd* number of periods, the period in the middle is assigned a zero value. If there is an *even* number, then -1 and $+1$ are assigned the two periods in the middle, so that again $\Sigma x = 0$.

With $\Sigma x = 0$, the formula for b and a reduces to the following:

$$b = \frac{n\Sigma xy}{n\Sigma x^2}$$
$$a = \Sigma y / n$$

EXAMPLE 9.6

Case 1 (odd number)

20×1	20×2	20×3	20×4	20×5	
x = −2	−1	0	+1	+2	

Case 2 (even number)

20×1	20×2	20×3	20×4	20×5	20×6
x = −3	−2	−1	+1	+2	+3

In each case, $\Sigma x = 0$.

EXAMPLE 9.7

Consider ABC Company whose historical earnings per share (EPS) follow:

Year	EPS
20×1	$1.00
20×2	1.20
20×3	1.30
20×4	1.60
20×5	1.70

Since the company has five years' of data, which is an odd number, the year in the middle is assigned a zero value.

EXAMPLE 9.7 *(continued)*

Year	x	EPS(y)	xy	x^2
20X1	−2	$1.00	−2.00	4
20X2	−2	1.20	−1.20	1
20X3	0	1.30	0	0
20X4	+1	1.60	1.60	1
20X5	+2	1.70	3.40	4
	0	$6.80	1.80	10

$$b = \frac{(5)(1.80)}{(5)(10)} = \frac{9}{50} = \$0.18$$

$$a = \frac{\$6.80}{5} = \$1.36$$

Therefore, the estimated trend equation is:

$$\hat{y} = \$1.36 + \$0.18x$$

where

$$\hat{y} = \text{estimated EPS}$$
$$x = \text{year index value}$$

To project 19×6 sales, we assign +3 to the x value for the year 19×6. Thus,

$$\hat{y} = \$1.36 + \$0.18(+3)$$
$$= \$1.36 + 54$$
$$= \$1.90$$

REGRESSION STATISTICS

Regression analysis uses a variety of statistics that tell us about the accuracy and reliability of the regression results. They include:

- Correlation coefficient (r) and coefficient of determination (r^2)
- Standard error of the estimate (s_e)
- Standard error of the regression coefficient (s_b) and t-statistic

What is the correlation between variables y and x?

The correlation coefficient, r, measures the degree of correlation between y and x. The range of values it takes on is between −1 and +1. More widely used, however, is the coefficient of determination, designated r^2 (read "r-squared"). Simply put, r^2 tells us how good the estimated regression equation is. In other words, it is a measure of "goodness of fit" in the regression. Therefore, the higher the r^2, the more confidence we have in the estimated cost formula.

More specifically, the coefficient of determination represents the proportion of the total variation in y that is explained by the regression equation. It has the range of values between 0 and 1.

EXAMPLE 9.8

The statement "factory overhead is a function of machine hours with $r^2 = 70\%$" can be interpreted as "70 percent of the total variation of factory overhead is explained by the regression equation or the change in machine hours" and "the remaining 30 percent is accounted for by something other than machine hours."

The coefficient of determination is computed as follows:

$$r^2 = 1 - \frac{\Sigma(y - y')^2}{\Sigma(y - \overline{y})^2}$$

In a simple regression situation, however, there is the short-cut method available:

$$r^2 = \frac{[n \cdot \Sigma xy - (\Sigma x)(\Sigma y)]^2}{[n\Sigma x^2 - (\Sigma x)^2] \cdot [n\Sigma y^2 - (\Sigma y)^2]}$$

Comparing this formula with the one for b in Example 9.5, we see the only additional information we need to compute r^2 is Σy^2.

EXAMPLE 9.9

From the table prepared in Example 9.5, $\Sigma y^2 = 4{,}359$. Using the shortcut method for r^2,

$$r^2 = \frac{(1{,}818)^2}{(3{,}228) \cdot [(12)(4{,}359) - (225)^2]}$$

$$= \frac{3{,}305{,}124}{(3{,}228)(52{,}308 - 50{,}625)}$$

$$= \frac{3{,}305{,}124}{(3{,}228)(1{,}683)} = \frac{3{,}305{,}124}{5{,}432{,}724}$$

$$= 0.6084 = 60.84\%$$

This means that about 60.84 percent of the total variation in total factory overhead is explained by Direct Labor Hours (DLH) and the remaining 39.16 percent is

---

EXAMPLE 9.9   *(continued)*

still unexplained. A relatively low r^2 indicates that there exists a lot of room for improvement in the estimated cost-volume formula ($y' = \$10.5836 + \$0.5632x$). Machine hours or a combination of DLH and machine hours might improve r^2.

How can I compute the standard error of the estimate?

The standard error of the estimate, s_e, is defined as the standard deviation of the regression. It is computed:

$$s_e = \sqrt{\frac{\Sigma(y - y')^2}{n-2}} = \sqrt{\frac{\Sigma y^2 - a\Sigma y - b\Sigma xy}{n-2}}$$

The statistics can be used to gain some idea of the accuracy of our predictions.

EXAMPLE 9.10

Going back to our example data, s_e is calculated as:

$$s_e = \sqrt{\frac{(4,359) - (10.5836)(225) - (0.5632)(3,414)}{12-2}}$$

$$= \sqrt{\frac{54.9252}{10}} = 2.3436$$

If a manager wants the prediction to be 95 percent confident, the confidence interval would be the *estimated cost* $\pm$ 2(2.3436).

More specifically, the confidence interval for the prediction given as 10 hours of direct labor time would be:

$$\$16.2156^* \pm 2\ (2.3436)$$

$$= \$16.2156 \pm 4.6872,\ \text{which means:}$$
$$\$11.5284 - \$20.9028$$

$^*y' = \$10.5836 + \$0.5632x = \$10.5836 + \$0.5632(10)$
$= \$10.5836 + \$5.632 = \$16.2156$

What is the relationship between the standard error of the coefficient and *t*-statistic?

The standard error of the coefficient, s_b, and the *t*-statistic are closely related s_b is calculated as:

$$s_b = \frac{s_e}{\sqrt{\Sigma(x - \bar{x})^2}}$$

or in short-cut form

$$s_b = \frac{s_e}{\sqrt{\Sigma x^2 - \bar{x}\Sigma x}}$$

s_b gives an estimate of the range in which the true coefficient "actually" is. The t-statistic shows the statistical significance of x in explaining y. It is developed by dividing the estimated coefficient, b, by its standard error, s_b. That is, t-statistic $= b/s_b$. Thus, the t-statistic really measures how many standard errors the coefficient is away from zero.

RECOMMENDATION

Generally, any t value greater than +2 or less than –2 is acceptable. The higher the t-value, the more significant the b is, and therefore, the greater the confidence in the coefficient as a predictor.

EXAMPLE 9.11

The s_b for our example is:

$$s_b = \frac{2.3436}{\sqrt{2,792 - (14.5)(174)}}$$

$$= \frac{2.3436}{\sqrt{2,792 - 2,523}} = \frac{2.3436}{\sqrt{269}}$$

$$= \frac{2.3436}{16.40} = 0.143$$

NOTE: $s_e = 2.3436$, $\Sigma x^2 = 2,792$, $\bar{x} = 14.5$, $\Sigma x = 174$.

Thus, t-statistic $= b/s_b = 0.5632/0.143 = 3.94$

Since $t = 3.94 > 2$, we conclude that the b coefficient is statistically significant.

How can I estimate cash collection rates using regression?

Credit sales affect cash collections with time lags. In other words, there is a time lag between point of credit sale and realization of cash. More specifically, the lagged effect of credit sales and cash inflows is distributed over a number of periods as follows:

$$C_t = b_1 S_{t-1} + b_2 S_{t-2} + \cdots + b_i S_{t-i}$$

where

C_t = cash collections

S_t = credit sales made in period t

$b_1, b_2, \ldots\, b_i$ = collection percentages
i = number of periods lagged

By using the regression method discussed previously, we will be able to estimate these collection rates (or payment proportions). We can use Data Regression of Lotus 1–2–3 or special packages such as STATPACK or SAS.

NOTE

The cash collection percentages $(b_1, b_2, \ldots, b_i)$ may not add up to 100 percent because of the possibility of bad debts. Once we estimate these percentages, we should be able to compute the bad debt percentage with no difficulty.

EXAMPLE 9.12

Exhibit 9.5 shows the regression results using actual monthly data on credit sales and cash inflows for a real company. Equation I can be written as follows:

$$C_t = 60.6\% \,(S_{t-1}) + 24.3\% \,(S_{t-2}) + 8.8\% \,(S_{t-3})$$

This result indicates that the receivables generated by the credit sales are collected at the following rates:

○ First month after sale, 60.6%
○ Second month after sale, 24.3%
○ Third month after sale, 8.8%

The bad debt percentage is computed as 6.3 percent $(100\% - 93.7\%)$.

CAUTION

These collection and bad debt percentages are probabilistic variables; that is, variables whose values cannot be known with precision. However, the standard error of the regression coefficient and the t-value permit us to assess a probability that the true percentage is between specified limits. The confidence interval takes the following form:

$$b \pm t\, s_b$$

Independent Variables	Equation I
S_{t-1}	0.606*
	(0.062)**
S_{t-2}	0.243*

Exhibit 9.5 REGRESSION RESULT FOR CASH COLLECTION (C_1)

Independent Variables	Equation I
	(0.085)
S_{t-3}	0.088
	(0.157)
S_{t-4}	
R^2	0.754
Durbin-Watson	2.52***
Standard error of the estimate (S_e)	11.63***
no. # of monthly observations	21
Bad debt percentages	0.063

*Statistically significant at the 5% significance level.
**This figure in the parentheses is the standard error of the estimate for the coefficient.
***No autocorrelation present at the 5% significance level.

Exhibit 9.5 REGRESSION RESULT FOR CASH COLLECTION (C_1) *(continued)*

EXAMPLE 9.13

To illustrate, assuming $t = 2$ as a rule of thumb at the 95 percent confidence level, we find, the true collection percentage from the prior month's sales will be:

$$60.6\% \pm 2 \ (6.2\%)$$
$$= 60.6\% \pm 12.4\%$$

Turning to the estimation of cash collections and allowance for doubtful accounts, we will use the following values for illustrative purposes:

$$S_{t-1} = \$77.6$$
$$S_{t-2} = \$58.5$$
$$S_{t-3} = \$76.4$$

and forecast average monthly net credit sales = $75.2

The forecast cash collection for period t would be:

$$C_t = 60.6\% \ (77.6) + 19.3\% \ (58.5) + 8.8\% \ (76.4)$$
$$= \$65.04$$

If the accountant wants to be 95 percent confident about this forecast value, then he or she would set the interval as follows:

$$C_t \pm t \, s_e$$

To illustrate, using $t = 2$ as a rule of thumb at the 95 percent confidence level, the true value for cash collections in period t will be:

$$\$65.04 \pm 2 \ (11.63)$$
$$= \$65.04 \pm 23.26$$

EXAMPLE 9.13 *(continued)*

The estimated allowance for uncollectible accounts for period t will be:

6.3% ($75.2) = $4.73

NOTE

By using the limit's discussed so far, accountants can:

- Develop flexible (or probabilistic) cash budgets, where the lower and upper limits can be interpreted as pessimistic and optimistic outcomes, respectively.
- Simulate the cash budget in an attempt to determine both the expected change in cash collections each period and the variation about this value.

QUANTITATIVE METHODS FOR ACCOUNTING

What types of quantitative methods are available?

The term *quantitative models*, also known as *operations research (OR)* or *management science*, describes sophisticated mathematical and statistical techniques for the solution of planning and decision-making problems.

What is the definition of "quantitative models"?

In recent years, much attention has been given to the use of a variety of quantitative models in accounting. Especially with the rapid development of microcomputers, accountants find them increasingly easy to use. It is becoming necessary to acquire knowledge about the use of those quantitative (mathematical and statistical) methods. The so-called Decision Support System (DSS) is in effect the embodiment of this trend. Numerous tools are available under these subject headings. We will explore six of the most important techniques that have broad applications in accounting:

- Decision making under uncertainty
- Linear programming and shadow prices
- Goal programming and multiple goals
- Learning curve
- Inventory planning and control
- Program Evaluation and Review Technique (PERT)

DECISION MAKING

What is the difference between certainty and uncertainty in decision making?

Decisions are made under *certainty* or under *uncertainty*. Decision making under certainty means that for each decision there is only one event and therefore only one outcome for each action. Decision making under uncertainty, which is more common in reality, involves several events for each action, each with its probability of occurrence.

Decision Making Under Certainty

What is an example of decision making under certainty?

An accountant is often faced with a decision situation in which for each decision alternative there is only one event and therefore only one outcome for each action.

EXAMPLE 9.14

Assume there is only one possible event for the two possible actions:

- ○ "Do nothing" at a future cost of $3.00 per unit for 10,000 units
- ○ "Rearrange" a facility at a future cost of $2.80 for the same number of units

We can set up the following table:

Actions	Possible Outcome with Certainty
Do nothing	$30,000 (10,000 units × $3.00)
Rearrange	28,000 (10,000 units × $2.80)

Since there is only one possible outcome for each action (with certainty), the decision is obviously to choose the action that will result in the more desirable outcome (least cost), that is, to "rearrange."

Decision Making Under Uncertainty

What measures do I take when making a decision under uncertainty?

When decisions are made in a world of *uncertainty*, it is often helpful to make the following computations:

- ○ Expected value
- ○ Standard deviation
- ○ Coefficient of variation

How do I compute expected value?

For decisions involving uncertainty, the concept of *expected value* ($\overline{A}$) provides a rational means for selecting the best course of action. The expected value of an alternative is an arithmetic mean, a weighted average using the probabilities as weights. More specifically, it is found by multiplying the probability of each outcome by its payoff.

$$\overline{A} = \Sigma A_x P_x$$

where

A_x = the outcome for the xth possible event

P_x = the probability of occurrence of that outcome

EXAMPLE 9.15

Consider two investment proposals, A and B, with the following probability distribution of cash flows in each of the next five years:

Cash Inflows

Probability	(0.2)	(0.3)	(0.4)	(0.1)
A	$50	200	300	400
B	$100	150	250	850

The expected value of the cash inflow in proposal A is:

$50 (0.2) + 200 (0.3) + 300 (0.4) + 400 (0.1)$
= $230

The expected value of the cash inflow in proposal B is:

$100 (0.2) + 150 (0.3) + 250 (0.4) + 850 (0.1)$
= $250

How is standard deviation determined?

The standard deviation (σ) measures the dispersion of a probability distribution. It is the square root of the mean of the squared deviations from the expected value.

$$\sigma = \sqrt{\sum_{x-1}^{n} (A_x - \overline{A})^2 \, P_x}$$

NOTE

The standard deviation is commonly used as an absolute measure of risk. The higher the standard deviation, the higher the risk.

EXAMPLE 9.16

Using the data from Example 9.16, we can compute the standard deviations of proposals A and B as follows:

For A:

$$\sigma = \sqrt{\begin{array}{l}[(\$50-230)^2(0.2) + (200-230)^2(0.3) \\ +(300-230)^2(0.4) + (400-230)^2(0.1)]\end{array}}$$

$$= \$107.70$$

For B:

$$\sigma = \sqrt{\begin{array}{l}[(\$100-250)^2(0.2) + (150-250)^2(0.3) \\ +(250-250)^2(0.4) + (850-250)^2(0.1)]\end{array}}$$

$$= \$208.57$$

Proposal B is riskier than proposal A, because its standard deviation is greater.

How is the coefficient of variation computed?

Coefficient of variation is a measure of relative dispersion, or relative risk. It is computed by dividing the standard deviation by the expected value:

$$CV = \frac{\sigma}{A}$$

EXAMPLE 9.17

Using the data from Examples 9.15 and 9.16, we calculate the coefficient of variation for each proposal as:

For A: $107.70/\$230 = \underline{0.47}$

For B: $208.57/\$250 = \underline{0.83}$

Therefore, because the coefficient is a relative measure of risk, B is said to have a greater degree of risk.

Decision Matrix

What is a decision matrix?

Although the statistics such as expected value and standard deviation are essential for choosing the best course of action under uncertainty, the decision problem can best be approached using *decision theory*. Decision theory is a systematic approach to making decisions especially under uncertainty.

Decision theory uses an organized approach such as a *payoff table* (or *decision matrix*), which is characterized by:

○ The *row* representing a set of alternative *courses of action* available to the decision maker
○ The *column* representing the *state of nature* or conditions that are likely to occur and the decision maker has no control over
○ The *entries* in the body of the table representing the outcome of the decision (*payoffs* in the form of costs, revenues, profits or cash flows)

By computing expected value of each action, we will be able to pick the best one.

EXAMPLE 9.18

Assume the following probability distribution of daily demand for strawberries:

Daily demand	0	1	2	3
Probability	0.2	0.3	0.3	0.2

Also assume that unit cost = $3, selling price = $5 (i.e., profit on sold unit = $2), and salvage value on unsold units = $2 (i.e., loss on unsold unit = $1). We can stock either 0, 1, 2, or 3 units.

How many units should be stocked each day? Assume that units from one day cannot be sold the next day. Then the payoff table can be constructed as follows:

State of Nature

Demand Stock	0	1	2	3	Expected Value
(probability)	(0.2)	(0.3)	(0.3)	(0.2)	
0	$0	0	0	0	$0
Actions 1	−1	2	2	2	1.40
2	−2	1*	4	4	1.90**
3	−3	0	3	6	1.50

*Profit for (stock 2, demand 1) equals (no. of units sold)(profit per unit) − (no. of units unsold)(loss per unit) = (1)($5 − 3) − (1)($3 − 2) = $1

**Expected value for (stock 2) is: −2(0.2) + 1(0.3) + 4(0.3) + 4(0.2) = $1.90

The optimal stock action is the one with the highest *expected monetary value*, that is, stock 2 units.

Expected Value of Perfect Information

How is expected value computed?

Suppose the decision maker can obtain a perfect prediction of which event (state of nature) will occur. The *expected value with perfect information (EVPI)* would be the total expected value of actions selected on the assumption of a perfect forecast. The EVPI can then be computed as:

EVPI = Expected value with perfect information
       – Expected value with existing information

EXAMPLE 9.19

From the payoff table in Example 9.18, the following analysis yields the expected value *with* perfect information:

State of Nature

Demand	0	1	2	3	Expected Value
Stock	(0.2)	(0.3)	(0.3)	(0.2)	
0	$0				$0
Actions 1		2			0.6
2			4		1.2
3				6	1.2
					$3.00

Alternatively,

$$\$0(0.2) + 2(0.3) + 4(0.3) + 6(0.2) = \$3.00$$

With existing information, the best that the decision maker could obtain was select (stock 2) and obtain $1.90. With perfect information (forecast), the decision maker could make as much as $3. Therefore, the expected value of perfect information is $3.00 – $1.90 = $1.10. This is the maximum price the decision maker is willing to pay for additional information.

Decision Tree

How does decision tree analysis work?

Decision tree is another approach used in discussions of decision making under uncertainty. It is a pictorial representation of a decision situation. As in the case of the *decision matrix* approach discussed earlier, it shows decision alternatives, states of nature, probabilities attached to the states of nature, and conditional benefits and losses. The decision tree approach is most useful in a sequential decision situation.

EXAMPLE 9.20

Assume XYZ Corporation wishes to introduce one of two products to the market this year. The probabilities and present values (PV) of projected cash inflows are given here.

Products	Initial Investment	PV of Cash Inflows	Probabilities
A	$225,000		1.00
		$450,000	0.40
		200,000	0.50
		−100,000	0.10
B	80,000		1.00
		320,000	0.20
		100,000	0.60
		−150,000	0.20

A decision tree analyzing the two products is given in Exhibit 9.6.

LINEAR PROGRAMMING AND SHADOW PRICES

What is linear programming?

Linear programming (LP) addresses the problem of allocating limited resources among competing activities in an optimal manner. Specifically, it is a technique used to:

o *Maximize* a revenue, contribution margin, or profit function subject to constraints

o *Minimize* a cost function subject to constraints

Linear programming consists of two important ingredients:

o Objective function

o Constraints (including *nonnegativity* constraints), which are typically inequalities

What are the applications of linear programming?

A firm may wish to:

o Find an optimal product mix so as to maximize its total contribution without violating restrictions imposed upon the availability of resources

o Determine a least-cost combination of input materials while satisfying production requirements, maintaining required inventory levels, staying within production capacities, and using available employees

Choice A or B	Initial Investment (1)	Probability (2)	PV of Cash Inflow (3)	PV of Cash Inflow (2 × 3) = (4)
Product A	$225,000	0.40	$450,000	$180,000
		0.50	$200,000	100,000
		0.10	-$100,000	10,000
			Expected PV of Cash Inflows	$270,000
Product B	$80,000	0.20	$320,000	$ 64,000
		0.60	$100,000	60,000
		0.20	-$150,000	30,000
			Expected PV of Cash Inflows	$ 94,000

For Product A:

Expected NPV = expected PV − 1 = $270,000 − $225,000 = $45,000

For Product B:

Expected NPV = $94,000 − $80,000 = $14,000

Based on the expected net present value, the company should choose product A over product B.

Exhibit 9.6

361

Other managerial applications include:

- ○ Selecting an investment mix
- ○ Blending chemical products
- ○ Scheduling flight crews
- ○ Assigning jobs to machines
- ○ Determining transportation routes
- ○ Determining distribution or allocation pattern

How do I formulate a linear programming problem?

To formulate the LP problem:

Step 1. Define the *decision variables* you are trying to solve for.

Step 2. Express the objective function and constraints in terms of these decision variables.

NOTE
As the name *linear* programming implies, all the expressions must be of *linear* form.

EXAMPLE 9.21

A firm produces two products, A and B. Both products require time in two processing departments, Assembly Department and Finishing Department. Data on the two products are as follows:

	Products		Available Hours
Processing	**A**	**B**	
Assembly	2	4	100
Finishing	3	2	90
Contribution Margin per Unit	$25	$40	

The firm wants to find the most profitable mix of these two products.

Step 1. Define the decision variables as follows:

A = the number of units of product A to be produced

B = the number of units of product B to be produced

Step 2. The objective function to maximize total contribution margin (CM) is expressed as:

Total CM = $25A + $40B

EXAMPLE 9.21 *(continued)*

Then, formulate the constraints as inequalities:

$$2A + 4B \leq 100 \quad \text{(Assembly constraint)}$$

$$3A + 2B \leq 90 \quad \text{(Finishing constraint)}$$

Do not forget to add the nonnegativity constraints:

$$A, B \geq 0$$

Our LP model is:

maximize subject to   Total CM = 25A + 40B
                          2A + 4B ≤ 100
                          3A + 2B ≤ 90
                          A, B ≥ 0

How are LP problems solved?

The solution methods available to solve LP problems include:

- o The simplex method
- o The graphical method

What is the simplex method?

The *simplex* method is the technique most commonly used to solve LP problems. It is an algorithm, which is an iteration method of computation, moving from one solution to another until it reaches the best solution. Virtually all computer software for LP uses this method of computation.

What is the graphical method?

The graphical solution is easier to use but limited to the LP problems involving two (or at most three) decision variables. The graphical method follows the steps:

Step 1. Change inequalities to equalities.

Step 2. Graph the equalities.

Step 3. Identify the correct side for the original inequalities.

Step 4. After all this, identify the feasible region, the area of feasible solutions. *Feasible solutions* are values of decision variables that satisfy all the restrictions simultaneously.

Step 5. Determine the contribution margin at all of the corners in the feasible region.

EXAMPLE 9.22

Using the data from Example 9.21, follow steps 1 through 4. We obtain the following feasible region (shaded area in Exhibit 9.7).

EXAMPLE 9.22 *(continued)*

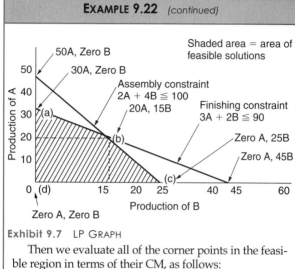

Exhibit 9.7 LP GRAPH

Then we evaluate all of the corner points in the feasible region in terms of their CM, as follows:

	Corner Points		Contribution Margin
	A	**B**	**$25A + $40B**
(a)	30	0	$25(30) + $40(0) = $ 750
(b)	20	15	25(20) + 40(15) = 1,100
(c)	0	25	25(0) + 40(25) = 1,000
(d)	0	0	25(0) + 40(0) = 0

The corner 20A, 15B produces the most profitable solution.

Shadow Prices (Opportunity Costs)

What are shadow prices?

An accountant who has solved an LP problem might wish to know whether it pays to add capacity in hours in a particular department. He or she might be interested in the monetary value to the firm of adding an hour per week of assembly time. This monetary value is the additional contribution margin that could be earned. This amount is called the *shadow price* of the given resource. A shadow price is in a way an opportunity cost, the contribution margin that would be lost by not adding an additional hour of capacity. To justify a decision in favor of a short-term capacity expansion, the accountant must be sure that the shadow price (or opportunity cost) exceeds the actual price of that expansion.

How are shadow prices determined?

Shadow prices are computed as follows:

Step 1.   Add one hour (preferably, more than an hour to make it easier to show graphically) to the constraint under consideration.

Step 2. Resolve the problem and find the maximum CM.
Step 3. Compute the difference between CM of the original LP problem and the CM determined in step 2, which is the shadow price.

Other methods (e.g., using the dual problem) are available to compute shadow prices.

EXAMPLE 9.23

Using the data in Example 9.21, compute the shadow price of the assembly capacity. To make it easier to show graphically, add eight hours of capacity to the assembly department rather than one hour. The new assembly constraint is shown in Exhibit 9.8.

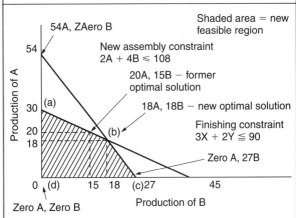

Shaded area = new feasible region

54A, ZAero B

New assembly constraint
2A + 4B ≤ 108

20A, 15B — former optimal solution

18A, 18B — new optimal solution

Finishing constraint
3X + 2Y ≤ 90

Zero A, 27B

Zero A, Zero B

Exhibit 9.8 LP GRAPH

	Corner Points		Contribution Margin
	A	**B**	**$25A + $40B**
(a)	30	0	$25(30) + $40(0) = $ 750
(b)	18	18	25(18) + 40(18) = 1,170
(c)	0	27	25(0) + 40(27) = 1,080
(d)	0	0	25(0) + 40(0) = 0

The new optimal solution of 18A, 18B has total CM of $1,170 per week. Therefore, the shadow price of the assembly capacity is $70 ($1,170 − $1,100 = $70). The firm would be willing to pay up to $70 to obtain an additional eight hours per week, or $8.75 *per hour* per week.

Can the computer be used for LP problem solving?

We can use a computer LP software package, for example, LINDO (Linear Interactive and Discrete Optimization), to quickly solve an LP problem. Exhibit 9.9 shows a computer output by an LP program for our LP model set up in Example 9.22.

** INFORMATION ENTERED **

NUMBER OF CONSTRAINTS	2
NUMBER OF VARIABLES	2
NUMBER OF <= CONSTRAINTS	2
NUMBER OF = CONSTRAINTS	0
NUMBER OF >= CONSTRAINTS	0

MAXIMIZATION PROBLEM

$$25 \times 1 \qquad + 40 \times 2$$

SUBJECT TO

$$2 \times 1 \qquad + 4 \times 2 \qquad \qquad <= 100$$
$$3 \times 1 \qquad + 2 \times 2 \qquad \qquad <= 90$$

NOTE:

$$x_1 = A$$
$$x_2 = B$$

** RESULTS **

VARIABLE	VARIABLE VALUE	ORIGINAL COEFF.	COEFF. SENS.
x 1	20	25	0
x 2	15	40	0

Solution:

$$x_1 = A = 20$$
$$x_2 = B = 15$$

CONSTRAINT NUMBER	ORIGINAL RHS	SLACK OR SURPLUS	SHADOW PRICE
1	100	0	8.75
2	90	0	2.5

OBJECTIVE FUNCTION VALUE: <u>1100</u> = CM

SENSITIVITY ANALYSIS

OBJECTIVE FUNCTION COEFFICIENTS

VARIABLE	LOWER LIMIT	ORIGINAL COEFFICIENT	UPPER LIMIT
x 1	20	25	60
x 2	16.67	40	50

RIGHT-HAND SIDE

CONSTRAINT NUMBER	LOWER LIMIT	ORIGINAL VALUE	UPPER LIMIT
1	60	100	180
2	50	90	150

NOTE: The printout shows the following optimal solution:

$$A = 20$$
$$B = 15$$
$$CM = \$1,100$$

Exhibit 9.9   COMPUTER PRINTOUT FOR LP

GOAL PROGRAMMING AND MULTIPLE GOALS

What is goal programming?

In the previous section, we saw how to develop an optimal program (or product mix) using LP. However, LP has one important drawback; it is limited primarily to solving problems where the objectives of management can be stated in a single goal (e.g., profit maximization or cost minimization). But management must now deal with multiple goals, which are often incompatible and in conflict with each other. Goal programming (GP) gets around this difficulty. In GP, unlike LP, the objective function may consist of multiple, incommensurable, and conflicting goals. Rather than maximizing or minimizing the objective criterion, the deviations from these set goals are minimized, often based on the priority factors assigned to each goal. The fact that management has multiple goals that are in conflict with each other means that management will look for a *satisfactory* solution rather than an *optimal* solution.

What are some examples of multiple conflicting goals?

Consider an investor who desires investments that will have a maximum return and minimum risk. These goals are generally incompatible and therefore unachievable. Other examples of multiple conflicting goals can be found in businesses that want to:

o Maximize profits and increase wages paid to employees
o Upgrade product quality and reduce product costs
o Pay larger dividends to shareholders and retain earnings for growth
o Increase control of channels of distribution and reduce working-capital requirements
o Reduce credit losses and increase sales

How is a goal programming problem solved?

EXAMPLE 9.24

In Example 9.23, the company during this planning period is facing a major organizational change and feels that maximizing contribution margin is not a realistic objective. However, it would like to achieve some satisfactory level of profit during this difficult period. Management feels that a CM of $750 would be satisfactory.

EXAMPLE 9.24 (continued)

The GP problem is to determine, given the production time and material constraints, the product mix that would yield this rate of profit contribution.

To incorporate the $1,500 profit contribution into the GP model, we first define the following *deviational* variables:

$d-$ = underachievement of the target profit
$d+$ = overachievement of the target profit

This profit goal is now written into the model as a goal constraint,

$25A + 40B + d- - d+ = \$750$ (profit goal constraint)

Then our GP model is as follows:

$$
\begin{aligned}
\text{Min } D = \quad & d- + d+ \\
\text{subject to} \quad & 2A + 4B && <100 \\
& 3A + 2B && < 90 \\
& 25A + 40B + d- - d+ && = 750 \\
& A, B, d-, d+ && > 0
\end{aligned}
$$

The solution is shown in Exhibit 9.10.

MINIMIZATION PROBLEM

0×1	$+ 0 \times 2$	$+ 1 \times 3$	$+ 1 \times 4$

SUBJECT TO

2×1	$+ 4 \times 2$	$+ 0 \times 3$	$+ 0 \times 4$
		$<= 100$	
3×1	$+ 2 \times 2$	$+ 0 \times 3$	$+ 0 \times 4$
		$<= 90$	
25×1	$+ 40 \times 2$	$+ 1 \times 3$	$- 1 \times 4$
		$= 750$	

Note:
$x_1 = A$
$x_2 = B$
$x_3 = d-$
$x_4 = d+$

** RESULTS **

VARIABLE	VARIABLE VALUE	ORIGINAL COEFF.	COEFF. SENS.
$\times 1$	0	0	0
$\times 2$	18.75	0	0
$\times 3$	0	1	1
$\times 4$	0	1	1

Exhibit 9.10 COMPUTER PRINTOUT FOR GP

MINIMIZATION PROBLEM

Solution:
$$x_1 = A = 0$$
$$x_2 = B = 18.75$$
$$x_3 = d- = 0$$
$$x_4 = d+ = 0$$

CONSTRAINT NUMBER	ORIGINAL RHS	SLACK OR SURPLUS	SHADOW PRICE
1	100	25	0
2	90	52.5	0
3	750	0	0

OBJECTIVE FUNCTION VALUE: 0

SENSITIVITY ANALYSIS
OBJECTIVE FUNCTION COEFFICIENTS

VARIABLE	LOWER LIMIT	ORIGINAL COEFFICIENT	UPPER LIMIT
$\times 1$	0	0	No Limit
$\times 2$	-40	0	40
$\times 3$	0	1	No Limit
$\times 4$	0	1	No Limit

RIGHT HAND SIDE

CONSTRAINT NUMBER	LOWER LIMIT	ORIGINAL VALUE	UPPER LIMIT
1	75	100	No Limit
2	37.5	90	No Limit
3	0	750	1000

The GP solution is:

$$A = 0, B = 18.75, d- = 0, d+ = 0$$

This means that the company should make 18.75 units of product B (drop product A) in order to fully achieve the target profit of $750.

Exhibit 9.10 COMPUTER PRINTOUT FOR GP *(continued)*

NOTE

One further step might be considered when formulating the GP model. The goal can be ranked according to "preemptive" priority factors. The deviational variables at the same priority level may be given different weights in the objective function, so that the deviational variables within the same priority have the different cardinal weights. (This topic is not treated here and should be referred to in an advanced text.)

LEARNING CURVE

What is the learning cave?

The *learning curve* is based on the proposition that labor hours decrease in a definite pattern as labor operations are repeated. More specifically, it is based on the statistical findings that as the cumulative output doubles, the cumulative average labor input time required per unit will be reduced by some constraint percentage, ranging between 10 percent and 40 percent. The curve is usually designated by its complement. If the rate of reduction is 20 percent, the curve is referred to as an *80 percent learning curve*. (See Exhibit 9.11.)

EXAMPLE 9.25

The following data illustrate the 80 percent learning curve relationship:

Quantity (in units)		Time (in hours)	
Per Lot	Cumulative	Total (Cumulative)	Average Time Per Unit
15	15	600	40.0
15	30	960	32.0 (40.0 × 0.8)
30	60	1,536	25.6 (32.0 × 0.8)
60	120	2,460	20.5 (25.6 × 0.8)
120	240	3,936	16.4 (20.5 × 0.8)

As can be seen, as production quantities double, the average time per unit decreases by 20 percent of its immediately preceding time.

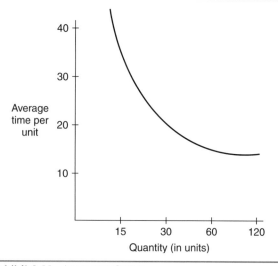

Exhibit 9.11   LEARNING CURVE

What are some applications of the learning curve?

Applications of learning curve theory include:

○ Scheduling labor requirements
○ Capital budgeting decisions
○ Setting incentive wage rates

EXAMPLE 9.26

Stanley Electronics Products, Inc. finds that new-product production is affected by an 80 percent learning effect. The company has just produced 50 units of output at 100 hours per unit. Costs were as follows:

Materials @ $20	$1,000
Labor and labor-related costs:	
Direct labor—100 hr @ $8	800
Variable overhead—100 hr @ $2	200
	$2,000

The company has just received a contract calling for another 50 units of production. It wants to add a 50 percent markup to the cost of materials and labor and labor-related costs. Determine the price for this job as follows:

Building up the table yields:

Quantity	Total Time (in hours)	Average time (per unit)
50 units	100 hr	2 hr
100	160	1.6 (80% × 2 hr)

Thus, for the new 50-unit job, it takes 60 hours total.

Materials @ $20	$1,000
Labor and labor-related costs:	
Direct labor—60 hr @ $8	480
Variable overhead—60 hr @ $2	120
	$1,600
50 percent markup	800
Contract price	$2,400

INVENTORY PLANNING AND CONTROL

How do I plan and control inventory?

One of the most common problems that faces managerial accountants is that of inventory planning and control. Inventory usually represents a sizable portion of a firm's total assets. Excess funds tied up in inventory are a drag on profitability. The purpose of inventory planning and control is to develop policies that will achieve an optimal investment in inventory. This objective is achieved by determining the optimal level of inventory necessary to minimize inventory related costs.

What types of inventory costs are there?

Inventory costs fall into three categories:

○ *Order costs* include all costs associated with preparing a purchase order.

○ *Carrying costs* include storage costs for inventory items plus opportunity cost (i.e., the cost incurred by investing in inventory).

○ *Shortage (stockout) costs* include those costs incurred when an item is out of stock. These include the lost contribution margin on sales plus lost customer goodwill.

What are the basic types of inventory models?

There are many inventory planning and control models available which try to answer the following basic questions:

○ How much to order?
○ When to order?

They include the:

○ Basic economic order quantity (EOQ) model
○ Reorder point
○ Determination of safety stock

Economic Order Quantity (EOQ)

What is the optimal amount to order?

The EOQ model determines the order size that minimizes the sum of carrying and ordering costs.

○ Demand is assumed to be a fixed amount and constant throughout the year.

○ Order cost is assumed to be a fixed amount.

○ Unit carrying costs are assumed to be constant.

NOTE: Since demand and lead time are assumed to be determinable, there are no shortage costs.

EOQ is computed as:

$$EOQ = \sqrt{\frac{2(\text{annual demand})\ (\text{ordering cost})}{\text{carrying cost per unit}}}$$

EXAMPLE: If the carrying cost is expressed as a percentage of average inventory value (e.g., 12 percent per year to hold inventory), then the denominator value in the EOQ formula would be 12 percent times the price of an item.

EXAMPLE 9.27

ABC Store buys sets of steel at $40 per set from an out-side vendor. ABC will sell 6,400 sets evenly throughout the year. ABC desires a 16 percent return on investment (cost of borrowed money) on its inventory investment. In addition, rent, taxes, and the likes for each set in inventory is $1.60. The ordering cost is $100 per order.

The carrying cost per dozen is 16% ($40) + $1.60 = $8.00. Therefore,

$$EOQ = \sqrt{\frac{2(6,400)(\$100)}{\$8.00}} = \sqrt{160,000} = 400 \text{ sets}$$

$$\begin{aligned}
\text{Total inventory costs} &= \frac{\text{Carrying cost}}{\text{per unit}} \times \frac{EOQ}{2} \\
&\quad + \frac{\text{Order}}{\text{per order}} \times \frac{\text{Annual demand}}{EOQ} \\
&= (\$8.00)(400/2) + (\$100)(6,400/400) \\
&= \$1,600 + \$1,600 = \$3,200
\end{aligned}$$

Total number of orders per year
= Annual demand / EOQ
= 6,400 / 400
= 16 orders

How is the EOQ model applied?

The EOQ model described here is appropriate for a pure inventory system, that is, for single-item, single-stage inventory decisions for which joint costs and constraints can be ignored. EOQ assumes that both lead time and demand rates are constant and known with certainty. CAUTION: This may be unrealistic. Nevertheless, these models have proven useful in inventory planning for many firms.

Many situations exist where such an assumption holds or nearly holds. EXAMPLES: Subcontractors who must supply parts on a regular basis to a primary contractor face a constant demand. Even where demand varies, the assumption of uniform usage is not unrealistic. For an auto dealer, demand for automobiles varies from week to week, but over a season the weekly fluctuations cancel each other out so that seasonal demand can be assumed constant.

How does EOQ handle quantity discounts?

The economic order quantity (EOQ) model does not take into account quantity discounts. This makes it unrealistic in many real-life cases. Usually, the more you order, the lower the unit price you pay. Quantity discounts are price reductions for large orders offered to buyers to induce them to buy in large quantities. If quantity discounts are offered, the buyer must weigh the potential benefits of reduced purchase price and fewer orders that will result from buying in large quantities against the increase in carrying costs caused by higher average inventories. Hence, the buyer's goal is to select the order quantity that will minimize total cost, where total cost is the sum of carrying cost, ordering cost, and purchase cost:

$$\text{Total cost} = \text{Carrying cost} + \text{Ordering cost} + \text{Purchase cost}$$
$$= C \times (Q/2) + O\,(D/Q) + PD$$

> where
> C = carrying cost per unit
> O = ordering cost per order
> D = annual demand
> P = unit price
> Q = order quantity

How do I calculate EOQ with quantity discounts?

To find the EOQ *with* quantity discounts:

Step 1. Compute the economic order quantity (EOQ) ignoring price discounts; and compute the corresponding costs using the new cost formula given above.

   NOTE: $\text{EOQ} = \sqrt{2OD/C}$.

Step 2. Compute the costs for those quantities greater than the EOQ at which price reductions occur.

Step 3. Select the value of Q that will result in the lowest total cost.

EXAMPLE 9.28

Using the data from Example 9.27, assume that ABC was offered the following price discount schedule:

Order Quantity (Q)	Unit Price (P)
1 to 499	$40.00
500 to 999	39.90
1000 or more	39.80

Step 1. The EOQ with no discounts is computed as follows:

$$\text{EOQ} = \sqrt{2(6,400)(100)/8.00} = \sqrt{160,000}$$
$$= 400 \text{ sets.}$$

EXAMPLE 9.28 (continued)

Total cost = $8.00 (400/2) + $100 (6,400/400)
         + $40.00 (6,400)
         = $1,600 + 1,600
         + $256,000
         = $259,200

Step 2. The value that minimized the sum of the carrying cost and the order cost but not the purchase cost was EOQ = 400 sets. As can be seen in Exhibit 9.12 the further we move from the point 400, the greater the sum of the carrying and ordering costs is. Thus, 400 is obviously the only candidate for the minimum total cost value within the first price range. Q = 500 is the only candidate within the $39.90 price range, and Q = 1,000 is the only candidate within the $39.80 price bracket.

Step 3. These three quantities are evaluated in Exhibit 9.13 and illustrated in Exhibit 9.12. The EOQ *with* price discounts is 500 sets. Hence, ABC is justified in going to the first price break, but the extra carrying cost of going to the second price break more than outweighs the savings in ordering and in the cost of the product itself.

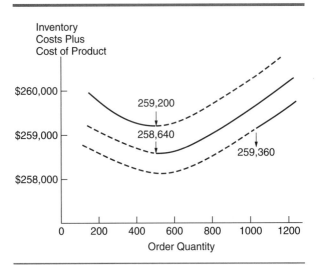

Exhibit 9.12 INVENTORY COST AND QUANTITY

Order Quantity	400	500	1,000
Ordering cost $100 × (6,400/order quantity)	$ 1,600	$ 1,280	$ 640
Carrying cost $8 × (order quantity/2)	1,600	2,000	4,000
Purchase cost Unit price × 6,400	256,000	255,360	254,720
Total cost	$259,200	$258,640	$259,360

Exhibit 9.13   ANNUAL COSTS WITH VARYING ORDER QUANTITIES

What are the pros and cons of quantity discounts?

Buying in large quantities has some favorable and some unfavorable features for a firm. The advantages are:

- Lower unit costs
- Lower ordering costs
- Fewer stockouts
- Lower transportation costs

The disadvantages are:

- Higher inventory carrying costs
- Greater capital requirement
- Higher probability of obsolescence and deterioration

Reorder Point (ROP)

When is the best time to place an order?

Reorder point (ROP), which answers *when* to place a new order, requires a knowledge of the *lead time*, the interval between placing an order and receiving delivery. ROP is calculated as follows:

> Reorder point = average usage per unit of lead time × lead time + safety stock

Step 1. Multiply average daily (or weekly) usage by the lead time in days (or weeks) yielding the lead time demand.

Step 2. Add safety stock to this to provide for the variation in lead time demand.

NOTE

If average usage and lead time are both certain, no safety stock is necessary and should be dropped from the formula.

EXAMPLE 9.29

Using the data in Example 9.27, assume lead time is constant at one week, and there are 50 working weeks in a year.

Step 1. Reorder point is 128 sets = (6,400 sets/50 weeks) × 1 week. Therefore, when the inventory level drops to 128 sets, the new order should be placed.

Step 2. Suppose, however, that the store is faced with variable usage for its steel and requires a safety stock of 150 additional sets to carry. Then the reorder point will be 128 sets *plus* 150 sets, or 278 sets.

Exhibit 9.14 shows this inventory system when the order quantity is 400 sets and the reorder point is 128 sets.

Safety Stock and Reorder Point

At what level should inventory be ordered?

When lead time and demand are not certain, the firm must carry extra units of inventory called *safety stock* as protection against possible stockouts. Stockouts can be quite expensive.

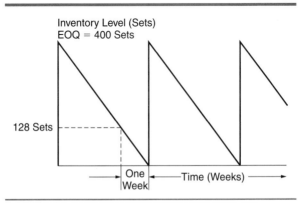

Exhibit 9.14 BASIC INVENTORY SYSTEM WITH EOQ AND REORDER POINT

EXAMPLES: Lost sales and disgruntled customers are external costs. Idle machine and disrupted production scheduling are internal costs.

The probability approach is used to show how the optimal stock size can be determined in the presence of stockout costs.

EXAMPLE 9.30

Using the data from Examples 9.27 and 9.28, assume that the total usage over a one-week period is expected to be:

Total Usage	Probability
78	0.2
128	0.4
178	0.2
228	0.1
278	0.1
	1.00

Further assume that a stockout cost is estimated at $12.00 per set. Recall that the carrying cost is $8.00 per set.

The computation shows that the total costs are minimized at $1,200, when a safety stock of 150 sets is maintained. Therefore, the reorder point is: 128 sets + 150 sets = 278 sets.

Computation of Safety Stock

Safety Stock Levels in Units	Stockout and Probability	Average Stockout in Units	Average Stockout Costs	No. of Orders	Total Annual Stockout Costs	Carrying Costs	Total
0	50 with 0.2	35[1]	$420[2]	16	$6,720[3]	0	$7,140
	100 with 0.1						
	150 with 0.1						
50	50 with 0.1	15	180	16	2,880	400[4]	3,280
	100 with 0.1						
100	50 with 0.1	5	60	16	960	800	1,760
150	0	0	0	16	0	1,200	1,200

[1] 50(0.2) + 100(0.1) + 150(0.1) = 10 + 10 + 15 = 35 units

[2] 35 units × $12.00 = $420

[3] $420 × 16 times = $6,720

[4] 50 units × $8.00 = $400

379

PROGRAM EVALUATION AND REVIEW TECHNIQUE (PERT)

What is PERT?

Program Evaluation and Review Technique (PERT) is a useful management tool for planning, scheduling, costing, coordinating, and controlling complex projects such as

- ○ Formulation of a master budget
- ○ Construction of buildings
- ○ Installation of computers
- ○ Scheduling the closing of books
- ○ Assembly of a machine
- ○ Research and development activities

Questions to be answered by PERT include:

- ○ When will the project be finished?
- ○ What is the probability that the project will be completed by any given time?

How do I schedule a project?

The PERT technique involves the diagrammatic representation of the sequence of activities comprising a project by means of a *network*. The network:

- ○ Visualizes all of the individual tasks (activities) to complete a given job or program.
- ○ Points out interrelationships.
- ○ Consists of activities (represented by arrows) and events (represented by circles).

In Exhibit 9.15.

- ○ *Arrows.* Arrows represent "tasks" or "activities" which are distinct segments of the project requiring time and resources.
- ○ *Nodes (circles).* Nodes symbolize "events" or milestone points in the project representing the completion of one or more activities and/or the initiation of one or more subsequent activities. An event is a point in time and does not consume any time in itself as does an activity.

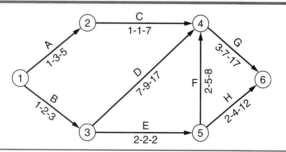

Exhibit 9.15 NETWORK DIAGRAM

When will the project be finished?

In a real-world situation, estimates of activity completion times will seldom be certain.

NOTE

To cope with the uncertainty in activity time estimates, the PERT proceeds by estimating *three* possible duration times for each activity. As shown in Exhibit 9.15, the numbers appearing on the arrows represent the three time estimates for activities needed to complete the various events. These time estimates are:

1. The most optimistic time, a
2. The most likely time, m
3. The most pessimistic time, b

EXAMPLE 9.31

For activity B:

- o The optimistic time for completing activity B is 1 day.
- o The most likely time is 2 days.
- o The pessimistic time is 3 days.

The next step is to calculate an expected time, which is determined as follows:

$$t_e \text{ (expected time)} = (a + 4m + b)/6$$

For activity B, the expected time is

$$t_e = (1 + 4(2) + 3)/6 = 12/6 = 2 \text{ days}$$

What quantitative calculations are involved in PERT?

As a measure of variation (uncertainty) about the expected time, the standard deviation is calculated as follows:

$$\sigma = (b - a)/6$$

The standard deviation of completion time for activity B is:

$$\sigma = (3 - 1)/6 = 2/6 = 0.33 \text{ day}$$

Expected activity times and their standard deviations are computed in this manner for all of the activities of the network and arranged in the tabular format as shown below:

Activity	Predecessors	a	m	b	t_e	σ
A	None	1	3	5	3.0	0.67
B	None	1	2	3	2.0	0.33
C	A	1	1	7	2.0	1.00

Activity	Predecessors	a	m	b	t_e	σ
D	B	7	9	17	10.0	1.67
E	B	2	2	2	2.0	0.00
F	E	2	5	8	5.0	0.67
G	C,D,F	3	7	17	8.0	2.33
H	E	2	4	12	5.0	1.67

What is a critical path?

To answer the first question—when will the project be finished—we need to determine the network's *critical path*. A path is a sequence of connected activities. In Exhibit 9.15, 1-2-4-6 is a path. The critical path for a project is the path that takes the longest time. The sum of the estimated activity times for all activities on the critical path is the total time required to complete the project. These activities are "critical," because any delay in their completion causes a delay in the project.

The critical path is also the minimum amount of time needed for the completion of the project. Thus, the activities along this path must be shortened in order to speed up the project. Activities not on the critical path are not critical; they will be worked on simultaneously with critical path activities, and their completion could be delayed up to a point without delaying the project as a whole.

How do I find the critical path?

An easy way to find the critical path involves the following two steps:

○ Identify all possible paths of a project and calculate their completion times.

○ Pick the one with the longest completion time; this is the critical path.

NOTE

When the network is large and complex, a more systematic and efficient approach is needed. Refer to an advanced management science text.

EXAMPLE 9.32

Given the data in Example 9.31, we have:

Path	Completion Time	
A-C-G	13 days	(3 + 2 + 8)
B-D-G	20 days	(2 + 10 + 8)

EXAMPLE 9.32 *(continued)*

B-E-F-G	17 days (2 + 2 + 5 + 8)
B-E-H	9 days (2 + 2 + 5)

The critical path is B-D-G, which means it takes 20 days to complete the project.

What is the probability that the project will be completed on time?

The next important information to obtain is the probability of the project being completed within a contract time. To obtain this information, use the standard deviation of total project time around the expected time, as follows:

Standard deviation (project)

$$= \sqrt{\begin{array}{l}\text{the sum of the squares of the standard} \\ \text{deviations of all critical path activities}\end{array}}$$

Using the standard deviation and table of areas under the normal distribution curve (Exhibit 9.16), the probability of completing the project within any given time period can be determined.

AREAS UNDER THE NORMAL CURVE

Z	0	1	2	3	4	5	6	7	8	9
.0	.5000	.5040	.5080	.5120	.5160	.5199	.5239	.5279	.5319	.5359
.1	.5398	.5438	.5478	.5517	.5557	.5596	.5636	.5675	.5714	.5753
.2	.5793	.5832	.5871	.5910	.5948	.5987	.6026	.6064	.6103	.6141
.3	.6179	.6217	.6255	.6293	.6331	.6368	.6406	.6443	.6480	.6517
.4	.6554	.6591	.6628	.6664	.6700	.6736	.6772	.6808	.6844	.6879
.5	.6915	.6950	.6985	.7019	.7054	.7088	.7123	.7157	.7190	.7224
.6	.7257	.7291	.7324	.7357	.7389	.7422	.7454	.7486	.7517	.7549
.7	.7580	.7611	.7642	.7673	.7703	.7734	.7764	.7794	.7823	.7852
.8	.7881	.7910	.7939	.7967	.7995	.8023	.8051	.8078	.8106	.8133
.9	.8159	.8186	.8212	.8238	.8264	.8289	.8315	.8340	.8365	.8389

.9648

Mean 1.81

Exhibit 9.16 NORMAL DISTRIBUTION TABLE

384

1.0	.8413	.8438	.8461	.8485	.8508	.8531	.8554	.8577	.8599	.8621
1.1	.8643	.8665	.8686	.8708	.8729	.8749	.8770	.8790	.8810	.8830
1.2	.8849	.8869	.8888	.8907	.8925	.8944	.8962	.8980	.8997	.9015
1.3	.9032	.9049	.9066	.9082	.9099	.9115	.9131	.9147	.9162	.9177
1.4	.9192	.9207	.9222	.9236	.9251	.9265	.9278	.9292	.9306	.9319
1.5	.9332	.9345	.9357	.9370	.9382	.9394	.9406	.9418	.9430	.9441
1.6	.9452	.9463	.9474	.9484	.9495	.9505	.9515	.9525	.9535	.9545
1.7	.9554	.9564	.9573	.9582	.9591	.9599	.9608	.9616	.9625	.9633
1.8	.9641	.9648	.9656	.9664	.9671	.9678	.9686	.9693	.9700	.9706
1.9	.9713	.9719	.9726	.9732	.9738	.9744	.9750	.9756	.9762	.9767
2.0	.9772	.9778	.9783	.9788	.9793	.9798	.9803	.9808	.9812	.9817
2.1	.9821	.9826	.9830	.9834	.9838	.9842	.9846	.9850	.9854	.9857
2.2	.9861	.9864	.9868	.9871	.9874	.9878	.9881	.9884	.9887	.9890
2.3	.9893	.9896	.9898	.9901	.9904	.9906	.9909	.9911	.9913	.9916
2.4	.9918	.9920	.9922	.9925	.9927	.9929	.9931	.9932	.9934	.9936
2.5	.9938	.9940	.9941	.9943	.9945	.9946	.9948	.9949	.9951	.9952
2.6	.9953	.9955	.9956	.9957	.9959	.9960	.9961	.9962	.9963	.9964
2.7	.9965	.9966	.9967	.9968	.9969	.9970	.9971	.9972	.9973	.9974
2.8	.9974	.9975	.9976	.9977	.9977	.9978	.9979	.9979	.9980	.9981
2.9	.9981	.9982	.9982	.9983	.9984	.9984	.9985	.9985	.9986	.9986
3.	.9987	.9990	.9993	.9995	.9997	.9998	.9998	.9999	.9999	1.0000

Exhibit 9.16   NORMAL DISTRIBUTION TABLE

EXAMPLE 9.33

Using the formula above and information in Exhibit 9.16, the standard deviation of completion time (the path B-D-G) for the project is as follows:

$$\sqrt{(0.33)^2 + (1.67)^2 + (2.33)^2}$$
$$= \sqrt{0.1089 + 2.7889 + 5.4289}$$
$$= \sqrt{8.3267\%} = 2.885 \text{ days}$$

Assume the expected delivery time is 21 days.

Step 1. Compute z, the number of standard deviations from the mean represented by our given time of 21 days. The formula for z is:

z = (delivery time – expected time)/
standard deviation

Therefore, z = (21 days – 20 days)/
2.885 days = 0.35

Step 2. Find the probability associated with the calculated value of z by referring to a table of areas under a normal curve (Exhibit 9.16)

From Exhibit 9.16 we see the probability is .63683, which means there is close to a 64 percent chance that the project will be completed in less than 21 days. To summarize:

○ The expected completion time of the project is 20 days.
○ There is a better than 60 percent chance of finishing before 21 days. The chances of meeting any other deadline can also be obtained, if desired.
○ Activities B-D-G are on the critical path; they must be watched more closely than the others. If they fall behind, the whole project falls behind.

What other considerations are there with critical path?

If extra effort is needed to finish the project on time or before the deadline, borrow resources (such as money and labor) from any activity not on the critical path.

It is possible to reduce the completion time of one or more activities. This will require an extra expenditure of cost. The benefit from reducing the total completion time of a project by accelerated efforts on certain activities must be balanced against this extra cost. A related problem is determining which activities must be accelerated in order to reduce the total project completion time. Critical Path Method (CPM), also known as PERT/COST, is widely used to deal with this subject. CAUTION: PERT is a technique for project management and control.

- o It is *not* an optimizing decision model, since the decision to undertake a project is initially assumed.
- o It won't evaluate an investment project according to its attractiveness or the time specifications observed.

PART 4

AUDITING, COMPILING, AND REVIEWING
FINANCIAL STATEMENTS

CHAPTER 10

AUDITING PROCEDURES

*T*he financial statement audit, commonly referred to as the *attest function*, involves (1) examination of financial statements through the gathering of sufficient competent evidential matter and (2) expression of an opinion on the fairness of the presentation of the financial statements in conformity with generally accepted accounting principles (or another comprehensive basis of accounting).

In planning a financial statement audit, the practitioner should develop an overall strategy for:

- ○ Considering a client's internal control
- ○ Performing substantive tests

This strategy should be documented in the audit work papers.

INTERNAL CONTROL

What are the components of internal control?

A client's internal control is a process designed to provide reasonable, but not absolute, assurance that the following entity objectives will be achieved:

- ○ Reliable financial reporting
- ○ Effective and efficient operations
- ○ Compliance with laws and regulations

A client's internal control consists of five interrelated components:

- ○ Control environment
- ○ Risk assessment
- ○ Control activities
- ○ Information and communication systems support
- ○ Monitoring

What is the control environment?

The control environment, which is the foundation for the other components of internal control, provides discipline and structure by setting the tone of an organization and influencing control consciousness. Factors to consider in assessing the client's control environment include:

○ Integrity and ethical values, including (1) management's actions to eliminate or mitigate incentives and temptations on the part of personnel to commit dishonest, illegal, or unethical acts, (2) policy statements, and (3) codes of conduct

○ Commitment to competence, including management's consideration of competence levels for specific tasks and how those levels translate into necessary skills and knowledge

○ Board of directors or audit committee participation, including interaction with internal and external (independent) auditors

○ Management's philosophy and operating style, such as management's attitude and actions regarding financial reporting, as well as management's approach to taking and monitoring risks

○ The entity's organizational structure

○ Assignment of authority and responsibility, including fulfilling job responsibilities

○ Human resource policies and practices, including those relating to hiring, orientation, training, evaluating, counseling, promoting, and compensating employees

What is meant by risk assessment?

An entity's risk assessment for financial reporting purposes is its identification, analysis, and management of risks pertaining to financial statement preparation. Accordingly, risk assessment may consider the possibility of executed transactions that remain unrecorded.

The following internal and external events and circumstances may be relevant to the risk of preparing financial statements that are not in conformity with generally accepted accounting principles (or another comprehensive basis of accounting):

○ Changes in operating environment, including competitive pressures

○ New personnel that have a different perspective on internal control

○ Rapid growth that can result in a breakdown in controls

○ New technology in information systems and production processes

- New lines, products, or activities
- Corporate restructuring that might result in changes in supervision and segregation of job functions
- Foreign operations
- Accounting pronouncements requiring adoption of new accounting principles

What control activities are applicable to a financial statement audit?

Control activities are the policies and procedures management has implemented in order to ensure that directives are carried out. Control activities that may be relevant to a financial statement audit may be classified into the following categories:

- Performance reviews, including comparisons of actual performance with budgets, forecasts, and prior period results.
- Information processing. Controls relating to information processing are generally designed to verify accuracy, completeness, and authorization of transactions. Specifically, controls may be classified as general controls or application controls. General controls might include controls over data center operations, systems software acquisition and maintenance, and access security; application controls apply to the processing of individual applications and are designed to ensure that transactions that are recorded are valid, authorized, and complete.
- Physical controls, which involve adequate safeguards over the access to assets and records, include authorization for access to computer programs and files and periodic counting and comparison with amounts shown on control records.
- Segregation of duties, which is designed to reduce opportunities that allow any person to be in a position to both perpetrate and conceal errors or fraud in the normal course of his or her duties, involves assigning different people the responsibilities of authorizing transactions, recording transactions, and maintaining custody of assets.

What knowledge about the "information and communication systems support" component should an auditor obtain?

The auditor should obtain sufficient knowledge about the information system relevant to financial reporting. The information system generally consists of the methods and records established to record, process, summarize, and report entity transactions and to maintain accountability of related assets, liabilities, and equity.

Communication involves providing an understanding of individual roles and responsibilities pertaining to internal control over financial reporting.

What is meant by monitoring?

Monitoring is management's process of assessing the quality of internal control performance over time. Accordingly, management must assess the design and operation of controls on a timely basis and take necessary corrective actions. Monitoring may involve (1) separate evaluations, (2) the use of internal auditors, and (3) the use of communications from outside parties (e.g., complaints from customers and regulator comments).

Is there a relationship between objectives and components?

There is a direct relationship between objectives and components. This results from the fact that objectives are what an entity strives to achieve, while components are what an entity needs to achieve the objectives. It is also important to remember that internal control is relevant not only to the entire entity, but also to an entity's operating units and business functions.

CAUTION

Not all of the objectives and related controls are relevant to a financial statement audit. Furthermore, an understanding of internal control relevant to each operating unit and business function may not be essential.

What objectives and controls are relevant to a financial statement audit?

In general, the auditor should consider the controls that pertain to the entity's objective of preparing financial statements for external use that are presented fairly in conformity with generally accepted accounting principles (GAAP) or some other comprehensive basis of accounting other than GAAP (OCBOA).

The controls relating to operations and compliance objectives may be relevant to a financial statement audit if they pertain to data the auditor evaluates or uses. For example, the auditor may consider the controls relevant to nonfinancial data (such as production statistics) used in analytical procedures.

What is the auditor's primary consideration with respect to the components of internal control?

The auditor's primary consideration is whether a specific control affects the financial statement assertions rather than its classification into any particular component.

Although the five components are applicable to every audit, they should be considered in the context of the following:

- o Entity size
- o Organization and ownership characteristics
- o Nature of the entity's business
- o Diversity and complexity of operations
- o Methods of transmitting, processing, maintaining, and accessing information
- o Applicable legal and regulatory requirements

How does information technology (IT) affect internal control?

- o An entity's use of IT may affect any of the five interrelated components of internal control.
- o Controls in systems that use IT consist of a combination of automated controls (e.g., controls embedded in computer programs) and manual controls.

What are the potential benefits of IT to internal control?

IT provides potential benefits of effectiveness and efficiency for internal control because it enables the entity to:

- o Consistently apply predefined rules and perform complex calculations in processing large volumes of transactions or data.
- o Enhance the timeliness, availability, and accuracy of information.
- o Facilitate the additional analysis of information.
- o Enhance the ability to monitor the performance of the entity's activities and its policies and procedures.
- o Reduce the risk that controls will be circumvented.
- o Enhance the ability to achieve effective segregation of duties by implementing security controls in applications, databases, and operating systems.

What risks does IT pose to internal control?

IT poses specific risks to internal control, including:

- o Reliance on inaccurate systems or programs
- o Unauthorized access to data that may result in destruction of data or improper alterations to data

- ○ Unauthorized changes to master files
- ○ Unauthorized changes to systems or programs
- ○ Failure to make necessary changes to systems or programs
- ○ Inappropriate manual intervention
- ○ Potential loss of data

NOTE: The extent and nature of these risks to internal control depend on the nature and characteristics of the entity's information system.

To what extent must I consider the client's internal control?

The practitioner must obtain a sufficient understanding of internal control to enable the proper planning of the audit. Whether controls have been placed in operations is of prime importance. Operating effectiveness is not to be judged by the practitioner. The understanding of the internal control should (1) provide a basis for identifying types of potential misstatements, (2) enable the assessment of the risk that such misstatements will occur, and (3) enable the auditor to design substantive tests.

What are the procedures used to obtain an understanding of internal control?

Ordinarily, a combination of the following procedures is used in obtaining a sufficient understanding of internal control:

- ○ Previous experience with the client
- ○ Inquiry of appropriate client personnel
- ○ Observation of client activities
- ○ Reference to prior year working papers
- ○ Inspection of client-prepared descriptions, such as organization charts and accounting manuals

How should I document my understanding of internal control?

The auditor must exercise professional judgment in determining the methods and extent of documentation. The most frequently used methods of documentation are:

- ○ Flowcharts
- ○ Questionnaires
- ○ Narrative memos (written descriptions)

How are flowcharts helpful?

A flowchart is a pictorial representation of the flow of transactions. Flowcharts use standardized symbols and enable the auditor to visualize strengths and weaknesses in internal control. (See Exhibits 10.1A, 10.1B, and 10.2A–D.)

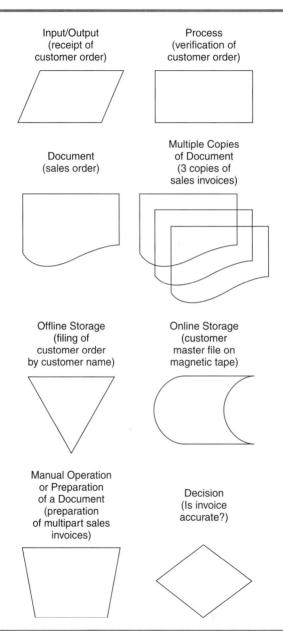

Exhibit 10.1A STANDARDIZED FLOWCHART SYMBOLS

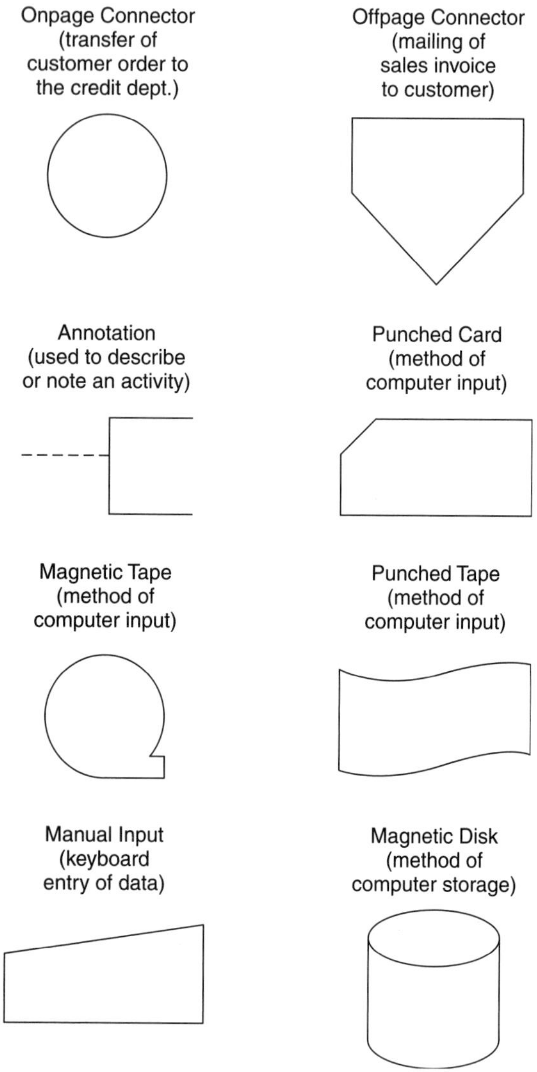

Onpage Connector
(transfer of
customer order to
the credit dept.)

Offpage Connector
(mailing of
sales invoice
to customer)

Annotation
(used to describe
or note an activity)

Punched Card
(method of
computer input)

Magnetic Tape
(method of
computer input)

Punched Tape
(method of
computer input)

Manual Input
(keyboard
entry of data)

Magnetic Disk
(method of
computer storage)

Exhibit 10.1B STANDARDIZED FLOWCHART SYMBOLS
(continued)

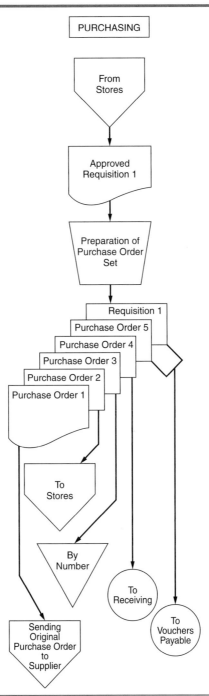

Exhibit 10.2A FLOWCHART FOR A TYPICAL PURCHASING AND CASH DISBURSEMENT SYSTEM

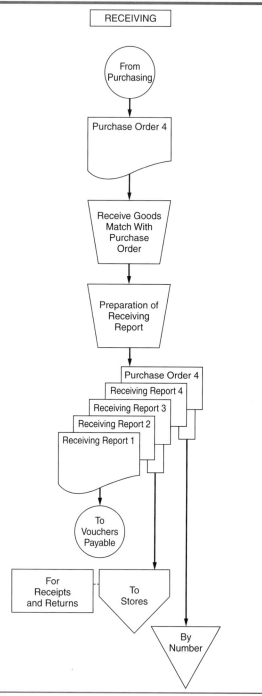

RECEIVING

From Purchasing

Purchase Order 4

Receive Goods Match With Purchase Order

Preparation of Receiving Report

Purchase Order 4
Receiving Report 4
Receiving Report 3
Receiving Report 2
Receiving Report 1

To Vouchers Payable

For Receipts and Returns

To Stores

By Number

Exhibit 10.2B FLOWCHART FOR A TYPICAL PURCHASING AND CASH DISBURSEMENT SYSTEM *(continued)*

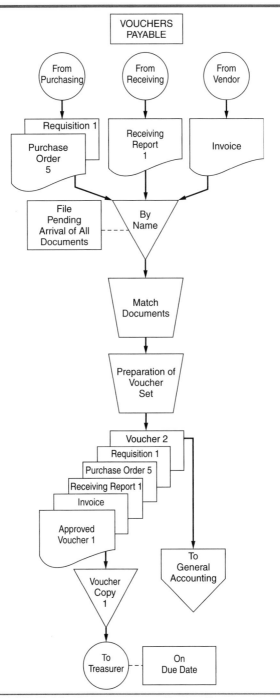

Exhibit 10.2C FLOWCHART FOR A TYPICAL PURCHASING AND CASH DISBURSEMENT SYSTEM *(continued)*

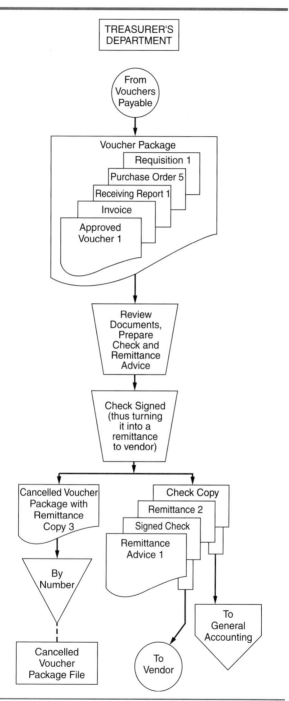

Exhibit 10.2D FLOWCHART FOR A TYPICAL PURCHASING AND
CASH DISBURSEMENT SYSTEM *(continued)*

How are questionnaires used?

A questionnaire is a series of questions designed to elicit a "yes" or "no" response as to whether a control exists. A "no" response, indicating a lack of the control, should prompt the auditor to pose another question in order to ascertain the existence of a compensating control. Questionnaires are useful because they can be tailored to fit a particular client. (See Exhibit 10.3.)

What is meant by assessing control risk?

The assessment of control risk is a process of evaluating the effectiveness of a client's internal controls in preventing or detecting material misstatements in the financial statements.

How do I assess control risk?

If the auditor concludes, based on his or her understanding of internal control, that controls are likely to be ineffective or that evaluation of their effectiveness would be inefficient, then the auditor may assess control risk at the maximum level for some or all financial statement assertions.

If specific controls are likely to prevent or detect material misstatements and the auditor performs tests of controls in order to evaluate the effectiveness of the controls identified, then assessment of control risk below the maximum level is permissible.

Authorized Execution of Transactions				
	Yes	No	Basis for Answer	Comments
1. Are investment transactions approved by the board of directors, the treasurer, or other responsible officer?				
2. Is authorization required for access to vaults or safe-deposit boxes?				
3. Is there proper documentation for initiation and approval of transactions?				
Limited Access to Assets				
	Yes	No	Basis for Answer	Comments
1. Are investment securities kept in safe-deposit boxes or vaults?				
2. If not, is a bonded custodian utilized?				

Exhibit 10.3 THE MAKE-A-MILLION-DOLLARS COMPANY SAMPLE INTERNAL CONTROL QUESTIONNAIRE FOR INVESTMENTS

Authorized Execution of Transactions				
	Yes	No	Basis for Answer	Comments
3. Are securities, other than bearer bonds, registered in the name of the company?				
4. Does the company require two authorized signatures for access to the securities?				

Comparison of Recorded Amounts with Assets in Existence				
	Yes	No	Basis for Answer	Comments
1. Is there periodic inspection of investment securities?				
2. Is there periodic comparison of recorded amounts with actual investment certificates?				
3. Is there periodic review of worthless securities for possible realization?				

Recording of Transactions				
	Yes	No	Basis for Answer	Comments
1. Is an investment ledger maintained?				
2. Are general ledger control totals compared to subsidiary investment ledgers?				
3. Does management record investments using the lower-of-cost-or-market-value method?				
4. Are investment transactions classified between current and long-term?				
5. Is the cost or equity method being utilized?				

Technically Trained and Competent Personnel				
	Yes	No	Basis for Answer	Comments
1. Are employees involved in the custody function bonded?				
2. Are employees involved in the custody function subjected to polygraph tests?				
3. Does the company maintain a prior work-experience requirement for all employees involved in custody and recording of transactions?				

Exhibit 10.3   THE MAKE-A-MILLION-DOLLARS COMPANY SAMPLE INTERNAL CONTROL QUESTIONNAIRE FOR INVESTMENTS *(continued)*

Authorized Execution of Transactions				
Segregation of Incompatible Functions				
	Yes	No	Basis for Answer	Comments
1. Are the following functions segregated:				
a. Custody of investment securities?				
b. Maintenance of subsidiary records?				
c. Journalizing transactions?				
d. Posting to general ledger accounts?				
e. Authorization for acquiring and disposing of investments?				
f. Execution of authorized transactions?				
g. Cash transactions?				

Exhibit 10.3   THE MAKE-A-MILLION-DOLLARS COMPANY SAMPLE INTERNAL CONTROL QUESTIONNAIRE FOR INVESTMENTS *(continued)*

What are tests of controls?

SAS 55 defines tests of controls as tests directed toward the design or operation of an internal control to assess its effectiveness in preventing or detecting material misstatements in a financial statement assertion. Inquiry of company personnel, inspection of client documents and records, observation of client activities, and reperformance of controls represent some of the procedures used in performing tests of controls.

In performing tests of controls, the auditor seeks answers to the following questions:

- o Who performed the control?
- o When was the control performed?
- o How was the control performed?
- o Was the control consistently applied?

What is the relationship between the assessed level of control risk and substantive testing?

Since the auditor's determination of the nature, extent, and timing of substantive tests is dependent on detection risk, the assessed level of control risk must be considered in conjunction with inherent risk (see SAS 47). There is an inverse relationship between detection risk and the assurances to be provided from substantive tests. Accordingly, as detection risk decreases, the auditor should consider the following:

- o Utilize more effective substantive tests.
- o Perform substantive tests at year-end rather than at interim dates.
- o Increase the amount of substantive testing.

Do I have to document the assessed level of control risk?

The assessed level of control risk must be documented in the working papers in every audit engagement. If the control risk is assessed at the maximum level, documentation may be limited to a statement to that effect. The basis for the auditor's conclusion is not required when control risk is assessed at the maximum level. If the control risk is assessed at below the maximum level, documentation must include the assessed level and the basis for the auditor's conclusion.

How do cycles figure in assessing control risk?

The second fieldwork standard under Generally Accepted Auditing Standards (GAAS) requires that the auditor obtain a sufficient understanding of internal control in order to plan the audit and to determine the nature, extent, and timing of tests to be performed.

RECOMMENDATION

The auditor should use the cycle approach, whereby broad areas of activity are selected and specific classes of transactions are identified. The main cycles and their related classes of transactions are:

- o *Revenue Cycle*: revenue and accounts receivable (order processing, credit approval, shipping, invoicing and recording) and cash receipts
- o *Expenditure Cycle*: purchasing, receiving, accounts payable, payroll and cash disbursements
- o *Production or Conversion Cycle*: inventories, cost of sales, and property, plant, and equipment
- o *Financing Cycle*: notes receivable and investments, notes payable, debt, leases, and other obligations and equity accounts
- o *External Reporting*: accounting principles and preparation of financial statements

---

Can I use statistical methods in performing tests of control?

To save time and money in performing tests of controls, auditors can use statistical sampling, in the form of attribute sampling. The following steps should prove useful in this regard:

Step 1. Determine the objective of the test, namely, to obtain reasonable assurance that a particular control is in place (e.g., mathematical accuracy of invoices is verified by an individual other than the preparer of the invoice).

Step 2. Define the deviation condition. A deviation condition is a departure from a prescribed control (sometimes referred to as an attribute), such as the failure to initial an invoice that was mathematically verified. *WARNING: Deviation conditions increase the likelihood of, but do not necessarily result in, financial statement misstatements.*

Step 3. Define the population:

- Define the period covered. If interim testing is performed, consider (a) inquiring about the period after testing and through the end of the year, and (b) the nature and amount of transactions and balances, and the length of the remaining period.
- Define the sampling unit. The sampling unit represents the item to be tested, e.g., a document, a journal page, a transaction, a line item.
- Determine the completeness of the population. The sample drawn must be representative of the population. *EXAMPLE: In testing purchase transactions, the population should include unpaid as well as paid invoices.*

Step 4. Determine the selection technique:

- Random number selection provides assurance that each and every item in the population has a chance of being picked.
- Systematic selection involves picking every nth item from the population. The *n*th item, often referred to as the skip interval, is determined by dividing the population size by the sample size. *EXAMPLE: If the population size is 10,000 and the sample size is 50, the skip interval is 200. Thus, the auditor would pick every 200th item, beginning with a blind start.*

Step 5. Determine the sample size by using the appropriate table.

- Select an acceptable level of risk of assessing control risk too low. Practically speaking, auditors select either a 5 percent or a 10 percent risk. These levels will provide the auditor 95 percent and 90 percent confidence, respectively, that the sample is representative of the population. *NOTE: The lower the risk the auditor selects, the bigger the sample size will be.*

- Select the tolerable rate. This is the maximum rate of deviation the auditor is willing to tolerate while still being able to reduce assessed control risk. The tolerable rate is dependent on professional judgment and the planned degree of reliance on the control.

Planned Degree of Reliance	Tolerable Rate
Substantial	2–7%
Moderate	6–12%
Little	11–20%

- Assess the expected population deviation rate. This may be based on (a) reference to actual deviation rates of the prior year, adjusted for current-year implementation of prior-year recommendations; (b) communication with prior-year accountants; or (c) a preliminary sample of 50 items.

Step 6.   Select the sample and perform tests of controls.
Step 7.   Interpret the sample results.

- Calculate the sample deviation rate—divide the actual number of deviations by the sample size.
- Determine the upper occurrence limit by using the appropriate table. Essentially the upper occurrence limit takes the sample deviation rate and adjusts it upward to reflect the fact that the population is likely to contain a greater rate of deviations.
- Determine whether the deviations are a result of errors (unintentional) or fraud (intentional).
- Accept or reject the sample as representative of the population:
    - If the sample deviation is greater than the tolerable rate, no reliance may be placed on the control.
    - If the upper occurrence limit is less than the tolerable rate, reliance may be placed upon the control.
    - If the upper occurrence limit is greater than the tolerable rate, no reliance should be placed on the control. In this case, the auditor might perform tests of controls on another control or proceed to substantive testing without modification.

EXAMPLE 10.1

In determining whether the credit department is performing properly, Margie Scott, CPA, utilizes attribute sampling in testing controls over sales orders. Scott determines:

- The deviation condition is the absence of the credit manager's initials on a sales order.
- The population consists of the duplicate sales orders for the entire fiscal year.
- The sampling unit is the sales order itself.

EXAMPLE 10.1 *(continued)*

○ Random number selection will be utilized.
○ A 5 percent risk of assessing control risk too low will be utilized.
○ The tolerable rate of deviation is 6 percent.
○ The expected population deviation rate is 2 percent.

Using Exhibit 10.4, we find that the sample size will be 127. Scott uses a random number table (Exhibit 10.8) to select the sample. Since the population consists of sales orders numbered 1 to 500, Scott decides to use the first three digits of items selected from the random number table. Using a blind start at column 5, line 6, Scott selects the following sales orders:

Number
277
188
174
496
482
312
⋮

After performing the sampling plan, Scott finds that four sales orders are missing the credit manager's signature (apparently an error on the part of the credit manager). The sample deviation rate is therefore 4/127 or 3.1 percentage. The upper occurrence limit, determined by using Exhibit 10.6, is 7.2. (The sample size of 125 is used for conservative results.) Since the upper occurrence limit is greater than the tolerable rate of 6 percentage, Scott rejects the control and attempts to identify a compensating control for additional testing.

Statistical Sample Sizes for Tests of Controls (for large populations)

Expected Population Deviation Rate	Tolerable Rate								
	2%	3%	4%	5%	6%	7%	8%	9%	10%
0.00%	149	99	74	59	49	42	36	32	29
.50	•	157	117	93	78	66	58	51	46
1.00	•	•	156	93	78	66	58	51	46
1.50	•	•	192	124	103	66	58	51	46
2.00	•	•	•	181	127	88	77	68	46
2.50	•	•	•	•	150	109	77	68	61
3.00	•	•	•	•	195	129	95	84	61
4.00	•	•	•	•	•	•	146	100	89
5.00	•	•	•	•	•	•	•	158	116
6.00	•	•	•	•	•	•	•	•	179

Exhibit 10.4   5 PERCENT RISK OF ASSESSING CONTROL RISK TOO LOW

Expected Population Deviation Rate	Tolerable Rate								
	2%	3%	4%	5%	6%	7%	8%	9%	10%
0.00%	114	76	57	45	38	32	28	25	22
.50	194	129	96	77	64	55	48	42	38
1.00	•	176	96	77	64	55	48	42	38
1.50	•	•	132	105	64	55	48	42	38
2.00	•	•	198	132	88	75	48	42	38
2.50	•	•	•	158	110	75	65	58	38
3.00	•	•	•	•	132	94	65	58	52
4.00	•	•	•	•	•	149	98	73	65
5.00	•	•	•	•	•	•	160	115	78
6.00	•	•	•	•	•	•	•	182	116

•Sample size is too large to be cost effective.

Exhibit 10.5   10 Percent Risk of Assessing Control Risk Too Low

Statistical Sample Results Evaluation Table for Tests of Controls
Upper Occurrence Limit (for large populations)

Sample Size	Actual Number of Occurrences Found								
	0	1	2	3	4	5	6	7	8
25	11.3	17.6	•	•	•	•	•	•	•
30	9.5	14.9	19.5	•	•	•	•	•	•
35	8.2	12.9	16.9	•	•	•	•	•	•
40	7.2	11.3	14.9	18.3	•	•	•	•	•
45	6.4	10.1	13.3	16.3	19.2	•	•	•	•
50	5.8	9.1	12.1	14.8	17.4	19.9	•	•	•
55	5.3	8.3	11.0	13.5	15.9	18.1	•	•	•
60	4.9	7.7	10.1	12.4	14.6	16.7	18.8	•	•
65	4.5	7.1	9.4	11.5	13.5	15.5	17.4	19.3	•
70	4.2	6.6	8.7	10.7	12.6	14.4	16.2	18.0	19.7
75	3.9	6.2	8.2	10.0	11.8	13.5	15.2	16.9	18.4
80	3.7	5.8	7.7	9.4	11.1	12.7	14.3	15.8	17.3
90	3.3	5.2	6.8	8.4	9.9	11.3	12.7	14.1	15.5
100	3.0	4.7	6.2	7.6	8.9	10.2	11.5	12.7	14.0
125	2.4	3.7	4.9	6.1	7.2	8.2	9.3	10.3	11.3
150	2.0	3.1	4.1	5.1	6.0	6.9	7.7	8.6	9.4
200	1.5	2.3	3.1	3.8	4.5	5.2	5.8	6.5	7.1

Exhibit 10.6   5 Percent Risk of Assessing Control Risk Too Low

| | Actual Number of Occurrences Found | | | | | | | | |
Sample Size	0	1	2	3	4	5	6	7	8
20	10.9	18.1	•	•	•	•	•	•	•
25	8.8	14.7	19.9	•	•	•	•	•	•
30	7.4	12.4	16.8	•	•	•	•	•	•
35	6.4	10.7	14.5	18.1	•	•	•	•	•
40	5.6	9.4	12.8	15.9	19.0	•	•	•	•
45	5.0	8.4	11.4	14.2	17.0	19.6	•	•	•
50	4.5	7.6	10.3	12.9	15.4	17.8	•	•	•
55	4.1	6.9	9.4	11.7	14.0	16.2	18.4	•	•
60	3.8	6.3	8.6	10.8	12.9	14.9	16.9	18.8	•
70	3.2	5.4	7.4	9.3	11.1	12.8	14.6	16.2	17.9
80	2.8	4.8	6.5	8.3	9.7	11.3	12.8	14.3	15.7
90	2.5	4.3	5.8	7.3	8.7	10.1	11.4	12.7	14.0
100	2.3	3.8	5.2	6.6	7.8	9.1	10.3	11.5	12.7
120	1.9	3.2	4.4	5.5	6.6	7.6	8.6	9.6	10.6
160	1.4	2.4	3.3	4.1	4.9	5.7	6.5	7.2	8.0
200	1.1	1.9	2.6	3.3	4.0	4.6	5.2	5.8	6.4

•Over 20%

Exhibit 10.7 10 PERCENT RISK OF ASSESSING CONTROL RISK TOO LOW

Line	(1)	(2)	(3)	(4)	(5)	(6)	(7)	(8)	(9)	(10)	(11)	(12)	(13)	(14)
1	50590	11592	10195	10244	81647	91646	69179	14194	62590	36207	20969	99570	91291	90700
2	22368	46573	25595	85393	30995	89198	27982	53402	93965	34095	52666	19174	39615	99505
3	24130	48360	22527	97265	76393	64809	15179	24830	49340	32081	30680	19655	63348	58629
4	42167	93093	06243	61680	07856	16376	39440	53537	71341	57004	00849	74917	97758	16379
5	37570	39975	81837	16656	06121	91782	60468	81305	49684	60672	14110	06927	01263	54613
6	77921	06907	11008	42751	27756	53498	18602	70659	90655	15053	21916	81825	44394	42880
7	99562	72905	56420	69994	98872	31016	71194	18738	44013	48840	63213	21069	10634	12952
8	96301	91977	05463	07972	18876	20922	94595	56869	69014	60045	18425	84903	42508	32307
9	89579	14342	63661	10281	17453	18103	57740	84378	25331	12566	58678	44947	05585	56941
10	85475	36857	53342	53988	53060	59533	38867	62300	08158	17983	16439	11458	18593	64952
11	28918	69578	88231	33276	70997	79936	56865	05859	90106	31595	01547	85590	91610	78188
12	63553	40961	48235	03427	49626	69445	18663	72695	52180	20847	12234	90511	33703	90322
13	09429	93969	52636	92737	88974	33488	36320	17617	30015	08272	84115	27156	30613	74952
14	10365	61129	87529	85689	48237	52267	67689	93394	01511	26358	85104	20285	29975	89868
15	07119	97336	71048	08178	77233	13916	47564	81056	97735	85977	29372	74461	28551	90707
16	51085	12765	51821	51259	77452	16308	60756	92144	49442	53900	70960	63990	75601	40719

Exhibit 10.8 RANDOM NUMBER TABLE

								Column							
Line	(1)	(2)	(3)	(4)	(5)	(6)	(7)	(8)	(9)	(10)	(11)	(12)	(13)	(14)
17	02368	21382	52404	60268	89368	19885	55322	44819	01188	63255	64835	44919	05944	55157
18	01011	54092	33362	94904	31273	04146	18594	29852	71585	85030	51132	01915	92747	64951
19	52162	53916	46369	58586	23216	14513	83149	98736	23495	64350	94738	17752	35156	35749
20	07056	97628	33787	09998	42698	06691	76988	13602	51851	46104	88916	19509	25625	58104
21	48663	91245	85828	14346	09172	30168	90229	04734	59193	22178	30421	61666	99904	32812
22	54164	58492	22421	74103	47070	25306	76468	26384	58151	06646	21524	15227	96909	44592
23	32639	32363	05597	24200	13363	38005	94342	28728	35806	06912	17012	64161	18296	22851
24	29334	27001	87637	87308	58731	00256	45834	15398	46557	41135	10367	07684	36188	18510
25	02488	33062	28834	07351	19731	92420	60952	61280	50001	67658	32586	86679	50720	94953
26	81525	72295	04839	96423	24878	82651	66566	14778	76797	14780	13300	87074	79666	95725
27	29676	20591	68086	26432	46901	20849	89768	81536	86645	12659	92259	57102	80428	25280
28	00742	57392	39064	66432	84673	40027	32832	61362	98947	96067	64760	64584	96096	98253
29	05366	04213	25669	26422	44407	44048	37937	63904	45766	66134	75470	66520	34693	90449
30	91921	26418	64117	94305	26766	25940	39972	22209	71500	64568	91402	42416	07844	69618
31	00582	04711	87917	77341	42206	35126	74087	99547	81817	42607	43808	76655	62028	76630
32	00725	69884	62797	56170	86324	88072	76222	36086	84637	93161	76038	65855	77919	88006
33	69011	65795	95876	55293	18988	27354	26575	08625	40801	59920	29841	80150	12777	48501

Exhibit 10.8 RANDOM NUMBER TABLE *(continued)*

413

Column

Line	(1)	(2)	(3)	(4)	(5)	(6)	(7)	(8)	(9)	(10)	(11)	(12)	(13)	(14)
34	25976	57948	29888	80604	67917	48708	18912	82271	65424	69774	33611	54262	85963	03547
35	09763	83473	73577	12908	30883	18317	28290	35797	05998	41688	34952	37888	38917	80050
36	91567	42595	29758	30134	04024	86385	29880	99730	55536	84855	29080	09250	79656	73211
37	17955	56349	90999	49127	20044	59931	06115	20542	18059	02008	73708	83517	36103	42791
38	46503	18584	18845	49618	02304	51038	20655	58727	28168	15475	56942	53389	20562	87338
39	92157	89634	94824	78171	84610	82834	09922	25417	44137	48413	25555	21246	35509	20468
40	14577	62765	35605	81263	39667	47358	56873	56307	61607	49518	89656	20103	77490	18062
41	98427	07523	33362	64270	01638	92477	66969	98420	04880	45585	46565	04102	46880	45709
42	34914	63976	88720	82765	34476	17032	87589	40836	32427	70002	70663	88863	77775	69348
43	70060	28277	39475	46473	23219	53416	94970	25832	69975	94884	19661	72828	00102	66794
44	53976	54914	06990	67245	68350	82948	11398	42878	80287	88267	47363	46634	06541	97809
45	76072	29515	40980	07391	58745	25774	22987	80059	39911	96189	41151	14222	60697	59583
46	90725	52210	83974	29992	65831	38857	50490	83765	55657	14361	31720	57375	56228	41546
47	64364	67412	33339	31926	14883	24413	59744	92351	97473	89286	38931	04110	23726	51900
48	08962	00358	31662	25388	61642	34072	81249	35648	56891	69352	48373	45578	78547	81788
49	95012	68379	93526	70765	10592	04542	76463	54328	02349	17247	28865	14777	62730	92277
50	15664	10493	20492	38391	91132	21999	59516	81652	27195	48223	46751	22923	32261	85653

Exhibit 10.8 RANDOM NUMBER TABLE (continued)

SUBSTANTIVE TESTING

What is the purpose of substantive testing?

To form the basis of an opinion on the fairness of the financial statements, the third generally accepted fieldwork standard requires the gathering of sufficient competent evidential matter. Substantive tests are the procedures by which auditors gather this evidential matter.

Although the nature, extent, and timing of substantive tests is a matter of professional judgment, effective client internal control is a positive influence. Accordingly, the auditor may decide to decrease the amount of substantive testing, omit certain procedures, and/or schedule interim testing. Conversely, weak internal control will likely result in increased substantive testing, the need for additional audit procedures, and/or scheduling testing at or after year-end.

What is involved in substantive testing?

In general, substantive tests include:

- Tests of transactions
- Tests of details of account balances
- Analytical procedures

In *testing transactions*, the auditor is concerned with tests of:

- Omitted transactions and account understatement (tracing source documents to the books of entry)
- Invalid or unsupported transactions and account overstatement (tracing recorded transactions to source documents)

Tests for omitted Transactions and Account Understatement

Documents $\longrightarrow$ Books

Tests for Invalid or Unsupported Transactions and Account Overstatement

In analyzing *details of account balances*, auditors use professional judgment in determining which accounts to scrutinize. Some of the accounts commonly requiring scrutiny are:

- Repairs and maintenance
- Fixed assets
- Officers' salaries
- Contributions
- Travel and entertainment
- Income tax provisions

Analytical procedures include the study and comparison of the relationships between data. This involves the comparison of current period financial information with:

- Prior period information
- Expected results
- Predictable pattern information
- Intra-industry information
- Nonfinancial information

How do I construct an audit program?

To facilitate the audit, audit work programs should be developed for each account subject to examination. Audit work programs are easily developed by considering:

- The auditor's objectives
- Generally accepted accounting principles
- Required actions or procedures

What are the audit objectives?

The following audit objectives provide the framework for any audit program a particular engagement may demand:

- *Presentation and disclosure*: Do the financial statements include all relevant footnote disclosures and are the statements appropriately classified?
- *Valuation or allocation*: Do accounts accurately reflect appropriate amounts?
- *Completeness*: Do accounts reflect all transactions executed in the accounting period?
- *Existence or occurrence*: Do recorded amounts of assets and liabilities actually exist? Have recorded transactions actually occurred in the accounting period?
- *Rights and obligations*: Does the entity maintain rights to its assets? Are the entity's liabilities its own obligations?
- *Related income statement effects*: Are there any income statement implications?

What else is needed in preparing an audit program?

The next steps in developing an audit work program are identifying the flow of transactions in the accounting process and developing an understanding of relevant generally accepted accounting principles.

Finally, you must select the appropriate audit procedures from among the following general procedures:

- Inspection of related documents
- Observation of procedures
- Confirmation of account balances and existence of assets, liabilities and transactions

- Inquiry of company personnel
- Retracing of transactions from books to records
- Recalculation of extensions and footings
- Vouching of documents to verify propriety and validity
- Counting of tangible assets
- Scanning ("eyeballing") of documents, schedules, and accounts
- Scrutinizing of documents, schedules, and accounts
- Reading or reviewing of documents, minutes of board meetings, and financial statements
- Comparison of perpetual records with physical assets
- Analysis of account balances (See Exhibit 10.9)

I. Substantive Tests of Cash Balances

   A. Presentation and Disclosure

      1. Read or review the financial statements to verify proper classification.

      2. Read or review the financial statements to verify disclosures such as those relating to compensation balances.

      3. Determine the conformity with GAAP.

   B. Valuation or Allocation

      1. Simultaneously count cash on hand and negotiable securities.

      2. Confirm directly with the bank:

      (a) Account balances

      (b) Direct liabilities to bank

      (c) Contingent liabilities to bank

      (d) Letters of credit

      (e) Security agreements under the Uniform Commercial Code

      (f) Authorized signatures

      3. Count petty cash fund and reconcile with vouchers.

   C. Completeness

      1. Obtain bank cutoff statement and determine propriety of year-end outstanding checks and deposits-in-transit.

      2. Examine or prepare year-end bank reconciliation.

      3. Prepare a proof of cash.

      4. Perform analytical procedures.

   D. Existence or Occurrence (See Valuation or Allocation.)

Exhibit 10.9 SAMPLE AUDIT WORK PROGRAMS

E. Rights and Obligations

   1. Read minutes of the board of directors' meetings.
   2. Determine existence of compensating balances, levies, etc.
   3. Verify names on accounts through confirmation requests.

F. Related Income Statement Effects—not truly relevant

II. Substantive Tests of Receivable Balances

   A. Presentation and Disclosure

      1. Determine appropriate classification of account balances.
      2. Read or review the financial statements in order to verify disclosure of
         a. Restrictions—pledging, factoring and discounting
         b. Related party transactions
      3. Trace amounts on trial balance to general ledger control accounts and subsidiary ledger totals.

   B. Valuation or Allocation

      1. Confirm account balances where reasonable and practicable using positive and/or negative confirmation requests.
      2. Examine collections in the subsequent period cash receipts journal.
      3. Examine and verify amortization tables.
      4. Examine aging schedules.
      5. Review adequacy of allowance for doubtful accounts.
      6. Review collectibility by checking credit ratings (e.g., Dun and Bradstreet ratings).
      7. Verify clerical accuracy and pricing of sales invoices.
      8. Foot daily sales summaries and trace to journals.
      9. Perform tests for omitted and invalid (or unsupported) transactions with respect to subsidiary ledger account balances.

   C. Completeness

      1. Perform sales and sales return cutoff tests.
      2. Perform analytical procedures.
      3. Test for omitted transactions.

Exhibit 10.9   SAMPLE AUDIT WORK PROGRAMS *(continued)*

D. Existence or Occurrence

   1. Inspect note agreements.

   2. Confirm accounts receivable and notes receivable balances.

   3. Review client documentation.

E. Rights and Obligations

   1. Read minutes of board of directors' meetings.

   2. Read leases for pledging agreements.

   3. Determine pledging and contingent liabilities to bank by using a standard bank confirmation.

F. Related Income Statement Effects

   1. Review installment sales profit recognition.

   2. Verify accuracy of sales discounts and term discounts.

   3. Review bad debt expense computations.

   4. Recalculate interest income on notes receivable.

III. Substantive Tests of Inventory

A. Presentation and Disclosure

   1. Read or review the financial statements to verify footnote disclosure of:

   (a) Valuation method and inventory flow, e.g., lower-of-cost-or-market value, first-in-first-out

   (b) Pledged inventory

   (c) Inventory in or out on consignment

   (d) Existence of and terms of major purchase commitments

B. Valuation or Allocation

   1. Verify the correct application of lower-of-cost-or-market value.

   2. Recalculate inventory valuation under the full absorption costing method.

   3. Verify the quality of inventory items.

   4. Vouch and test inventory pricing.

   5. Perform analytical procedures.

   6. Verify the propriety of inventory flow.

   7. Consider using the services of a specialist to corroborate the valuation of inventory (e.g., a gemologist to corroborate the valuation of precious stones).

Exhibit 10.9 SAMPLE AUDIT WORK PROGRAMS (continued)

C. Completeness

1. Perform cutoff tests for purchases, sales, purchase returns, and sales returns.

2. With respect to tagged inventory, perform tests for omitted transactions and tests for invalid transactions.

3. Verify the clerical and mathematical accuracy of inventory listings.

4. Reconcile physical inventory amounts with perpetual records.

5. Reconcile physical counts with general ledger control totals.

D. Existence or Occurrence

1. Observe client inventory counts.

2. Confirm inventory held in public warehouses.

3. Confirm existence of inventory held by others on consignment.

E. Rights and Obligations

1. Determine existence of collateral agreements.

2. Read consignment agreements.

3. Review major purchase commitment agreements.

4. Examine invoices for evidence of ownership.

5. Review minutes of the board of directors' meetings.

F. Related Income Statement Effects

1. Verify that ending inventory on the balance sheet is identical to ending inventory in the Cost of Goods Sold section.

IV. Substantive Tests for Fixed Assets

A. Presentation and Disclosure

1. Read the financial statements in order to verify:

a. Disclosure of historical cost

b. Disclosure of depreciation methods under GAAP

c. Financial statement classification

d. Disclosure of restrictions

B. Valuation or Allocation

1. Examine invoices.

Exhibit 10.9 SAMPLE AUDIT WORK PROGRAMS *(continued)*

2. Inspect lease agreements and ascertain the proper accounting treatment (e.g., capital vs. operating lease).

3. Analyze repairs and maintenance accounts.

4. Analyze related accumulated depreciation accounts.

5. Vouch entries in fixed asset accounts.

6. Test extensions and footings on client-submitted schedules.

C. Completeness

1. Perform analytical procedures.

2. Inspect fixed assets.

3. Examine subsidiary schedules.

4. Reconcile subsidiary schedules with general ledger control.

D. Existence or Occurrence

1. Inspect fixed assets.

2. Examine supporting documentation.

E. Rights and Obligations

1. Inspect invoices.

2. Inspect lease agreements.

3. Inspect insurance policies.

4. Inspect title documents.

5. Inspect personal property tax returns.

6. Read minutes of the board of directors' meetings.

F. Related Income Statement Effects

1. Recalculate depreciation expenses.

2. Recalculate gain or loss on disposal of fixed assets.

Exhibit 10.9 SAMPLE AUDIT WORK PROGRAMS *(continued)*

AUDIT REPORTS

How does the auditor report?

After the auditor gathers sufficient competent evidential matter, pursuant to the fourth generally accepted reporting standard, he or she must form an opinion on the fairness of the presentation of the financial statements, or disclaim an opinion.

The auditor's standard unqualified opinion can be modified when warranted.

How should the auditor's standard report be worded?

The wording of the auditor's report depends on whether it relates to the audit of (1) a private company or (2) a public company regulated by the Public Company Accounting Oversight Board (PCAOB).

An audit report on the financial statements of a private company should include a reference to either U.S. generally accepted auditing standards or auditing standards generally accepted in the United States of America.

EXAMPLE 10.2 A STANDARD REPORT—PRIVATE COMPANY

INDEPENDENT AUDITOR'S REPORT

I (we) have audited the accompanying balance sheet of [company name] as of (at) [date] and the related statements of income, retained earnings, and cash flows for the year then ended. These financial statements are the responsibility of the Company's management. My (our) responsibility is to express an opinion on these financial statements based on my (our) audit.

I (we) conducted my (our) audit in accordance with U.S. generally accepted auditing standards (or, auditing standards generally accepted in the United States of America). Those standards require that I (we) plan and perform the audit to obtain reasonable assurance about whether the financial statements are free of material misstatement. An audit includes examining, on a test basis, evidence supporting the amounts and disclosures in the financial statements. An audit also includes assessing the accounting principles used and significant estimates made by management, as well as evaluating the overall financial statement presentation. I (we) believe that my (our) audit provides a reasonable basis for my (our) opinion.

In my (our) opinion, the financial statements referred to above present fairly, in all material respects, the financial position of [company name] as of (at) [date], and the results of its operations and its cash flows for the year then ended in conformity with U.S. generally accepted accounting principles (or accounting principles generally accepted in the United States of America)

[Signature]

[Date]

An audit report on the financial statements of a public company regulated by the PCAOB should (1) be titled "Report of Independent Registered Public Accounting Firm," (2) refer to "the standards of the Public Company Accounting Oversight Board (United States)," (3) not include any reference to generally accepted auditing standards, and (4) include the city and state (or country, if a non-U.S. auditor) from which the audit report is issued.

EXAMPLE 10.3 A STANDARD REPORT—PUBLIC COMPANY

REPORT OF INDEPENDENT REGISTERED PUBLIC ACCOUNTING FIRM

We have audited the accompanying balance sheet of [company name] as of (at) [date] and the related statements of income, retained earnings, and cash flows for the year then ended. These financial statements are the responsibility of the Company's management. Our responsibility is to express an opinion on these financial statements based on our audit.

We conducted our audit in accordance with the standards of the Public Company Accounting Oversight Board (United States). Those standards require that we plan and perform the audit to obtain reasonable assurance about whether the financial statements are free of material misstatement. An audit includes examining, on a test basis, evidence supporting the amounts and disclosures in the financial statements. An audit also includes assessing the accounting principles used and significant estimates made by management, as well as evaluating the overall financial statement presentation. We believe that our audit provides a reasonable basis for our opinion.

In our opinion, the financial statements referred to above present fairly, in all material respects, the financial position of [company name] as of (at) [date], and the results of its operations and its cash flows for the year then ended in conformity with accounting principles generally accepted in the United States of America.

[Signature]

[City and State or Country]

[Date]

NOTE

The independent auditor's report should be addressed to the company or its board of directors or stockholders.

How may the standard report be modified?

Using the auditor's standard report as a guideline, the practitioner can easily make modifications depending upon the circumstances. These modifications can be classified by the type of report being issued. They are:

- ○ Unqualified opinion
- ○ Qualified opinion
- ○ Disclaimer of opinion
- ○ Adverse opinion

IMPORTANT NOTE

All sample audit reports that follow contain wording applicable to financial statements of a private company. When reporting on financial statements of a public company, the practitioner is required to modify the audit report as indicated on page 422 and 423.

Unqualified Opinion

When does a division of responsibility apply?

A division of responsibility occurs, for instance, when the auditor of a consolidated group of companies is unable to audit one of the subsidiaries included in the group. Another auditor, however, is able to conduct that audit. The principal auditor has the choice of referring to the other auditor if he or she:

- ○ Is satisfied as to the professional reputation of the other auditor
- ○ Has obtained a representation letter from the other auditor confirming his or her independence
- ○ Is satisfied that the other auditor is familiar with generally accepted auditing standards and generally accepted accounting principles
- ○ Coordinates the audit activities of the two auditors

REQUIREMENT

If reference is to be made, then all paragraphs are modified to reflect the division of responsibility. The introductory paragraph should indicate the magnitude or the size of the portion of the financial statements audited by the other auditor. This may be accomplished through the use of dollars or percentages of total assets and revenues.

EXAMPLE 10.4 DIVISION OF RESPONSIBILITY

INDEPENDENT AUDITOR'S REPORT

I (We) have audited the consolidated balance sheets of KJB Company as of (at) December 31, 20XX, and the related consolidated statements of income, retained earnings, and cash flows for the year then ended. These financial statements are the responsibility of the Company's management. My (Our) responsibility is to express an opinion on these financial statements based on my (our) audit. I (We) did not audit the financial statements of KJB Company, a wholly owned subsidiary, which statements reflect total assets of $_____ as of December 31, 20XX and total revenues of $_____ for the year then ended. Those statements were audited by other auditors whose report has been furnished to me (us), and my (our) opinion, insofar as it relates to the amounts included for KJB Company, is based solely on the report of the other auditors.

I (We) conducted my (our) audit in accordance with U.S. generally accepted auditing standards. Those standards require that I (we) plan and perform the audit to obtain reasonable assurance about whether the financial statements are free of material misstatement. An audit includes examining, on a test basis, evidence supporting the amounts and disclosures in the financial statements. An audit also includes assessing the accounting principles used and significant estimates made by management, as well as evaluating the overall financial statement presentation. I (We) believe that my (our) audit and the report of the other auditors provide a reasonable basis for my (our) opinion.

In my (our) opinion, based on my (our) audit and the report of other auditors, the consolidated financial statements referred to above present fairly, in all material respects, the financial position of KJB as of (at) December 31, 20XX, and the results of its operations and its cash flows for the year then ended in conformity with U.S. generally accepted accounting principles.

How may I emphasize a disclosure?

The practitioner, in his or her report, may emphasize a matter that is already disclosed and properly accounted for in the financial statements. Emphasis of a matter, such as a type II subsequent event (discussed later), should be made in a separate paragraph between the scope and opinion paragraphs. No modification should be made to either the scope or the opinion paragraph.

How do I handle breaks in consistency?

When financial statements reflect a change in accounting principles, the auditor must modify the audit report by adding an explanatory paragraph following the opinion paragraph:

EXAMPLE 10.5 EXPLANATORY PARAGRAPH

As discussed in Note X to the financial statements, the company changed its method of computing depreciation in 20X5.

CAUTION

In general, if the year of change is reported on in subsequent years, the additional paragraph must be presented.

When is the consistency modification required?

Changes in accounting principles requiring the consistency modification include a change:

○ From one generally accepted accounting principle (GAAP) or method to another
○ In reporting entity
○ From a non-GAAP method to a method or principle that is generally accepted
○ In principle which is inseparable from a change in accounting estimate

Changes in the following, however, do not require consistency modifications:

○ Accounting estimates
○ Correction of an error not involving a principle
○ Financial statement classification, format, and terminology
○ Reporting entity as a result of an accounting transaction

Qualified Opinion

When is the scope of the examination limited?

A scope limitation arises when the auditor is unable to do one or more of the following:

○ Gather enough evidential matter to afford the expression of an unqualified opinion
○ Apply a required auditing procedure
○ Apply one or more auditing procedures considered necessary under the circumstances

What if the limitation is not a serious one?

When the scope limitation is not severe enough to warrant the expression of a disclaimer of an opinion, an "except for" qualified opinion should be issued. The necessary modifications to the report include:

- o Adding the phrase "Except as discussed in the following paragraph" to the beginning or end of the second sentence of the scope paragraph.
- o Adding a paragraph before the opinion paragraph that explains the nature of the scope limitation.
- o Modifying the opinion paragraph for the possible effects of the scope limitation on the financial statements.

EXAMPLE 10.6 REPORT MODIFIED TO INDICATE A SCOPE LIMITATION

INDEPENDENT AUDITOR'S REPORT

I (We) have audited the accompanying balance sheet of SMR Company as of (at) December 31, 20XX, and the related statements of income, retained earnings, and cash flows for the year then ended. These financial statements are the responsibility of the Company's management. My (Our) responsibility is to express an opinion on these financial statements based on my (our) audit.

Except as discussed in the following paragraph, I (we) conducted my (our) audit in accordance with U.S. generally accepted auditing standards. Those standards require that I (we) plan and perform the audit to obtain reasonable assurance about whether the financial statements are free of material misstatement. An audit includes examining, on a test basis, evidence supporting the amounts and disclosures in the financial statements. An audit also includes assessing the accounting principles used and significant estimates made by management, as well as evaluating the overall financial statement presentation. I (We) believe that my (our) audit provides a reasonable basis for my (our) opinion.

I was (We were) unable to obtain audited financial statements supporting the Company's investment in a foreign affiliate stated at $_____ at December 31, 20XX, or its equity in earnings of that affiliate of $_____, which is included in net income for the year then ended as described in Note X to the financial statements; nor was I (were we) able to satisfy myself (ourselves) as to the carrying value of the investment in the foreign affiliate or the equity in its earnings by other auditing procedures.

EXAMPLE 10.6 REPORT MODIFIED TO INDICATE A SCOPE LIMITATION *(continued)*

In my (our) opinion, except for the effects of such adjustments, if any, as might have been determined to be necessary had I (we) been able to examine evidence regarding the foreign affiliate investment and earnings, the financial statements referred to in the first paragraph above present fairly, in all material respects, the financial position of SMR Company as of (at) December 31, 20XX, and the results of its operations and its cash flows for the year then ended in conformity with U.S. generally accepted accounting principles.

How do I handle a departure from GAAP?

When financial statements contain a departure from GAAP, and the client refuses to make the necessary modifications, the auditor will express a qualified opinion, unless the effects of the departure warrant the issuance of an adverse opinion. Departures from GAAP include the lack of adequate disclosure (e.g., the omission of the summary of significant accounting policies), the omission of the statement of cash flows (which results in incomplete presentation), as well as the use of an accounting method that does not reflect the substance of a particular transaction (e.g., the failure to capitalize lease obligations).

The necessary modifications to the report include:

○ Adding an explanatory paragraph between the scope and opinion paragraphs describing the departure, the treatment required under GAAP, and the principal effects on the financial statements (or, if not practicable, a statement so indicating)

○ Modifying the opinion paragraph by adding the phrase "except for" and including a reference to the explanatory paragraph

---

EXAMPLE 10.7 REPORT MODIFIED TO DISCLOSE A DEPARTURE FROM GAAP

INDEPENDENT AUDITOR'S REPORT

I (We) have audited the accompanying balance sheet of SR Company as of (at) December 31, 20XX and the related statements of income, retained earnings, and cash flows for the year then ended. These financial statements are the responsibility of the Company's management. My (Our) responsibility is to express an opinion on these financial statements based on my (our) audit.

EXAMPLE 10.7 REPORT MODIFIED TO DISCLOSE A DEPARTURE FROM GAAP *(continued)*

I (We) conducted my (our) audit in accordance with U.S. generally accepted auditing standards. Those standards require that I (we) plan and perform the audit to obtain reasonable assurance about whether the financial statements are free of material misstatement. An audit includes examining, on a test basis, evidence supporting the amounts and disclosures in the financial statements. An audit also includes assessing the accounting principles used and significant estimates made by management, as well as evaluating the overall financial statement presentation. I (We) believe that my (our) audit provides a reasonable basis for my (our) opinion.

The Company has excluded from property and debt in the accompanying balance sheet certain lease obligations, which in my (our) opinion should be capitalized in order to conform with generally accepted accounting principles. If these lease obligations were capitalized, property would be increased (decreased) by $_____, long-term debt by $_____, and retained earnings by $_____ as of December 31, 20XX, and net income and earnings per share would be increased (decreased) by $_____ and $_____, respectively, for the year then ended.

In my (our) opinion, except for the effects of not capitalizing certain lease obligations as discussed in the preceding paragraph, the financial statements referred to above present fairly, in all material respects, the financial position of SR Company as of (at) December 31, 20XX, and the results of its operations and its cash flows for the year then ended in conformity with U.S. generally accepted accounting principles.

NOTE

If the departure from GAAP is adequately disclosed in the notes to the financial statements, the explanatory paragraph may be shortened by referring to the applicable note (see Example 10.8).

EXAMPLE 10.8 EXPLANATORY PARAGRAPH

As more fully described in Note X to the financial statements, the Company has excluded certain lease obligations from property and debt in the accompanying balance sheet. In my (our) opinion, generally accepted accounting principles require that such obligations be included in the balance sheet.

What if an uncertainty exists?

Uncertainties involve matters that are expected to be resolved at a future date, at which time conclusive evidential matter concerning their outcome would be expected to become available. Uncertainties include, but are not limited to, situations pertaining to:

- ○ Loss contingencies resulting from litigation, claims, and assessments.
- ○ Substantial doubt about the entity's ability to continue as a going concern for a reasonable period of time (i.e., "going concern uncertainties").

Do I have to modify the audit report for an uncertainty?

In general, management has the responsibility to estimate the effect of future events on financial statements (or determine that an estimate is not reasonably estimable) and to make the required disclosures under generally accepted accounting principles.

If the auditor concludes that sufficient evidential matter supports management's assertions about the nature of matters involving uncertainties (other than "going concern" uncertainties) and their financial statement presentation and disclosure, then a standard unqualified opinion is normally warranted; accordingly, no modification is necessary.

If sufficient evidential matter concerning uncertainties exists, but is not made available to the auditor, then a scope limitation exists. As is generally the case with a scope limitation, the auditor should modify the audit report by issuing a qualified opinion or a disclaimer of opinion.

If the auditor concludes that financial statements are materially misstated due to GAAP departures concerning uncertainties, then the auditor should modify the audit report by issuing a qualified or adverse opinion.

NOTE
For a discussion of "going concern" uncertainties, see the summary of SAS 59 in Chapter 12.

Disclaimer of Opinion

When is a disclaimer of opinion issued?

When a severe scope limitation exists and the auditor does not wish to express a qualified opinion, a disclaimer of opinion is warranted. A disclaimer of opinion indicates the practitioner's inability to form an opinion on the fairness of the financial statements.

The necessary modifications to the report are as follows:

o Modify the introductory paragraph.

o Omit the scope (second) paragraph of the standard report.

o Add an explanatory paragraph describing the reasons why the audit was not in conformity with generally accepted auditing standards.

o In lieu of an opinion paragraph, draft a disclaimer paragraph which includes wording to the effect that "I (we) do not express an opinion on these financial statements."

EXAMPLE 10.9 AUDIT REPORT CONTAINING A DISCLAIMER OF OPINION

INDEPENDENT AUDITOR'S REPORT

I was (We were) engaged to audit the accompanying balance sheet of Harold Corporation as of (at) December 31, 20XX, and the related statements of income, retained earnings, and cash flows for the year then ended. These financial statements are the responsibility of the Company's management.

The Company did not make a count of its physical inventory in 20XX, stated in the accompanying financial statements at $_____. Further, evidence supporting the cost of property and equipment acquired prior to December 31, 20XX, is no longer available. The Company's records do not permit the application of other auditing procedures to inventories or property and equipment.

Since the Company did not take physical inventories and I was (we were) not able to apply other auditing procedures to satisfy myself (ourselves) as to inventory quantities and the cost of property and equipment, the scope of my (our) work was not sufficient to enable me (us) to express, and I (we) do not express, an opinion on these financial statements.

CAUTION

In disclaiming an opinion, never identify the audit procedures that were actually performed.

WARNING

A severe client-imposed scope limitation might warrant withdrawal from the audit engagement. Severe client-imposed scope limitations include the client's refusal to provide a representation letter required under SAS 85 and the client's refusal to send a letter of audit inquiry to the outside legal counsel as required under SAS 12.

Adverse Opinion

When is an adverse opinion warranted?

An adverse opinion should be expressed when financial statements do *not* present fairly in conformity with GAAP an entity's

- Financial position
- Results of operations
- Retained earnings
- Cash flows

Issued when financial statements are misleading, the adverse opinion should include the following modifications:

- Add a paragraph between the scope and opinion paragraphs disclosing all of the substantive reasons for the issuance of the adverse opinion as well as the principal effects on the financial statements. If the principal effects cannot be reasonably determined, the report should so state.
- Modify the opinion paragraph to indicate that the statements are not presented fairly in conformity with generally accepted accounting principles.

EXAMPLE 10.10 REPORT REFLECTING THE AUDITOR'S ADVERSE OPINION

INDEPENDENT AUDITOR'S REPORT

I (We) have audited the accompanying balance sheet of X Company as of (at) December 31, 20XX and the related statements of income, retained earnings, and cash flows for the year then ended. These financial statements are the responsibility of the Company's management. My (Our) responsibility is to express an opinion on these financial statements based on my (our) audit.

I (We) conducted my (our) audit in accordance with U.S. generally accepted auditing standards. Those standards require that we plan and perform the audit to obtain reasonable assurance about whether the financial statements are free of material misstatement. An audit includes examining, on a test basis, evidence supporting the amounts and disclosures in the financial statements. An audit also includes assessing the accounting principles used and significant estimates made by management, as well as evaluating the overall financial statement presentation. I (We) believe that my (our) audit provides a reasonable basis for my (our) opinion.

EXAMPLE 10.10 REPORT REFLECTING THE AUDITOR'S ADVERSE OPINION (continued)

As discussed in Note X to the financial statements, the Company carries its property, plant and equipment accounts at appraisal values, and provides depreciation on the basis of such values. Further, the Company does not provide for income taxes with respect to differences between financial income and taxable income arising because of the use, for income tax purposes, of the installment method of reporting gross profit from certain types of sales. Generally accepted accounting principles, in my (our) opinion, require that property, plant and equipment be stated at an amount not in excess of cost, reduced by depreciation based on such amount, and that deferred income taxes be provided. Because of the departures from generally accepted accounting principles identified above, as of December 31, 20XX, inventories have been increased $_____ by inclusion in manufacturing overhead of depreciation in excess of that based on cost; property, plant and equipment, less accumulated depreciation, is carried at $_____ in excess of an amount based on the cost to the Company; and allocated income tax of $_____ has not been recorded; resulting in an increase of $_____ in retained earnings and in appraisal surplus of _____. For the year ended December 31, 20XX, cost of goods sold has been increased $_____ because of the effects of the depreciation accounting referred to above and deferred income taxes of $_____ have not been provided, resulting in an increase in net income and earnings per share of $_____ and $_____, respectively.

In my (our) opinion, because of the effects of the matters discussed in the preceding paragraph, the financial statements referred to above do not present fairly, in conformity with U.S. generally accepted accounting principles, the financial position of X Company as of December 31, 20XX, or the results of its operations and its cash flows for the year then ended.

CHAPTER 11

COMPILATION, REVIEW, AND OTHER REPORTING SERVICES

A practitioner whose client's stock is not publicly traded is often requested to compile or review financial statements. When an accountant is involved in the compilation or review of a client's financial statements, he or she is generally required to issue a report at the conclusion of the engagement.

Compilation and review services represent two types of engagements that practitioners face daily. This chapter will explain these services and the reporting practices associated with them, in addition to special reports generally associated with audit engagements.

Engagements involving prospective financial statements and attestation services, which are also discussed, should be viewed by the practitioner as an important area for practice expansion.

COMPILATION OF FINANCIAL STATEMENTS

What is a compilation of financial statements?

A compilation of financial statements is limited to presenting in the form of financial statements information that is the representation of management or owners. A key characteristic of a compilation is that *no opinion* or any other form of assurance is expressed on the fairness of the presentation of the financial statements. Accordingly, the accountant is not required to make inquiries or perform procedures to verify or review management—furnished information.

How is a compilation conducted?

Inasmuch as a compilation engagement does not result in the expression of any assurance, the procedures to be performed are quite limited.

> **RECOMMENDATION**
>
> To facilitate the compilation engagement and to demonstrate that due care has been exercised, the practitioner should consider the following procedures:

Step 1.   If desired, obtain an engagement letter.

Step 2.   Research the accounting principles and practices applicable to the client's industry.

Step 3.   Obtain a general understanding of the flow and nature of the transactions underlying the client's financial records.

Step 4.   Obtain a general understanding of the client's accounting records.

Step 5.   Inquire about the stated qualifications of the client's accounting personnel.

Step 6.   Determine the basis of accounting used—GAAP or another comprehensive basis of accounting (e.g., cash basis, modified cash basis, income tax basis, etc.).

Step 7.   Determine the necessity of performing the following accounting services:

   • Adjustment of client books
   • Consultation with appropriate personnel regarding accounting-related matters
   • Bookkeeping services when the client's manual or automated bookkeeping does not produce financial statements as the end result

Step 8.   Although it is not required to verify or corroborate representations made by management and personnel, obtain satisfaction as to representations that appear incorrect, incomplete, or otherwise unsatisfactory.

Step 9.   When financial statements depart from the basis of accounting in use, and the client refuses to make the necessary adjustments, modify the accountant's report to disclose this fact.

Step 10.   Read the financial statements to confirm that the statements are free from obvious material errors. (EXAMPLES: Mathematical mistakes, omission of relevant disclosures, and departures from relevant accounting principles.)

Step 11.   If a higher level of service was performed (e.g., a review or an audit), issue the report that relates to the highest level of service performed.

Step 12.   If the accountant is not independent with respect to the client, indicate this fact, but not the reasons therefor, in the compilation report.

What reports may be issued on a compilation engagement?

At the conclusion of a compilation engagement, the accountant generally must issue a report that includes the following:

○ An identification of the financial statements

○ A statement that the compilation was performed in accordance with *Statements on Standards for Accounting and Review Services* issued by the American Institute of Certified Public Accountants

○ The definition of a compilation, stating that a compilation is limited to presenting in the form of financial statements information that is the representation of management (owners)

○ A statement that the financial statements have not been subjected to an audit or a review and, accordingly, no opinion or any other form of assurance on them is provided

○ The date of the report, which should coincide with the date on which the compilation was completed

○ The accountant's signature

RECOMMENDATIONS

Each page of the financial statements must be labeled "See accountant's compilation report." If desired, expand the label to include "and the Notes to the Financial Statements," since the notes are an integral part of the financial statements.

In order to avoid misinterpretation, mark each page of the financial statements "unaudited."

EXAMPLE 11.1 A STANDARD COMPILATION REPORT

I (We) have compiled the accompanying balance sheet of Debit Company as of (at) December 31, 20XX, and the related statements of income, retained earnings, and cash flows for the year then ended, in accordance with *Statements on Standards for Accounting and Review Services* issued by the American Institute of Certified Public Accountants.

A compilation is limited to presenting in the form of financial statements information that is the representation of management (owners). I (We) have not audited or reviewed the accompanying financial statements and, accordingly, do not express an opinion or any other form of assurance on them.

NOTE
It is permissible to compile and report on only one of the financial statements normally included in the complete set.

When should the standard compilation report be modified?

The following circumstances warrant modification of the standard compilation report:

- ○ *Omission of substantially all disclosures.* When financial statements which purport to be in conformity with generally accepted accounting principles (or another comprehensive basis of accounting) lack the necessary disclosures (e.g., notes to the financial statements, parenthetical comments on the face of the statements, etc.), the accountant should add the following paragraph immediately after the standard two-paragraph report:

  Management has elected to omit substantially all of the disclosures required by generally accepted accounting principles. If the omitted disclosures were included in the financial statements, they might influence the user's conclusions about the company's financial position, results of operations, and cash flows. Accordingly, these financial statements are not designed for those who are not informed about such matters.

- ○ *Selected information presented.* When notes to the financial statements include only a few matters, the presentation of this information should be labeled "Selected Information—Substantially all of the Disclosures Required by Generally Accepted Accounting Principles Are Not Included." The compilation report should include the additional paragraph stated above.

- ○ *Omission of the statement of cash flows.* See the first departure above. Modify the first sentence of the additional paragraph to reflect the omission of either the statement of cash flows alone or the statement of cash flows and substantially all of the disclosures required by GAAP:

  Management has elected to omit the statement of cash flows (and substantially all of the disclosures) required by generally accepted accounting principles...

NOTE
Financial statements, which are prepared using a comprehensive basis of accounting other than GAAP, do not *require* presentation of a statement of cash flows.

○ *Lack of independence.* While an accountant who is not independent with respect to a client's financial statements *may* issue a compilation report, he or she must state in the report that, "I am (we are) not independent with respect to Debit Company." CAUTION: The accountant should not disclose the reasons as to why it is believed that independence is lacking.

○ *Departure from generally accepted accounting principles.* Although the accountant is under no obligation to search for departures from GAAP, such departures, if uncovered and not corrected, must be disclosed in the accountant's report. This is accomplished by adding to the standard report a middle explanatory paragraph, which either discloses the effects of the departure or states that the effects of such departure have not been determined.

○ *Financial statements are based on a comprehensive basis of accounting other than generally accepted accounting principles.* If a client uses a comprehensive basis of accounting other than GAAP, it is necessary to appropriately modify the titles of the financial statements, and disclose the basis of accounting used if the financial statements do not include the necessary disclosure.

EXAMPLE 11.2 COMPILATION REPORT ON CASH BASIS FINANCIAL STATEMENTS WITH OMISSION OF SUBSTANTIALLY ALL DISCLOSURES

I (We) have compiled the accompanying statement of assets and liabilities arising from cash transactions of Credit Incorporated as of (at) December 31, 20XX, and the related statement of revenue collected and expenses paid for the year then ended, in accordance with *Statements on Standards for Accounting and Review Services* issued by the American Institute of Certified Public Accountants. The financial statements have been prepared on the cash basis of accounting which is a comprehensive basis of accounting other than generally accepted accounting principles.

A compilation is limited to presenting in the form of financial statements information that is the representation of management (owners). I (We) have not audited or reviewed the accompanying financial statements and, accordingly, do not express an opinion or any other form of assurance on them.

Management has elected to omit substantially all of the informative disclosures ordinarily included in financial statements. If the omitted disclosures were included

> **EXAMPLE 11.2 COMPILATION REPORT ON CASH BASIS FINANCIAL STATEMENTS WITH OMISSION OF SUBSTANTIALLY ALL DISCLOSURES** *(continued)*
>
> in the financial statements, they might influence the user's conclusions about the Company's assets, liabilities, equity, revenue, and expenses. Accordingly, these statements are not designed for those who are not informed about such matters.

○ *Supplementary Information.* When both the basic financial statements and other data presented for supplementary analysis purposes is compiled, the compilation report should refer to the other data. Alternatively, the accountant may issue a separate report on the supplementary data that states that (1) the other data are presented for supplementary analysis purposes only, (2) the information has been compiled without audit or review from information that is the representation of management, and (3) no opinion of any other assurance on the data is expressed.

What communications are necessary when an accountant compiles financial statements that are not expected to be used by a third party?

If an accountant submits unaudited financial statements to a client that are not expected to be used by a third party, a decision must be made to either (1) issue a compilation report, or (2) document an understanding with the client in an engagement letter, preferably signed by management, regarding the services to be performed and the limitations on the use of the financial statements.

What statements or descriptions should be included in the written understanding regarding an engagement in which a compilation report is not issued?

The written understanding should include the following statements or descriptions:

○ The nature and limitations of the engagement.
○ The definition of a compilation.
○ The financial statements will not be audited or reviewed.
○ No opinion or any other form of assurance on the financial statements will be expressed.
○ Management possesses knowledge of the nature of the procedures performed and the basis of accounting

and assumptions utilized in the preparation of the financial statements.

o Acknowledgment of management's representation and agreement that the financial statements are not to be used by any third party.

o The engagement cannot be relied upon to disclose errors, illegal acts, or fraud.

o Material departures from generally accepted accounting principles (or another comprehensive basis of accounting, if applicable) may exist, and their related financial statement effects may not be disclosed.

o If applicable, substantially all disclosures (and the statement of cash flows, if applicable) required by generally accepted accounting principles (or another comprehensive basis of accounting) may be omitted.

o The accountant's lack of independence, if applicable.

o Reference to supplementary information, if applicable.

What action is necessary if the accountant does not establish an understanding with the client?

An accountant should not accept or perform the engagement if he or she fails to establish an understanding with the client.

If the accountant decides not to issue a compilation report on financial statements not expected to be used by third parties, do the financial statements require any special marking?

Each page of the financial statements that are not accompanied by a compilation report and that are not expected to be used by third parties should be marked "Restricted for Management's Use Only," or "Solely for the information and use by the management of [name of entity] and not intended to be and should not be used by any third party."

What should an accountant do if he or she becomes aware that the "restricted" financial statements have been distributed to third parties?

If the accountant becomes aware that the "restricted" financial statements have been distributed to third parties, then he or she should discuss the matter with the client and request the return of the financial statements. The client's failure to comply should cause the accountant to notify known third parties that the financial statements are not intended for their use.

REVIEW OF FINANCIAL STATEMENTS

What constitutes a review of financial statements?

A review is a step up in the level of service from a compilation engagement, since some form of assurance on the financial statements will be expressed.

Review procedures generally are limited to inquiries of company personnel and analytical procedures applied to financial data. These provide the accountant with a reasonable basis for expressing *limited assurance* that no material modifications need be made to the financial statements in order for them to be in conformity with generally accepted accounting principles (or another comprehensive basis of accounting).

Since review procedures do not include consideration of the client's internal control or the gathering of competent evidential matter, an opinion may not be expressed. In a review, the practitioner may identify matters that significantly affect the financial statements. However, the review engagement may not be relied upon to disclose all significant matters that would surface in an audit.

What are the steps in a review engagement?

The steps in a review engagement should be tailored to each engagement, but generally include the following:

Step 1. If desired, obtain an engagement letter.

Step 2. Obtain a satisfactory level of knowledge of the accounting principles, methods, and practices of the industry in which the client operates.

Step 3. Obtain a general understanding of:

- The client's organization
- The client's operating characteristics
- The nature of the client's assets, liabilities, equity, revenues, and expenses
- The client's production, distribution, and compensation methods
- The types of products and services offered
- The client's operating locations
- Any material related-party transactions

Step 4. Perform analytical procedures. Analytical procedures should be performed in order to identify and provide a basis for inquiries about unusual relationships and individual items that may be indicative of material misstatement.

An accountant should:

- Develop expectations by identifying and using plausible relationships that are reasonably expected to exist based on the accountant's understanding of the entity and the industry in which the entity operates.

- Compare recorded amounts, or ratios developed from recorded amounts, to accountant-developed expectations.

RECOMMENDATION: To identify unusual relationships and individual items, an accountant should consider performing the following analytical procedures:

- Compare current period financial information with that of prior periods.

- Compare current period financial information with anticipated results. EXAMPLE: Budgeted and forecasted amounts.

- Compare current financial information with pertinent nonfinancial information. EXAMPLE: Number of units of inventory to square footage of a storage facility.

- Compare current period financial ratios and other indicators with prior period expectations. EXAMPLES: current ratio, gross margin, accounts receivable turnover, and debt to equity.

- Compare current-period financial ratios and other indicators to industry norms.

- Compare relationships among current period financial statement elements with corresponding prior period relationships. EXAMPLE: a specific expense item as a percentage of sales.

Analytical procedures may also encompass statistical techniques, including trend analysis and regression analysis.

Step 5. Consider making the following inquiries of management personnel who have financial and accounting oversight:

- Whether the financial statements have been prepared in conformity with generally accepted accounting principles (or an other comprehensive basis of accounting) on a consistent basis

- The accounting principles and practices and the methods followed in applying them and procedures for recording, classifying, and summarizing transactions, and accumulating information relevant to financial statement disclosure

- Unusual or complex situations that may affect the financial statements
- Significant transactions occurring or recognized near the end of the accounting period
- Uncorrected misstatements identified during the previous engagement
- Questions that have surfaced during the application of review procedures
- Subsequent events that could have a material effect on the financial statements
- Their knowledge of any fraud or suspected fraud affecting the entity involving management or others that could have a material effect on the financial statements, for example, communications received from employees, former employees, or others
- Significant journal entries and other adjustments
- Communications from regulatory agencies
- Actions taken at meetings of shareholders, board of directors, committees of the board of directors, or comparable meetings that may affect the financial statements

Step 6. Perform other review procedures including:

- Reading the financial statements to consider, on the basis of information coming to the accountant's attention, whether the financial statements appear to conform with generally accepted accounting principles or an other comprehensive basis of accounting
- Obtaining reports from other accountants, if any, who have been engaged to audit or review the financial statements of significant components of the reporting entity, its subsidiaries, and other investees

Step 7. Obtain a representation letter from management.

Step 8. Document the review engagement

Are illustrative inquiries available?

The *Appendix to Statement on Accounting and Review Services No.10* contains guidance on the inquiries applicable to review engagements.

The list of illustrative inquiries presented in Exhibit 11.1 (by permission of the American Institute of Certified Public Accountants) should not be construed as a mandatory work program or all-inclusive checklist. The practitioner must be guided by professional judgment in tailoring inquiries and procedures to the needs of the client given all facts and circumstances.

1. General
   (a) Have there been any changes in the entity's business activities?
   (b) Are there any unusual or complex situations that may have an effect on the financial statements (for example, business combinations, restructuring plans, or litigation)?
   (c) What procedures are in place related to recording, classifying, and summarizing transactions and accumulating information related to financial statement disclosures?
   (d) Have the financial statements been prepared in conformity with generally accepted accounting principles or, if appropriate, a comprehensive basis of accounting other than generally accepted accounting principles? Have there been any changes in accounting principles and methods of applying those principles?
   (e) Have there been any instances of fraud or illegal acts within the entity?
   (f) Have there been any allegations or suspicions that fraud or illegal acts might have occurred or might be occurring within the entity? If so, where and how?
   (g) Are any entities, other than the reporting entity, commonly controlled by the owners? If so, has an evaluation been performed to determine whether those other entities should be consolidated into the financial statements of the reporting entity?
   (h) Are there any entities other than the reporting entity in which the owners have significant investments (for example, variable interest entities)? If so, has an evaluation been performed to determine whether the reporting entity is the primary beneficiary related to the activities of these other entities?
   (i) Have any significant transactions occurred or been recognized near the end of the reporting period?
2. Cash and cash equivalents
   (a) Is the entity's policy regarding the composition of cash and cash equivalents in accordance with Financial Accounting Standards Board Statement of Financial Accounting Standards No. 95, Statement of Cash Flows (paragraphs 7–10)? Has the policy been applied on a consistent basis?

Exhibit 11.1 ILLUSTRATIVE INQUIRIES

(b) Are all cash and cash equivalents accounts reconciled on a timely basis?

(c) Have old or unusual reconciling items between bank balances and book balances been reviewed and adjustments made where necessary?

(d) Has there been a proper cutoff of cash receipts and disbursements?

(e) Has a reconciliation of intercompany transfers been prepared?

(f) Have checks written but not mailed as of the financial statement date been properly reclassified into the liability section of the balance sheet?

(g) Have material bank overdrafts been properly reclassified into the liability section of the balance sheet?

(h) Are there compensating balances or other restrictions on the availability of cash and cash equivalents balances? If so, has consideration been given to reclassifying these amounts as noncurrent assets?

(i) Have cash funds been counted and reconciled with control accounts?

3. Receivables

(a) Has an adequate allowance for doubtful accounts been properly reflected in the financial statements?

(b) Have uncollectible receivables been written off through a charge against the allowance account or earnings?

(c) Has interest earned on receivables been properly reflected in the financial statements?

(d) Has there been a proper cutoff of sales transactions?

(e) Are there receivables from employees or other related parties? Have receivables from owners been evaluated to determine if they should be reflected in the equity section (rather than the asset section) of the balance sheet?

(f) Are any receivables pledged, discounted, or factored? Are recourse provisions properly reflected in the financial statements?

(g) Have receivables been properly classified between current and noncurrent?

Exhibit 11.1   ILLUSTRATIVE INQUIRIES *(continued)*

(h) Have there been significant numbers of sales returns or credit memoranda issued subsequent to the balance sheet date?

(i) Is the accounts receivable subsidiary ledger reconciled to the general ledger account balance on a regular basis?

4. Inventory

(a) Are physical inventory counts performed on a regular basis, including at the end of the reporting period? Are the count procedures adequate to ensure an appropriate count? If not, how have amounts related to inventories been determined for purposes of financial statement presentation? If so, what procedures were used to take the latest physical inventory and what date was that inventory taken?

(b) Have general ledger control accounts been adjusted to agree with the physical inventory count? If so, were the adjustments significant?

(c) If the physical inventory counts were taken at a date other than the balance sheet date, what procedures were used to determine changes in inventory between the date of the physical inventory counts and the balance sheet date?

(d) Were consignments in or out considered in taking physical inventories?

(e) What is the basis of valuing inventory for purposes of financial statement presentation?

(f) Does inventory cost include material, labor, and overhead where applicable?

(g) Has inventory been reviewed for obsolescence or cost in excess of net realizable value? If so, how are these costs reflected in the financial statements?

(h) Have proper cutoffs of purchases, goods in transit, and returned goods been made?

(i) Are there any inventory encumbrances?

(j) Is scrap inventoried and controlled?

5. Prepaid Expenses

(a) What is the nature of the amounts included in prepaid expenses?

(b) How are these amounts being amortized?

Exhibit 11.1   ILLUSTRATIVE INQUIRIES *(continued)*

6. Investments

   (a) What is the basis of accounting for investments reported in the financial statements (for example, securities, joint ventures, or closely-held businesses)?

   (b) Are derivative instruments properly measured and disclosed in the financial statements? If those derivatives are utilized in hedge transactions, have the documentation or assessment requirements related to hedge accounting been met?

   (c) Are investments in marketable debt and equity securities properly classified as trading, available-for-sale, and held-to-maturity?

   (d) How were fair values of the reported investments determined? Have unrealized gains and losses been properly reported in the financial statements?

   (e) If the fair values of marketable debt and equity securities are less than cost, have the declines in value been evaluated to determine whether the declines are other than temporary?

   (f) For any debt securities classified as held-to-maturity, does management have the positive ability and intent to hold the securities until they mature? If so, have those debt securities been properly measured?

   (g) Have gains and losses related to disposal of investments been properly reflected in the financial statements?

   (h) How was investment income determined? Is investment income properly reflected in the financial statements?

   (i) Has appropriate consideration been given to the classification of investments between current and noncurrent?

   (j) For investments made by the reporting entity, have consolidation, equity, or cost method accounting requirements been considered?

   (k) Are any investments encumbered?

7. Property and Equipment

   (a) Are property and equipment items properly stated at depreciated cost or other proper value?

   (b) When was the last time a physical inventory of property and equipment was taken?

Exhibit 11.1 ILLUSTRATIVE INQUIRIES *(continued)*

(c) Are all items reflected in property and equipment held for use? If not, have items that are held for sale been properly reclassified from property and equipment?

(d) Have gains or losses on disposal of property and equipment been properly reflected in the financial statements?

(e) What are the criteria for capitalization of property and equipment? Have the criteria been consistently and appropriately applied?

(f) Are repairs and maintenance costs properly reflected as an expense in the income statement?

(g) What depreciation methods and rates are utilized in the financial statements? Are these methods and rates appropriate and applied on a consistent basis?

(h) Are there any unrecorded additions, retirements, abandonments, sales, or trade-ins?

(i) Does the entity have any material lease agreements? If so, have those agreements been properly evaluated for financial statement presentation purposes?

(j) Are there any asset retirement obligations associated with tangible long-lived assets? If so, has the recorded amount of the related asset been increased because of the obligation and is the liability properly reflected in the liability section of the balance sheet?

(k) Has the entity constructed any of its property and equipment items? If so, have all components of cost been reflected in measuring these items for purposes of financial statement presentation, including, but not limited to, capitalized interest?

(l) Has there been any significant impairment in value of property and equipment items? If so, has any impairment loss been properly reflected in the financial statements?

(m) Are any property and equipment items mortgaged or otherwise encumbered? If so, are these mortgages and encumbrances properly reflected in the financial statements?

8. Intangibles and Other Assets

(a) What is the nature of the amounts included in other assets?

Exhibit 11.1 ILLUSTRATIVE INQUIRIES *(continued)*

(b) Do these assets represent costs that will benefit future periods? What is the amortization policy related to these assets? Is this policy appropriate?

(c) Have other assets been properly classified between current and noncurrent?

(d) Are intangible assets with finite lives being appropriately amortized?

(e) Are the costs associated with computer software properly reflected as intangible assets (rather than property and equipment) in the financial statements?

(f) Are the costs associated with goodwill (and other intangible assets with indefinite lives) properly reflected as intangible assets in the financial statements? Has amortization ceased related to these assets?

(g) Has there been any significant impairment in value of these assets? If so, has any impairment loss been properly reflected in the financial statements?

(h) Are any of these assets mortgaged or otherwise encumbered?

9. Accounts and Short-Term Notes Payable and Accrued Liabilities

(a) Have all payables been reflected in the financial statements?

(b) Are loans from financial institutions and other short-term liabilities properly classified in the financial statements?

(c) Have all significant accruals (for example, payroll, interest, provisions for pension and profit-sharing plans, or other postretirement benefit obligations) been properly reflected in the financial statements?

(d) Has a liability for employees' compensation for future absences been properly accrued and disclosed in the financial statements?

(e) Are any liabilities collateralized or subordinated? If so, are those liabilities disclosed in the financial statements?

(f) Are there any payables to employees and related parties?

10. Long-Term Liabilities

(a) Are the terms and other provisions of long-term liability agreements properly disclosed in the financial statements?

Exhibit 11.1   ILLUSTRATIVE INQUIRIES *(continued)*

  (b) Have liabilities been properly classified between current and noncurrent?

  (c) Has interest expense been properly accrued and reflected in the financial statements?

  (d) Is the company in compliance with loan covenants and agreements? If not, is the non compliance properly disclosed in the financial statements?

  (e) If so, are these facts disclosed in the financial statements?

  (f) Are there any obligations that, by their terms, are due on demand within one year from the balance sheet date? If so, have these obligations been properly reclassified into the current liability section of the balance sheet?

11. Income and Other Taxes

  (a) Do the financial statements reflect an appropriate provision for current and prior-year federal income taxes payable?

  (b) Have any assessments or reassessments been received? Are there tax authority examinations in process?

  (c) Are there any temporary differences between book and tax amounts? If so, have deferred taxes on these differences been properly reflected in the financial statements?

  (d) Do the financial statements reflect an appropriate provision for taxes other than income taxes (for example, franchise, sales)?

  (e) Have all required tax payments been made on a timely basis?

12. Other Liabilities, Contingencies, and Commitments

  (a) What is the nature of the amounts included in other liabilities?

  (b) Have other liabilities been properly classified between current and noncurrent?

  (c) Are there any guarantees, whether written or verbal, whereby the entity must stand ready to perform or is contingently liable related to the guarantee? If so, are these guarantees properly reflected in the financial statements?

  (d) Are there any contingent liabilities (for example, discounted notes, drafts, endorsements, warranties, litigation, and unsettled asserted claims)? Are there any potential

Exhibit 11.1 ILLUSTRATIVE INQUIRIES *(continued)*

unasserted claims? Are these contingent liabilities, claims, and assessments properly measured and disclosed in the financial statements?

(e) Are there any material contractual obligations for construction or purchase of property and equipment and or any commitments or options to purchase or sell company securities? If so, are these facts clearly disclosed in the financial statements?

(f) Is the entity responsible for any environmental remediation liability? If so, is this liability properly measured and disclosed in the financial statements?

(g) Does the entity have any agreement to repurchase items that previously were sold? If so, have the repurchase agreements been taken into account in determining the appropriate measurements and disclosures in the financial statements?

(h) Does the entity have any sales commitments at prices expected to result in a loss at the consummation of the sale? If so, are these commitments properly reflected in the financial statements?

(i) Are there any violations, or possible violations, of laws or regulations the effects of which should be considered for financial statement accrual or disclosure?

13. Equity

(a) What is the nature of any changes in equity accounts during each reporting period?

(b) What classes of stock (other ownership interests) have been authorized?

(c) What is the par or stated value of the various classes of stock (other ownership interests)?

(d) Do amounts of outstanding shares of stock (other ownership interests) agree with subsidiary records?

(e) Have pertinent rights and privileges of ownership interests been properly disclosed in the financial statements?

(f) Does the entity have any mandatorily redeemable ownership interests? If so, have these ownership interests been evaluated so that a proper determination has been made related to whether these ownership interests should be measured and reclassified to

Exhibit 11.1 ILLUSTRATIVE INQUIRIES *(continued)*

the liability section of the balance sheet? Are redemption features associated with ownership interests clearly disclosed in the financial statements?

(g) Have dividend (distribution) and liquidation preferences related to ownership interests been properly disclosed in the financial statements?

(h) Do disclosures related to ownership interests include any applicable call provisions (prices and dates), conversion provisions (prices and rates), unusual voting rights, significant terms of contracts to issue additional ownership interests, or any other unusual features associated with the ownership interests?

(i) Are syndication fees properly reflected in the financial statements as a reduction of equity (rather than an asset)?

(j) Have any stock options or other stock compensation awards been granted to employees or others? If so, are these options or awards properly measured and disclosed in the financial statements?

(k) Has the entity made any acquisitions of its own stock? If so, are the amounts associated with these reacquired shares properly reflected in the financial statements as a reduction in equity? Is the presentation in accordance with applicable state laws?

(l) Are there any restrictions or appropriations on retained earnings or other capital accounts? If so, are these restrictions or appropriations properly reflected in the financial statements?

14. Revenue and Expenses

(a) What is the entity's revenue recognition policy? Is the policy appropriate? Has the policy been consistently applied and appropriately disclosed?

(b) Are revenues from sales of products and rendering of services recognized in the appropriate reporting period (that is, when the products have been delivered and when the services have been performed)?

(c) Were any sales recorded under a "bill and hold" arrangement? If yes, have the criteria been met to record the transaction as a sale?

(d) Are purchases and expenses recognized in the appropriate reporting period (that is,

Exhibit 11.1 ILLUSTRATIVE INQUIRIES *(continued)*

matched against revenue) and properly classified in the financial statements?

(e) Do the financial statements include discontinued operations items that might he considered extraordinary, or both? If so, are amounts associated with discontinued operations, extraordinary items, or both properly displayed in the income statement?

(f) Does the entity have any gains or losses that would necessitate the display of comprehensive income (for example, gains/losses on available-for-sale securities or cash flow hedge derivatives)? If so, have these items been properly displayed within comprehensive income (rather than included in the determination of net income)?

15. Other

(a) Have events occurred subsequent to the balance sheet date that would require adjustment to, or disclosure in, the financial statements?

(b) Have actions taken at stockholders, board of directors, committees of directors, or comparable meetings that affect the financial statements been reflected in the financial statements?

(c) Are significant estimates and material concentrations (for example, customers or suppliers) properly disclosed in the financial statements?

(d) Are there plans or intentions that may materially affect the carrying amounts or classification of assets and liabilities reflected in the financial statements?

(e) Have there been material transactions between or among related parties (for example, sales, purchases, loans, or leasing arrangements)? If so, are these transactions properly disclosed in the financial statements?

(f) Are there uncertainties that could have a material impact on the financial statements? Is there any change in the status of previously disclosed material uncertainties? Are all uncertainties, including going concern matters, that could have a material impact on the financial statements properly disclosed in the financial statements?

(g) Are barter or other nonmonetary transactions properly recorded and disclosed?

Exhibit 11.1 ILLUSTRATIVE INQUIRIES *(continued)*

What should be included in the representation letter obtained from management?

It is important that the representation letter obtained from management cover all financial statements and periods that the accountant is reporting on. Although the specific items to be addressed in the representation letter will vary depending on the circumstances of the engagement and the nature and basis of financial statement presentation, representations pertaining to GAAP financial statements should relate to the following:

- o Management's acknowledgment of its responsibility for the fairness of the financial statement presentation
- o Management's belief that the financial statements are fairly presented in conformity with GAAP
- o Management's acknowledgement of its responsibility for the prevention and detection of fraud
- o Knowledge of any fraud or suspected fraud involving members of management or others that could materially affect the financial statements, including communications received from current or former employees, or others
- o Management's full and truthful response to all accountant inquiries
- o Completeness of information
- o Subsequent events

In general, the representation letter should be (1) dated no earlier than the date of the accountant's review report and (2) signed by the chief executive officer and chief financial officer. In the event that the current management team is different from the management team of prior periods on which the accountant is reporting on a comparative basis, the current management team is responsible for all of the representations.

What are the documentation requirements applicable to a review engagement?

The form and content of the documentation should be tailored to meet the circumstances of the engagement. A review report may also be supported by other means in addition to the documentation of the review. For example, documentation of a compilation engagement and documentation contained in quality control files may supplement the documentation of the review engagement.

Specifically, the documentation of the review should include:

- Significant findings or issues that could result in material misstatement of the financial statements, including actions to address such findings or issues, and the accountant's basis for his or her final conclusion
- The matters covered in the accountant's inquiry
- The analytical procedures performed
- The accountant-developed expectations where significant expectations are not otherwise readily determinable from the documentation of the work performed, and factors considered in the development of those expectations
- Results of the comparison of the expectations to the recorded amounts or ratios developed from recorded amounts
- Additional procedures performed in response to significant unexpected differences arising from analytical procedures and the results of such additional procedures
- Unusual matters identified by the accountant and their disposition
- The representation letter

Reports on Reviewed Financial Statements

What should the review report contain?

The accountant's review report should include:

- An identification of the financial statements
- A statement that a review was performed in accordance with *Statements on Standards for Accounting and Review Services* issued by the American Institute of Certified Public Accountants
- A statement that all the information included in the financial statements is the representation of management (or owners)
- The definition of a review stating that a review consists principally of inquiries of company personnel and of analytical procedures applied to financial data
- A statement that a review is substantially less in scope than an audit, the objective of which is the expression of an opinion on the financial statements taken as a whole, and that no such opinion is expressed
- If warranted, the issuance of limited assurance; that is, a statement that the accountant is not aware of any material modifications that should be made to the financial statements in order for them to be in

conformity with generally accepted accounting principles (or other comprehensive basis of accounting)

o Disclosure of any material modifications, if any, that should be made to the financial statements for them to be in conformity with generally accepted accounting principles (or other comprehensive basis of accounting)

o The date of the report, which should coincide with the completion of the inquiries and analytical procedures

o The accountant's signature

RECOMMENDATIONS

Each page of the reviewed financial statements must be labeled "See Accountant's Review Report." If desired, expand the label to include "and the Notes to the Financial Statements." It is also permissible to label each page of the financial statements as "unaudited."

What does a standard review report look like?

EXAMPLE 11.3 STANDARD REVIEW REPORT

I (We) have reviewed the accompanying balance sheet of Credit Corporation as of (at) December 31, 20XX, and the related statements of income, retained earnings, and cash flows for the year then ended, in accordance with *Statements of Standards for Accounting and Review Services* issued by the American Institute of Certified Public Accountants. All information included in these financial statements is the representation of the management (owners) of Credit Corporation.

A review consists principally of inquiries of company personnel and analytical procedures applied to financial data. It is substantially less in scope than an audit in accordance with generally accepted auditing standards, the objective of which is the expression of an opinion regarding the financial statements taken as a whole. Accordingly, I (we) do not express such an opinion.

Based on my (our) review, I am (we are) not aware of any material modifications that should be made to the accompanying financial statements in order for them to be in conformity with generally accepted accounting principles.

What should I be cautious about in review engagements?

If the practitioner is precluded from performing review procedures that he or she considers necessary, then a review report should *not* be issued. In such circumstances, the accountant might consider issuing a compilation report.

CAUTION
Professional judgment must be exercised in considering the circumstances that precluded the review report.

Independence is a requirement for the issuance of a review report.

An accountant may undertake an engagement to review less than a complete set of financial statements. **EXAMPLE: The practitioner may accept an engagement to review only a client's balance sheet.**

Under certain circumstances, a client may request that an accountant, who was engaged to perform an audit under GAAS, change the engagement to a lower level of service, namely a change to a compilation or a review. Before undertaking the step down, the accountant should take into consideration:

- ○ The client's reasons for the steps down, including any client-imposed scope limitations.
- ○ The extent of any additional procedures to complete the audit engagement.
- ○ The cost to the client of performing the additional auditing procedures.

When justification exists for the step-down, as in the case of a client who no longer requires an audit report to secure a bank loan because alternative financing was arranged, the accountant's report should not refer to the step-down or to the application of any audit procedures performed. Accordingly, the standard compilation or review report is appropriate.

CAUTION
If the accountant is precluded from discussing litigation, claims, and assessments with the client's legal counsel because the client refuses to authorize the communication or the client refuses to furnish a representation letter, then the situation is tantamount to a scope limitation sufficient to preclude the issuance of an opinion. Such scope limitations similarly preclude the accountant from issuing a review or compilation report on the financial statements.

When must the standard report be modified?

Departures from Generally Accepted Accounting Principles. When the accountant becomes aware of a material departure from generally accepted accounting principles, it is necessary to modify the standard report by:

- ○ Beginning the third paragraph with wording such as "Based on my (our) review, with the exception of the matter(s) described in the following paragraph(s), I am (we are) not aware of any material modifications…"
- ○ Presenting an additional paragraph in order to disclose the effects of the departure

In situations where the principal effects of the departure cannot reasonably be determined, the practitioner should state this in the report.

SUPPLEMENTARY INFORMATION

When the basic financial statements are accompanied by additional information, such as a supporting schedule of selling, general and administrative expenses, the accountant should indicate the responsibility he or she is taking with respect to this supplementary information. This may be accomplished by presenting either of two reports:

- ○ One report that covers both the basic financial statements and the supplementary information
- ○ Separate reports on the basic financial statements and the supplementary information

Whichever approach is followed, the report should include a statement that the additional information is presented for the purpose of analysis only and was or was not subjected to the review procedures applicable to the review of the basic financial statements.

NOTE

If the additional information was reviewed, the report should contain the expression of limited assurance; that is, that the accountant is not aware of any material modifications that should be made to the additional information. On the other hand, if the practitioner did not review the supplementary information, the report should state this fact. In this circumstance, it would be appropriate to state that the additional information was compiled from information that is the representation of management, without audit or review, and that no opinion or any other form of assurance is being expressed.

REPORTING ON PRESCRIBED FORMS

How do I report on compiled financial statements included in certain prescribed forms?

A prescribed form is a preprinted form designed and adopted by the body to which it is to be submitted (e.g., forms used by industry trade associations and banks). Generally, the accountant has no responsibility to advise the designer of the prescribed form of departures from GAAP.

EXAMPLE 11.4 COMPILATION REPORT APPLICABLE TO COMPILED FINANCIAL STATEMENTS INCLUDED IN A PRESCRIBED FORM

I (We) have compiled the (identification of financial statements, including name of entity and period covered) included in the accompanying prescribed form in accordance with *Statements on Standards for Accounting and Review Services* issued by the American Institute of Certified Public Accountants.

My (Our) compilation was limited to presenting in the form prescribed by (name of body) information that is the representation of management (owners). I (We) have not audited or reviewed the financial statements referred to above and, accordingly, do not express an opinion or any other form of assurance on them.

These financial statements (including related disclosures) are presented in accordance with the requirements of (name body), which differ from generally accepted accounting principles. Accordingly, these financial statements are not designed for those who are not informed about such differences.

WARNING
Do not sign a preprinted report form that does not conform to the reporting standards contained in the *Statements on Standards for Accounting and Review Services* issued by the American Institute of Certified Public Accountants.

COMMUNICATION BETWEEN SUCCESSOR AND PREDECESSOR ACCOUNTANTS

If I am a successor accountant, do I have a responsibility to communicate with the predecessor accountant in either a compilation or review engagement?

The successor accountant ("successor") must decide whether or not to communicate with the predecessor accountant ("predecessor") regarding acceptance of a compilation or review engagement. If the successor decides to contact the predecessor, after permission is granted by the client to both the successor and predecessor, inquiry may be made about the following:

○ Facts that bear on the integrity of management
○ Disagreements about accounting principles
○ Disagreements about the performance of relevant procedures
○ Cooperation of management in providing additional or revised information
○ The predecessor's understanding of the reason for the change in accountants

It is generally expected that the predecessor will respond promptly and fully. However, unusual conditions, such as impending litigation, may preclude a full response. In such cases, the predecessor should indicate that his or her response is limited.

The successor may also request that the predecessor release copies of certain working papers. If the client grants permission for such release, the predecessor should provide access to working papers relating to (1) matters of continuing accounting significance and (2) contingencies. It should be noted, however, that valid business reasons may lead the predecessor to decide not to provide the requested access.

Finally, if the successor becomes aware of information that may require revision of the financial statements reported on by the predecessor, the successor has a responsibility to request his or her client to communicate this information to the predecessor. The client's refusal to communicate with the predecessor regarding such information should result in the successor contacting his or her attorney.

REPORTS ON PROSPECTIVE FINANCIAL STATEMENTS

What are prospective financial statements?

Prospective financial statements encompass financial forecasts and financial projections. Pro forma financial statements and partial presentations are specifically excluded from this category.

Financial forecasts are prospective financial statements that present, to the best of the responsible party's knowledge and belief, an entity's expected financial position, results of operations, and cash flows. They are based on assumptions about conditions *actually* expected to exist and the course of action expected to be taken.

Financial projections are prospective financial statements that present, to the best of the responsible party's knowledge and belief, an entity's expected financial position, results of operations, and cash flows. They are based on assumptions about conditions expected to exist and the course of action expected to be taken, given one or more hypothetical (i.e., "what-if") assumptions.

Responsible parties are those who are responsible for the underlying assumptions. While the responsible party is usually management, it may be a third party. EXAMPLE: If a client is negotiating with a bank for a large loan, the bank may stipulate the assumptions to be used. Accordingly, in this case, the bank would represent the responsible party.

What are my reporting responsibilities regarding prospective financial statements?

Statement on Standards for Attestation Engagements #10 specifically precludes an accountant from compiling, examining, or applying agreed-upon procedures to prospective financial statements that fail to include a summary of significant assumptions. The practice standards in the *Statement* are *not* applicable:

- To engagements involving prospective financial statements that are restricted to internal use

- To those used solely in litigation support services (e.g., in circumstances where the practitioner is serving as an expert witness)

How are prospective financial statements used?

The intended use of an entity's prospective financial statements governs the type of prospective financial statements to be presented.

- ○ When an entity's prospective financial statements are for *general use*, only a financial forecast is to be presented. "General use" means that the statements will be used by persons not negotiating directly with the responsible party. EXAMPLE: In a public offering of a tax shelter interest.

- ○ When an entity's prospective financial statements are for *limited use*, either a financial forecast or a financial projection may be presented. "Limited use" refers to situations where the statements are to be used by the responsible party alone or by the responsible party and those parties negotiating directly with the responsible party. EXAMPLE: If a client is negotiating directly with a bank, either a forecast or a projection is appropriate.

How do I compile prospective statements?

Compilation procedures applicable to prospective financial statements are not designed to provide any form of assurance on the presentation of the statements or the underlying assumptions.

They are essentially the same as those applicable to historical financial statements. Additional procedures:

- ○ Inquire of the responsible party as to the underlying assumptions developed.
- ○ Compile or obtain a list of the underlying assumptions and consider the possibility of obvious omissions or inconsistencies.
- ○ Verify the mathematical accuracy of the assumptions.
- ○ Read the prospective financial statements in order to identify departures from AICPA presentation guidelines.
- ○ Obtain a client representation letter in order to confirm that the responsible party acknowledges its responsibility for the prospective statements (including the underlying assumptions).

CAUTION

An accountant is precluded from compiling forecasts and projections that do not present the summary of significant assumptions. Furthermore, the practitioner should not compile a projection that fails to identify the underlying hypothetical assumptions or describe the limitations on the utility of the projection.

What do I include in a compilation report on prospective statements?

The accountant's report on compiled prospective financial statements should include:

o An identification of the prospective financial statements presented

o A statement as to the level of service provided and the fact that the prospective financial statements were compiled in accordance with attestation standards established by the AICPA

o A statement describing the limited scope of a compilation and the fact that no opinion or any other form of assurance is being expressed

o A warning that the prospective results may not materialize

o A statement that the accountant is under no responsibility to update his or her report for conditions occurring after the compilation report is issued

o The date of the report, which should coincide with the completion of the compilation procedures

o The accountant's signature

o In the case of a projection, a separate middle paragraph describing the limitations on the utility of the statements

o A separate paragraph when the statements present the expected results in the form of a range of values

o If the accountant is not independent, a statement as to this fact (No disclosure should be made as to the reasons why the accountant feels that he or she is not independent.)

o A separate explanatory paragraph when the prospective statements contain a departure from AICPA presentation guidelines or omit disclosures unrelated to the significant assumptions

---

EXAMPLE 11.5 STANDARD REPORT ON COMPILED FORECASTS

I (We) have compiled the accompanying forecasted balance sheet, statement of income, retained earnings, and cash flows of Future Corporation as of (at) December 31, 20XX and for the year then ending, in accordance with attestation standards established by the American Institute of Certified Public Accountants.

A compilation is limited to presenting in the form of a forecast information that is the representation of management (or other responsible party) and does not include

EXAMPLE 11.5 STANDARD REPORT ON COMPILED FORECASTS (continued)

evaluation of the support for the assumptions underlying the forecast. I (We) have not examined the forecast and, accordingly, do not express an opinion or any other form of assurance on the accompanying statements or assumptions. Furthermore, there will usually be differences between the forecasted and actual results, because events and circumstances frequently do not occur as expected, and those differences may be material. I (We) have no responsibility to update this report for events and circumstances occurring after the date of this report.

EXAMPLE 11.6 STANDARD REPORT ON COMPILED PROJECTIONS

I (We) have compiled the accompanying projected balance sheet, statements of income, retained earnings, and cash flows of Future Corporation as of December 31, 20XX, and for the year then ending, in accordance with attestation standards established by the American Institute of Certified Public Accountants.

The accompanying projection, and this report, were prepared for [state special purpose, for example, "the Takeover Corporation for the purpose of negotiating a buyout of the Company,"] and should not be used for any other purpose.

A compilation is limited to presenting in the form of a projection information that is the representation of management (or other responsible party) and does not include evaluation of the support for the assumptions underlying the projection. I (We) have not examined the projection and, accordingly, do not express an opinion or any other form of assurance on the accompanying statements or assumptions. Furthermore, even if [describe hypothetical assumption, for example, "the buyout is consummated"] there will usually be differences between the projected and actual results, because events and circumstances frequently do not occur as expected, and those differences may be material. I (We) have no responsibility to update this report for events and circumstances occurring after the date of this report.

EXAMPLE 11.7 PARAGRAPH INCLUDED WHEN STATEMENTS CONTAIN A RANGE OF VALUES

As described in the summary of significant assumptions, management of Future Corporation (or another responsible party) has elected to portray forecasted (or projected) [describe financial statement element(s) for which expected results of one or more assumptions fall within a range, and identify the assumptions expected to fall within a range, for example, "revenue at the amounts of $XXX, XXX and $YYY, YYY, which is based on a buyout purchase price of X% of 20XX net income and Y% of 20XX net income,"] rather than as a single point estimate. Accordingly, the accompanying forecast (projection) presents forecasted (projected) financial position, results of operations, and cash flows [describe assumption(s) expected to fall within a range, for example, "at such buyout rates"]. However, there is no assurance that the actual results will fall within the range of [describe assumption(s) expected to fall within a range, for example, "buyout rates"] presented.

EXAMPLE 11.8 SAMPLE PARAGRAPH INCLUDED WHEN PROSPECTIVE FINANCIAL STATEMENTS DEPART FROM AICPA PRESENTATION GUIDELINES

Management (or another responsible party) has elected to omit the summary of significant accounting policies required by the guidelines for presentation of a financial forecast (or projection) established by the American Institute of Certified Public Accountants. If the omitted disclosures were included in the forecast (projection), they might influence the user's conclusions about the Company's financial position, results of operations, and cash flows for the forecasted (projected) period. Accordingly, this forecast (projection) is not designed for those who are not informed about such matters.

What is involved in an examination of prospective financial statements?

An examination of prospective financial statements evaluates:

o The preparation of the statements
o The support of the related underlying assumptions
o The conformity of the statements with AICPA presentation guidelines

The practitioner's report should contain an opinion as to whether:

o The statements are presented in conformity with the AICPA guidelines
o The underlying assumptions provide a reasonable basis for the forecast
o The underlying assumptions provide a reasonable basis for the projection in light of the hypothetical assumptions

How do I conduct an examination of prospective financial statements?

In performing an examination of prospective financial statements, the practitioner should:

Step 1. Assess inherent and control risk as well as limit his or her detection risk.

Step 2. Consider the sufficiency of external sources (such as government and industry publications) and internal sources (such as management-prepared budgets) of information supporting the underlying assumptions.

Step 3. Determine the consistency of the assumptions and the sources from which they are predicated.

Step 4. Determine the consistency of the assumptions themselves.

Step 5. Determine the reliability and consistency of the historical financial information used.

Step 6. Evaluate the preparation and presentation of the prospective financial statements:

- Does the presentation reflect the underlying assumptions?
- Are the assumptions mathematically accurate?
- Do the assumptions reflect an internally consistent pattern?
- Do the accounting principles in use reflect those expected to be in effect in the prospective period?
- Are the AICPA presentation guidelines followed?
- Is there adequate disclosure of the assumptions?

Step 7. Obtain a client representation letter to confirm that the responsible party acknowledges its responsibility for the presentation of the prospective financial statements *and* the underlying assumptions.

What is included in examination reports on prospective statements?

The accountant's report on examined prospective financial statements should include:

- A title that includes the word *independent*
- Identification of the prospective financial statements presented
- Identification of the responsible party and a statement that the prospective financial statements are the responsibility of the responsible party
- A statement that the practitioner's responsibility is to express an opinion on the prospective financial statements based on his or her examination
- A statement that the examination was performed in accordance with attestation standards established by the AICPA and, accordingly, included such procedures as the practitioner considered necessary in the circumstances
- A statement that the practitioner believes that the examination provides a reasonable basis for his or her opinion
- An opinion on the presentation of the prospective financial statements in terms of their conformity with AICPA presentation guidelines
- An opinion as to whether the underlying assumptions provide a reasonable basis for the prospective financial statements
- A warning that the prospective results may not materialize
- A statement that the accountant is under no responsibility to update his or her report for conditions occurring after the examination report is issued
- The accountant's signature, which may be manual or printed
- The date of the report, which should coincide with the completion of the examination procedures

EXAMPLE 11.9 STANDARD REPORT ON EXAMINED FORECASTS

INDEPENDENT ACCOUNTANT'S REPORT

(I) We have examined the accompanying forecasted balance sheet, statements of income, retained earnings, and cash flows of Travis Company as of December 31, 20XX,

EXAMPLE 11.9 STANDARD REPORT ON EXAMINED FORECASTS *(continued)*

and for the year then ending. Travis Company's management is responsible for the forecast. (My) Our responsibility is to express an opinion on the forecast based on (my) our examination.

(My) Our examination was conducted in accordance with attestation standards established by the American Institute of Certified Public Accountants and, accordingly, included such procedures as (I) we considered necessary to evaluate both the assumptions used by management and the preparation and presentation of the forecast. (I) We believe that (my) our examination provides a reasonable basis for (my) our opinion.

In (my) our opinion, the accompanying forecast is presented in conformity with guidelines for presentation of a forecast established by the American Institute of Certified Public Accountants, and the underlying assumptions provide a reasonable basis for management's forecast. However, there will usually be differences between the forecasted and actual results, because events and circumstances frequently do not occur as expected, and those differences may be material. (I) We have no responsibility to update this report for events and circumstances occurring after the date of this report.

[Signature]

[Date]

EXAMPLE 11.10 STANDARD REPORT ON EXAMINED PROJECTIONS

INDEPENDENT ACCOUNTANT'S REPORT

I(We) have examined the accompanying projected balance sheet, statements of income, retained earnings, and cash flows of Jordan Company as of December 31, 20xx, and for the year then ending. Jordan Company's management is responsible for the projection, which was prepared for *[state special purpose, for example, "the purpose of negotiating a loan to expand Jordan Company's plant"]*. (My) Our responsibility is to express an opinion on the projection based on (my) our examination.

(My) Our examination was conducted in accordance with attestation standards established by the American Institute of Certified Public Accountants and, accordingly, included such procedures as (I) we considered necessary to evaluate both the assumptions used by management

EXAMPLE 11.10 STANDARD REPORT ON EXAMINED PROJECTIONS *(continued)*

and the preparation and presentation of the projection. (I) We believe that (my) our examination provides a reasonable basis for (my) our opinion.

In (my) our opinion, the accompanying projection is presented in conformity with guidelines for presentation of a projection established by the American Institute of Certified Public Accountants, and the underlying assumptions provide a reasonable basis for managements projection *[describe the hypothetical assumption, for example, assuming the granting of the requested loan for the purpose of expanding Jordan Company's plant as described in the summary of significant assumptions."]* However, even if *[describe hypothetical assumption, for example, "the loan is granted and the plant is expanded,"]* there will usually be differences between the projected and actual results, because events and circumstances frequently do not occur as expected, and those differences may be material. (I) We have no responsibility to update this report for events and circumstances occurring after the date of this report.

The accompanying projection and this report are intended solely for the information and use of *[identify specified parties, for example, "Jordan Company and DEF National Bank"]* and is not intended to be and should not be used by anyone other than these specified parties.

[Signature]

[Date]

When should the standard examination report be modified?

RANGE OF VALUES

When prospective financial statements contain a range of values, the report should contain an additional paragraph clearly indicating this. The explanatory paragraph should be similar to the one added to compilation reports on prospective financial statements containing a range of values.

DEPARTURE FROM AICPA PRESENTATION GUIDELINES

When the prospective financial statements contain a departure from the AICPA presentation guidelines, issue either an "except for" qualified opinion or an adverse opinion. An "except for" qualified opinion should contain an explanatory middle paragraph which describes the departure. The opinion paragraph should specifically refer to the explanatory middle paragraph.

In my (our) opinion, except for [describe the departure, for example, the omission of the disclosures of the reasons for significant variation in the relationship between income tax expense and pretax accounting income as discussed in the preceding paragraph,] ...

NOTE
The issuance of an adverse opinion is mandated if the prospective financial statements fail to disclose the significant underlying assumptions.

SIGNIFICANT ASSUMPTION DOES NOT PROVIDE REASONABLE BASIS

When the accountant believes that one or more significant assumptions (including hypothetical assumptions) do not provide a reasonable basis for the prospective financial statements, the issuance of an adverse opinion is justified.

NOTE
The examination report should include a middle paragraph that discloses all of the substantive reasons for the issuance of the adverse opinion. The opinion paragraph should specifically refer to the middle explanatory paragraph.

EXAMPLE 11.11 PARAGRAPH USED WHEN EXPRESSING AN ADVERSE OPINION

In my (our) opinion, the accompanying forecast is not presented in conformity with guidelines for presentation of a financial forecast established by the American Institute of Certified Public Accountants because management's (or another responsible party's) assumptions, as discussed in the preceding paragraph, do not provide a reasonable basis for management's (or another responsible party's) forecast. I (We) have no responsibility to update this report for events or circumstances occurring after the date of this report.

SCOPE LIMITATION

When the accountant is unable to perform one or more examination procedures considered necessary for the particular engagement, a disclaimer of an opinion should be expressed. The disclaimer should clearly describe the scope limitation in a separate explanatory paragraph.

NOTE

The scope paragraph of the examination report should be modified to indicate the existence of a scope limitation and the explanatory middle paragraph.
EXAMPLE: "Except as explained in the following paragraph, ..." The disclaimer paragraph should also refer to the explanatory paragraph.

EXAMPLE 11.12 SAMPLE DISCLAIMER

Because, as described in the preceding paragraph, I am (we are) unable to evaluate management's (or another responsible party's) assumptions regarding income from an equity investee and other assumptions depend thereon, I (we) express no opinion with respect to the presentation of or the assumptions underlying the accompanying forecast. I (We) have no responsibility to update this report for events and circumstances occurring after the date of this report.

EMPHASIS OF A MATTER

The accountant may emphasize a matter in a separate paragraph while simultaneously expressing an unqualified opinion. This is accomplished in a manner similar to emphasizing a matter already disclosed in historical financial statements.

DIVISION OF RESPONSIBILITY

When another auditor is involved and the principal auditor wishes to divide the responsibility for the overall examination report, the principal auditor should modify the report in a manner similar to the modifications pertinent to historical financial statements.

Agreed-Upon Procedures

When may I undertake an engagement with agreed-upon procedures?

It is permissible to undertake an engagement involving the application of agreed-upon procedures to prospective financial statements provided that:

- The accountant is independent
- The procedures performed or to be performed are agreed upon by the accountant and the specified users
- The specified users take responsibility for the sufficiency of the agreed-upon procedures

- A summary of significant assumptions is included in the prospective financial statements
- The prospective financial statements are subject to reasonably consistent estimation or measurement
- The accountant and the specified users agree upon the criteria to be used in the determination of findings
- The procedures to be applied are expected to result in reasonably consistent findings
- Evidential matter is expected to exist to provide a reasonable basis for expressing the accountant's findings
- A description of any agreed-upon materiality limits for reporting purposes is included in the accountant's report
- The accountant's report is restricted to use by the specified users

How do I report on the results of applying agreed-upon procedures?

The accountant's report on prospective financial statements subjected to agreed-upon procedures should include:

- A title including the word "independent"
- An identification of the specified parties
- A reference to the prospective financial statements and the character of the engagement
- A statement that the procedures performed were those agreed to by the specified parties
- An identification of the responsible party and a statement that the prospective financial statements are the responsibility of the responsible party
- A statement that the agreed-upon procedures engagement was conducted in accordance with attestation standards established by the American Institute of Certified Public Accountants
- A statement that the specified users are responsible for the sufficiency of the procedures and a disclaimer of responsibility for the sufficiency of those procedures
- A listing of the procedures performed (or a reference thereto) and the related findings
- A description of any agreed-upon materiality limits
- A statement that the accountant was not engaged to, and did not, examine the prospective financial statements; a disclaimer of opinion; a statement that if the accountant had performed additional procedures, other matters might have been reported
- A restriction on the use of the report because it is generally intended to be used solely by the specified parties
- A description of any reservations or restrictions concerning procedures or findings

- A warning that the prospective results might not materialize
- A statement that the accountant is under no responsibility to update his or her report for conditions occurring after the report is issued
- A description of the nature of the assistance provided by any specialists
- The accountant's signature, which may be manual or printed
- The date of the report

CAUTION

Negative assurance should not be expressed; the results of an agreed-upon procedures engagement should be presented in the form of findings.

EXAMPLE 11.13 REPORT AFTER APPLYING AGREED-UPON PROCEDURES

INDEPENDENT ACCOUNTANT'S REPORT ON APPLYING AGREED-UPON PROCEDURES

Board of Directors—Katie Corporation
Board of Directors—Mike Company

At your request, we have performed certain agreed-upon procedures, as enumerated below, with respect to the forecasted balance sheet and the related forecasted statements of income, retained earnings, and cash flows of Karen Company, a subsidiary of Mike Company, as of December 31, 20XX, and for the year then ending. These procedures, which were agreed to by the Boards of Directors of Katie Corporation and Mike Company, were performed solely to assist you in evaluating the forecast in connection with the proposed sale of Karen Company to Katie Corporation. This agreed-upon procedures engagement was performed in accordance with attestation standards established by the American Institute of Certified Public Accountants. The sufficiency of these procedures is solely the responsibility of the specified users of the report. Consequently, we make no representation regarding the sufficiency of the procedures described below either for the purpose for which this report has been requested or for any other purpose.

[Include paragraphs to enumerate procedures and findings.]
We were not engaged to, and did not, perform an examination, the objective of which would be the expression of an opinion on the accompanying prospective financial statements. Accordingly, we do not express

> ### EXAMPLE 11.13 REPORT AFTER APPLYING AGREED-UPON PROCEDURES (continued)
>
> an opinion on whether the prospective financial statements are presented in conformity with AICPA presentation guidelines or on whether the underlying assumptions provide a reasonable basis for the presentation. Had we performed additional procedures, other matters might have come to our attention that would have been reported to you. Furthermore, there will usually be differences between the forecasted and actual results, because events and circumstances frequently do not occur as expected, and those differences may be material. We have no responsibility to update this report for events and circumstances occurring after the date of this report.
>
> This report is intended solely for the use of the Boards of Directors of Mike Company and Katie Corporation and is not intended to be and should not be used by anyone other than these specified parties.
>
> *[Signature]*
>
> *[Date]*

What are the minimum items to be included in prospective financial statements?

Financial forecasts and financial projections may be in the form of either complete basic financial statements or financial statements containing the following minimum 12 items:

1. Sales or gross revenues
2. Gross profit or cost of sales
3. Unusual or infrequently occurring items
4. Provision for income taxes
5. Discontinued operations or extraordinary items
6. Income from continuing operations
7. Net income
8. Basic and fully diluted earnings per share
9. Significant changes in financial position
10. Management's (or another responsible party's) intent as to what the prospective statements present, a statement indicating that management's (or another responsible party's) assumptions are predicated on facts and circumstances in existence when the statements were prepared, and a warning that the prospective results may not materialize
11. Summary of significant assumptions
12. Summary of significant accounting policies

ATTEST ENGAGEMENTS

What is an attest engagement?

An *attest engagement* is when an accountant is engaged to issue or does issue an examination, a review, or an agreed-upon procedures, report on subject matter, or an assertion about the subject matter that is the responsibility of another party. EXAMPLES: Assertions that may require attest engagements include:

o A client write-up computer program is capable of generating a monthly, quarterly, and year-to-date payroll ledger without the need for a separate payroll module

o The value of stocks and bonds in a particular mutual fund has grown at the rate of 48 percent over the last two years

How do I conduct an attestation engagement?

In performing an attestation engagement, the practitioner must:

o Possess sufficient knowledge of the subject matter of the assertion.

o Only perform engagements if the assertion is capable of evaluation (or measurement) against reasonable criteria, *and* the assertion can be consistently estimated or measured.

o Be independent in fact (i.e., possess independence in mental attitude).

o Exercise due professional care.

o Plan the engagement and supervise any assistants.

o Obtain sufficient competent evidence in order to express the written conclusion.

What constitutes subject matter?

Subject matter, which may be as of a point in time or for a period of time, may exist in many forms, including:

o Historical or prospective performance or condition, such as a mutual fund's performance

- Physical characteristics, such as the square footage of a warehouse
- Historical events, such as the price of goods at a particular date
- Analyses, such as breakeven analysis
- Systems or processes, such as internal control over financial reporting
- Behavior, such as compliance with terms of an agreement

Must the practitioner obtain a representation letter in an attest engagement?

If the attest engagement constitutes either an examination or a review, the practitioner should obtain a representation letter from the responsible party. The representation letter should cover both oral and written representations pertinent to the engagement.

Examination Engagements

What is the purpose of an examination engagement?

The purpose of an examination engagement is to express an opinion about whether the (1) subject matter is based on (or in conformity with) the criteria in all material respects, or (2) written assertion is presented (or fairly stated), in all material respects, based on the criteria. If necessary, the practitioner may express a qualified opinion or a disclaimer of opinion. NOTE: The practitioner may modify the report in order to emphasize a matter.

What items should be included in the examination report?

- A title that includes the word *independent*
- An identification of the subject matter or an identification of the assertion (or a statement of the assertion, if the assertion does not accompany the examination report) and the responsible party
- A statement that the subject matter (or the assertion) is the responsibility of the responsible party
- A statement that the practitioner's responsibility is to express an opinion on the subject matter (or the assertion) based on his or her examination
- A statement that the examination was conducted in accordance with attestation standards established by the American Institute of Certified Public Accountants, and, accordingly, included procedures that the practitioner considered necessary in the circumstances

- A statement that the practitioner believes the examination provides a reasonable basis for his or her opinion
- The practitioner's opinion on whether—
  - The subject matter is based on (or in conformity with) the criteria in all material respects, or
  - The assertion is presented (or fairly stated), in all material respects, based on the criteria
- A statement restricting the use of the report to specified parties when:
  - The criteria used to evaluate the subject matter are determined by the practitioner to be appropriate only for a limited number of parties who either participated in their establishment or can be presumed to have an adequate understanding of the criteria
  - The criteria used to evaluate the subject matter are available only to the specified parties, or
  - A written assertion has not been provided by the responsible party. (A statement to that effect should also be included in the explanatory paragraph of the report.)
- The practitioner's signature, which may be manual or printed.
- The date of the examination report

EXAMPLE 11.14 STANDARD REPORT FOR AN EXAMINATION ENGAGEMENT ON SUBJECT MATTER

INDEPENDENT ACCOUNTANT'S REPORT

I (We) have examined the *[identify the subject matter for example, the accompanying Schedule of Investment Performance Statistics of Reap the Benefits Fund for the year ended December 31, 20XX]*. Reap the Benefits Fund's management is responsible for the schedule of investment performance statistics. My (Our) responsibility is to express an opinion based on my (our) examination.

My (Our) examination was conducted in accordance with attestation standards established by the American Institute of Certified Public Accountants and, accordingly, included examining, on a test basis, evidence supporting *[identify the subject matter for example, Reap the Benefit Fund's Schedule of Investment Performance Statistics]* and performing such other procedures as (I) we considered necessary in the circumstances. I (We) believe that my (our) examination provides a reasonable basis for my (our) opinion.

[Additional paragraph(s) may be added to emphasize certain matters relating to the attest engagement or the subject matter.]

EXAMPLE 11.14 STANDARD REPORT
FOR AN EXAMINATION ENGAGEMENT
ON SUBJECT MATTER (continued)

In my (our) opinion, the schedule referred to above presents, in all material respects, [identify the subject matter for example, the investment performance statistics of Reap the Benefits Fund for the year ended December 31, 20XX] based on [identify criteria-for example, the ABC criteria set forth in Note 1].

[Signature]

[Date]

EXAMPLE 11.14.1 STANDARD REPORT FOR AN
EXAMINATION ENGAGEMENT ON AN ASSERTION

INDEPENDENT ACCOUNTANT'S REPORT

(I) We have examined management's assertion that [identify the assertion for example, the accompanying Schedule of Investment Performance Statistics of Reap the Benefits Fund for the year ended December 31, 20XX is presented in accordance with ABC criteria set forth in Note 1]. Reap the Benefits Fund's management is responsible for the assertion. My (Our) responsibility is to express an opinion on the assertion based on my (our) our examination.

My (Our) examination was conducted in accordance with attestation standards established by the American Institute of Certified Public Accountants and, accordingly, included examining, on a test basis, evidence supporting management's assertion and performing such other procedures as I (we) considered necessary in the circumstances. I (We) believe that my (our) examination provides a reasonable basis for my (our) opinion.

[Additional paragraph(s) may be added to emphasize certain matters relating to the attest engagement or the assertion.]

In my (our) opinion, management's assertion referred to above is fairly stated, in all material respects, based on [identify established or stated criteria for—example, the ABC criteria set forth in Note 1].

[Signature]

[Date]

Review Engagements

What is the objective of a review engagement?

The purpose of a review engagement is to express *negative* assurance.

What items should be included in the review report?

○ A title that includes the word *independent*

○ An identification of the subject matter or an identification of the assertion (or a statement of the assertion, if the assertion does not accompany the examination report) and the responsible party

○ A statement that the subject matter (or the assertion) is the responsibility of the responsible party

○ A statement that the review was conducted in accordance with attestation standards established by the American Institute of Certified Public Accountants

○ A statement that a review is substantially less in scope than an examination, the objective of which is the expression of opinion on the subject matter (or the assertion), and accordingly, no such opinion is expressed

○ A statement about whether the practitioner is aware of any material modifications that should be made to:

● The subject matter in order for it to be based on (or in conformity with), in all material respects, the criteria, other than those modifications, if any, indicated in the review report, or

● The assertion in order for it to be presented (or fairly stated), in all material respects, based on (or in conformity with) the criteria, other than those modifications, if any, indicated in the review report

○ A statement restricting the use of the report to specified parties when:

● The criteria used to evaluate the subject matter are determined by the practitioner to be appropriate only for a limited number of parties who either participated in their establishment or can be presumed to have an adequate understanding of the criteria

● The criteria used to evaluate the subject matter are available only to the specified parties, or

● A written assertion has not been provided by the responsible party (A statement to that effect should also be included in the explanatory paragraph of the report)

○ The practitioner's signature, which may be manual or printed

○ The date of the review report

EXAMPLE 11.15 STANDARD REPORT FOR A REVIEW ENGAGEMENT ON SUBJECT MATTER

INDEPENDENT ACCOUNTANT'S REPORT

I (We) have reviewed the accompanying *[identify the subject matter — for example, the accompanying schedule of investment returns of Reap the Benefits Fund for the year ended December 31, 20XX]*. Reap the Benefit Fund's management is responsible for the schedule of investment returns.

My (Our) review was conducted in accordance with attestation standards established by the American Institute of Certified Public Accountants. A review is substantially less in scope than an examination, the objective of which is the expression of an opinion on *[identify the subject matter—for example, Reap the Benefit Fund's schedule of investment returns]*. Accordingly, I (we) do not express such an opinion.

[If desired, the practitioner may present additional paragraphs to emphasize matters pertaining to the attest engagement or the subject matter.]

Based on my (our) review, nothing came to my (our) attention that caused me (us) to believe that the *[identify the subject matter—for example, schedule of investment returns of Reap the Benefit Fund for the year ending December 31, 20XX]* is not presented, in all material respects, in conformity with [identify the criteria—for example, the ABC criteria set forth in Note X].

[Signature]

[Date]

EXAMPLE 11.15.1 STANDARD REPORT FOR A REVIEW ENGAGEMENT ON AN ASSERTION

INDEPENDENT ACCOUNTANT'S REPORT

I (We) have reviewed management's assertion that *[identify the assertion—for example, the accompanying schedule of investment returns of Reap the Benefits Fund for the year ended December 31, 20XX is presented in accordance with the ABC criteria referred to in Note X]*. Reap the Benefit Fund's management is responsible for the assertion.

My (Our) review was conducted in accordance with attestation standards established by the American Institute of Certified Public Accountants. A review is substantially less in scope than an examination, the objective of which is the expression of an opinion on management's

---

EXAMPLE 11.15.1 STANDARD REPORT FOR A REVIEW ENGAGEMENT ON AN ASSERTION *(continued)*

assertion. Accordingly, I (we) do not express such an opinion.

[If desired, the practitioner may present additional paragraphs to emphasize matters pertaining to the attest engagement or the assertion.]

Based on my (our) review, nothing came to my (our) attention that caused me (us) to believe that management's assertion referred to above is not stated fairly, in all material respects, based on *[identify the criteria—for example, the ABC criteria referred to in the investment management agreement between Reap the Benefit Fund and Holdem Investment Managers, dated November 15, 20XX].*

[Signature]

[Date]

Engagements to Apply Agreed-Upon Procedures

How do I report when applying agreed-upon procedures to subject matter?

The results of applying agreed-upon procedures should be in the form of findings. Accordingly, neither an opinion nor negative assurance should be provided.

All findings should be reported unless a definition of materiality is agreed upon by the specified users and described in the practitioner's report.

The practitioner's report should include:

○ A title including the word "independent"
○ Identification of the specified parties
○ Identification of the subject matter and the character of the engagement
○ Identification of the responsible party
○ A statement that the subject matter is the responsibility of the responsible party
○ A statement that the procedures performed were those agreed to by the specified parties identified in the report
○ A statement that the agreed-upon procedures engagement was conducted in accordance with attestation standards established by the AICPA
○ A statement that the sufficiency of the procedures is solely the responsibility of the specified parties and a disclaimer of responsibility for the sufficiency of those procedures

- A list of the procedures performed (or reference thereto) and related findings; negative assurance should *not* be provided
- If applicable, the agreed-upon materiality limits
- A statement that the practitioner was not engaged to, and did not perform an examination of the subject matter; a disclaimer of opinion; and a statement that if the practitioner had performed additional procedures, other matters might have come to his or her attention that would have been reported
- A statement of restrictions on the use of the report because it is intended to be used solely by the specified parties
- Any reservations or restrictions concerning procedures or findings
- Where applicable, a description of the nature of the assistance provided by a specialist
- The practitioner's signature which may be manual or printed
- The date of the agreed-upon procedures report

EXAMPLE 11.16 REPORT ON APPLYING AGREED-UPON PROCEDURES

INDEPENDENT ACCOUNTANT'S REPORT ON APPLYING AGREED-UPON PROCEDURES

To the Audit Committees and Managements of ME Inc. and YOU Fund:

We have performed the procedures enumerated below, which were agreed to by the audit committees and managements of ME Inc. and YOU Fund, solely to assist you in evaluating the accompanying Statement of Investment Performance Statistics of YOU Fund (prepared in accordance with the criteria specified therein) for the year ended December 31, 20X1. YOU Fund's management is responsible for the statement of investment performance statistics. This agreed-upon procedures engagement was conducted in accordance with attestation standards established by the American Institute of Certified Public Accountants. The sufficiency of these procedures is solely the responsibility of those parties specified in this report. Consequently, we make no representation regarding the sufficiency of the procedures described below either for the purpose for which this report has been requested or for any other purpose.

[Include paragraphs to enumerate procedures and findings.]

EXAMPLE 11.16 REPORT ON APPLYING AGREED-UPON PROCEDURES *(continued)*

We were not engaged to and did not conduct an examination, the objective of which would be the expression of an opinion on the accompanying Statement of Investment Performance Statistics of YOU Fund. Accordingly, we do not express such an opinion. Had we performed additional procedures, other matters might have come to our attention that would have been reported to you.

This report is intended solely for the information and use of the audit committees and managements of ME Inc. and YOU Fund, and is not intended to be and should not be used by anyone other than these specified parties.

[Signature]

[Date]

REPORTING ON AN ENTITY'S INTERNAL CONTROL OVER FINANCIAL REPORTING

What conditions are necessary to examine and report on an entity's internal control over financial reporting?

According to SSAE 10, the following conditions are necessary for an examination of management's assertion about the effectiveness of its internal control over financial reporting:

o Management accepts responsibility for the effectiveness of its internal control
o Management evaluates the effectiveness of its internal control using suitable criteria ("control criteria")
o Sufficient evidential matter exists or could be developed to support management's evaluation
o Management presents an assertion in writing in either (1) a separate report that will accompany the practitioner's report, or (2) a representation letter to the practitioner.

What steps are involved in examining management's assertion about the effectiveness of an entity's internal control over financial reporting?

o Plan the engagement.
o Obtain an understanding of internal control.
o Evaluate the design effectiveness of the controls.

- ○ Perform tests of controls and evaluate the operating effectiveness of the controls.
- ○ Express an opinion on the effectiveness of the entity's internal control, or management's assertion thereon, based on the control criteria.

Is it necessary to obtain written representations from management?

The practitioner *should* obtain written representations from management.

The following items should be included in the representation letter required under SSAE 10:

- ○ Management's acknowledgment of its responsibility to establish and maintain internal control
- ○ A statement that management has evaluated the effectiveness of its internal control based on specified control criteria
- ○ Management's assertion about the effectiveness of its internal control over financial reporting based upon the control criteria
- ○ A statement that management has disclosed all significant deficiencies in the design or operation of internal control, including those considered to be material weaknesses in internal control
- ○ A description of any material fraud involving management or other employees having a significant role in internal control
- ○ A statement of whether there were, after the date of management's report, changes in internal control, including corrective actions taken by management.

WARNING

Management's refusal to provide the necessary written representations is tantamount to a scope limitation sufficient to preclude the issuance of an unqualified opinion. Accordingly, a qualified opinion or a disclaimer of opinion would normally be appropriate. Furthermore, the practitioner might consider withdrawing from the engagement because of his or her possible impaired ability to rely on other management representations.

What items should be included in the examination report?

- ○ A title that includes the word "independent"
- ○ An identification of the subject matter (i.e., internal control over financial reporting) (or the written assertion thereon) and the responsible party (i.e., management)

○ A statement that the responsible party is responsible for maintaining effective internal control over financial reporting (or the assertion thereon)

○ A statement that the practitioner's responsibility is to express an opinion on the effectiveness of an entity's internal control (or management's assertion) based on his or her examination

○ A statement that the examination was conducted in accordance with attestation standards established by the American Institute of Certified Public Accountants and, accordingly, included obtaining an understanding of internal control over financial reporting, testing and evaluating the design and operating effectiveness of internal control, and performing such other procedures as the practitioner considered necessary in the circumstances

○ A statement that the practitioner believes the examination provides a reasonable basis for his or her opinion.

○ A paragraph stating that, because of inherent limitations of any internal control, misstatements due to error or fraud may occur and not be detected (In addition, the paragraph should state that projections of any evaluation of internal control over financial reporting to future periods are subject to the risk that internal control may become inadequate because of changes in conditions, or that the degree of compliance with the policies or procedures may deteriorate.)

○ An opinion on whether (a) the entity has maintained, in all material respects, effective internal control as of the specified date, or during a period of time, based on the control criteria or (b) management's assertion about the effectiveness of the entity's internal control over financial reporting is fairly stated, in all material respects, based on the control criteria

○ A statement restricting the use of the report to the specified parties under the following circumstances:

  ● When the criteria used to evaluate internal control over financial reporting are determined by the practitioner to be appropriate only for a limited number of parties who either participated in their establishment or can be presumed to have an adequate understanding of the criteria

  ● When the criteria used to evaluate internal control over financial reporting are available only to specified parties

○ The practitioner's signature, which may be manual or printed

○ The date of the examination report

What report is generally appropriate when expressing an opinion directly on the effectiveness of an entity's internal control as of a specified date?

EXAMPLE 11.17 REPORT ON ENTITY'S INTERNAL CONTROL AS OF A SPECIFIED DATE

INDEPENDENT ACCOUNTANT'S REPORT

[Introductory paragraph]

We have examined the effectiveness of Michael Company's internal control over financial reporting as of December 31, 20XX, based on *[identify criteria]*. Michael Company's management is responsible for maintaining effective internal control over financial reporting. Our responsibility is to express an opinion on the effectiveness of internal control based on our examination.

[Scope paragraph]

Our examination was conducted in accordance with attestation standards established by the American Institute of Certified Public Accountants and, accordingly, included obtaining an understanding of the internal control over financial reporting, testing and evaluating the design and operating effectiveness of the internal control, and performing such other procedures as we considered necessary in the circumstances. We believe that our examination provides a reasonable basis for our opinion.

[Inherent limitations paragraph]

Because of inherent limitations in any internal control, misstatements due to error or fraud may occur and not be detected. Also, projections of any evaluation of the internal control over financial reporting to future periods are subject to the risk that the internal control may become inadequate because of changes in conditions, or that the degree of compliance with the policies or procedures may deteriorate.

[Opinion paragraph]

In our opinion, Michael Company maintained, in all material respects, effective internal control over financial reporting as of December 31, 20XX, based on

[identify criteria].

[Signature]

[Date]

What report is generally appropriate when expressing an opinion on a written assertion about the effectiveness of an entity's internal control as of a specified date?

EXAMPLE 11.18 REPORT ON ASSERTION ABOUT ENTITY'S INTERNAL CONTROL AS OF A SPECIFIED DATE

INDEPENDENT ACCOUNTANT'S REPORT

[Introductory paragraph]

We have examined management's assertion, included in the accompanying *[title of management report]*, that Michael Company maintained effective internal control over financial reporting as of December 31, 20XX, based on *[identify criteria]*. Michael Company's management is responsible for maintaining effective internal control over financial reporting. Our responsibility is to express an opinion on management's assertion based on our examination.

[Scope paragraph]

Our examination was conducted in accordance with attestation standards established by the American Institute of Certified Public Accountants and, accordingly, included obtaining an understanding of the internal control over financial reporting, testing and evaluating the design and operating effectiveness of the internal control, and performing such other procedures as we considered necessary in the circumstances. We believe that our examination provides a reasonable basis for our opinion.

[Inherent limitations paragraph]

Because of inherent limitations in any internal control, misstatements due to error or fraud may occur and not be detected. Also, projections of any evaluation of the internal control over financial reporting to future periods are subject to the risk that the internal control may become inadequate because of changes in conditions, or that the degree of compliance with the policies or procedures may deteriorate.

[Opinion paragraph]

In our opinion, management's assertion that Michael Company maintained effective internal control over financial reporting as of December 31, 20XX, is fairly stated, in all material respects, based on [identify criteria].

[Signature]

[Date]

What should a practitioner do if one or more material weaknesses are identified during the examination engagement?

When one or more material weaknesses are identified during the examination, the practitioner should either express (1) a qualified opinion or (2) an adverse opinion if the material weakness(es) is (are) so pervasive that the control objectives are not achieved.

NOTE

The identification of one or more material weaknesses in an engagement to report on management's assertion about the effectiveness of internal control over financial reporting should cause the practitioner to report directly on the effectiveness of internal control, and not the assertion. Furthermore, a qualified or an adverse opinion should be expressed.

 ## COMPLIANCE ATTESTATION

SSAE 10 provides guidance for engagements related to an entity's (1) compliance with specified requirements (i.e., requirements of specified laws, regulations, rules, contracts, or grants), and (2) the effectiveness of an entity's internal control over compliance with specified requirements.

What levels of service are applicable to engagements pertaining to compliance attestation?

The practitioner may be engaged to examine (1) an entity's compliance with specified requirements (or a written assertion thereon), or (b) the effectiveness of the entity's internal control over compliance (or a written assertion thereon). Alternatively, the practitioner may be engaged to perform an agreed-upon procedures engagement. NOTE: A review engagement may not be performed.

What report should a practitioner use when expressing an opinion directly on an entity's compliance with specified requirements during a period of time?

EXAMPLE 11.19 EXPRESSING OPINION DIRECTLY ON AN ENTITY'S COMPLIANCE WITH SPECIFIED REQUIREMENTS DURING A PERIOD OF TIME

INDEPENDENT ACCOUNTANT'S REPORT

[Introductory paragraph]

We have examined *[name of entity]*'s compliance with *[list specified compliance requirements]* during the *[period]*

EXAMPLE 11.19 EXPRESSING OPINION DIRECTLY ON AN ENTITY'S COMPLIANCE WITH SPECIFIED REQUIREMENTS DURING A PERIOD OF TIME *(continued)*

---

ended *[date]*. Management is responsible for *[name of entity]*'s compliance with those requirements. Our responsibility is to express an opinion on *[name of entity]*'s compliance based on our examination.

[Scope paragraph]

Our examination was conducted in accordance with attestation standards established by the American Institute of Certified Public Accountants and, accordingly, included examining, on a test basis, evidence about *[name of entity]*'s compliance with those requirements and performing such other procedures as we considered necessary in the circumstances. We believe that our examination provides a reasonable basis for our opinion. Our examination does not provide a legal determination on *[name of entity]*'s compliance with specified requirements.

[Opinion paragraph]

In our opinion, *[name of entity]* complied, in all material respects, with the aforementioned requirements for the year ended December 31, 20XX.

[Signature]

[Date]

What report should a practitioner use when expressing an opinion on management's assertion about compliance with specified requirements during a period of time?

EXAMPLE 11.20 EXPRESSING AN OPINION ON MANAGEMENT'S ASSERTION ABOUT COMPLIANCE WITH SPECIFIED REQUIREMENTS DURING A PERIOD OF TIME

INDEPENDENT ACCOUNTANT'S REPORT

[Introductory paragraph]

We have examined management's assertion, included in the accompanying *[title of management report]*, that *[name of entity]* complied with *[list specified compliance requirements]* during the *[period]* ended *[date]*. Management is responsible for *[name of entity]*'s compliance with those requirements. Our responsibility is to express an opinion

---

EXAMPLE 11.20 EXPRESSING AN OPINION ON MANAGEMENT'S ASSERTION ABOUT COMPLIANCE WITH SPECIFIED REQUIREMENTS DURING A PERIOD OF TIME *(continued)*

on management's assertion about *[name of entity]*'s compliance based on our examination.

[Scope paragraph]

Our examination was conducted in accordance with attestation standards established by the American Institute of Certified Public Accountants and, accordingly, included examining, on a test basis, evidence about *[name of entity]*'s compliance with those requirements and performing such other procedures as we considered necessary in the circumstances. We believe that our examination provides a reasonable basis for our opinion. Our examination does not provide a legal determination on *[name of entity]*'s compliance with specified requirements.

[Opinion paragraph]

In our opinion, management's assertion that *[name of entity]* complied, in all material respects, with the aforementioned requirements during the *[period]* ended *[date]* is fairly stated, in all material respects.

[Signature]

[Date]

MANAGEMENT'S DISCUSSION AND ANALYSIS

What is Management's Discussion and Analysis?

Management's Discussion and Analysis (MD&A) is a document that needs to be prepared in accordance with rules and regulations of the Securities and Exchange Commission. MD&A, which is usually presented in annual reports to shareholders, generally covers three years of audited financial statements as well as any available interim-period financial statements. MD&A is designed to provide users with a useful analysis of significant changes in a publicly-traded company's financial condition and results of operations.

What types of attest services may a practitioner perform with respect to MD&A?

A practitioner may accept an engagement to examine, review, or apply agreed-upon procedures to MD&A. An attest engagement with respect to MD&A should be performed in accordance with the general attestation rules previously discussed in this chapter.

PERSONAL FINANCIAL STATEMENTS INCLUDED IN WRITTEN PERSONAL FINANCIAL PLANS

What are my responsibilities when personal financial statements are included in a financial plan?

When the accountant prepares personal financial statements that are included in a written personal financial plan, the accountant may:

○ Follow the compilation standards applicable to compilation engagements involving historical basic financial statements.

○ Issue the report specified in *Statement on Standards for Accounting and Review Services 6.*

In order to make use of the exemption provided in SSARS 6, the accountant must reach an understanding with the client that the personal financial statements:

○ Are prepared only to assist in the development of goals and objectives pertaining to the client's personal finances

○ Will not be used in securing credit

CAUTION

If the accountant, during the engagement, discovers that the personal financial statements are to be used to obtain credit or for some purpose other than to develop a financial strategy, the accountant may not utilize the exemption from SSARS 1.

EXAMPLE 11.21 REPORT BASED ON EXEMPTION FROM SSARS 1

The following is the standard report for personal financial statements in financial plans based on exemption from SSARS 1:

The accompanying Statement of Financial Condition of Karen B, as of December 31, 20XX, was prepared solely to help you develop your personal financial plan. Accordingly, it may be incomplete or contain other departures from generally accepted accounting principles and should not be used to obtain credit or for any other purposes other than developing your financial plan. I (We) have not audited, reviewed, or compiled the statement.

What must I do when examining personal financial statements?

Engagements to examine personal financial statements are subject to the standards applicable to examinations of historical financial statements. Accordingly, the auditor must gather sufficient competent evidential matter to form the basis of his or her opinion. While the accountant normally expresses the opinion on a statement of financial condition, the accountant may report on:

o A statement of changes in net worth
o Comparative financial statements

NOTE
If warranted, the practitioner may express a qualified opinion, an adverse opinion or a disclaimer of opinion on personal financial statements.

EXAMPLE 11.22 REPORT BASED ON AUDIT OF PERSONAL FINANCIAL STATEMENTS

INDEPENDENT AUDITOR'S REPORT

I (we) have audited the accompanying statement of financial condition of Marc and Susan Janes as of December 31, 20XX, and the related statement of changes in net worth for the year then ended. These financial statements are the responsibility of Marc and Susan Janes. Our responsibility is to express an opinion on these financial statements based on our audit.

We conducted our audit in accordance with auditing standards generally accepted in the United States of America. Those standards require that we plan and perform the audit to obtain reasonable assurance about whether the financial statements are free of material misstatement. An audit includes examining, on a test basis, evidence supporting the amounts and disclosures in the financial statements. An audit also includes assessing the accounting principles used and significant estimates made by the individuals, as well as evaluating the overall financial statement presentation. We believe that our audit provides a reasonable basis for our opinion.

In our opinion, the financial statements referred to above present fairly, in all material respects, the financial condition of Marc and Susan Janes as of December 31, 20XX, and the changes in their net worth for the year

> ### EXAMPLE 11.22 REPORT BASED ON AUDIT OF
> ### PERSONAL FINANCIAL STATEMENTS (continued)
>
> then ended in conformity with accounting principles
> generally accepted in the United States of America.
>
> *[Signature]*
>
> *[Date]*

REPORTING ON COMPARATIVE STATEMENTS

What are the reporting requirements for comparative statements?

Guidance for reporting on audited comparative financial statements is provided in *Statement on Auditing Standards 58*.

The practitioner may report on financial statements of one or more prior periods that are presented with financial statements of the current period.

If the accountant is the *continuing auditor* having performed the audit of the current period and immediately preceding period(s), he or she has the responsibility of updating the report on the financial statements of the prior period(s).

> ### NOTE
>
> In updating the audit report, the practitioner should either re-express a previous opinion or express an opinion different from the one previously expressed. The latter circumstance may arise when, for example, prior period financial statements are subsequently restated.

> ### EXAMPLE 11.23 CONTINUING AUDITOR'S
> ### STANDARD REPORT ON COMPARATIVE FINANCIAL
> ### STATEMENTS
>
> #### INDEPENDENT AUDITOR'S REPORT
>
> I (We) have audited the accompanying balance sheets of M Corporation as of (at) December 31, 20X4 and 20X3, and the related statements of income, retained earnings, and cash flows for the years then ended. These financial statements are the responsibility of the Company's management. My (Our) responsibility is to express an opinion on these financial statements based on my (our) audits.
>
> I (We) conducted my (our) audits in accordance with auditing standards generally accepted in the United States

---

EXAMPLE 11.23 CONTINUING AUDITOR'S STANDARD REPORT ON COMPARATIVE FINANCIAL STATEMENTS *(continued)*

---

of America. Those standards require that I (we) plan and perform the audit to obtain reasonable assurance about whether the financial statements are free of material misstatement. An audit includes examining, on a test basis, evidence supporting the amounts and disclosures in the financial statements. An audit also includes assessing the accounting principles used and significant estimates made by management, as well as evaluating the overall financial statement presentation. I (We) believe that my (our) audits provide a reasonable basis for my (our) opinion.

In my (our) opinion, the financial statements referred to above present fairly, in all material respects, the financial position of M Corporation as of (at) December 31, 20X4 and 20X3, and the results of its operations and its cash flows for the years then ended in conformity with accounting principles generally accepted in the United States of America.

How may the continuing auditor's standard report be modified?

The practitioner may issue a report that contains differing opinions. EXAMPLE: A qualified opinion on the current year's financial statements and an unqualified opinion on the prior year's financial statements.

If the practitioner deems it necessary to modify the opinion expressed on prior period financial statements, he or she should include an explanatory paragraph (preceding the opinion paragraph) in the updated report. The explanatory paragraph should disclose:

- o Date of the original audit report
- o Type of the original report (e.g., unqualified, qualified)
- o Reasons for the change in the type of report
- o Statement that the updated report is different from the report previously expressed

---

EXAMPLE 11.24 EXPLANATORY PARAGRAPH ADDED WHEN THE STANDARD REPORT NEEDS TO BE MODIFIED

In my (our) report dated April 3, 20X5, I (we) expressed an opinion that the 20X4 financial statements did not present fairly financial position, results of operations, and cash flows in conformity with generally accepted accounting

> **EXAMPLE 11.24 EXPLANATORY PARAGRAPH**
> **ADDED WHEN THE STANDARD REPORT NEEDS**
> **TO BE MODIFIED** (continued)
>
> principles because of two departures from such princi-
> ples: (1) the Company carried its property, plant, and
> equipment at appraisal values, and provided for depre-
> ciation on the basis of such values, and (2) the Company
> did not provide for deferred income taxes with respect
> to differences between income for financial reporting
> purposes and taxable income. As described in Note X,
> the Company has changed its method of accounting for
> these items and restated its 20X4 financial statements to
> conform with generally accepted accounting principles.
> Accordingly, my (our) present opinion on the 20X4
> financial statements, as presented herein, is different
> from that expressed in my (our) previous report.

When may I reissue a report on prior period statements?

If a client requests that a predecessor auditor reissue a
report on prior period financial statements, he or she must
first:

- Read the current period financial statements.
- Compare the original prior period financial statements with the statements to be presented.
- Obtain a representation letter from the successor
  auditor.

> **NOTE**
>
> The representation letter should disclose events and cir-
> cumstances that came to the successor's attention
> which might have a significant effect on the predeces-
> sor's report or on the prior period financial statements.

- If events and circumstances arose after the original
  report was issued, perform inquiry and other necessary procedures.

> **NOTE**
>
> The date of a reissued report should coincide with the
> date of the original report. However, if the predecessor
> revises his or her report, or if the financial statements of
> the prior period need to be restated, the practitioner
> should utilize dual dating in the report.

What if the predecessor auditor's report is not with the successor's?

When the report of the predecessor auditor is not presented with the report of the successor auditor, add the following to the introductory paragraph of the successor auditor's report:

- ○ A statement that another auditor audited the financial statements of the prior period(s)
- ○ The date of the predecessor's report
- ○ A statement as to the type of opinion expressed by the predecessor
- ○ If the predecessor's report was not standard, a statement of the substantive reasons for the type of opinion

---

EXAMPLE 11.25 ADDITIONAL WORDING FOR INTRODUCTORY PARAGRAPH OF THE SUCCESSOR'S REPORT

The financial statements of KJB Company as of December 31, 20X4 were audited by other auditors whose report, dated April 1, 20X5, on those statements included an explanatory paragraph that described the litigation discussed in Note X to the financial statements.

How do I compile and review comparative statements?

If a client requests that the practitioner report on comparative financial statements of a nonpublicly traded entity, the practitioner should be guided by the provisions of SSARS 2. Accordingly, the accountant must reissue or update the report issued in connection with the financial statements of the prior period.

SAME LEVEL OF SERVICE

When a continuing accountant performs the same level of service for each of the comparative periods (e.g., compilation for all periods or review for all periods), the accountant's report is modified by merely including the comparative dates.

HIGHER LEVEL OF SERVICE

When the continuing accountant is requested to step up the level of service, the resulting report must be modified to reflect the levels of service provided and the responsibility the practitioner is taking.

GUIDELINE

If the prior period involved a compilation and the current period involves a review, the report should contain the standard wording of a review report for the current period and the following additional paragraph as shown in Example 11.26:

EXAMPLE 11.26 WORDING ADDED TO THE COMPARATIVE REPORT FOR STEP-UP TO A REVIEW

The accompanying 20X4 financial statements of SJD Corporation were compiled by me (us). A compilation is limited to presenting in the form of financial statements information that is the representation of management (owners). I (We) have not audited or reviewed the 20X1 financial statements and, accordingly, do not express an opinion or any other form of assurance on them.

LOWER LEVEL OF SERVICE

The accountant may be involved in a step-down in the level of service provided. Accordingly, the accountant may perform an audit with respect to the financial statements of one period and a review or compilation in a subsequent period.

In a step-down *from an audit to a compilation or a review,* the practitioner should issue the appropriate compilation or review report with respect to the statements of the current period. An additional paragraph should:

○ Describe the responsibility assumed for the prior periods.

○ Indicate the date of the previous report.

○ State the type of opinion expressed in the audit report.

○ State that subsequent to the date of the audit report no additional auditing procedures have been performed.

Similarly, if an engagement involves a step-down *from a review to a compilation,* the comparative report should contain the standard compilation report and an additional paragraph that:

○ Describes responsibility for the prior period.

○ Indicates the date of the review report.

○ Provides the limited assurance normally expressed in a standard review report.

○ States that no additional review procedures have been performed subsequent to the date of the review report.

> ### EXAMPLE 11.27 WORDING ADDED TO THE COMPARATIVE REPORT FOR STEP-DOWN TO A COMPILATION
>
> The accompanying 20X4 financial statements of SJD Company were previously reviewed by me (us), and my (our) report dated April 1, 20X5, stated that I was (we were) not aware of any material modifications that should be made to those statements in order for them to be in conformity with generally accepted accounting principles. I (We) have not performed any procedures in connection with that review engagement after the date of my (our) report on the 20X4 financial statements.

SPECIAL REPORTS

What is a special report?

SAS 62 states that a special report is an auditor's report issued in connection with any of the following:

- Financial statements based on a comprehensive basis of accounting other than GAAP
- Specified elements, accounts, or items contained in a basic set of financial statements
- Compliance with contractual agreements or regulations related to financial statements subjected to an audit
- Special-purpose financial presentations to comply with contractual agreements or regulatory provisions
- Financial information included in prescribed forms

What constitutes a comprehensive basis of accounting other than GAAP?

A comprehensive basis of accounting other than generally accepted accounting principles includes:

- The cash basis of accounting, which recognizes income when collected and expenses when paid.
- The modified cash basis of accounting, which recognizes income when collected and expenses when paid, except for the capitalization of fixed assets and the recognition of depreciation expense, which is a noncash item.
- A basis of accounting that follows the requirements of a regulatory agency.
- Any basis of accounting that uses a definite set of criteria having substantial support, such as the price-level basis of accounting.

NOTE
With respect to financial statements based on a comprehensive basis of accounting other than GAAP, an auditor may perform an audit in conformity with generally accepted auditing standards.

What should a special report include?

The report issued at the conclusion of the audit engagement should include:

○ A title that includes the word "independent."

○ An identification of the financial statements audited and a statement as to whether the audit was performed in accordance with generally accepted auditing standards.

○ An opinion on the fairness of presentation of the financial statements. "Fairness of presentation" is considered in light of the comprehensive basis of accounting used.

An additional paragraph placed before the opinion paragraph should:

○ Identify the basis of accounting utilized.

○ Refer to the note to the financial statement that describes the basis of accounting used.

○ State that the basis of accounting is a comprehensive basis of accounting other than GAAP.

RECOMMENDATION
Change the titles of financial statements based on a comprehensive basis of accounting other than GAAP. EXAMPLE: In the cash basis of accounting, use "statement of assets and liabilities arising from cash transactions" instead of "balance sheet."

EXAMPLE 11.28 REPORT FOR INCOME TAX BASIS FINANCIAL STATEMENTS
INDEPENDENT AUDITOR'S REPORT I (We) have audited the accompanying statements of assets, liabilities, and capital—income tax basis of ABC Partnership as of December 31, 20X2 and 20X1, and the related statements of revenue and expenses—income tax basis and of changes in partners' capital accounts—income tax basis for the years then ended. These financial statements are the responsibility of the Partnership's

EXAMPLE 11.28 REPORT FOR INCOME TAX BASIS FINANCIAL STATEMENTS (continued)

management. My (Our) responsibility is to express an opinion on these financial statements based on my (our) audits.

I (We) conducted my (our) audits in accordance with auditing standards generally accepted in the United States of America. Those standards require that I (we) plan and perform the audit to obtain reasonable assurance about whether the financial statements are free of material misstatement. An audit includes examining, on a test basis, evidence supporting the amounts and disclosures in the financial statements. An audit also includes assessing the accounting principles used and significant estimates made by management, as well as evaluating the overall financial statement presentation. I (We) believe that my (our) audits provide a reasonable basis for my (our) opinion.

As described in Note X, these financial statements were prepared on the basis of accounting the Partnership uses for income tax purposes, which is a comprehensive basis of accounting other than generally accepted accounting principles.

In my (our) opinion, the financial statements referred to above present fairly, in all material respects, the assets, liabilities, and capital of ABC Partnership as of [at] December 31, 20X2 and 20X1, and its revenue and expenses and changes in partners' capital accounts for the years then ended, on the basis of accounting described in Note X.

EXAMPLE 11.29 SAMPLE REPORT FOR CASH BASIS FINANCIAL STATEMENTS

INDEPENDENT AUDITOR'S REPORT

I (We) have audited the accompanying statements of assets and liabilities arising from cash transactions of XYZ Company as of December 31, 20X2 and 20X1, and the related statements of revenue collected and expenses paid for the years then ended. These financial statements are the responsibility of the Company's management. My (our) responsibility is to express an opinion on these financial statements based on my (our) audits.

I (We) conducted my (our) audits in accordance with auditing standards generally accepted in the United States of America. Those standards require that I (we) plan and perform the audit to obtain reasonable assurance

> **EXAMPLE 11.29 SAMPLE REPORT FOR CASH BASIS FINANCIAL STATEMENTS** *(continued)*
>
> about whether the financial statements are free of material misstatement. An audit includes examining, on a test basis, evidence supporting the amounts and disclosures in the financial statements. An audit also includes assessing the accounting principles used and significant estimates made by management, as well as evaluating the overall financial statement presentation. I (We) believe that my (our) audits provide a reasonable basis for my (our) opinion.
>
> As described in Note X, these financial statements were prepared on the basis of cash receipts and disbursements, which is a comprehensive basis of accounting other than generally accepted accounting principles.
>
> In my (our) opinion, the financial statements referred to above present fairly, in all material respects, the assets and liabilities arising from cash transactions of XYZ Company as of December 31, 20X2 and 20X1, and its revenue collected and expenses paid during the years then ended, on the basis of accounting described in Note X.

What about the statement of cash flows?

The presentation of a statement of cash flows is required under GAAP. Accordingly, when financial statements are intended to be in conformity with a comprehensive basis of accounting other than GAAP, a statement of cash flows need not be presented.

Specific Elements, Accounts, or Items in a Basic Set of Financial Statements

What should I do when asked to evaluate specific elements or items?

With respect to specific elements, accounts, or items (such as rentals, royalties, and the provision for income tax expense) contained in a basic set of financial statements, an accountant may undertake an engagement to:

- Express an opinion.
- Apply agreed-upon procedures.

What report should generally be issued in connection with an engagement to express an opinion on specified elements, accounts, or items of a financial statement?

EXAMPLE 11.30 REPORT FOR ADEQUACY OF PROVISION FOR INCOME TAXES IN THE BASIC FINANCIAL STATEMENTS

INDEPENDENT AUDITOR'S REPORT

I (We) have audited, in accordance with auditing standards generally accepted in the United States of America, the financial statements of XYZ Company, Inc., for the year ended June 30 20XX, and have issued my (our) report thereon dated August 15, 20XX. I (We) have also audited the current and deferred provision for the Company's federal and state income taxes for the year ended June 30, 20XX, included in those financial statements, and the related asset and liability tax accounts as of June 30, 20XX. This income tax information is the responsibility of the Company's management. My (Our) responsibility is to express an opinion on it based on my (our) audit.

I (We) conducted my (our) audit of the income tax information in accordance with auditing standards generally accepted in the United States of America. Those standards require that I (we) plan and perform the audit to obtain reasonable assurance about whether the federal and state income tax accounts are free of material misstatement. An audit includes examining, on a test basis, evidence supporting the amounts and disclosures related to the federal and state income tax accounts. An audit also includes assessing the accounting principles used and significant estimates made by management, as well as evaluating the overall presentation of the federal and state income tax accounts. I (We) believe that my (our) audit provides a reasonable basis for my (our) opinion.

In my (our) opinion, the Company has paid or, in all material respects, made adequate provision in the financial statements referred to above for the payment of all federal and state income taxes and for related deferred income taxes that could be reasonably estimated at the time of my (our) audit of the financial statements of XYZ Company, Inc., for the year ended June 30, 20XX.

> **CAUTION**
>
> In general, do not express an opinion on specified elements, accounts, or items included in financial statements if you expressed an adverse opinion or disclaimed an opinion on the basic financial statements.

May agreed-upon procedures be used on specific items?

An engagement to apply agreed-upon procedures to specific elements, accounts, or items is more limited in scope than an audit that leads to the expression of an opinion. Accordingly, the practitioner should issue a disclaimer of opinion.

CAUTION: Engagements involving the application of agreed-upon procedures may be accepted provided that:

- o An understanding between the accountant and client has been reached regarding the specific procedures to be performed.
- o The accountant's report is to be distributed only to the named parties involved.
- o The accountant follows the guidance in SSAE #10 relative to agreed-upon engagements.

Compliance with Contracts or Regulations Relating to Audited Financial Statements

What are my responsibilities regarding compliance with contracts?

Clients sometimes request an independent accountant to issue a report concerning compliance with contractual agreements or regulations. EXAMPLE: A report on compliance with the terms, provisions, and covenants of bond indentures. Such a report should express the requisite negative assurance either in a separate report or as part of the audit report on the basic financial statements.

In either reporting situation, the report should specifically state that the negative assurance is being expressed in connection with the audit (of the financial statements). NOTE: The practitioner should state that the "audit was not directed primarily toward obtaining knowledge of such noncompliance."

What format should generally be used if the report on contractual provisions related to audited financial statements is given in a separate report?

The separate report to be used in connection with contractual provisions should contain negative assurance.

EXAMPLE 11.31 SEPARATE REPORT ISSUED IN CONNECTION WITH CONTRACTUAL PROVISIONS

INDEPENDENT AUDITOR'S REPORT

I (We) have audited, in accordance with auditing standards generally accepted in the United States of America, the balance sheet of XYZ Company as of December 31, 20X2, and the related statement of income, retained earnings, and cash flows for the year then ended, and have issued my (our) report thereon dated February 16, 20X3.

In connection with my (our) audit, nothing came to my (our) attention that caused me (us) to believe that the Company failed to comply with the terms, covenants, provisions, or conditions of sections XX to YY, inclusive, of the Indenture dated July 21, 20X0, with ABC Bank insofar as they relate to accounting matters. However, my (our) audit was not directed primarily toward obtaining knowledge of such noncompliance.

This report is intended solely for the information and use of the boards of directors and management of XYZ Company and ABC Bank and should not be used for any other purpose.

What is meant by special-purpose financial presentations to comply with contractual agreements or regulatory provisions?

Special-purpose financial presentations are intended to be used only by the parties to the agreement, regulatory agencies, or other specified parties. Accordingly, such presentations

- ○ May not represent a complete presentation of assets, liabilities, revenues, and expenses, but may nevertheless be in conformity with GAAP or OCBOA
- ○ May represent a complete presentation of assets, liabilities, revenues, and expenses that is not in conformity with GAAP or OCBOA

What report should generally be issued in connection with special-purpose financial presentations?

EXAMPLE 11.32 REPORT ISSUED IN CONNECTION WITH A STATEMENT OF ASSETS SOLD AND LIABILITIES TRANSFERRED TO COMPLY WITH A CONTRACTUAL AGREEMENT

INDEPENDENT AUDITOR'S REPORT

I (We) have audited the accompanying statement of net assets sold of ABC Company as of June 8, 20XX. This

> ## EXAMPLE 11.32 REPORT ISSUED IN CONNECTION WITH A STATEMENT OF ASSETS SOLD AND LIABILITIES TRANSFERRED TO COMPLY WITH A CONTRACTUAL AGREEMENT *(continued)*
>
> statement of net assets sold is the responsibility of ABC Company's management. My (Our) responsibility is to express an opinion on the statement of net assets sold based on my (our) audit.
>
> I (We) conducted my (our) audit in accordance with auditing standards generally accepted in the United States of America. Those standards require that I (we) plan and perform the audit to obtain reasonable assurance about whether the statement of net assets sold is free of material misstatement. An audit includes examining, on a test basis, evidence supporting the amounts and disclosures in the statement. An audit also includes assessing the accounting principles used and significant estimates made by management, as well as evaluating the overall presentation of the statement of net assets sold. I (We) believe that my (our) audit provides a reasonable basis for my (our) opinion.
>
> The accompanying statement was prepared to present the net assets of ABC Company sold to XYZ Corporation pursuant to the purchase agreement described in Note X, and is not intended to be a complete presentation of ABC Company's assets and liabilities.
>
> In our opinion, the accompanying statement of net assets sold presents fairly, in all material respects, the net assets of ABC Company as of June 8, 20XX sold pursuant to the purchase agreement referred to in Note X, in conformity with accounting principles generally accepted in the United States of America.
>
> This report is intended solely for the information and use of the boards of directors and managements of ABC Company and XYZ Corporation and should not be used for any other purpose.

Financial Information Included in Prescribed Forms

What are the requirements for financial information in prescribed forms?

Accountants often accept engagements to audit financial information included in prescribed forms.

EXAMPLE
The accountant may be requested to certify the financial information presented in forms prescribed by the United States government for the reimbursement of expenses paid by health care facilities.

In such circumstances, the practitioner must be satisfied that the form prescribed for the auditor's report adheres to relevant reporting standards. When the prescribed audit report contains inappropriate or unacceptable wording, the practitioner should either modify the wording or attach a separate report that conforms to the relevant reporting standards.

CHAPTER 12

AUDITING STANDARDS

*T*his chapter provides the practitioner with a handy reference guide to the major practical provisions of the Statements on Auditing Standards (SAS) and Auditing Standards (AS) of the Public Company Accounting Oversight Board (PCAOB) not previously covered.

Statements on Auditing Standards set forth authoritative guidance for properly conducting an audit of a nonpublic company. Audits of publicly-headed companies should also be based on SASs unless provisions are superseded by Auditing Standards issued by the PCAOB. In applying the substantive material of these Statements, the practitioner must exercise professional judgment and due professional care.

 ## SAS 1—CODIFICATION OF AUDITING STANDARDS AND PROCEDURES

This statement covers the material contained in Statements on Auditing Procedures 33 through 54. While much of SAS 1 has been superseded by subsequent pronouncements, the information presented below remains in effect.

What are subsequent events?

Subsequent events are events that occur after the balance sheet date but before the issuance of the financial statements and the auditor's report. They provide additional information about conditions or circumstances:

- Existing at or before the balance sheet date (Type I)
- Arising after the balance sheet date (Type II)

How should subsequent events be handled?

- Type I subsequent events require adjustment of the financial statements.
- Type II subsequent events may require disclosure in the financial statements in order to prevent readers from being misled.

EXAMPLE 12.1 TYPE I SUBSEQUENT EVENT

A client has advised you that one of their accounts receivable is deemed to be uncollectible as of the balance sheet date. Accordingly, the client has made an adjusting entry to record the bad debt expense and to remove the account receivable from the subsidiary ledger. However, while examining the cash receipts of the period subsequent to the balance sheet date you find a partial collection of the receivable. Accordingly, the practitioner should suggest to the client that an adjusting entry be made to properly reflect the receivable at its net realizable value.

EXAMPLE 12.2 TYPE II SUBSEQUENT EVENT

Fifteen days after the end of the year, a client's building is completely destroyed in a fire. Since the building was in existence as of the balance sheet date, no adjusting entry is necessary. In order to prevent the readers from being misled, the casualty should be disclosed in the notes to the financial statements.

How do I handle the subsequent discovery of facts existing at the date of the auditor's report?

Subsequent discovery of facts existing at the date of the auditor's report differs from subsequent events in that the audit report is already issued in the case of subsequent discovery of facts.

In such a case, the auditor should:

○ Determine the reliability of the facts and verify their existence as of the date of the audit report.
○ Ascertain whether the audit report would have been affected had the facts been known at the date of the report.
○ Determine whether readers of the financial statements might be materially influenced.
○ Advise the client that disclosure is necessary through revised financial statements.

The audit report may need to be modified, especially if the client refuses to make the necessary disclosures. In such circumstances, the practitioner should withdraw from the engagement and take steps to recall the financial statements.

SAS 2—REPORTS ON AUDITED FINANCIAL STATEMENTS

Superseded by SAS 58.

SAS 3—THE EFFECTS OF EDP ON THE AUDITOR'S STUDY AND EVALUATION OF INTERNAL CONTROL

Superseded by SAS 48.

SAS 4—QUALITY CONTROL CONSIDERATIONS FOR A FIRM OF INDEPENDENT AUDITORS

Superseded by SAS 25.

SAS 5—THE MEANING OF "PRESENT FAIRLY IN CONFORMITY WITH GENERALLY ACCEPTED ACCOUNTING PRINCIPLES" IN THE INDEPENDENT AUDITOR'S REPORT

Superseded by SAS 69.

SAS 6—RELATED PARTY TRANSACTIONS

Superseded by SAS 45.

SAS 7—COMMUNICATION BETWEEN PREDECESSOR AND SUCCESSOR AUDITOR

Superseded by SAS 84.

SAS 8—OTHER INFORMATION IN DOCUMENTS CONTAINING AUDITED FINANCIAL STATEMENTS

When other information is presented in client-prepared documents containing audited financial statements (e.g., annual reports), the auditor's responsibility is to read *all* of the information contained in the document. In doing so, the practitioner's objective is to identify material inconsistencies between the information in the document and the information presented in the audited financial statements.

The auditor has the responsibility of notifying the client of any material inconsistencies. The auditor should request that the client appropriately modify the "other information."

If the client refuses to do so, the auditor should consider modifying the audit report by adding an explanatory paragraph that describes the material inconsistency. The inclusion of this explanatory paragraph generally does not affect the opinion expressed on the financial statements.

CAUTION: Depending upon the materiality of the inconsistency, the auditor may consider withholding the use of the audit report in the document and/or withdrawing from the current engagement.

SAS 9—THE EFFECT OF AN INTERNAL AUDIT FUNCTION ON THE SCOPE OF THE INDEPENDENT AUDITOR'S EXAMINATION

Superseded by SAS 65.

SAS 10—LIMITED REVIEW OF INTERIM FINANCIAL INFORMATION

Superseded by SAS 24 and later superseded by SAS 36. SAS 36 was subsequently superseded by SAS 71.

SAS 11—USING THE WORK OF A SPECIALIST

Superseded by SAS 73.

SAS 12—INQUIRY OF A CLIENT'S LAWYER CONCERNING LITIGATION, CLAIMS, AND ASSESSMENTS

The independent auditor must obtain sufficient competent evidential matter concerning the existence of a possible loss from litigation, claims, and assessments. In this connection, he or she should identify the period in which the underlying cause occurred, the probability of an unfavorable outcome, and an estimate of the potential loss.

The auditing procedures to be performed by the independent auditor include:

- Inquiry of management personnel
- Obtaining a client-prepared description of litigation, claims, and assessments
- Examination of documents in the possession of the client
- Obtaining written assurance from management as to the disclosure and proper accounting of all unasserted claims
- Reading the minutes of the board of directors' meetings
- Reading contracts, loan agreements, leases, and correspondence with governmental agencies and legal counsel

How do I corroborate information furnished by the client?

The auditor's primary means of corroborating information provided by the client concerning litigation, claims, and assessments is a letter of audit inquiry sent to the client's legal counsel. The client's legal counsel, after obtaining the permission of the client to respond, is expected to respond promptly and fully. The client's lawyer, however, may limit his or her response to the matters to which he or she has devoted substantial attention.

EXAMPLE 12.3 LETTER OF AUDIT INQUIRY

[*Prepared on client's letterhead—See Note A*]

Date [*See Note B*]

[*Name of lawyer*]

[*Address of lawyer*]

Dear ....:

In connection with an audit of our financial statements at (balance sheet date) and for the (period) then ended, management of the Company has prepared, and furnished to our auditors (name and address of auditors), a description and evaluation of certain contingencies, including those set forth below involving matters with respect to which you have been engaged and to which you have devoted substantive attention on behalf of the Company in the form of legal consultation or representation. These contingencies are regarded by management of the Company as material for this purpose (management may indicate a materiality limit if an understanding has been reached with the auditor). Your response should include matters that existed at (balance sheet date) and during the period from that date to the date of your response.

PENDING OR THREATENED LITIGATION

[*excluding unasserted claims*]

[Ordinarily the information would include the following: (1) the nature of the litigation, (2) the progress of the case to date, (3) how management is responding or intends to respond to the litigation (for example, to contest the case vigorously or to seek an out-of-court settlement), and (4) an evaluation of the likelihood of an unfavorable outcome and an estimate, if one can be made, of the amount or range of potential loss.]

Example 12.3 Letter of Audit Inquiry *(continued)*

Please furnish to our auditors such explanation, if any, that you consider necessary to supplement the foregoing information, including an explanation of those matters as to which your views may differ from those stated and an identification of the omission of any pending or threatened litigation, claims, and assessments or a statement that the list of such matters is complete.

Unasserted Claims and Assessments

(considered by management to be probable of assertion, and that, if asserted, would have at least a reasonable possibility of an unfavorable outcome)

[Ordinarily management's information would include the following: (1) the nature of the matter, (2) how management intends to respond if the claim is asserted, and (3) an evaluation of the likelihood of an unfavorable outcome and an estimate, if one can be made, of the amount or range of potential loss.]

Please furnish to our auditors such explanation, if any, that you consider necessary to supplement the foregoing information, including an explanation of those matters as to which your views may differ from those stated.

We understand that whenever, in the course of performing legal services for us with respect to a matter recognized to involve an unasserted possible claim or assessment that may call for financial statement disclosure, if you have formed a professional conclusion that we should disclose or consider disclosure concerning such possible claim or assessment, as a matter of professional responsibility to us, you will so advise us and will consult with us concerning the question of such disclosure and the applicable requirements of Statement of Financial Accounting Standards No. 5. Please specifically confirm to our auditors that our understanding is correct.

Please specifically identify the nature of and reasons for any limitation on your response.

[The auditor may request the client to inquire about additional matters, for example, unpaid or unbilled charges or specified information on certain contractually assumed obligations of the company, such as guarantees of indebtedness of others.]

Very truly yours,

[*Authorized signature for client*]

EXAMPLE 12.3 LETTER OF AUDIT INQUIRY *(continued)*

NOTES TO USER:

(A) Auditors should carefully consider the provisions of SAS No. 12 in drafting this letter.

(B) Sending of this letter should be timed so that the lawyer's response is dated as close to the auditor's opinion date as practicable. However, the auditor and client should consider early mailing of a draft inquiry as a convenience for the lawyer in preparing a timely response to the formal inquiry letter.

What if the lawyer does not respond to the inquiry?

The lawyer's refusal to respond to the letter of audit inquiry is tantamount to a scope limitation sufficient to preclude the issuance of an unqualified opinion.

 ## SAS 13—REPORTS ON A LIMITED REVIEW OF INTERIM FINANCIAL INFORMATION

Superseded by SAS 24 and subsequently superseded by SAS 36. SAS 36 was subsequently superseded by SAS 71.

 ## SAS 14—SPECIAL REPORTS

Superseded by SAS 62.

 ## SAS 15—REPORTS ON COMPARATIVE FINANCIAL STATEMENTS

Superseded by SAS 58.

 ## SAS 16—THE INDEPENDENT AUDITOR'S RESPONSIBILITY FOR THE DETECTION OF ERRORS OR IRREGULARITIES

Superseded by SAS 53.

 ## SAS 17—ILLEGAL ACTS BY CLIENTS

Superseded by SAS 54.

 ## SAS 18—UNAUDITED REPLACEMENT COST INFORMATION

Withdrawn by the Auditing Standards Board.

SAS 19—CLIENT REPRESENTATIONS

Superseded by SAS 85.

SAS 20—REQUIRED COMMUNICATION OF MATERIAL WEAKNESSES IN INTERNAL ACCOUNTING CONTROL

Superseded by SAS 60.

SAS 21—SEGMENT INFORMATION

Rescinded by the Auditing Standards Board.

SAS 22—PLANNING AND SUPERVISION

How do I develop an audit work program?

This statement provides guidance in planning the audit (including supervision of assistants) as required by the first standard of fieldwork.

The nature, extent, and timing of planning depends on the size and complexity of the client organization and the auditor's prior experience with the organization and business. The audit must be based on a written audit work program. This is a detailed listing of the procedures to be performed during the course of the engagement.

The following are considerations for developing an audit work program:

- ○ Matters that pertain to the client's business and type of industry. EXAMPLES: types of products and services offered by the client, the client's capital structure, the existence of related parties, the location of the client's facilities, and any pertinent governmental regulations
- ○ The accounting policies, procedures, and methods used by the client
- ○ The auditor's understanding of the client's internal control and the auditor's assessment of control risk
- ○ The auditor's preliminary estimates of materiality levels
- ○ Items included in the financial statements likely to require adjustment or modification
- ○ Circumstances that may need extensive or additional auditing procedures
- ○ The report expected to be issued in connection with the engagement

The actual procedures for planning an audit engagement should be based on professional judgment. Some common procedures are:

- A review of prior years' working papers, financial statements, and audit reports
- A discussion about matters affecting the audit with firm personnel responsible for nonaudit services. EXAMPLES: Consulting services and tax services
- Inquiry about current business developments
- Reading and reviewing interim financial statements of the current year
- A discussion with client management, the board of directors, or audit committee concerning the type, scope, and timing of the audit engagement
- Determining the effect of related auditing and accounting promulgations
- Determining staff requirements and assigning audit personnel
- Determining the timing of specific audit procedures
- Considering the use of outside consultants, specialists, and internal auditors
- Coordinating the assistance of client personnel in the data preparation process

How are the auditor's assistants to be supervised?

With respect to the supervision of assistants, the auditor with final responsibility should:

- Instruct the assistants.
- Review their work at every critical level of supervision.
- Resolve any differences of opinion.

Differences of opinion concerning auditing and accounting matters, when resolved, should be documented in the audit work papers.

SAS 23—ANALYTICAL REVIEW PROCEDURES

Superseded by SAS 56.

SAS 24—REVIEW OF INTERIM FINANCIAL INFORMATION

Superseded by SAS 36 and later superseded by SAS 71.

SAS 25—THE RELATIONSHIP OF GENERALLY ACCEPTED AUDITING STANDARDS TO QUALITY CONTROL STANDARDS

Am I responsible for quality control?

When performing an audit, the independent auditor is responsible for complying with generally accepted auditing standards.

When conducting an audit practice, an independent auditor (or firm of independent auditors) is responsible for complying with quality control standards in order to provide assurance of compliance with generally accepted auditing standards.

NOTE

Refer to Quality Control Statements issued by the AICPA for guidance in establishing an effective system of quality control.

SAS 26—ASSOCIATION WITH FINANCIAL STATEMENTS

When am I considered associated with financial statements?

An accountant is deemed to be associated with financial statements when:

○ He or she has consented to the use of his or her name in a report, document, or any written communication containing the financial statements.

○ The accountant has prepared or assisted in the preparation of the financial statements, even though his or her name is not on the financial statements.

NOTE: This statement applies to association with audited or unaudited financial statements of a public entity.

RECOMMENDATION

The practitioner engaged to compile or review unaudited financial statements of a nonpublic entity should comply with Statements on Standards for Accounting and Review Services.

May I use a disclaimer?

When the practitioner is associated with unaudited financial statements of a public entity, it is appropriate to issue a disclaimer of opinion. Such a disclaimer may be in the form of a report on the financial statements, or the disclaimer may be placed directly on the statements. In addition to providing the disclaimer of opinion, the practitioner should clearly mark every page of the financial statements "unaudited."

SAS 27–28—SUPPLEMENTARY INFORMATION REQUIRED BY THE FINANCIAL ACCOUNTING STANDARDS BOARD; SUPPLEMENTARY INFORMATION ON THE EFFECTS OF CHANGING PRICES

SAS 27 is superseded by SAS 52. SAS 28 was withdrawn by the Auditing Standards Board.

SAS 29—REPORTING ON INFORMATION ACCOMPANYING THE BASIC FINANCIAL STATEMENTS IN AUDITOR-SUBMITTED DOCUMENTS

Must I report on information accompanying the statements?

When an independent auditor submits to a client or other third party a document that includes information in addition to the basic financial statements, he or she must report on all information contained in that document.

What information must the report cover?

The auditor's report covering the information accompanying the basic financial statements should:

○ State that the audit was for the purpose of forming an opinion on the basic financial statements taken as a whole.

○ Identify the accompanying information. This may be by descriptive title, such as "Supporting Schedule—Administrative Expenses," or by reference to the page number of the document.

○ State that the information accompanying the basic financial statements is presented for analysis purposes and is not part of the basic financial statements.

○ Express an opinion as to whether the accompanying information is presented fairly in all material respects in relation to the basic financial statements taken as a whole. If the accompanying information was not subjected to auditing procedures, a disclaimer of opinion should be expressed.

NOTE: The report on the accompanying information may be included as part of the opinion on the basic financial statements or presented as a separate report in the auditor-submitted document.

EXAMPLE 12.4 REPORT ON AUDITED INFORMATION

My (Our) audit was made for the purpose of forming an opinion on the basic financial statements taken as a whole. The [*identify accompanying information*] is presented for purposes of additional analysis and is not a required part of the basic financial statements. Such information has been subjected to the auditing procedures applied in the audit of the basic financial statements and, in my (our) opinion, is fairly stated in all material respects in relation to the basic financial statements taken as a whole.

EXAMPLE 12.5 DISCLAIMER ON ALL ACCOMPANYING INFORMATION

My (Our) audit was made for the purpose of forming an opinion on the basic financial statements taken as a whole. The [*identify accompanying information*] is presented for purposes of additional analysis and is not a required part of the basic financial statements. Such information has not been subjected to the auditing procedures applied in the audit of the basic financial statements, and, accordingly, I (we) express no opinion on it.

SAS 30—REPORTING ON INTERNAL ACCOUNTING CONTROL

Superseded by SSAE 2, which was later Superseded by SSAE 10.

SAS 31—EVIDENTIAL MATTER

What constitutes evidential matter?

Evidential matter consists of:

- Underlying accounting data (e.g., books of original entry)
- Related accounting manuals and informal worksheets supporting computations
- Corroborating evidential matter (e.g., client-prepared documents, minutes of board meetings, and information obtained through inquiry, observation, inspection, and confirmation)

How much evidential matter is enough?

Professional judgment must be exercised in determining the nature, extent, and timing of substantive tests the auditor should perform in gathering sufficient competent evidential matter needed to enable the expression of an opinion.

When is evidential matter competent?

Evidential matter is deemed to be competent if it is valid and relevant.

SAS 32—ADEQUACY OF DISCLOSURE IN FINANCIAL STATEMENTS

How much disclosure is enough?

If the independent auditor concludes that the audited financial statements omit information required by GAAP, the auditor should express either a qualified opinion or an adverse opinion.

RECOMMENDATION

If practicable, present the omitted information in an explanatory paragraph of the audit report. "Practicable" means that the information is obtainable from the client's records and the auditor is not put in the position of being the preparer of the information.

SAS 33—SUPPLEMENTARY OIL AND GAS RESERVE INFORMATION

Superseded by SAS 45.

SAS 34—THE AUDITOR'S CONSIDERATIONS WHEN A QUESTION ARISES ABOUT AN ENTITY'S CONTINUED EXISTENCE

Superseded by SAS 59.

SAS 35—SPECIAL REPORTS: APPLYING AGREED-UPON PROCEDURES TO SPECIFIED ELEMENTS, ACCOUNTS, OR ITEMS OF A FINANCIAL STATEMENT

Superseded by SAS 75.

SAS 36—REVIEW OF INTERIM FINANCIAL INFORMATION

Superseded by SAS 71.

SAS 37—FILLINGS UNDER FEDERAL SECURITIES STATUTES

What are my responsibilities in filings under Federal Securities Statutes?

The accountant involved in filings under the Federal Securities Statutes is considered to be an expert. Therefore, the accountant's responsibility is based on the "reasonable man standard."

The "subsequent events" period is extended from the date of the audit report to the effective date of the filing under the Federal Securities Statutes. In addition, if the accountant finds that any unaudited information is not in conformity with generally accepted accounting principles, he or she should insist that an appropriate revision be made.

SAS 38—LETTERS FOR UNDERWRITERS

Superseded by SAS 49. SAS 49 was subsequently superseded by SAS 72.

SAS 39—AUDIT SAMPLING

What risks are involved in statistical sampling?

This statement provides guidance in situations where the independent auditor decides to utilize statistical or non-statistical sampling plans or approaches in performing tests of controls or substantive tests or both.

While sampling plans create uncertainty, the uncertainty is justified due to the cost/benefit relationship since a well-designed sample is presumed to be representative of a population.

In performing sampling plans, the auditor should assess and control *sampling risk*, which is the risk that a sample may not be representative of a population and therefore cause the auditor to draw an invalid conclusion.

- In *substantive testing*, sampling risk involves the risk of incorrect acceptance and the risk of incorrect rejection.
- In *tests of controls*, it includes the risk of assessing control risk too low and the risk of assessing control risk too high.

Nonsampling risk should also be controlled. Nonsampling risk includes the risk that the auditor will fail to detect material misstatements due to nonapplication of a required procedure or the application of a procedure inconsistent with a given audit objective. EXAMPLE: The audit objective is the detection of unrecorded liabilities and the audit procedure is the confirmation of recorded account balances.

Audit risk is a combination of sampling and nonsampling risks.

SAS 40—SUPPLEMENTARY MINERAL RESERVE INFORMATION

Superseded by SAS 52.

SAS 41—WORKING PAPERS

Superseded by SAS 96.

SAS 42—REPORTING ON CONDENSED FINANCIAL STATEMENTS AND SELECTED FINANCIAL DATA

What about client-prepared documents?

This statement is applicable to reporting on a client-prepared document containing:

○ Condensed financial statements that are derived from audited financial statements
○ Selected financial data derived from audited financial statements

---

NOTE

The practitioner should refer to SAS 29 when reporting on an auditor-submitted document that contains condensed financial statements or selected financial data.

Condensed Financial Statements

What should be in the report on condensed financial statements?

The auditor's report on condensed financial statements should contain:

○ A statement that the auditor has audited, in accordance with auditing standards, generally accepted in the United States of America, the complete set of financial statements

- An indication that an opinion has been expressed on the complete set of financial statements
- The date of the auditor's report on the complete set of financial statements
- The type of opinion expressed on the complete set of financial statements
- An opinion as to whether the information contained in the condensed financial statements is presented fairly in all material respects in relation to the complete set of financial statements

---

CAUTION

To prevent readers from being misled, condensed financial statements should be so marked.

EXAMPLE 12.6 WORDING OF A REPORT ON CONDENSED FINANCIAL STATEMENTS

I (We) have audited, in accordance with auditing standards, generally accepted in the United States of America the consolidated balance sheet of Mat Corporation as of December 31, 20X3, and the related statements of income, retained earnings, and cash flows for the year then ended (not presented herein); and in my (our) report dated March 2, 20X4, I (we) expressed an unqualified opinion on those financial statements.

In my (our) opinion, the information set forth in the accompanying condensed financial statements is fairly stated in all material respects in relation to the consolidated financial statements from which it has been derived.

Selected Financial Data

Since selected financial data are not a required part of the basic financial statements, the auditor's report on such data should be limited to data that are derived from financial statements subjected to an audit.

What should be in the report on selected financial data?

The auditor's report on selected financial data should include:

- A statement that the auditor has audited, in accordance with auditing standards, generally accepted in the United States of America the complete set of financial statements.
- An indication that an opinion has been expressed on the complete set of financial statements.

- The type of opinion expressed on the complete set of financial statements.
- An opinion as to whether the information contained in the selected financial data is presented fairly in all material respects in relation to the complete set of financial statements.

EXAMPLE 12.7 WORDING OF ADDITIONAL PARAGRAPH ADDED TO THE AUDITOR'S STANDARD REPORT

I (We) have also previously audited, in accordance with generally accepted auditing standards, the balance sheets as of December 31, 20X3, 20X2, and 20X1, and the related statements of income, retained earnings, and cash flows for the years ended December 31, 20X3, 20X2, and 20X1 (none of which are presented herein); and I (we) expressed unqualified opinions on those consolidated financial statements. In my (our) opinion, the information set forth in the selected financial data for each of the five years in the period ended December 31, 20X5, appearing on page xx, is fairly stated, in all material respects, in relation to the consolidated financial statements from which it has been derived.

SAS 43—OMNIBUS STATEMENT ON AUDITING STANDARDS

This statement amends parts of selected Statements on Auditing Standards. These amendments have been incorporated into the summaries of the pertinent Statements.

SAS 44—SPECIAL-PURPOSE REPORTS ON INTERNAL ACCOUNTING CONTROL AT SERVICE ORGANIZATIONS

Superseded by SAS 70.

SAS 45—OMNIBUS STATEMENT ON AUDITING STANDARDS—1983

This statement amends parts of selected Statements on Auditing Standards.

Substantive Tests Prior to the Balance Sheet Date

How do I control incremental audit risk?

Auditors may perform substantive tests prior to the balance sheet date. However, interim testing increases the likelihood that material misstatements will occur between the interim-testing date and the balance sheet date. Accordingly, the auditor should assess the difficulty in controlling this risk ("incremental audit risk"). In order to control this risk, the auditor should consider whether:

○ Business conditions have changed in the remaining period to such an extent that management would be more likely to perpetrate fraud.

○ Accounts selected for interim testing are expected to adhere to predictable patterns.

RECOMMENDATION
The auditor should design substantive tests that will enable the extension of interim conclusions to the balance sheet date. Accordingly, the auditor should consider: ○ Comparing interim results with those at the balance sheet date.   ○ Performing other types of analytical procedures.   ○ Performing substantive tests of details.

Any significant fluctuations between interim results and those as of the balance sheet date warrant investigation.

Related Parties

How do I handle related party transactions?

With respect to related party transactions, the auditor should be aware that the substance of a particular transaction could be significantly different from its legal form. Whenever a client transacts business with another entity at terms more favorable than would be afforded under usual circumstances, it is possible that a related party relationship exists.

RECOMMENDATION
The auditor should design substantive tests in order to identify the existence and terms of related party transactions. This is crucial, since FASB Statement 57 requires that related party information be disclosed in financial statements.

How do I identify related party transactions?

In order to identify transactions with related parties, the auditor should review:

○ The minutes of meetings of the board of directors

○ Transactions with major customers, suppliers, borrowers, and lenders

○ Large, unusual, and nonrecurring transactions

Once identified, related party transactions should be examined in order for the auditor to gain satisfaction as to the purpose, extent, and nature of the transactions. In addition, the practitioner must be satisfied with the related party disclosures contained in the financial statements.

SAS 46—CONSIDERATION OF OMITTED PROCEDURES AFTER THE REPORT DATE

What if one or more procedures were omitted?

Under certain circumstances, such as peer review, the auditor may conclude, after the issuance of an audit report, that he or she omitted one or more auditing procedures. In these situations, the auditor has the responsibility of assessing the importance of the omitted procedures to his or her present ability to support the previously expressed opinion. In making this assessment, the auditor should consider any alternative auditing procedures performed.

If the auditor still feels that the omitted procedures impair the present ability to support the audit report, he or she should undertake to apply the omitted or alternative procedures. If the auditor is unable to apply the necessary procedures, he or she should contact legal counsel in order to discuss the appropriate course of action.

SAS 47—AUDIT RISK AND MATERIALITY IN CONDUCTING AN AUDIT

What constitutes audit risk?

The risk that the independent auditor may unknowingly fail to modify his or her audit opinion on materially misstated financial statements is known as *audit risk*.

In considering audit risk, the auditor must be aware of the following:

○ *Inherent risk* is the "built-in" susceptibility of an account balance or class of transactions to misstatements, regardless of internal control. EXAMPLE: Cash has a high inherent risk due to its liquidity.

○ *Control risk* is the risk that an account balance or class of transactions will contain misstatements that will not be detected or prevented by the client's internal controls.

○ *Detection risk* is the risk that the auditor will fail to identify material misstatements.

NOTE

There should be an inverse relationship between detection risk and inherent and control risks. In other words, the greater the inherent and control risk, the less the detection risk the auditor can and should accept.

RECOMMENDATION

The auditor can control detection risk by applying the appropriate auditing procedures. On the other hand, it is management's responsibility to minimize control risk by establishing and maintaining effective internal control.

What is materiality?

Materiality relates to the financial importance of an item or group of items in the financial statements. There is no quantitative definition of materiality; rather, materiality is qualitatively defined.

CRITERION

An item (or group of items) should be considered material if the inclusion or omission of the item (or group of items) will affect the reader of the financial statements.

What must I do with respect to audit risk and materiality?

Both audit risk and materiality must be considered in planning an audit and expressing an opinion on the financial statements. Needless to say, the auditor should limit audit risk to a relatively low level.

In addition, audit risk and materiality are inversely related. Accordingly, the risk that an account may be materially misstated may be low, although the risk that an account may be misstated by a small amount may be very high.

SAS 48—THE EFFECTS OF COMPUTER PROCESSING ON THE AUDIT OF FINANCIAL STATEMENTS

What effect does automation have on an audit?

An auditor should consider the following in planning an engagement to audit an entity that records its transactions by computer:

- ○ The extent of electronic data processing
- ○ The complexity of the electronic data processing operations

- The organizational structure of the electronic data processing department
- The availability of financial data
- The application of computer-assisted audit techniques
- The need for a specialist to explain the effects of electronic data processing

How do automated and manual systems differ?

When considering a client's internal control in an electronic data processing environment, the auditor should consider the characteristics that distinguish computer processing from manual recording:

- *Transaction trails:* Audit trails in a computerized environment are either nonexistent or short lived.

- *Uniform processing of transactions:* If a computer handles a particular type of transaction correctly, then it will handle all subsequent transactions of the same type in the same manner. CAUTION: The converse is also true. If a transaction is handled incorrectly, all subsequent similar transactions processed will also be incorrectly handled.

- *Segregation of functions:* Since many functions are performed internally by the computer, there is an inherent lack of segregation of functions in a computerized environment. To compensate for this situation, job functions should be segregated within the electronic data processing activities.

- *Potential for errors and fraud:* The potential for errors and fraud in a computerized environment depends on the human involvement in the computerized applications and the extent of the segregation of functions.

- *Potential for increased management supervision:* Given that a computer can generate data more quickly than manual preparation, financial information is provided on a more timely basis. This enables management to use information before it outlives its utility.

- *Initiation or subsequent execution of transactions by computer:* Authorization for initiation or subsequent execution of transactions is built into the computer. Documentation for this authorization is therefore not always apparent.

- *Dependence of other controls on controls over computer processing:* The output derived from computer processing is often useful in performing manual control procedures.

SAS 49—LETTERS FOR UNDERWRITERS

Superseded by SAS 72.

SAS 50—REPORTS ON THE APPLICATION OF ACCOUNTING PRINCIPLES

When might I have to report on the application of accounting principles?

An accountant may be requested to prepare a written report on:

- ○ The application of accounting principles to specified transactions
- ○ The type of opinion that may be expressed on an entity's financial statements

---

NOTE

An accountant should not prepare a written report on a hypothetical transaction.

What should be in a report on the application of accounting principles?

The accountant's report on the application of accounting principles should include:

- ○ The appropriate address (it should be addressed to the principal to the transaction or to the intermediary)
- ○ A statement describing the type of engagement
- ○ An indication that the engagement was performed in accordance with the relevant standards of the American Institute of Certified Public Accountants
- ○ A description of the transaction and its related facts, circumstances, and assumptions (including their source)
- ○ An identification of the principals to the transaction
- ○ A description of the relevant accounting principles
- ○ A statement fixing the responsibility for the proper accounting treatment with the preparers of the financial statements, who should consult with their continuing accountants
- ○ A warning that the report may change if differences of facts, circumstances, or assumptions arise
- ○ A statement restricting the use of the report to the specified parties

EXAMPLE 12.8 WORDING FOR A REPORT ON ACCOUNTING APPLICATIONS

I (We) have been engaged to report on the appropriate application of accounting principles generally accepted in the United States of America to the specific transaction described below. This report is being issued to the Karen Company (DBA Intermediaries) for assistance in evaluating accounting principles for the described specific transaction. My (Our) engagement has been conducted in accordance with standards established by the American Institute of Certified Public Accountants.

The facts, circumstances, and assumptions relevant to the specific transaction as provided to me (us) by the management of the Karen Company (DBA Intermediaries) are as follows:

[*Description of Transaction*]

[*Description of Appropriate Accounting Principles*]

The ultimate responsibility for the decision on the appropriate application of accounting principles generally accepted in the United States of America for an actual transaction rests with the preparers of financial statements, who should consult with their continuing accountants. My (our) judgment on the appropriate application of accounting principles generally accepted in the United States of America for the described specific transaction is based solely on facts provided to me (us) as described above; should these facts and circumstances differ, my (our) conclusion may change.

This report is intended solely for the information and use of the board of directors and management of the Karen Company (DBA Intermediaries) and is not intended to be and should not be used by anyone other than these specified parties.

SAS 51—REPORTING ON FINANCIAL STATEMENTS PREPARED FOR USE IN OTHER COUNTRIES

When reporting on financial statements for overseas use, what should I do?

Generally accepted auditing standards as developed in the United States should be adhered to when examining financial statements of a U.S. entity prepared in conformity with accounting principles accepted in another country. Under certain circumstances, the auditor may also have to adhere to the auditing standards of the foreign country.

If the financial statements are for use *only* in a foreign country, the auditor may issue:

- o A U.S.-style report modified for reporting on the foreign country's accounting principles
- o A report based on the foreign country's standards

EXAMPLE 12.9 UNITED STATES-STYLE REPORT MODIFIED FOR USE IN A FOREIGN COUNTRY

INDEPENDENT AUDITOR'S REPORT

I (We) have audited the accompanying balance sheet of Transcontinental Company as of December 31, 20XX and the related statements of income, retained earnings, and cash flows for the year then ended which, as described in Note X, have been prepared on the basis of accounting principles accepted in [*name of country*]. These financial statements are the responsibility of the Company's management. My (our) responsibility is to express an opinion on these financial statements based on my (our) audit.

I (We) conducted my (our) audit in accordance with auditing standards generally accepted in the United States of America (and in [*name of country*]). U.S. standards require that I (we) plan and perform the audit to obtain reasonable assurance about whether the financial statements are free of material misstatement. An audit includes examining, on a test basis, evidence supporting the amounts and disclosures in the financial statements. An audit also includes assessing the accounting principles used and significant estimates made by management, as well as evaluating the overall financial statement presentation. I (We) believe that my (our) audit provides a reasonable basis for my (our) opinion.

In my (our) opinion, the financial statements referred to above present fairly, in all material respects, the financial position of Transcontinental Company as of [at] December 31, 20XX, and the results of its cash flows for the year then ended in conformity with accounting principles generally accepted in [*name of country*].

SAS 52—OMNIBUS STATEMENT ON AUDITING STANDARDS—1987

Essentially modified SAS 5 (superseded by SAS 69) to recognize various publications of the Government Accounting Standards Board (GASB) as a source of generally accepted accounting principles.

This pronouncement also (a) recognizes supplementary information required by the GASB and (b) reflects changes in light of the issuance of FASB Statement 89, Financial Reporting and Changing Prices, which no longer makes it mandatory to disclose supplementary information pertaining to the effects of changing prices.

Since supplementary information required by the FASB or GASB is not a required part of the basic financial statements, the auditor is not required to modify his or her audit report to refer to the supplementary information unless:

- o It is omitted.
- o Its measurement or presentation is not in conformity with prescribed guidelines.
- o The auditor is unable to apply prescribed procedures.
- o The auditor is precluded from removing substantial doubt as to the conformity with prescribed guidelines.

RECOMMENDATION

The auditor's opinion should not be modified due to the circumstances described above. Accordingly, even though the auditor may deem it necessary to add an explanatory paragraph; the auditor may still issue an unqualified opinion.

SAS 53—THE AUDITOR'S RESPONSIBILITY TO DETECT AND REPORT ERRORS AND IRREGULARITIES

Superseded by SAS 82.

SAS 54—ILLEGAL ACTS BY CLIENTS

What is an illegal act?

An illegal act is a violation of law or government regulations by the client.

CAUTION

The auditor should seek legal counsel when determining what is an illegal act.

What is my responsibility for the detection and reporting of illegal acts?

The auditor's responsibility is essentially the same as his or her responsibility to detect and report errors and fraud (as discussed in SAS 99).

NOTE

The auditor is concerned with the illegal act's effect on the financial statements as opposed to the illegality itself.

What if I detect an illegal act that does not have a material effect on the financial statements?

If the client refuses to take appropriate action with respect to *any* illegal act, material or otherwise, the auditor should consider withdrawing from the engagement.

SAS 55—CONSIDERATION OF INTERNAL CONTROL IN A FINANCIAL STATEMENT AUDIT

Modified by SAS 78 and SAS 94; refer to Chapter 10.

SAS 56—ANALYTICAL PROCEDURES

Analytical procedures must be performed in the planning and overall review stages of all audits. Because analytical procedures enable identification of unusual relationships and fluctuations, the auditor can better determine the nature and extent of substantive tests.

NOTE
Analytical procedures do not have to be used in substantive testing. This is a matter of professional judgment.

What are analytical procedures?

Analytical procedures include comparison of recorded amounts, or ratios based on recorded amounts, to expectations derived by the auditor. Accordingly, analytical procedures include comparison of current period financial information with

- o Prior period information
- o Expected results
- o Predictable pattern information
- o Intra-industry information
- o Nonfinancial information

SAS 57—AUDITING ACCOUNTING ESTIMATES

What is meant by an accounting estimate?

An accounting estimate is an approximation of a financial statement element, item, or account.
EXAMPLES:

- o Net realizable values of inventory
- o Pension and warranty expenses

o Obsolete inventories
o Amount of a probable loss contingency

What is my responsibility with respect to accounting estimates?

Whereas management is responsible for developing accounting estimates, the auditor is responsible for evaluating the reasonableness of such estimates.

The auditor must evaluate accounting estimates in order to obtain reasonable assurance that (a) all material accounting estimates have been developed, (b) the accounting estimates are reasonable, (c) the accounting estimates are in conformity with GAAP, and (d) the accounting estimates are properly disclosed in the financial statements.

How do I evaluate the reasonableness of accounting estimates?

The auditor should review and test the process employed by management in developing a particular accounting estimate. Furthermore, the auditor should develop an independent expectation of the estimate to corroborate the reasonableness of the client's estimate. Finally, the auditor should review subsequent events.

SAS 58—REPORTS ON AUDITED FINANCIAL STATEMENTS

Modified by SAS 79; refer to Chapter 10.

SAS 59—THE AUDITOR'S CONSIDERATION OF AN ENTITY'S ABILITY TO CONTINUE AS A GOING CONCERN

The auditor is responsible for evaluating whether there is substantial doubt about the entity's ability to continue as a going concern for a reasonable time period, not to exceed one year beyond the date of the audited financial statements.

What conditions and events may indicate a going-concern problem?

The following might be considered indicative of a going-concern problem:

o *Negative trends*—such as a poor current working capital ratio
o *Indicators of possible financial trouble*—such as defaults on note agreements
o *Internal matters*—such as a strike by employees
o *External matters*—pending or actual litigation or legislation

> **CAUTION**
>
> The auditor should consider mitigating circumstances by evaluating management's plans. For example, management may be planning to restructure its debt in a manner that will increase equity ownership.

Do going-concern problems affect financial statements?

Certain informative disclosures might be necessary if the client is experiencing a going-concern problem. These disclosures include:

- The conditions and events causing the going-concern problem
- The possible effects of such conditions
- Management's evaluation of the significance of those conditions and events along with any mitigating factors
- The possible cessation of operations
- Management's plans for overcoming the going-concern problem
- Significant information regarding the recoverability or classification of assets and liabilities

What is my reporting responsibility?

If the auditor concludes that there is substantial doubt about the entity's ability to continue as a going concern for a reasonable time period, then the audit report should be modified to include an additional paragraph (to be inserted after the opinion paragraph) that reflects the auditor's conclusion.

> **EXAMPLE**
>
> The following represents sample wording of such an additional paragraph:
>
> The accompanying financial statements have been prepared assuming that the Company will continue as a going concern. As discussed in Note X to the financial statements, the Company has suffered recurring losses from operations and has a net capital deficiency that raise substantial doubt about its ability to continue as a going concern. Management's plans in regard to these matters are also described in Note X. The financial statements do not include any adjustments that might result from the outcome of this uncertainty.

> **CAUTION**
>
> A going-concern problem should not result in a qualified opinion. It would still be appropriate to issue an unqualified opinion.

	WARNING
	Do not use conditional language (e.g; "if the company. ..., then. ...) in the additional paragraph.

 ## SAS 60—COMMUNICATION OF INTERNAL CONTROL RELATED MATTERS NOTED IN AN AUDIT

While performing an audit, an auditor is under no obligation to search for reportable conditions (i.e., matters pertaining to significant deficiencies in the client's internal control that could have an adverse affect on the recording, processing, summarizing, and reporting of financial data).

What is my responsibility if I do identify reportable conditions?

If reportable conditions are identified, the auditor should communicate with the audit committee (or its equivalent). Such communication may be oral or written, although the latter is preferable.

What should be included in a report issued on reportable conditions?

A report on reportable conditions should:

- ○ Include a statement that the purpose of the audit was to report on the financial statements and not to provide assurance relating to internal control.
- ○ Define reportable conditions.
- ○ Describe the reportable conditions identified.
- ○ Restrict the distribution of the report.

EXAMPLE 12.10
A REPORT ON REPORTABLE CONDITIONS

In planning and performing my (our) audit of the financial statements of the ABC Corporation for the year ended December 31, 20XX, I (we) considered its internal control in order to determine my (our) auditing procedures for the purpose of expressing my (our) opinion on the financial statements and not to provide assurance on internal control. However, I (we) noted certain matters involving internal control and its operation that I (we) consider to be reportable conditions under standards established by the American Institute of Certified Public Accountants. Reportable conditions involve matters coming to my (our) attention relating to significant deficiencies in the design or operation of internal control

---

EXAMPLE 12.10
A REPORT ON REPORTABLE CONDITIONS *(continued)*

that, in my (our) judgment, could adversely affect the organization's ability to record, process, summarize, and report financial data consistent with the assertions of management in the financial statements.

[Include paragraph(s) to describe reportable conditions noted.]

This report is intended solely for the information and use of the audit committee (board of directors, board of trustees, or owners in owner-managed enterprises), management, and others within the organization (or specified regulatory agency and is not intended to be and should not be used by anyone other than the specified parties.

CAUTION

Never issue a report containing a representation that no reportable conditions were noted during the audit.

RECOMMENDATION

The CPA should exercise professional judgment in determining when to communicate reportable conditions. Interim communication may be warranted.

What if I identify a material weakness?

A material weakness in internal control is a reportable condition in which the design or operation of the internal control components does not reduce to a relatively low level the risk that material misstatements may occur and go undetected by employees in the normal course of performing their assigned functions.

The auditor is not responsible for separately identifying and reporting material weaknesses.

Since material weaknesses are reportable conditions, the auditor may communicate them as such.

SAS 61—COMMUNICATION WITH AUDIT COMMITTEES

Certain matters pertaining to an audit must be communicated to the audit committee (or those having responsibility for oversight of the financial reporting process).

What matters are to be included in a communication with the audit committee?

Some of the matters to be communicated concern:

- The auditor's responsibility for the audited financial statements
- The significant accounting policies of the entity
- Management judgments and accounting estimates
- Significant audit adjustments
- Other information in documents containing audited financial statements
- Disagreements with management
- Client consultations with other accountants
- Major issues discussed with management prior to retention
- Difficulties encountered in performing the audit

SAS 62—SPECIAL REPORTS

See Chapter 11.

SAS 63—COMPLIANCE AUDITING APPLICABLE TO GOVERNMENTAL ENTITIES AND OTHER RECIPIENTS OF GOVERNMENTAL FINANCIAL ASSISTANCE

Superseded by SAS 68.

SAS 64—OMNIBUS STATEMENT ON AUDITING STANDARDS

This statement amends parts of selected Statements on Auditing Standards. These amendments have been incorporated into the summaries of the pertinent statements.

SAS 65—THE AUDITOR'S CONSIDERATION OF THE INTERNAL AUDIT FUNCTION IN AN AUDIT OF FINANCIAL STATEMENTS

What is required of me as an independent auditor?

The work performed by a client's *internal* auditors may affect the nature, extent, and timing of the *independent* auditor's procedures. Internal auditors may provide direct assistance to the independent auditor. Accordingly, the practitioner should review the competency and objectivity of the internal auditors as well as evaluate their work.

- ○ *Competency* of the internal auditors may be evaluated in light of their:
  - Education
  - Experience
  - Professional certification
  - Audit programs, policies, and procedures
  - Supervision and review
  - Working-paper documentation, including recommendations
- ○ In judging *objectivity*, the independent auditor should consider:
  - The organizational level to which the internal audit reports are sent
  - Whether the internal audit staff has direct access (and reports) to the board of directors, the audit committee, or its equivalent

---

CAUTION

Given that the independent auditor is responsible for expressing an opinion on the financial statements, the independent auditor is responsible for all judgments concerning risks associated with the audit, materiality levels, sufficiency of tests performed, and evaluations of audit evidence. Furthermore, the practitioner should not allow internal auditors to gather evidence that the independent auditor cannot corroborate.

EXAMPLE: The practitioner should not allow internal auditors to prepare and mail the accounts receivable confirmations. Rather, the internal auditors may be requested to prepare the confirmations, but the practitioner should both verify the balances (by inspecting the subsidiary ledger) and mail the confirmations.

SAS 66—COMMUNICATION OF MATTERS ABOUT INTERIM FINANCIAL INFORMATION FILED OR TO BE FILED WITH SPECIFIED REGULATORY AGENCIES

Superseded by SAS 71.

SAS 67—THE CONFIRMATION PROCESS

What is the confirmation process?

Confirmation is the process of obtaining and evaluating a direct communication from a third party in response to a request for information about an item relating to financial statement assertions. Throughout the confirmation process, the auditor should exercise professional skepticism.

What forms of confirmation exist?

The two types of confirmations that may be used are:

- o Positive forms that request a response whether or not the recipient is in agreement with the information stated on the confirmation request. A positive form may be a blank form that requests the recipient to fill in requested information.
- o Negative forms that request a response only if the recipient disagrees with the information stated on the confirmation request.

Is there risk involved in using the negative form?

The use of negative confirmation requests may increase audit risk. Accordingly, judgment should be exercised in considering their use. In general, negative confirmation requests may be used when:

- o The combined assessed level of inherent and control risk is low.
- o Many small balances are involved.
- o The auditor believes that the recipients are likely to give them consideration.

What should be done if a response to a confirmation request is not received?

- o If a negative confirmation request was used, and no response is received, the auditor ordinarily concludes that the recipient is in agreement with the stated information; accordingly, no additional procedures are necessary.
- o If a positive confirmation request was used, and no response is received, the auditor should perform alternative procedures. For example, in auditing accounts receivable, alternative procedures might include examination of subsequent period cash receipts and inspection of shipping documents.

Are there any special considerations in evaluating the results of confirmation procedures?

In evaluating the results of the confirmation process, the auditor should consider the following:

- o The reliability of the confirmations and/or applicable alternative procedures

- ○ The nature and cause of exceptions
- ○ The evidence generated from the application of other procedures
- ○ The need for additional information

What guidance does SAS 67 provide in connection with the confirmation of accounts receivable?

The definition of accounts receivable is rather narrow. Accounts receivable include an entity's claims against customers created from the sale of goods or services in the normal course of business operations. Also included are a financial institution's loans.

Confirmation of accounts receivable is generally required.

NOTE

Confirmation of accounts receivable may not be necessary when (1) accounts receivable are immaterial, (2) the use of the confirmations is not likely to be effective, and (3) the combined assessed level of inherent and control risk is low.

CAUTION

If the auditor does not confirm accounts receivable, he or she should document in the working papers the justification for the omission and any details of any relevant alternative procedures performed.

SAS 68—COMPLIANCE AUDITING APPLICABLE TO GOVERNMENTAL ENTITIES AND OTHER RECIPIENTS OF GOVERNMENTAL FINANCIAL ASSISTANCE

Superseded by SAS 74.

SAS 69—THE MEANING OF PRESENT FAIRLY IN CONFORMITY WITH GENERALLY ACCEPTED ACCOUNTING PRINCIPLES IN THE INDEPENDENT AUDITOR'S REPORT

The phrase "present fairly" contained in the opinion paragraph of the auditor's report should be applied within the framework of generally accepted accounting principles (GAAP).

When is a principle, method, or practice in accordance with GAAP?

In deciding whether an accounting principle, practice, or method is in conformity with GAAP, the practitioner should consider whether:

1. The accounting principle, practice or method has general acceptance. SAS 69 (as amended) provides three hierarchical structures to be used in determining whether an accounting principle, practice, or method is based on an acceptable source. The classification of sources into categories included in the hierarchies determines the source's level of authority. One hierarchy relates to nongovernmental entities, the second hierarchy applies to state and local governmental entities, and the third hierarchy applies to federal governmental entities.

With respect to nongovernmental entities, appropriate sources of GAAP include, but are not limited to:

- FASB Statements of Financial Accounting Standards and Interpretations
- APB Opinions
- AICPA Research Bulletins
- FASB Technical Bulletins
- AICPA Industry Audit and Accounting Guides
- AICPA Statements of Position

With respect to state and local government entities, appropriate sources of GAAP include, but are not limited to:

- GASB Statements and Interpretations
- AICPA and FASB pronouncements specifically directed to state and local governments
- GASB Technical Bulletins
- Relevant AICPA Industry Audit and Accounting Guides
- AICPA Statements of Position
- Implementation guides issued by GASB

With respect to federal governmental entities, appropriate sources of GAAP include, but are not limited to:

- Federal Accounting Standards Advisory Board (FASAB) Statements and Interpretations
- AICPA and FASB pronouncements specifically directed to federal governmental entities
- FASAB Technical Bulletins
- FASAB implementation guides
- FASAB Concepts Statements

2. The accounting principle, practice, or method is appropriate in the circumstances. The rule of thumb is "substance over form." EXAMPLE: If a client's lease (of machinery) provides for a bargain purchase price (e.g., $1) at the expiration of the lease, the lease should be treated as a capital lease, and not as an operating lease.

3. The financial statements are informative. Accordingly, the accountant must gain assurance that the financial statements include all of the disclosures, including notes, necessary to prevent the reader from being misled.

4. The financial statements are classified and summarized.

5. The information contained in the financial statements is presented within limits. The cost/benefit relationship should prevail. As such, the benefit of presenting the information must exceed the cost of providing it.

SAS 70— SERVICE ORGANIZATIONS

What is a service organization?

A service organization is an entity that provides a service to a client of the practitioner (i.e., "user organization"). EXAMPLE: A company that processes the payroll for a client of the CPA.

What is the responsibility of an auditor of a user organization?

If an auditor wants to assess control risk below the maximum level, he or she should obtain, from the auditor of the service organization, a report on controls placed in operation and tests of operating effectiveness.

CAUTION
The auditor of a service organization may issue a report only on controls placed in operation; this report does not cover tests of operating effectiveness. Accordingly, it may not be sufficient to enable the user auditor to assess control risk below the maximum level.

SAS 71—INTERIM FINANCIAL INFORMATION

Superseded by SAS 100.

SAS 72—LETTERS FOR UNDERWRITERS AND OTHER REQUESTING PARTIES

What is a comfort letter?

A CPA may issue a letter for an underwriter, called a *comfort letter*. A comfort letter may refer to one or more of the following:

○ The accountant's independence
○ Compliance of the financial statements included in the registration statement with the Securities Act of 1933
○ Unaudited financial statements, condensed financial statements, capsule information, pro forma financial information, and forecasts
○ Changes in financial statement items after the date of the financial statements included in the registration statement
○ Tables and statistics

NOTE

A typical comfort letter includes (1) an opinion as to whether the audited financial statements and related schedules included in a registration statement are in compliance with applicable accounting requirements of the Securities Act of 1933 and pertinent accounting requirements adopted by the SEC and (2) negative assurance as to whether the unaudited condensed interim financial information included in a registration statement is in compliance with applicable accounting requirements of the Securities Act of 1933 and pertinent accounting requirements adopted by the SEC.

SAS 73—USING THE WORK OF A SPECIALIST

How is a specialist used?

During the course of an audit, the independent auditor may need to employ a specialist. A specialist has expertise in an area other than accounting or auditing. Matters that might require the use of a specialist include:

○ Valuation of assets. EXAMPLE: A gemologist may be consulted in valuing inventories consisting of diamonds or other precious stones.
○ Determination of physical characteristics. EXAMPLE: A specialist may be consulted in connection with mineral reserves.
○ Determination or verification of amounts determined through the use of specialized methods and techniques.

EXAMPLE: An actuary may be consulted in order to corroborate a client's accrual for contributions to a defined benefit pension plan.

○ Interpretation of technical requirements, regulations, or agreements. EXAMPLE: An attorney may be consulted in connection with contracts or other legal documents.

What must be considered before using a specialist?

○ Consider the professional competency and reputation of the specialist.

○ Consider the relationship, if any, of the specialist to the client to determine if objectivity is impaired. NOTE: Independence of the specialist from the client is not required, but a lack of independence may require additional auditing procedures.

○ Understand the nature of the work of the specialist, including:

- The objectives and scope of the work
- The accounting assumptions and methods used
- The appropriateness of using the work for the intended purpose
- The form and content of the report to be issued by the specialist

Does using a specialist affect reporting requirements?

If the findings of the specialist support the representations or assertions made by management, then the auditor could appropriately express a standard unqualified opinion. In such circumstances, the auditor should not refer to the use of the specialist.

The auditor may make reference to and identify the specialist if he or she decides to:

○ Add explanatory language to the standard audit report. EXAMPLE: The findings of the specialist raise substantial doubt about the entity's ability to continue as a going concern for a reasonable period of time.

○ Issue a qualified opinion or adverse opinion because the findings of the specialist do not corroborate the representations or assertions made by management.

○ Disclaim an opinion because of the inability to obtain sufficient competent evidential matter regarding a material client representation or assertion. EXAMPLE: When a difference of opinion exists among specialists and the auditor cannot perform alternate auditing procedures.

SAS 74—COMPLIANCE AUDITING CONSIDERATIONS IN AUDITS OF GOVERNMENTAL ENTITIES AND RECIPIENTS OF GOVERNMENTAL FINANCIAL ASSISTANCE

This statement provides guidance for testing and reporting on compliance with laws and regulations applicable to certain governmental audits. In general, when performing governmental auditing, the practitioner has a responsibility to follow generally accepted auditing standards and certain supplemental standards known as generally accepted government auditing standards.

SUGGESTION
Practitioners undertaking a governmental audit engagement would be well advised to refer to "Government Auditing Standards" (known as the "Yellow Book") issued by the Comptroller General of the United States, The Single Audit Act of 1984, OMB Circular A-128, "Audits of State and Local Governments" and circular A-133, "Audits of Institutions of Higher Education and Other Nonprofit Institutions."

SAS 75—ENGAGEMENTS TO APPLY AGREED-UPON PROCEDURES TO SPECIFIED ELEMENTS, ACCOUNTS, OR ITEMS OF A FINANCIAL STATEMENT

Withdrawn by SAS 93.

SAS 76—AMENDMENTS TO STATEMENT ON AUDITING STANDARDS NO. 72, LETTERS FOR UNDERWRITERS, AND CERTAIN OTHER REQUESTING PARTIES

Refer to the summary of SAS 72, which includes the appropriate amendments.

SAS 77—AMENDMENTS TO STATEMENTS ON AUDITING STANDARDS NO. 22, PLANNING AND SUPERVISION, NO. 59, THE AUDITOR'S CONSIDERATION OF AN ENTITY'S ABILITY TO CONTINUE AS A GOING CONCERN, AND NO. 62, SPECIAL REPORTS

Amendments in this pronouncement have been incorporated into the summaries of SAS 22 and SAS 59 as well as Chapter 11.

SAS 78—CONSIDERATION OF INTERNAL CONTROL IN A FINANCIAL STATEMENT AUDIT: AN AMENDMENT TO SAS 55

Refer to Chapter 10, which includes the appropriate amendments.

SAS 79—AMENDMENT TO STATEMENT ON AUDITING STANDARDS 58, REPORTS ON AUDITED FINANCIAL STATEMENTS

Refer to Chapter 10, which includes the appropriate amendments.

SAS 80—AMENDMENT TO STATEMENT ON AUDITING STANDARDS NO. 31, EVIDENTIAL MATTER

Refer to the summary of SAS 31, which includes the appropriate amendments.

SAS 81—AUDITING INVESTMENTS

Superseded by SAS 92.

SAS 82—CONSIDERATION OF FRAUD IN A FINANCIAL STATEMENT AUDIT

Superseded by SAS 99.

SAS 83—ESTABLISHING AN UNDERSTANDING WITH THE CLIENT

What are the documentation requirements relative to the understanding established with the client?

The understanding should be documented in the working papers, preferably by means of a written communication with the client.

NOTE

While an engagement letter is highly recommended, it is not required. It should be stressed that an engagement should not be accepted unless an understanding with the client has been established.

What are the matters that should be considered when establishing an understanding with a client?

The understanding should cover (1) the objective(s) of the engagement, (2) management's responsibilities, and (3) the limitations of the engagement.

What are management's responsibilities that should be addressed in the understanding?

Management's responsibilities include:

- The financial statements
- Establishing and maintaining effective internal control
- Compliance with laws and regulations
- Making all financial records and related information available to the auditor
- Providing the auditor with a representation letter at the conclusion of the audit
- Adjusting the financial statements for those items that are deemed to be individually or collectively material to the financial statements
- Affirming in the representation letter that the financial statements have not been adjusted for those items that are deemed to be individually or collectively immaterial to the financial statements

What other matters may be relevant to the understanding?

Other matters that may be part of the understanding include:

- Terms of the engagement, including the timing of the audit, assistance of client personnel, fees and billing
- Any arrangements involving the use of specialists (see SAS 73) and internal auditors (see SAS65)
- Any arrangements involving a predecessor auditor (see SAS 84)
- Any additional services to be performed
- Any limitations of or arrangements regarding liability of either the auditor or the client
- Conditions under which access to audit documentation may be granted to others

SAS 84—COMMUNICATIONS BETWEEN PREDECESSOR AND SUCCESSOR ACCOUNTANTS

As a successor auditor, are there any required communications with the predecessor auditor?

Yes. An auditor should not accept an engagement until the required communications with the predecessor have been properly evaluated. Note: The communications addressed in this pronouncement are not required if the most recent audited financial statements are more than two years prior to the beginning of the earliest period the successor auditor is requested to audit.

The successor auditor should communicate with the predecessor primarily to determine whether there are any reasons the engagement should not be accepted. Accordingly, the successor is interested in:

- Reasons for the change in auditors, including any facts that bear on the integrity of management
- Any disagreements the predecessor may have had with the client regarding application of generally accepted auditing principles and/or generally accepted auditing standards
- Any phases of the predecessor's audit that required an unusually large amount of time, possibly indicative of problems with the client's financial records
- Any communications to audit committees (or their equivalent) regarding fraud (see SAS 99), illegal acts (see SAS 54) and reportable conditions (see SAS 60)

The successor should also request that the client authorize the predecessor to allow a review of the predecessor's working papers that may have continuing and auditing significance.

The predecessor's response should be prompt and full. However, the predecessor's response may indicate that the response is limited due to, for example, impending, threatened, or potential litigation, or disciplinary proceedings.

Do the required communications violate confidentiality?

There is no violation of confidentiality as long as the client authorizes (1) the successor to communicate with the predecessor and (2) the predecessor to respond to the successor's inquiries. The authorization may be oral or in writing.

What action is appropriate if a prospective client will not allow the predecessor to respond fully?

The refusal of a prospective client to allow the predecessor auditor to respond fully should cause the successor auditor to (1) question the reason(s) therefore and (2) consider declining the engagement.

What should the successor do if he or she becomes aware of information that may require the revision of the financial

statements reported on by the predecessor?

If the successor becomes aware of information that leads him or her to conclude that the financial statements reported on by the predecessor may require revision, then the successor should request that the client inform the predecessor and arrange a meeting of the three parties in order to discuss the matter and arrive at an appropriate resolution.

CAUTION

A client's refusal to inform the predecessor of the need to revise prior financial statements should cause the successor to consider whether withdrawal from the engagement is appropriate. Furthermore, the successor should consider the need to consult with his or her legal counsel.

SAS 85—MANAGEMENT REPRESENTATIONS

What type of representations do I need from the client?

At the conclusion of the audit, the auditor must obtain from the client a representation letter confirming oral and written representations or assertions made by the client during the course of the audit. The representation letter, to be addressed to the auditor, is usually signed by the chief executive officer and chief financial officer. The representation letter should cover all financial statements and periods covered by the audit report. It should be dated no earlier than the audit report date, which is usually the conclusion of the fieldwork.

What items should be included in the representation letter?

The items included in the client representation letter will vary depending on the engagement and the nature and basis of financial statement presentation. Some commonly included items are:

- ○ Management's acknowledgment of its responsibility for the fair presentation in the financial statements of financial position, results of operations, and cash flows in conformity with generally accepted accounting principles

○ Management's belief that the financial statements are fairly presented in conformity with generally accepted accounting principles

○ Availability of all financial records and related data

○ Completeness and availability of all minutes of meetings of stockholders, directors, and committees of directors

○ Communication from regulatory agencies concerning noncompliance with or deficiencies in financial reporting practices

○ Absence of unrecorded transactions

○ Management's belief that the effects of any uncorrected financial statement misstatements aggregated by the auditor during the current engagement and pertaining to the latest period presented are immaterial, both individually and in the aggregate, to the financial statements taken as a whole (A summary of such items should be included in or attached to the letter.)

○ Management's acknowledgment of its responsibility for the design and implementation of programs and controls to prevent and detect fraud

○ Knowledge of fraud or suspected fraud affecting the entity involving (1) management, (2) employees who have significant roles in internal control, or (3) others where the fraud could have a material effect on the financial statements

○ Knowledge of any allegations of fraud or suspected fraud affecting the entity received in communications from employees, former employees, analysts, regulators, short sellers, or others

○ Plans or intentions that may affect the carrying value or classification of assets or liabilities.

○ Information concerning related-party transactions and amounts receivable from or payable to related parties

○ Guarantees, whether written or oral, under which the entity is contingently liable

○ Significant estimates and material concentrations known to management that are required to be disclosed in accordance with the AICPA's Statement of Position 94-6, *Disclosure of Certain Significant Risks and Uncertainties*

○ Violations or possible violations of laws or regulations whose effects should be considered for disclosure in the financial statements or as a basis for recording a loss contingency

○ Unasserted claims or assessments that the entity's lawyer has advised are probable of assertion and must be disclosed in accordance with Financial Accounting

Standards Board (FASB) Statement No. 5, *Accounting for Contingencies*

○ Other liabilities and gain or loss contingencies that are required to be accrued or disclosed by FASB Statement No. 5

○ Satisfactory title to assets, liens, or encumbrances on assets, and assets pledged as collateral

○ Compliance with aspects of contractual agreements that may affect the financial statements

○ Information concerning subsequent events

Can a representation letter replace audit procedures?

Although the management representation letter is a form of evidential matter, it is *not* a substitute for the application of auditing procedures.

CAUTION

Management's refusal to furnish the representation letter to the auditor is tantamount to a scope limitation sufficient to preclude the issuance of an unqualified opinion. The refusal to issue a representation letter ordinarily will lead the auditor to doubt the integrity of management. As a result, the auditor should reconsider his or her ability to rely on other management assertions or representations. This will usually result in a disclaimer of opinion.

EXAMPLE 12.11
ILLUSTRATIVE REPRESENTATION LETTER

(PREPARED ON CLIENT'S LETTERHEAD)

[Date]

To *[Independent Auditor]*

We are providing this letter in connection with your audit(s) of the *[identification of financial statements]* of *[name of entity]* as of *[dates]* and for the *[periods]* for the purpose *of* expressing an opinion as to whether the *[consolidated]* financial statements present fairly, in all material respects, the financial position, results *of* operations, and cash flows *of [name of entity]* in conformity with accounting principles generally accepted in the United States of America. We confirm that we are responsible for the fair presentation in the *[consolidated]* financial statements of financial position, results of operations, and cash flows in conformity with generally accepted accounting principles.

EXAMPLE 12.11
ILLUSTRATIVE REPRESENTATION LETTER *(continued)*

Certain representations in this letter are described as being limited to matters that are material. Items are considered material, regardless of size, if they involve an omission or misstatement of accounting information that, in the light of surrounding circumstances, makes it probable that the judgment of a reasonable person relying on the information would be changed or influenced by the omission or misstatement.

We confirm, to the best of our knowledge and belief, *[as of (date of auditor's report),]* the following representations made to you during your audit(s).

1. The financial statements referred to above are fairly presented in conformity with accounting principles generally accepted in the United States *of* America.

2. We have made available to you all
   (a) Financial records and related data.
   (b) Minutes *of* the meetings *of* stockholders, directors, and committees *of* directors, or summaries *of* actions *of* recent meetings for which minutes have not yet been prepared.

3. There have been no communications from regulatory agencies concerning noncompliance with or deficiencies in financial reporting practices.

4. There are no material transactions that have not been properly recorded in the accounting records underlying the financial statements.

5. We believe that the effects of the uncorrected financial statement misstatements summarized in the accompanying schedule are immaterial, both individually and in the aggregate, to the financial statements taken as a whole.

6. We acknowledge our responsibility for the design and implementation of programs and controls to prevent and detect fraud.

7. We have no knowledge of any fraud or suspected fraud affecting the entity involving
   (a) Management,
   (b) Employees who have significant roles in internal control, or
   (c) Others where the fraud could have a material effect on the financial statements.

EXAMPLE 12.11
ILLUSTRATIVE REPRESENTATION LETTER (continued)

The company has no plans or intentions that may materially affect the carrying value or classification of assets and liabilities.

8. We have no knowledge of any allegations of fraud or suspected fraud affecting the entity received in communications from employees, analysts, regulators, short sellers, or others.

9. The company has no plans or intentions that may materially affect the carrying value or classification of assets and liabilities.

10. The following have been properly recorded or disclosed in the financial statements:

    (a) Related-party transactions, including sales, purchases, loans, transfers, leasing arrangements, and guarantees, and amounts receivable from or payable to related parties.

    (b) Guarantees, whether written or oral, under which the company is contingently liable.

    (c) Significant estimates and material concentrations known to management that are required to be disclosed in accordance with the AICPA's Statement of Position 94–6, *Disclosure of Certain Significant Risks and Uncertainties*. [*Significant estimates are estimates at the balance sheet date that could change materially within the next year. Concentrations refer to volumes of business, revenues, available sources of supply, or markets or geographic areas for which events could occur that would significantly disrupt normal finances within the next year.*]

11. There are no

    (a) Violations or possible violations of laws or regulations whose effects should be considered for disclosure in the financial statements or as a basis for recording a loss contingency

    (b) Unasserted claims or assessments that our lawyer has advised us are probable of assertion and must be disclosed in accordance with Financial Accounting Standards Board (FASB) Statement No. 5, *Accounting for Contingencies.*

    (c) Other liabilities or gain or loss contingencies that are required to be accrued or disclosed by FASB Statement No. 5.

EXAMPLE 12.11
ILLUSTRATIVE REPRESENTATION LETTER *(continued)*

---

12. The company has satisfactory title to all owned
    assets, and there are no liens or encumbrances
    on such assets nor has any asset been pledged as
    collateral.

13. The company has complied with all aspects of
    contractual agreements that would have a
    material effect on the financial statements in the
    event of noncompliance.

*[Add additional representations that are unique to the
entity's business or industry.]*

To the best of our knowledge and belief, no events have
occurred subsequent to the balance-sheet date and
through the date of this letter that would require adjustment to or disclosure in the aforementioned financial
statements.

[Name of Chief Executive Officer and Title]

[Name of Chief Financial Officer and Title]

SAS 86—AMENDMENT TO STATEMENT ON AUDITING STANDARDS NO. 72, LETTERS FOR UNDERWRITERS AND CERTAIN OTHER REQUESTING PARTIES

Refer to the summary of SAS 72, which includes the appropriate amendments.

SAS 87—RESTRICTING THE USE OF AN AUDITOR'S REPORT

What is the difference between general-use and restricted-use reports?

General-use reports are auditor's reports that are not
restricted as to use by specified parties—for example, audit
reports on historical financial statements.

Restricted-use reports, on the other hand, are auditor's
reports that are intended only for specified parties.

When may an auditor issue a restricted-use report?

An auditor may issue a restricted-use report in the following circumstances:

○ The subject matter of the report or the presentation
  being reported on is based on measurement or disclosure criteria included in contractual agreements or

regulatory provisions not in conformity with generally accepted accounting principles or an other comprehensive basis of accounting.

o The report is based on agreed-upon procedures.

o The report is a byproduct of a financial statement audit—for example, communication of internal control related matters noted in an audit (see SAS 60) and communications with audit committees (see SAS 61).

What is the appropriate language to include in restricted-use reports?

An example of appropriate language is: "This report is intended solely for the information and use of [*the specified parties*] and is not intended to be and should not be used by anyone other than these specified parties."

SAS 88—SERVICE ORGANIZATIONS AND REPORTING ON CONSISTENCY

Refer to the summary of SAS 70 and Chapter 10, which include the appropriate amendments.

SAS 89—AUDIT ADJUSTMENTS

The amendments contained in this pronouncement have been integrated within other areas of this book.

SAS 90—AUDIT COMMITTEE COMMUNICATIONS

The amendments contained in this pronouncement have been integrated within other areas of this book.

SAS 91—FEDERAL GAAP HIERARCHY

Refer to the summary of SAS 69, which includes the appropriate amendments.

SAS 92—AUDITING DERIVATIVE INSTRUMENTS, HEDGING ACTIVITIES, AND INVESTMENTS IN SECURITIES

What special skills or knowledge are required in order to audit derivative instruments, hedging activities, and other investments in securities?

o Obtain an understanding of an entity's information system for derivative instruments and securities,

○ including services provided by a service organization when significant information about them is transmitted, processed, maintained, or accessed electronically.

○ Identify controls placed in operation by the entity's service organization that are part of the entity's information system for derivative instruments and securities.

○ Obtain special knowledge to evaluate the measurement, disclosure, and other U.S. GAAP requirements for derivative instruments and securities.

○ Obtain an understanding of the determination of the fair values, including the appropriateness of various types of valuation models and the reasonableness of key factors and assumptions used in such models.

○ Obtain an understanding of the general risk management concepts and typical asset/liability management strategies to assess inherent risk and control risk for assertions about derivatives used in hedging activities.

How may inherent risk be affected in the audit of derivative instruments, hedging activities, and other investments in securities?

The assessment of inherent risk for assertions pertaining to derivative instruments, hedging activities, and other investments in securities may be affected by the following:

○ Accounting requirements based on management's objectives

○ The complexity of the features of the derivative financial instruments or securities, which may impact the measurement disclosure requirements

○ Derivatives without an initial exchange of cash that may be inadvertently ignored for valuation and disclosure considerations

○ An entity's inexperience with derivative instruments or securities

○ Embedded derivatives, which are less likely to be identified by management

○ Risks related to external factors, including:

• *Credit risk*—risk of loss as a result of the issuer of a debt security or the counterparty to a derivative failing to meet its obligation

• *Market risk*—risk of loss from adverse changes in market factors that affect the fair value of a derivative instrument or security (i.e., changes in interest rates, *foreign exchange rates*, market indexes for equity securities)

- *Basis risk*—risk of loss from ineffective hedging activities. Basis risk is the difference between the fair value (or cash flows) of the hedged item and the fair value (or cash flows) of the hedging derivative. The risk is that fair values (or cash flows) will change so that the hedge will no longer be effective.
- *Legal risk*—risk of loss from a legal or regulatory action that invalidates or otherwise precludes performance by one or both parties to the derivative instrument or security

What control risk considerations should the auditor be aware of when auditing derivative instruments, hedging activities, and other investments in securities?

The auditor's understanding of internal controls over derivative instruments and securities will not only encompass controls of the entity but may also include those of service organizations; outside services may be part of the entity's information system.

It may not be practicable or possible to reduce audit risk to an acceptable level without identifying controls placed in operation by a service organization and gathering evidential matter about the operating effectiveness of those controls.

What substantive auditing procedures should the auditor consider with respect to financial statement assertions for derivative instruments and other investments?

Substantive procedures for the financial statement assertions for derivative instruments and other investments include:

EXISTENCE OR OCCURRENCE

- Confirmation with the issuer of the derivative instrument or security
- Confirmation with the holder or with the counterparty to the derivative instrument or security
- Confirmation of settled transactions with the broker-dealer or counterparty
- Confirmation of unsettled transactions with the broker-dealer or counterparty
- Physical inspection of the derivative instrument or security contract
- Reading executed partnership or similar agreements
- Inspecting underlying agreements and other forms of supporting documentation, in paper or electronic

form, to determine amounts reported, evidence that might preclude "sales" treatment of a transfer, unrecorded repurchase agreements

- Inspecting supporting documentation for subsequent realization or settlement after the balance sheet date
- Performing analytical procedures

COMPLETENESS

- Requesting the counterparty to a derivative instrument or the holder of a security to provide information such as whether there are any side agreements or agreements to repurchase securities sold
- Requesting counterparties or holders who are frequently used, but with whom there are presently no record of derivative instruments or securities, to state whether they are counterparties to derivative instruments with the entity or holders of its securities
- Inspecting agreements to identify embedded derivatives
- Inspecting documentation in paper or electronic form for activity subsequent to the balance sheet date
- Performing analytical procedures
- Comparing previous and current account detail to determine whether assets removed from the accounts met the criteria for "sales" treatment
- Reading other information, such as minutes of meetings of the board of directors or finance, asset/liability, investment, or other committees

RIGHTS AND OBLIGATIONS

- Confirming significant terms with the counterparty, including the absence of any side agreements
- Inspecting agreements and other forms of supporting documentation, in paper or electronic form
- Considering whether the findings of other auditing procedures, such as reviewing minutes of meetings of the board of directors and reading contracts and other agreements, provide evidence about rights and obligations, such as pledging of securities as collateral or selling securities with a commitment to repurchase them

VALUATION

- Evidence about the cost of securities may include inspection of documentation of the purchase price, confirmation with issuer or holder, and testing discount or premium amortization, either by recomputation or analytical procedures.
- For valuations based on an investee's financial results, including but not limited to the equity method of accounting, the auditor should read

available financial statements of the investee and the accompanying audit report, if any. Financial statements of the investee that have been audited by an auditor whose report is satisfactory to the investor's auditor may constitute sufficient evidential matter. If additional evidential matter is needed, the auditor should review information in the investor's files that relates to the investee such as investee minutes and budgets and cash flows information about the investee. The auditor should also inquire of investor management about the investee's financial results. If the investee's financial statements are not audited, or if the report of the investee's auditor is not satisfactory, the investor's auditor should apply, or should request to have another auditor apply, appropriate auditing procedures to such financial statements.

○ For valuations based on fair value, the auditor should determine whether a specified valuation method is to be used to determine the fair value of the entity's derivative instruments and securities. The auditor should evaluate whether the determination of fair value is consistent with the specified method. Quoted market prices for derivative instruments and securities listed on national ex-changes or over-the-counter markets are generally considered to provide sufficient evidence of their fair value.

- If quoted market prices are not available for the derivative instruments or securities, estimates of fair value may be obtained from broker-dealer or other third-party sources based on proprietary valuation models or from the entity based on internally or externally developed valuation models. The auditor should understand the method used, and may determine that it is necessary to obtain estimates from more than one pricing source. This may be appropriate if:

  ○ The pricing source has a relationship with an entity that might impair its objectivity, such as an affiliate or a counterparty involved in selling or structuring the product.

  ○ The valuation is based on assumptions that are highly subjective or particularly sensitive to changes in the underlying circumstances.

○ If the estimated value of the derivative instrument or security is from valuation model, the auditor is not expected to substitute his or her judgment for that of management. The auditor should obtain evidence by performing procedures such as:

- Assessing the reasonableness and appropriateness of the model

- Calculating the value; for example, using a model developed by the auditor or by a specialist engaged by the auditor, to develop an independent expectation to corroborate the reasonableness of the value calculated by the entity's model
- Comparing the fair value with subsequent or recent transactions

IMPAIRMENT LOSSES

Management is required to determine whether to recognize an impairment loss for a decline in fair value that is other than temporary. Accordingly, the auditor should determine whether factors indicating an impairment loss exist, such as:

- Fair value is significantly below cost.

  - The decline is attributable to adverse conditions specifically related to the security or to specific conditions in an industry or in a geographic area.
  - The decline has existed for an extended period of time.
  - Management does not possess both the intent and the ability to hold the security for a period of time sufficient to allow for any anticipated recovery in fair value.

- The security has been downgraded by a rating agency.
- The financial condition of the issuer has deteriorated.
- Dividends have been reduced or eliminated, or scheduled interest payments have not been made.
- The entity recorded losses from the security subsequent to the end of the reporting period.

> ### What additional considerations should the auditor be aware of in connection with hedging activities?

The auditor should determine whether management complied with the hedge accounting requirements, including designation and documentation requirements, to support management's expectation at the inception of the hedge that the hedging relationship would be highly effective. The auditor should also review management's periodic assessment of the ongoing effectiveness of the hedging relationship.

When the entity designates a derivative as a fair value hedge, management is required to adjust the carrying amount of the hedged item for the change in the hedged item's fair value that is attributable to the hedged risk.

For a cash flow hedge of a forecasted transaction, management must determine that the forecasted transaction has probability of occurrence, and that the likelihood is not based solely on management's intent. The transaction's probability should be supported by facts and circumstances, such as the following:

- The frequency of similar past transactions.
- The financial and operational ability of the entity to carry out the transaction.
- The extent of loss that could result if the transaction does not occur.
- The likelihood that transactions with substantially different characteristics might be used to achieve the same business purpose.
- The auditor should evaluate management's determination of whether a forecasted transaction is probable.

What additional considerations should the auditor be aware of in connection with assertions about securities based on management's intent and ability?

Management's intent and ability is a key factor in valuing certain securities, such as:

- Debt securities classified as held-to-maturity and reported at cost depending on management's intent and ability to hold them to their maturity
- Equity securities reported using the equity method depending on management's ability to significantly influence the investee
- Equity securities classified as trading or available-for-sale based on management's intent and objectives

In order to evaluate management's intent and ability, the auditor should:

- Obtain an understanding of the process used by management to classify securities as trading, available-for-sale, or held-to-maturity.
- For an investment accounted for using the equity method, inquire of management as to whether the entity has the ability to exercise significant influence over the operating and financial policies of the investee.
- If the entity accounts for the investment contrary to the presumption established by generally accepted accounting principles for use of the equity method, determine whether that presumption has been overcome and whether appropriate disclosure is made regarding the reasons for not accounting for the investment in keeping with that presumption.
- Consider whether management's activities corroborate or conflict with its stated intent.
- Determine whether management's activities, contractual agreements, or the entity's financial condition

provide evidence of its ability. This can be done by auditor review of:

- The entity's financial position, working capital needs, operating results, debt agreements, guarantees, alternate sources of liquidity, and other relevant contractual obligations, as well as laws and regulations.
- Management's cash flow projections.
- Management's ability to obtain information from an investee.

SAS 93—OMNIBUS STATEMENT ON AUDITING STANDARDS—2000

This pronouncement includes amendments to existing pronouncements that have been integrated within other areas of this book.

SAS 94—THE EFFECT OF INFORMATION TECHNOLOGY ON THE AUDITOR'S CONSIDERATION OF INTERNAL CONTROL IN A FINANCIAL STATEMENT AUDIT

Refer to Chapter 10.

SAS 95—GENERALLY ACCEPTED AUDITING STANDARDS

This pronouncement indicates that interpretive publications (1) are not auditing standards, but rather recommendations on application of the SASs in specific circumstances and (2) consist of auditing interpretations of the SASs, auditing guidance in AICPA Audit and Accounting Guides, and AICPA Statements of Position. Furthermore, although other auditing publications have no authoritative status, they may assist the auditor in understanding and applying the SASs. Other auditing publications include auditing articles in professional journals, continuing professional education programs, textbooks, and state CPA society publications.

SAS 96—AUDIT DOCUMENTATION

What is audit documentation?

Audit documentation, which may be referred to as working papers, is the main record of the audit procedures performed, the evidential matter gathered from those procedures, and the judgments and evaluations made throughout the audit.

What are the purposes of audit documentation?

Audit documentation has three essential purposes:

o To support the auditor's report
o To document the auditor's observance of the field-work standards under generally accepted auditing standards
o To assist in the conduct and supervision of the audit

In what format should audit documentation be maintained?

Audit documentation may be in paper form, electronic format, or other suitable media.

What should be the content of audit documentation?

The auditor should use professional judgment when determining the content of audit documentation. Factors in this determination include the risk of material misstatement, the nature of the auditing procedures, the significance of the evidence obtained, the nature and extent of exceptions identified, and the need to document a conclusion and basis for that conclusion.

Does SAS 96 include any specific audit document requirements?

According to SAS 96, audit documentation should include:

o Copies or abstracts of significant contracts or agreements pertaining to significant transactions.
o Identification of specific items subjected to tests of controls and substantive tests of details involving inspection of documents or confirmation.
o Indication of the engagement team member(s) who performed and reviewed the audit work.
o Significant audit findings or issues, the auditor's response, and the basis for his or her final conclusions. Significant audit findings or issues include (1) matters that are significant and involve the selection, application, and consistency of accounting principles, (2) results of auditing procedures that indicate possible financial statement misstatement or the need to significantly modify auditing procedures, (3) circumstances that result in significant difficulty in applying auditing procedures, and (4) matters that might suggest the need to modify the auditor's report.

To whom does audit documentation belong?

Since the auditor prepares the audit documentation, he or she is the owner and is responsible for adopting reasonable retention procedures in order to maintain confidentiality and prevent unauthorized access.

NOTE

Audit documentation is not part of, or a substitute for, a client's records. However, audit documentation may sometimes serve as a reference source for a client.

What is the difference between a current file and a permanent file?

SAS 96 does not specifically address the distinction between a current file and a permanent file. However, many practitioners split their audit documentation into these two types of files. A current file consists of documentation that pertains only to the current year's engagement. A permanent file, sometimes referred to as a continuing file, includes documents that are pertinent to the current audit engagement as well as to future audit engagements.

SAS 97—AMENDMENT TO STATEMENT ON AUDITING STANDARDS NO. 50, REPORTS ON THE APPLICATION OF ACCOUNTING PRINCIPLES

Refer to the summary of SAS 50, which includes the appropriate amendments.

SAS 98—OMNIBUS STATEMENT ON AUDITING STANDARDS—2002

The provisions in this pronouncement have been integrated within other areas of this book.

SAS 99—CONSIDERATION OF FRAUD IN A FINANCIAL STATEMENT AUDIT

What is the difference between error and fraud?

The distinction between error and fraud is dependent on whether the underlying action that results in financial statement misstatement is intentional or unintentional.

Error refers to unintentional misstatements or omissions of financial statement amounts or disclosures—for example, misinterpretation, mistakes, and use of incorrect accounting estimates. Fraud, on the other hand, refers to acts that are intentional.

What types of misstatements are relevant to an auditor's consideration of fraud?

o Misstatements arising from fraudulent financial reporting, including manipulation, falsification, or alteration of accounting records or supporting documents, and intentional misapplication of accounting principles, practices, and methods

o Misstatements arising from misappropriation of assets (i.e., defalcation), including outright theft, embezzlement schemes, and causing an entity to pay for goods or services that the entity does not actually receive

What conditions are usually present when fraud occurs?

o Pressure or incentive to commit fraud
o Opportunity to perpetrate fraud
o Ability to rationalize or justify committing fraud

Is an auditor responsible for detecting fraud in a financial statement audit?

An auditor is responsible for planning and performing a financial statement audit in order to obtain reasonable, but not absolute, assurance about whether the financial statements are free of material misstatement, whether caused by fraud (or error).

NOTE

An auditor is not trained as, or normally expected to be, an expert in authentication. Accordingly, an auditor might not discover material misstatements caused by fraud that is concealed through falsified (forged) documents. Collusion might also prevent an auditor's detection.

Because of the characteristics of fraud, the auditor is advised to exercise professional judgment. Accordingly, the auditor should have a questioning mind and critically assess evidence obtained throughout the conduct of the audit.

What is meant by brainstorming?

SAS 99 requires members of the audit team to discuss the potential for material misstatement due to fraud. Brainstorming, or exchange of ideas, is therefore emphasized. Audit team members should brainstorm about

o How and where the financial statements might be susceptible to material misstatement due to fraud

- How management could perpetrate and conceal fraudulent financial reporting
- How an entity's assets could be misappropriated
- The need to emphasize professional skepticism throughout the audit
- The risk of management override of internal controls
- How the audit team might respond to the susceptibility of the financial statements to material misstatement caused by fraud

In general, how may an auditor identify risks that may result in material misstatement caused by fraud?

An auditor should consider the attributes of the risk of material misstatement caused by fraud:

- Type of risk—that is, whether the risk involves fraudulent financial reporting or misappropriation of assets
- Significance of risk—that is, whether it is of a magnitude that could result in material misstatement
- Likelihood of risk
- Pervasiveness of risk—that is, is the risk isolated to a particular assertion, account, or class of transaction, or does the risk have a potentially pervasive effect on the financial statements?

How should an auditor respond to the results of the assessment of the risk of material misstatement caused by fraud?

An auditor generally responds to the risk of material misstatement caused by fraud by:

- Developing a response that has an overall effect on the conduct of the audit
- Modifying the nature, extent, and timing of specific auditing procedures
- Performing additional auditing procedures to address the risk of material misstatement due to fraud arising from management override of internal controls

How might the risk of material misstatement caused by fraud have an overall effect on the audit?

Judgments about the risk of material misstatement caused by fraud may have an overall effect on the audit in the following ways:

- Assignment of personnel—The knowledge, skill, and ability of audit personnel should be commensurate with the assessed level of risk

- Accounting principles—The auditor should be more skeptical about management's selection and application of accounting principles, practices, and methods
- Predictability of auditing procedures—The auditor should incorporate an element of unpredictability in selecting auditing procedures performed from year to year

What procedures should be performed to address the risk of management override of internal controls?

The auditor should examine journal entries and other adjustments. More specifically, the auditor should:

- Obtain an understanding of the financial reporting process and the relevant internal controls.
- Identify and select journal entries and other adjustments for substantive testing.
- Determine the timing of substantive tests, with special focus on journal entries and other adjustments made at the end of the reporting period.
- Make inquiries of individuals involved in the financial reporting process about inappropriate or unusual activity concerning the processing of journal entries and other adjustments.

What should an auditor be aware of when evaluating audit evidence?

It is important to keep in mind that the assessment of the risk of material misstatement caused by fraud is not a one-time assessment, but rather should be ongoing through the conduct of the audit.

Accordingly, on an ongoing basis, the auditor should watch out for the following:

- Discrepancies in the accounting records
- Conflicting or missing evidential matter
- Problematic or unusual relationships between management and the auditor

The auditor should also:

- Evaluate whether analytical procedures in the substantive testing and overall review stages of the audit indicate previously unrecognized risks of material misstatement caused by fraud.
- At or near the end of fieldwork, evaluate the accumulated results of audit tests to determine the effect on the auditor's earlier risk assessment.

What actions should an auditor take if he or she believes that financial statement misstatements are or may be caused by fraud?

If the auditor believes that the effect of the misstatement is immaterial, he or she should nevertheless evaluate the implications, especially those dealing with the organizational position of the individual(s) involved.

If the auditor believes that the effect of the misstatement is material, or is unable to determine the materiality of the misstatement, the following actions are appropriate:

o Undertake to obtain additional evidential matter in order to ascertain whether material fraud has occurred, or is likely to have occurred, and if so, its related effects on the financial statements as well as the auditor's report.

o Consider the possible effects on other aspects of the audit.

o Discuss the matter as well as the approach for further investigation with an appropriate level of management that is at least one level above those involved, and with senior management, and the audit committee.

o Consider whether it is appropriate to advise the client to consult with its legal counsel.

What communications concerning fraud or its possibility are necessary?

An appropriate level of management should be notified if the auditor determines that there is evidence of fraud, even if the fraud is inconsequential.

The audit committee should be notified directly if the auditor determines that there is:

o Fraud involving senior management
o Fraud that results in material misstatement in the financial statements

If the auditor concludes that identified fraud risk factors have continuing internal control implications, the auditor should determine whether such factors represent reportable conditions requiring communication to senior management or the audit committee.

Although an auditor is generally precluded from communicating with nonclient personnel about fraud, he or she is permitted to disclose such information when:

o Permitted by law or regulatory requirements
o A predecessor auditor communicates with a successor auditor pursuant to the provisions of SAS 84
o Responding to a subpoena

o Required to notify a funding agency or other specified agency pursuant to requirements for the audits of entities that receive governmental financial assistance

Does SAS 99 contain any specific documentation requirements?

Yes. The auditor is required to document the following:

o The details of the required brainstorming
o The procedures performed to identify and assess the risks of material misstatement caused by fraud
o Specific risks of material misstatement caused by fraud that the auditor identified as well as a description of the auditor's response thereto
o If the auditor has not identified in a particular circumstance improper revenue recognition as a risk of material misstatement caused by fraud, the basis for the conclusion
o The results of the procedures to further address the risk of management override of internal controls
o Other conditions and results of analytical procedures that led the auditor to believe that additional audit procedures were necessary, as well as any further responses the auditor considered necessary
o The nature of the communications concerning fraud made to management, the audit committee, and others

Does SAS 99 provide lists of risk factors relating to misstatements arising from fraudulent financial reporting and misappropriation of assets?

The following list of risk factors are derived from the Appendix to SAS 99.

EXAMPLES OF FRAUD RISK FACTORS

RISK FACTORS RELATING TO MISSTATEMENTS ARISING FROM FRAUDULENT FINANCIAL REPORTING

Incentives/Pressures

A. Financial stability or profitability is threatened by economic, industry, or entity operating conditions, such as (or as indicated by):

1. High degree of competition or market saturation, accompanied by declining margins
2. High vulnerability to rapid changes, such as changes in technology, product obsolescence, or interest rates

---

EXAMPLES OF FRAUD RISK FACTORS *(continued)*

    3. Significant declines in customer demand and increasing business failures in either the industry or overall economy

    4. Operating losses making the threat of bankruptcy, foreclosure, or hostile takeover imminent

    5. Recurring negative cash flows from operations or an inability to generate cash flows from operations while reporting earnings and earnings growth

    6. Rapid growth or unusual profitability, especially compared to that of other companies in the same industry

    7. New accounting, statutory, or regulatory requirements

B. Excessive pressure exists for management to meet the requirements or expectations of third parties due to the following:

    1. Profitability or trend level expectations of investment analysts, institutional investors, significant creditors, or other external parties (particularly expectations that are unduly aggressive or unrealistic), including expectations created by management in, for example, overly optimistic press releases or annual report messages

    2. Need to obtain additional debt or equity financing to stay competitive—including financing of major research and development or capital expenditures

    3. Marginal ability to meet exchange listing requirements or debt repayment or other debt covenant requirements

    4. Perceived or real adverse effects of reporting poor financial results on significant pending transactions, such as business combinations or contract awards

C. Information available indicates that management or the board of directors' personal financial situation is threatened by the entity's financial performance arising from the following:

    1. Significant financial interests in the entity

    2. Significant portions of their compensation (for example, bonuses, stock options, and earn-out arrangements) being contingent upon achieving aggressive targets for stock price, operating results, financial position, or cash flow

    3. Personal guarantees of debts of the entity

EXAMPLES OF FRAUD RISK FACTORS *(continued)*

D. There is excessive pressure on management or operating personnel to meet financial targets set up by the board of directors or management, including sales or profitability incentive goals.

Opportunities

A. The nature of the industry or the entity's operations provides opportunities to engage in fraudulent financial reporting that can arise from the following:

1. Significant related-party transactions not in the ordinary course of business or with related entities not audited or audited by another firm

2. A strong financial presence or ability to dominate a certain industry sector that allows the entity to dictate terms or conditions to suppliers or customers that may result in inappropriate or non-arm's-length transactions

3. Assets, liabilities, revenues, or expenses based on significant estimates that involve subjective judgments or uncertainties that are difficult to corroborate

4. Significant, unusual, or highly complex transactions, especially those close to period end that pose difficult "substance over form" questions

5. Significant operations located or conducted across international borders in jurisdictions where differing business environments and cultures exist

6. Significant bank accounts or subsidiary or branch operations in tax-haven jurisdictions for which there appears to be no clear business justification

B. There is ineffective monitoring of management as a result of the following:

1. Domination of management by a single person or small group (in a nonowner-managed business) without compensating controls

2. Ineffective board of directors or audit committee oversight over the financial reporting process and internal control

C. There is a complex or unstable organizational structure, as evidenced by the following:

1. Difficulty in determining the organization or individuals that have controlling interest in the entity

EXAMPLES OF FRAUD RISK FACTORS *(continued)*

   2. Overly complex organizational structure involving unusual legal entities or managerial lines of authority

   3. High turnover of senior management, counsel, or board members

D. Internal control components are deficient as a result of the following:

   1. Inadequate monitoring of controls, including automated controls and controls over interim financial reporting (where external reporting is required)

   2. High turnover rates or employment of ineffective accounting, internal audit, or information technology staff

   3. Ineffective accounting and information systems, including situations involving reportable conditions

Attitudes/Rationalizations

- Ineffective communication, implementation, support, or enforcement of the entity's values or ethical standards by management or the communication of inappropriate values or ethical standards

- Nonfinancial management's excessive participation in or preoccupation with the selection of accounting principles or the determination of significant estimates

- Known history of violations of securities laws or other laws and regulations, or claims against the entity, its senior management, or board members alleging fraud or violations of laws and regulations

- Excessive interest by management in maintaining or increasing the entity's stock price or earnings trend

- A practice by management of committing to analysts, creditors, and other third parties to achieve aggressive or unrealistic forecasts

- Management failing to correct known reportable conditions on a timely basis

- An interest by management in employing inappropriate means to minimize reported earnings for tax-motivated reasons

- Recurring attempts by management to justify marginal or inappropriate accounting on the basis of materiality

EXAMPLES OF FRAUD RISK FACTORS *(continued)*

- The relationship between management and the current or predecessor auditor is strained, as exhibited by the following:
- Frequent disputes with the current or predecessor auditor on accounting, auditing, or reporting matters
- Unreasonable demands on the auditor, such as unreasonable time constraints regarding the completion of the audit or the issuance of the auditor's report
- Formal or informal restrictions on the auditor that inappropriately limit access to people or information or the ability to communicate effectively with the board of directors or audit committee
- Domineering management behavior in dealing with the auditor, especially involving attempts to influence the scope of the auditor's work or the selection or continuance of personnel assigned to or consulted on the audit engagement

RISK FACTORS RELATING TO MISSTATEMENTS ARISING FROM MISAPPROPRIATION OF ASSETS

Incentives/Pressures

A. Personal financial obligations may create pressure on management or employees with access to cash or other assets susceptible to theft to misappropriate those assets.

B. Adverse relationships between the entity and employees with access to cash or other assets susceptible to theft may motivate those employees to misappropriate those assets. For example, adverse relationships may be created by the following:

   1. Known or anticipated future employee layoffs
   2. Recent or anticipated changes to employee compensation or benefit plans
   3. Promotions, compensation, or other rewards inconsistent with expectations

Opportunities

A. Certain characteristics or circumstances may increase the susceptibility of assets to misappropriation. For example, opportunities to misappropriate assets increase when there are the following:

   1. Large amounts of cash on hand or processed

2. Inventory items that are small in size, of high value, or in high demand

3. Easily convertible assets, such as bearer bonds, diamonds, or computer chips

4. Fixed assets that are small in size, marketable, or lacking observable identification of ownership

B. Inadequate internal control over assets may increase the susceptibility of misappropriation of those assets. For example, misappropriation of assets may occur because there is the following:

1. Inadequate segregation of duties or independent checks

2. Inadequate management oversight of employees responsible for assets, for example, inadequate supervision or monitoring of remote locations

3. Inadequate job applicant screening of employees with access to assets

4. Inadequate recordkeeping with respect to assets

5. Inadequate system of authorization and approval of transactions (for example, in purchasing)

6. Inadequate physical safeguards over cash, investments, inventory, or fixed assets

7. Lack of complete and timely reconciliations of assets

8. Lack of timely and appropriate documentation of transactions, for example, credits for merchandise returns

9. Lack of mandatory vacations for employees performing key control functions

10. Inadequate management understanding of information technology, which enables information technology employees to perpetrate a misappropriation

11. Inadequate access controls over automated records, including controls over and review of computer systems event logs.

Attitudes/Rationalizations

Risk factors reflective of employee attitudes/rationalizations that allow them to justify misappropriations of assets, are generally not susceptible to observation by the auditor. Nevertheless, the auditor who becomes aware of the existence of such information should consider it in

---

EXAMPLES OF FRAUD RISK FACTORS *(continued)*

identifying the risks of material misstatement arising from misappropriation of assets. For example, auditors may become aware of the following attitudes or behavior of employees who have access to assets susceptible to misappropriation:

- o Disregard for the need for monitoring or reducing risks related to misappropriations of assets
- o Disregard for internal control over misappropriation of assets by overriding existing controls or by failing to correct known internal control deficiencies
- o Behavior indicating displeasure or dissatisfaction with the company or its treatment of the employee
- o Changes in behavior or lifestyle that may indicate assets have been misappropriated

---

SAS 100—INTERIM FINANCIAL INFORMATION

To which entities is this pronouncement applicable?

This statement applies to reviews of interim financial statements of a publicly traded entity.

Is there a difference between a review of a publicly traded entity's financial statements and a review of a nonpublicly traded entity's financial statements?

The review procedures and reporting requirements applicable to reviews of financial statements of a publicly traded entity are essentially the same as those applicable to reviews of financial statements of nonpublicly traded entities governed by *Statements on Standards for Accounting and Review Services* (discussed in Chapter 11). However, with respect to a review of interim financial information of a publicly traded entity, the following should be noted:

- o The accountant must have sufficient knowledge of the client's internal controls as they relate to both annual and interim information. If the accountant has performed the audit for the most recent annual period, he or she may have the requisite knowledge pertinent to the latest annual information. CAUTION: Even if the accountant has audited the financial statements of the most recent annual period, he or she should inquire about any significant changes in internal control.
- o Each page of the financial statements should be labeled "unaudited."

SAS 101—AUDITING FAIR VALUE MEASUREMENTS AND DISCLOSURES

How is fair value defined?

The fair value of an asset (or liability) is the amount at which that asset (or liability) could be bought (or incurred) or sold (or settled) in a current transaction between willing parties—that is, other than in a forced sale or liquidation sale.

NOTES
Observable market pricing is the preferable method for measuring an item's fair value.
Management is responsible for establishing an accounting and reporting process for determining fair value measurements.
Management is responsible for making the fair value measurements and disclosures in its financial statements.

What is an auditor's responsibility with respect to fair value measurements and disclosures included in financial statements?

An auditor must obtain sufficient competent audit evidence that fair value measurements and disclosures included in financial statements are in conformity with generally accepted accounting principles.

Accordingly, an auditor should:

o Obtain an understanding of the entity's process for determining fair value measurements and disclosures and the relevant controls.

o Evaluate management's intent and ability to carry out specific courses of action where intent is relevant to the use and disclosure of fair value measurements. Therefore, an auditor might

• Consider management's past history of carrying out its stated intentions.

• Review written plans and other documentation (e.g., budgets and minutes).

• Consider management's stated reasons for its choice of a particular course of action.

• Consider the entity's economic circumstances.

o Evaluate whether (1) the entity's method for determining fair value measurements is applied consistently and (2) consistency is appropriate in light of changing circumstances.

o Consider the need to engage a specialist when auditing fair value measurements.

o Test the entity's fair value measurements and disclosures to evaluate whether

- Management's assumptions are reasonable and reflect, or are not inconsistent with, market information.

- The fair value measurement was determined using an appropriate model, if applicable.

- Management used relevant information that was reasonably available at the time.

NOTE

The auditor may make an independent estimate of fair value to corroborate the entity's fair value measurement.

AS 1—REFERENCES IN AUDITOR'S REPORTS TO THE STANDARDS OF THE PUBLIC COMPANY ACCOUNTING OVERSIGHT BOARD

Refer to Chapter 11.

AS 2—AN AUDIT OF INTERNAL CONTROL OVER FINANCIAL REPORTING PERFORMED IN CONJUNCTION WITH AN AUDIT OF FINANCIAL STATEMENTS

What is a client's reporting responsibility in connection with internal control over financial reporting?

A client's annual report must include a management report that contains management's assessment of the effectiveness of the company's internal control over financial reporting as of the end of the company's most recent fiscal year, including a statement as to whether the internal control is effective.

What is an auditor's reporting responsibility in connection with internal control over financial reporting?

An auditor is required to attest to (audit) and report on management's assessment of internal control over financial reporting if the auditor audits the company's financial statements included in the company's annual report. The auditor's attestation report must then be included in the annual report.

What is the objective of the audit of internal control over financial reporting?

The objective of the audit of internal control over financial reporting is to obtain reasonable, but not absolute, assurance that no material weaknesses exist as of the date specified in management's assessment. To achieve this objective, an auditor must evaluate management's assessment and obtain and evaluate evidence regarding the design and operating effectiveness of internal control.

What is the definition of a "material weakness?"

The definition of a material weakness is slightly different from the definition included in SAS 60. Under AS2, a material weakness is a significant deficiency, or combination of significant deficiencies, that results in more than a remote likelihood that a material misstatement of the annual or interim financial statements will not be prevented or detected.

What established criteria should management use in assessing the effectiveness of its internal control?

Management is required to base its assessment on a suitable recognized framework. Generally, in the United States, the framework to be utilized is the framework contained in *Internal Control—Integrated Framework* (the COSO Report), published by the Committee of Sponsoring Organizations (COSO) of the Treadway Commission.

NOTE

The criteria contained in the COSO Report served as the basis for developing the SASs relevant to internal control issued by the Auditing Standards Board of the AICPA.

What are management's responsibilities in an audit of internal control over financial reporting?

Management's responsibilities in an audit of internal control are essentially the same as those specified in the Statements on Standards for Attestation Engagements issued by the AICPA.

How should an auditor evaluate management's assessment process?

An auditor is required to obtain an understanding of, and evaluate, management's process for assessing the effectiveness of internal control over financial reporting. Accordingly, an auditor needs to determine whether management has considered the following elements:

- Determining which controls should be tested, including controls over all relevant assertions related to all significant accounts and disclosures.
- Evaluating the likelihood that failure of the control could result in a misstatement, the magnitude of such a misstatement, and the degree to which other controls, if effective, achieve the same control objectives.
- Determining the locations or business units to include in the evaluation for a company with multiple locations or business units.
- Evaluating the design effectiveness of controls.
- Evaluating the operating effectiveness of controls based on procedures sufficient to assess their operating effectiveness. To evaluate the effectiveness of the company's internal control over financial reporting, management must have evaluated controls over all relevant assertions related to all significant accounts and disclosures.
- Determining the deficiencies in internal control over financial reporting that are of such a magnitude and likelihood of occurrence that they constitute significant deficiencies or material weaknesses.
- Communicating findings to the auditor and to others, if applicable.
- Evaluating whether findings are reasonable and support management's assessment.

NOTE

In order to obtain a sufficient understanding of management's process for assessing internal control, an auditor should perform at least one walkthrough for each major class of transactions. A walkthrough involves tracing a transaction from its initiation through its reporting in the company's financial reports.

When auditing internal control over financial reporting, may an auditor use the work of others?

While an auditor is required to perform enough of the audit testing himself or herself so that his or her own work provides the principal basis for the opinion, an auditor is allowed to use the work of others to modify the nature, extent, and timing of the work he or she would have performed.

When may an auditor issue an unqualified opinion?

An unqualified opinion may be issued only when there are no identified material weaknesses and when there have been no scope restrictions.

What type of opinion should be issued if a material weakness is identified?

An adverse opinion must be issued if a material weakness is identified.

What type of opinion should be issued if the scope of the auditor's work has been restricted?

Depending on the significance of the scope restriction, a qualified opinion or a disclaimer of opinion should be issued.

What should be included in management's assessment of the effectiveness the company's internal control over financial reporting?

The items required to be included in management's assessment of the effectiveness the company's internal control over financial reporting are:

- o A statement of management's responsibility for establishing and maintaining adequate internal control over financial reporting
- o A statement identifying the framework used by management to conduct the required assessment of the effectiveness of the company's internal control over financial reporting
- o An assessment of the effectiveness of the company's internal control over financial reporting as of the end of the company's most recent fiscal year, including an explicit statement as to whether that internal control over financial reporting is effective
- o A statement that the registered public accounting firm that audited the financial statements included in the annual report has issued an attestation report on

management's assessment of the company's internal control over financial reporting

What should an auditor consider in evaluating management's report on its assessment of internal control over financial reporting?

In order to properly evaluate management's report on its assessment of internal control over financial reporting, an auditor should consider whether:

- Management has properly stated its responsibility for establishing and maintaining adequate internal control over financial reporting
- The framework used by management to conduct the evaluation is suitable
- Management's assessment of the effectiveness of internal control over financial reporting, as of the end of the company's most recent fiscal year, is free of material misstatement
- Management has expressed its assessment in acceptable form; that is, management must state whether the company's internal control over financial reporting is effective
- Material weaknesses identified in the company's internal control over financial reporting, if any, have been properly disclosed, including material weaknesses corrected during the period

What should be included in the auditor's report on management's assessment of internal control over financial reporting?

The following elements must be included in the auditor's report:

- A title that includes the word *independent*
- An identification of management's conclusion about the effectiveness of the company's internal control over financial reporting as of a specified date based on the control criteria [for example, criteria established in *Internal Control—Integrated Framework* issued by the Committee of Sponsoring Organizations of the Treadway Commission (COSO)]
- An identification of the title of the management report that includes management's assessment (The auditor should use the same description of the company's internal control over financial reporting as management uses in its report.)

- A statement that the assessment is the responsibility of management
- A statement that the auditor's responsibility is to express an opinion on the assessment and an opinion on the company's internal control over financial reporting based on his or her audit.
- A definition of internal control over financial reporting
- A statement that the audit was conducted in accordance with the standards of the Public Company Accounting Oversight Board (United States)
- A statement that the standards of the Public Company Accounting Oversight Board require that the auditor plan and perform the audit to obtain reasonable assurance about whether effective internal control over financial reporting was maintained in all material respects
- A statement that an audit includes obtaining an understanding of internal control over financial reporting, evaluating management's assessment, testing and evaluating the design and operating effectiveness of internal control, and performing such other procedures as the auditor considered necessary in the circumstances
- A paragraph stating that, because of inherent limitations, internal control over financial reporting may not prevent or detect misstatements and that projections of any evaluation of effectiveness to future periods are subject to the risk that controls may become inadequate because of changes in conditions, or that the degree of compliance with the policies or procedures may deteriorate
- The auditor's opinion on whether management's assessment of the effectiveness of the company's internal control over financial reporting as of the specified date is fairly stated, in all material respects, based on the control criteria
- The auditor's opinion on whether the company maintained, in all material respects, effective internal control over financial reporting as of the specified date, based on the control criteria
- The manual or printed signature of the auditor's firm
- The city and state (or city and country, in the case of non-U.S. auditors) from which the auditor's report has been issued
- The date of the audit report, which should coincide with the date of the audit report on the company's financial statements (This is required because an audit of internal control over financial reporting cannot be performed without auditing the company's financial statements)

NOTES

Instead of issuing separate reports on the company's financial statements and on internal control, the auditor may issue a combined report that contains both an opinion on the financial statements and an opinion on internal control over financial reporting.

A separate report on internal control over financial reporting necessitates the inclusion of the following paragraph to the auditor's report on the company's financial statements:

We also have audited, in accordance with the standards of the Public Company Accounting Oversight Board (United States), the effectiveness of W Company's internal control over financial reporting as of December 31, 20X3, based on *[identify control criteria]* and our report dated *[date of report, which should be the same as the date of the report on the financial statements]* expressed *[include nature of opinions]*.

In addition, the following paragraph must be added to the report on internal control over financial reporting:

We have also audited, in accordance with the standards of the Public Company Accounting Oversight Board (United States), the *[identify financial statements]* of W Company and our report dated *[date of report, which should be the same as the date of the report on the effectiveness of internal control over financial reporting]* expressed *[include nature of opinion]*.

When is it appropriate to modify the standard report?

The standard report should be modified if:

- o Management's assessment is inadequate or management's report is inappropriate. (The auditor should qualify or disclaim an opinion.)
- o There is a material weakness in the company's internal control over financial reporting. (In this, an adverse opinion should be expressed.)
- o There is a restriction on the scope of the engagement. (The issuance of a qualified opinion or a disclaimer of opinion is appropriate; withdrawal from the engagement might need to be considered.)
- o The auditor decides to refer to the report of other auditors as the basis, in part, for the auditor's own report. (The auditor should consider the appropriateness of dividing responsibility with another auditor.)

o   A significant subsequent event has occurred since the date being reported on. (If the effectiveness of internal control is adversely affected, an adverse opinion should be issued.)

What are an auditor's responsibilities for evaluating management's Quarterly Certification Disclosures about internal control over financial reporting?

An auditor is required only to perform the following limited procedures on a quarterly basis to become aware of any material modifications that should be made to the disclosures about changes in internal control over financial reporting in order for management's certification to be accurate:

o   Inquire of management about significant changes in the design or operation of internal control as it relates to the preparation of annual as well as interim financial information that could have occurred since the preceding annual audit or prior review of interim financial information.

o   Evaluate the implications of misstatements identified during the required review of interim financial information.

o   Determine, through inquiry and observation, whether any change in internal control has materially affected, or is reasonably likely to materially affect, internal control.

What communications are required in an audit of internal control over financial reporting?

All identified significant deficiencies and material weakness must be communicated in writing to management and the audit committee before the auditor's report on internal control over financial reporting is issued. It is important that the communication distinguish the significant deficiencies from the material weaknesses.

The communication should be made directly to the board of directors if the auditor determines that the matters identified were based on the ineffectiveness of the oversight of the audit committee.

All deficiencies in internal control over financial reporting other than those considered to be significant deficiencies should be communicated, in writing, to management. The audit committee should be notified that this type of communication occurs.

Any of the communications described above should include a statement restricting the use of communication to the board of directors, audit committee, management, and others within the organization.

EXAMPLE 12.12 COMBINED REPORT EXPRESSING AN UNQUALIFIED OPINIONS ON MANAGEMENT'S ASSESSMENT OF EFFECTIVENESS OF INTERNAL CONTROL OVER FINANCIAL REPORTING, AND ON EFFECTIVENESS OF INTERNAL CONTROL OVER FINANCIAL REPORTING (SEPARATE REPORT)

REPORT OF INDEPENDENT REGISTERED PUBLIC ACCOUNTING FIRM

[Introductory paragraph]

We have audited management's assessment, included in the accompanying *[title of management's report]*, that W Company maintained effective internal control over financial reporting as of December 31, 20X3, based on *[Identify control criteria, for example, "criteria established in Internal Control—Integrated Framework issued by the Committee of Sponsoring Organizations of the Treadway Commission (COSO)."]*. W Company's management is responsible for maintaining effective internal control over financial reporting and for its assessment of the effectiveness of internal control over financial reporting. Our responsibility is to express an opinion on management's assessment and an opinion on the effectiveness of the company's internal control over financial reporting based on our audit.

[Scope paragraph]

We conducted our audit in accordance with the standards of the Public Company Accounting Oversight Board (United States). Those standards require that we plan and perform the audit to obtain reasonable assurance about whether effective internal control over financial reporting was maintained in all material respects. Our audit included obtaining an understanding of internal control over financial reporting, evaluating management's assessment, testing and evaluating the design and operating effectiveness of internal control, and performing such other procedures as we considered necessary in the circumstances. We believe that our audit provides a reasonable basis for our opinion.

[Definition paragraph]

A company's internal control over financial reporting is a process designed to provide reasonable assurance regarding the reliability of financial reporting and the preparation of financial statements for external purposes in accordance with generally accepted accounting principles. A company's internal control over financial reporting includes those policies and procedures that

(1) pertain to the maintenance of records that, in reasonable detail, accurately and fairly reflect the transactions and dispositions of the assets of the company; (2) provide reasonable assurance that transactions are recorded as necessary to permit preparation of financial statements in accordance with generally accepted accounting principles, and that receipts and expenditures of the company are being made only in accordance with authorizations of management and directors of the company; and (3) provide reasonable assurance regarding prevention or timely detection of unauthorized acquisition, use, or disposition of the company's assets that could have a material effect on the financial statements.

[Inherent limitations paragraph]

Because of its inherent limitations, internal control over financial reporting may not prevent or detect misstatements. Also, projections of any evaluation of effectiveness to future periods are subject to the risk that controls may become inadequate because of changes in conditions, or that the degree of compliance with the policies or procedures may deteriorate.

[Opinion paragraph]

In our opinion, management's assessment that W Company maintained effective internal control over financial reporting as of December 31, 20X3, is fairly stated, in all material respects, based on *[Identify control criteria, for example, "criteria established in Internal Control—Integrated Framework issued by the Committee of Sponsoring Organizations of the Treadway Commission (COSO)."]*. Also in our opinion, W Company maintained, in all material respects, effective internal control over financial reporting as of December 31, 20X3, based on *[Identify control criteria, for example, "criteria established in Internal Control—Integrated Framework issued by the Committee of Sponsoring Organizations of the Treadway Commission (COSO)."]*.

[Explanatory paragraph]

We have also audited, in accordance with the standards of the Public Company Accounting Oversight Board (United States), the *[identify financial statements]* of

EXAMPLE 12.12 COMBINED REPORT EXPRESSING AN UNQUALIFIED OPINIONS ON MANAGEMENT'S ASSESSMENT OF EFFECTIVENESS OF INTERNAL CONTROL OVER FINANCIAL REPORTING, AND ON EFFECTIVENESS OF INTERNAL CONTROL OVER FINANCIAL REPORTING (SEPARATE REPORT) *(continued)*

W Company and our report dated *[date of report, which should be the same as the date of the report on the effectiveness of internal control over financial reporting]* expressed *[include nature of opinion]*.

[Signature]

[City and State or Country]

[Date]

EXAMPLE 12.13 COMBINED REPORT EXPRESSING UNQUALIFIED OPINIONS ON FINANCIAL STATEMENTS; ON MANAGEMENT'S ASSESSMENT OF EFFECTIVENESS OF INTERNAL CONTROL OVER FINANCIAL REPORTING, AND ON EFFECTIVENESS OF INTERNAL CONTROL OVER FINANCIAL REPORTING

REPORT OF INDEPENDENT REGISTERED PUBLIC ACCOUNTING FIRM

[Introductory paragraph]

We have audited the accompanying balance sheets of W Company as of December 31, 20X3 and 20X2, and the related statements of income, stockholders' equity and comprehensive income, and cash flows for each of the years in the three-year period ended December 31, 20X3. We also have audited management's assessment, included in the accompanying *[title of management's report]*, that W Company maintained effective internal control over financial reporting as of December 31, 20X3, based on *[Identify control criteria, for example, "criteria established in Internal Control—Integrated Framework issued by the Committee of Sponsoring Organizations of the Treadway Commission (COSO)."]*. W Company's management is responsible for these financial statements, for maintaining effective internal control over financial reporting, and for its assessment of the effectiveness of internal control over financial reporting. Our responsibility is to express an opinion on these financial statements, an opinion on management's assessment, and an opinion on the effectiveness of the company's internal control over financial reporting based on our audits.

> **EXAMPLE 12.13 COMBINED REPORT EXPRESSING UNQUALIFIED OPINIONS ON FINANCIAL STATEMENTS; ON MANAGEMENT'S ASSESSMENT OF EFFECTIVENESS OF INTERNAL CONTROL OVER FINANCIAL REPORTING, AND ON EFFECTIVENESS OF INTERNAL CONTROL OVER FINANCIAL REPORTING** (continued)

[Scope paragraph]

We conducted our audits in accordance with the standards of the Public Company Accounting Oversight Board (United States). Those standards require that we plan and perform the audits to obtain reasonable assurance about whether the financial statements are free of material misstatement and whether effective internal control over financial reporting was maintained in all material respects. Our audit of financial statements included examining, on a test basis, evidence supporting the amounts and disclosures in the financial statements, assessing the accounting principles used and significant estimates made by management, and evaluating the overall financial statement presentation. Our audit of internal control over financial reporting included obtaining an understanding of internal control over financial reporting, evaluating management's assessment, testing and evaluating the design and operating effectiveness of internal control, and performing such other procedures as we considered necessary in the circumstances. We believe that our audits provide a reasonable basis for our opinions.

[Definition paragraph]

A company's internal control over financial reporting is a process designed to provide reasonable assurance regarding the reliability of financial reporting and the preparation of financial statements for external purposes in accordance with generally accepted accounting principles. A company's internal control over financial reporting includes those policies and procedures that (1) pertain to the maintenance of records that, in reasonable detail, accurately and fairly reflect the transactions and dispositions of the assets of the company; (2) provide reasonable assurance that transactions are recorded as necessary to permit preparation of financial statements in accordance with generally accepted accounting principles, and that receipts and expenditures of the company are being made only in accordance with authorizations of management and directors of the company; and (3) provide reasonable assurance regarding prevention or timely detection of unauthorized acquisition, use, or disposition of the company's assets that could have a material effect on the financial statements.

EXAMPLE 12.13 COMBINED REPORT EXPRESSING UNQUALIFIED OPINIONS ON FINANCIAL STATEMENTS; ON MANAGEMENT'S ASSESSMENT OF EFFECTIVENESS OF INTERNAL CONTROL OVER FINANCIAL REPORTING, AND ON EFFECTIVENESS OF INTERNAL CONTROL OVER FINANCIAL REPORTING *(continued)*

[Inherent limitations paragraph]

Because of its inherent limitations, internal control over financial reporting *may* not prevent or detect misstatements. Also, projections of any evaluation of effectiveness to future periods are subject to the risk that controls may become inadequate because of changes in conditions, or that the degree of compliance with the policies or procedures may deteriorate.

[Opinion paragraph]

In our opinion, the financial statements referred to above present fairly, in all material respects, the financial position of W Company as of December 31, 20X3 and 20X2, and the results of its operations and its cash flows for each of the years in the three-year period ended December 31, 20X3 in conformity with accounting principles generally accepted in the United States of America. Also in our opinion, management's assessment that W Company maintained effective internal control over financial reporting as of December 31, 20X3, is fairly stated, in all material respects, based on *[Identify control criteria, for example, "criteria established in Internal Control—Integrated Framework issued by the Committee of Sponsoring Organizations of the Treadway Commission (COSO)."]*. Furthermore, in our opinion, W Company maintained, in all material respects, effective internal control over financial reporting as *of* December 31, 20X3, based on *[Identify control criteria, for example, "criteria established in Internal Control—Integrated Framework issued by the Committee of Sponsoring Organizations of the Treadway Commission (COSO)."]*.

[Signature]

[City and State or Country]

[Date]

AS 3—AUDIT DOCUMENTATION

When are the documentation requirements in this pronouncement applicable?

The documentation requirements in this pronouncement are applicable to financial statement audits, audits of internal control over financial reporting (see AS 2), and reviews of interim financial information.

Under AS 3, an auditor must document "significant findings or issues." What does the PCAOB consider to be "significant findings or issues"?

The PCAOB defines "significant findings or issues" as substantive matters that are important to the procedures performed, evidence obtained, or conclusions reached. Examples of significant findings or issues include:

- ○ Significant matters pertaining to the selection, application, and consistency of accounting principles, including related disclosures
- ○ Results of auditing procedures that indicate a need for significant modification of the audit program
- ○ Audit adjustments
- ○ Disagreements among audit team members
- ○ Difficulties encountered in applying auditing procedures
- ○ Significant changes in the auditor's assessed level of audit risk
- ○ Matters that might impact the auditor's report
- ○ The existence of significant deficiencies in internal control, including material weaknesses

NOTE
All significant findings or issues must be identified in an engagement completion document.

What retention requirements should an auditor be aware of?

- ○ In general, audit documentation must be retained for a period of seven years, which commences on the date that the auditor grants permission to use the audit report in connection with the issuance of the company's financial statements (report release date). A specific law, however, may require a longer retention period.

- A complete and final set of audit documentation is required to be assembled for retention not more than 45 days after the report release date (documentation completion date).
- No audit documentation is permitted to be deleted or discarded after the document completion date.
- Information may be added after the documentation completion date provided that the documentation includes the date of addition, the name of the preparer of the additional documentation, and the reason for the addition.
- The office of the firm issuing the auditor's report is responsible for the documentation and its retention.

CHAPTER 13

THE SARBANES-OXLEY ACT OF 2002

*T*he Sarbanes-Oxley Act of 2002 (SOX) was enacted, in part, in response to the accounting scandals of several publicly traded companies. SOX resulted in changes to corporate governance, increased corporate reporting (disclosure), and partial regulation of the accounting profession. This chapter focuses on the impact that SOX has on independent auditors of publicly traded entities.

In general, what are the major provisions of SOX that impact auditors of publicly traded entities?

Major provisions in SOX that impact auditors of publicly traded entities include:

- Stricter rules regarding independence of the auditor
- Partner rotation
- Creation of the Public Company Accounting Oversight Board
- A requirement to attest to, and report on, management's assessment of the effectiveness of internal control over financial reporting (discussed in Chapter 12)

AUDITOR INDEPENDENCE

What employment situations impair auditor independence?

Under SOX, an auditor will lose independence if an employee of the company being audited was part of the audit engagement team at any time during the "cooling-off period." In order for the loss of independence to occur, the employee of the auditee must have had a financial accounting oversight role. Accordingly, prohibited employee positions include the chief executive officer, the chief financial officer, the controller, the chief accounting officer, as well as any other position in which the individual can impact the preparation or contents of the entity's financial statements.

The "cooling-off period" is generally the one-year period that precedes the commencement of audit procedures.

What are the services under SOX that impair auditor independence?

Under SOX, independence is impaired if an auditor performs the following services for a client:

- Bookkeeping
- Design and implementation of financial information systems
- Appraisal or valuation
- Expression of fairness opinions
- Issuance of contribution-in-kind reports
- Actuarial advice concerning amounts included in financial statements
- Internal audit outsourcing
- Legal advice
- Providing expert opinions in litigation or in regulatory or administrative proceedings or investigations

---

NOTES

Under SOX, an auditor may provide tax services, including providing tax advice and preparing tax returns. However, the services must be preapproved by the client's audit committee. Furthermore, the fees for tax services must be disclosed in the client's annual reports and proxy statements.

- As under prior SEC rules, auditor independence is lost if the auditor
- Provides management functions, such as serving as a director or officer of the auditee.
- Conducts human resource functions for the auditee.
- Serves as a broker-dealer, promoter, or underwriter for the auditee.

PARTNER ROTATION

What are the new partner rotation rules under SOX?

SOX classifies partners into two categories:

- Lead and concurring audit partners
- All other audit partners

Lead and concurring partners must be rotated after five years and are subject to a "time-out" period of five years.

All other audit partners must be rotated after seven years and are subject to a "time-out" period of two years.

PUBLIC COMPANY ACCOUNTING OVERSIGHT BOARD (PCAOB)

What is the PCAOB?

The PCAOB is a nongovernmental organization established under Title I of SOX. As an independent organization, the PCAOB is charged with oversight of audits of public companies and their auditors. Specifically, the PCAOB is responsible for:

- Registering auditors of publicly traded entities
- Disciplining auditors of publicly traded entities
- Investigating financial irregularities of publicly traded entities
- Establishing auditing and accounting standards

How will the PCAOB discipline auditors?

Public accounting firms registered with the PCAOB will be subject to inspections to ensure compliance with SOX. National audit firms will be subjected to inspection annually; other firms will be inspected every three years. The PCAOB is empowered to impose disciplinary action (including sanctions on accepting new audit clients) on firms that have unsatisfactory inspections.

Will the PCAOB replace existing auditing and accounting standards?

Currently, the PCAOB has no plans to take away the power of the Financial Accounting Standards Board (FASB) to promulgate accounting standards. Accordingly, the PCAOB intends to adopt the current and future accounting standards of FASB.

The PCAOB has stated that it will establish its own auditing standards. However, it has temporarily adopted the promulgations issued by the Auditing Standard Board of the AICPA, which no longer is empowered to set rules applicable to audits of public companies. It should be noted that promulgations of the PCAOB are not effective until approved by the SEC.

Has the PCAOB issued new auditing standards?

Yes. To date, the PCAOB has issued three new auditing standards, which are applicable only to audits of publicly traded companies. The new standards are as follows:

o Auditing Standard No. 1—References in Auditor's Reports to the Standards of the Public Company Accounting Oversight Board
o Auditing Standard No. 2—An Audit of Internal Control over Financial Reporting Performed in Conjunction with an Audit of Financial Statements
o Auditing Standard No. 3—Audit Documentation

PART 5

TAXATION

CHAPTER 14

TAX RESEARCH

*O*ne of the greatest assets for an accountant is the ability to conduct tax research. Whether the accountant is attempting to solve an existing tax problem or is formulating suggestions for proposed tax transactions, the practitioner should be familiar with the many sources of tax information.

SOURCES OF TAX LAW

What is the Internal Revenue Code?

The Internal Revenue Code represents the tax law. Amendments to the Internal Revenue Code must be approved by both the House of Representatives and the Senate before the president signs them into law.

How are committee reports helpful?

The legislative intent of the law may be found in the committee reports of the House Ways and Means Committee, the Senate Finance Committee, and the Joint Conference Committee. Committee reports often provide examples that may closely approximate your client's transactions and proposals.

When defending positions in court, the use of congressional intent is quite forceful. Each section in the Code includes a reference to the legislative history of the law, that is, a reference to *Revenue Acts* and their years of enactment. Standard tax services, such as those published by RIA and CCH, reprint congressional committee reports upon issuance. Another source for the committee reports is the *Cumulative Bulletin* issued twice a year by the Internal Revenue Service (IRS). The *Cumulative Bulletin* is the hardbound version containing 26 weekly *Internal Revenue Bulletins*.

What is the importance of Treasury Department regulations?

Treasury Department regulations represent the government's interpretation of the Internal Revenue Code. Regulations are issued in three forms:

- *Proposed Regulations* are not authoritative since their adoption has not been finalized.
- *Temporary Regulations*, though not in their final form, do represent an authoritative source for the practitioner.
- *Final Regulations* are completely authoritative and are published in the *Federal Register*.

What is a Revenue Ruling?

- *Revenue rulings*, which are interpretive in nature, are issued by the National Office of the Internal Revenue Service in Washington, D.C. They are published weekly in the *Internal Revenue Bulletin* and are reprinted in the semiannual *Cumulative Bulletin*.
- A *letter ruling* is issued in response to a taxpayer's request for a ruling on a particular transaction. If the IRS feels that the substance of the ruling could affect the public, it converts the letter ruling into a revenue ruling.

What should you know about revenue procedures?

Revenue procedures offer guidance on practices and procedures of the IRS. **EXAMPLE:** A revenue procedure may instruct the practitioner on how to apply for a ruling on a particular type of tax transaction.

Revenue procedures are published in the same manner as revenue rulings.

What is the purpose of Treasury Decisions?

Published in the weekly *Internal Revenue Bulletin* and the semi-annual *Cumulative Bulletin, Treasury Decisions* are issued to:

- Promulgate new regulations.
- Amend current regulations.
- Announce the Treasury's position relative to certain court decisions.

How are Technical Information Releases useful?

This source of tax information is used to locate announcements of various publications.

How about Technical Advice Memoranda?

Technical Advice Memoranda represent responses to requests made by auditors of the IRS. *Technical Advice Memoranda* are not published officially and may not be cited or used as precedent since they are applicable to specific audit situations.

THE COURT SYSTEM

What should I know about the Tax Court?

Taxpayers may wish to seek relief in the Tax Court since it only hears cases involving tax law. Therefore, the Tax Court specializes in tax matters.

Although most Tax Court cases are ruled upon by one of 19 judges, all 19 judges will rule upon a case ("*sit en banc*") when novel issues are of concern. Furthermore, Tax Court judges travel around the country in order to hear cases.

Decisions issued by the Tax Court are either regular decisions or memorandum decisions.

- ○ The *Regular* decisions involve new issues never before resolved by the Court. They are published in semiannual volumes of *Tax Court of the United States Reports*.
- ○ *Memorandum Decisions* involve only the application of existing doctrines of law. They are published only in mimeograph form.

An important distinction between regular and memorandum decisions is that with respect to regular decisions the IRS will publicly announce, in its *Internal Revenue Bulletin*, its decision as to whether it will or will not acquiesce. Acquiescence means that the Internal Revenue Service has agreed to follow the Tax Court's Decision in all subsequent cases.

NOTES
Taxpayers do not have to pay tax assessments before they bring suit in the Tax Court. Suits of $50,000 or less are the jurisdiction of the Small Claims Division of the U.S. Tax Court.

How does U.S. Claims Court differ from Tax Court?

The U.S. Claims Court, like the U.S. Tax Court, is a court of original jurisdiction. The U.S. Claims Court may rule upon any claim against the United States that involves constitutional law, Congressional Acts, or executive department regulations. Accordingly, the decisions of the U.S. Claims Court are not restricted to tax matters.

NOTE
To bring suit in the U.S. Claims Court, taxpayers must first pay the tax assessed.

What is the role of U.S. District Courts?

District Court cases are ruled upon by only one judge. A minimum of one District Court is found in every state. Like the U.S. Claims Court, the District Courts rule upon nontax matters.

A distinguishing characteristic of a District Court is that a jury trial is available in cases involving only questions of fact. Questions of law must be decided by a judge. Decisions of District Courts are only valid in the court's geographic jurisdiction.

NOTE
To bring suit in a U.S. District Court, a taxpayer must first pay the deficiency assessed by the government.

How do I appeal a court decision?

When a taxpayer loses a case in either U.S. Tax Court or U.S. District Court, an appeal may be made to a Regional Circuit of the U.S. Court of Appeals. Losses in the U.S. Claims Court may be appealed by seeking relief in the Court of Appeals for the Federal Circuit.

Trial courts (District Courts, the Tax Court and the Claims Court) are bound by the decisions established by the Court of Appeals having jurisdiction. A Court of Appeals, however, does not have to follow the decisions handed down by a Court of Appeals in a different jurisdiction.

Can a tax case go to the Supreme Court?

The U.S. Supreme Court represents the highest appellate court. The U.S. Supreme Court decides which cases it will hear by granting a *Writ of Certiorari*. Although the U.S. Supreme Court will not usually hear cases involving tax matters, it will agree to resolve conflicts between Courts of Appeals.

NOTE
All courts must abide by the decisions of the U.S. Supreme Court.

Which court should be used in a particular case?

The decision to use a particular court for tax litigation depends on many factors, including:

- o The expertise in tax matters possessed by the judges.
- o The ability to request a jury trial.
- o The requirement that the assessed tax be paid before legal action may be taken.

INDEX